Economic Accounts and Their Uses

Economic Accounts and Their Uses

JOHN W. KENDRICK
Professor of Economics
The George Washington University, and
The National Bureau of Economic Research

assisted by **Carol S. Carson**

McGRAW-HILL BOOK COMPANY
NEW YORK·ST. LOUIS·SAN FRANCISCO·DÜSSELDORF·JOHANNESBURG·KUALA LUMPUR·LONDON
MEXICO·MONTREAL·NEW DELHI·PANAMA·RIO DE JANEIRO·SINGAPORE·SYDNEY·TORONTO

Economic Accounts and Their Uses

Library of Congress Catalog Card Number 71-163299

07-033960-0

1234567890MAMM7987654321

This book was set in Century Schoolbook by
John C. Meyer & Son, and printed and bound by
The Maple Press Company. The tables were set in
Century Medium by Universal Graphics. The designer
was Edward Zytko; the drawings were done by John
Cordes. J. & R. Technical Services, Inc. The editors
were Jack R. Crutchfield and Claudia A. Hepburn.
Robert R. Laffler supervised production.

Contents

v

Preface

Much of the success of economics in recent decades has been due to the development of economic accounts, providing an empirical summary description of economic aggregates and structure and their changes through time. The accounts have made possible quantitative macroeconomic analysis, which has led to the refinement of theory, and provided a necessary background for economic projections and policy formation.

Along with economic theory and the tool subjects of mathematics, statistics, and econometrics, the field of economic accounts is becoming increasingly recognized as one in which separate university courses should be offered for both majors and beginning graduate students in economics. This volume is intended primarily to meet the growing need and demand in this area; its aim is to help prepare students for the quantitative analysis required for most basic research and for the applied research performed by economists in government, business firms, and other organizations. It will also be useful as a refresher and reference work for established economists.

Conceptual and statistical work in national income and product has a long history, dating back to Sir William Petty in the seventeenth century. But it was only in the 1930s that a significant number of countries began preparing official estimates of national income on a regular basis. During World War II, these estimates were expanded to show both the income and product sides of a national production account, and then still further elaborated to show income and outlay by significant economic sectors, and tied into the production account and with each other by accounting relationships. In a parallel development, industry income and product estimates were prepared, and interindustry purchase and sale relationships were shown by means of input-output tables. After the war, sector income and outlay accounts were elaborated to show separate capital and capital-finance (flow-of-funds) accounts, even though in the United States these were developed separately and not integrated with the official income and product accounts. Finally, both national and sector balance sheets and wealth statements were developed—again, independently, by private investigators, and also not tied into the official national accounts.

This book explains the various types of economic accounts from the standpoint of how they fit together in a comprehensive, integrated system. The chief conceptual and statistical problems and issues connected with the structure and estimates for each of the accounts and for the system as a whole are discussed. Particular reference is made to the national income accounts of the United States and to the United Nations revised standard system of national accounts. A dynamic, evolutionary viewpoint is taken: existing systems are examined critically, and suggestions made for their improvement. Throughout the discussions, references are made to practical uses of the estimates; the final chapters are devoted entirely to a survey of uses, with special treatment of aggregate demand analysis and short-term forecasting and growth analysis and long-term economic projections.

Existing textbooks on national income accounts, or the parts of macroeconomic texts devoted to the accounts, are generally deficient in a number of respects. They usually present the official United States income accounts more or less uncritically. They do not point out to the student that the field of economic accounts is in a dynamic, evolutionary state, much less stimulate him to think creatively about how the accounts could be improved or adapted for special purposes. To the extent that the various related types of economic accounts are presented, they are not treated as interrelated parts of a comprehensive system. Finally, in many textbooks the accounts are presented primarily as background for theoretical expositions, rather than as useful tools for quantitative analysis as well.

Further, most other treatments of the subject are out of date, if not actually obsolete. This volume takes off from the 1965 version of the United States income accounts and the United Nations revised standard system of national accounts, published in late 1968. It refers extensively to the pioneering and suggestive monograph by Richard and Nancy Ruggles, *The Design of Economic Accounts*, which parallels the author's approach in many important respects. The present volume also draws on the author's current work for the National Bureau of Economic Research on expansion of imputations and expansion of the concepts of investment and capital; this work is especially useful in the analysis of processes of economic growth and development.

It may be noted that "economic" accounting is used, rather than the broader term "social" accounting. A section on the efforts to develop social accounts and indicators is included, but these developments are still highly experimental. In any case, a full treatment of social accounts would require a separate volume extending considerably beyond the field of economics. It will also be noted that the word "national" has been dropped from the title. Economic accounts do not need to be confined to national economic statistics; the framework may be used as well to present regional and supranational estimates. Indeed, the volume contains separate chapters on regional accounts and on both international comparisons and combined income and product estimates for the world.

The author believes that this volume is the most comprehensive and up-to-date presentation of the subject of economic accounts now available. It is hoped that, in addition to being useful to students, professors, and practitioners of economics, the book will stimulate further advances in the field of economic accounts.

PREVIEW OF THE VOLUME

A preview of the organization of the volume will help the reader understand how each of the chapters fits into a logical sequence. Further, as a quick summary, this section provides an initial view of the economic accounts as a comprehensive and integrated whole, of great value for the various applications surveyed in the final chapters.

The first chapter describes the nature of economic accounts and explains their chief structural features. Chapter 2 summarizes the history of national income estimates and accounts.

The cornerstone of an economic accounting system, the production account, is covered in Chapter 3. The national and domestic product or expenditure is discussed with respect to its boundaries and content. The other side of the coin, factor costs and nonfactor charges, is likewise examined. In Chapter 4, the third approach to national income and product is developed—value added, or income and product originating, in the various sectors or industries. This approach is extended in Chapter 5 by an explanation of how the industry product accounts may be further disaggregated to show interindustry sales and purchase relationships in the form of input-output matrices.

The final topic under the production approach to the economic accounts, covered in Chapter 6, is the "deflation" of product and factor flows, in order to reveal the price and quantity components of current-dollar changes. *Real* product and factor-cost estimates and the correlative price indexes for the economy and its industrial divisions are essential for purposes of analyzing production, productivity, and cost-price relationships.

Beginning with Chapter 7, the accounts are further developed from the viewpoint of the appropriation and disposition of income, including acquisition of real and financial assets. First, the principles of institutional sectoring, appropriate for this approach, are set forth, and sector income and outlay accounts discussed in terms of their relationship to the basic production account and to each other. In Chapter 8, capital accumulation accounts are presented as a disaggregation by sector of the national saving-investment account or as an extension of the sector appropriation accounts to show saving, tangible investment, and net financial investment. The rationale for expanding the concept of nonfinancial investment to include intangibles, such as outlays for research and development and for education and training, is developed, and an illustrative set of "total investment" accounts is presented.

Net financial investment provides the link with the financing, or "flow-of-funds," accounts. This subject is treated in Chapter 9. These accounts are seen to break down the net changes in financial assets and liabilities by type and to show the intersectoral lending and borrowing relationships. The accumulation and financing accounts lead into the topic of Chapter 10—national and sector balance sheets and wealth statements. Sector balance sheets are seen as reflecting the net changes in real and financial assets, and liabilities, plus revaluations due to the price changes of nonfinancial assets and financial claims. The national wealth statement which emerges when sector balance sheets are consolidated is shown to equate net worth with the sum of domestic nonfinancial assets plus net foreign claims.

Thus far, the economic accounts have been viewed largely at the national level, with reference chiefly to United States statistics and the UN standard system. In Chapter 11, the problems of international accounts and comparisons are presented, including rough estimates of gross world product (GWP) for a recent year. Chapter 12 discusses the possibilities of disaggregation on a regional basis, to permit analysis of subnational economies. The subject of estimating methods and data sources is treated in Chapter 13, including a discussion of the reliability of the national income and product estimates of the United States.

To tie together the presentation of the various types of economic accounts in the preceding chapters, Chapter 14 summarizes the main features of the accounts from the standpoint of an integrated system. The designs of the United States and UN systems are critically examined, and suggestions for improvement are recapitulated.

Chapter 15 is a survey of the various uses and users of the economic accounts, with reference to representative articles and books in which the accounts furnish the basis for economic analyses, projections, and policy recommendations. Chapter 16 goes in some depth into the use of economic accounts for analysis of aggregate demand and for short-term projections. Chapter 17 has a parallel treatment of economic growth and long-term projections. The official United States estimates are supplemented in these uses by the author's estimates for the National Bureau of Economic Research of intangible investments and stocks, which are presented as a chief explanation of productivity advance.

After each chapter, a list of questions is provided to aid the student in reviewing the chief points covered. There is also a list of Selected References for each chapter.

ACKNOWLEDGMENTS

Every scientific author is indebted to his intellectual ancestors, and in this I am no exception. But my greatest debts are to my professional colleagues, since the flowering of economic accounting systems began only shortly before my own entry into the field in 1941. At that time, while engaged in national income analysis at the National Resources Planning Board, I made the acquaintance of the economists in the National Income Division of the U.S. Department of Commerce, notably, Milton Gilbert, Edward Denison, George Jaszi, and Charles Schwartz, who were in the process of developing the new GNP estimates. In 1946, I joined the staff of the Office of Business Economics (OBE), and later collaborated with Mr. Jaszi in preparation of the first set of official estimates of GNP in constant prices, by component. I subsequently developed estimates of gross farm product, in current and constant dollars, applying the "double-deflation" technique. My lasting interest in national income accounts is largely due to my work in OBE and the stimulating contacts there.

My work on real product led me to develop estimates of real factor costs and productivity, which I have always considered an aspect of the economic accounts. While working on my summary volume in this field, *Productivity Trends in the United States*, for the National Bureau of Economic Research, I was privileged to become acquainted with other pioneers in the economic accounts, Simon Kuznets, Solomon Fabricant, Morris Copeland, Wassily Leontief, Raymond Goldsmith, and others, who further stimulated my interest in the field. Later, Goldsmith persuaded me to become research director of the Wealth Inventory Planning Study, which, under a grant from the Ford Foundation, produced the report *Measuring the Nation's Wealth*. While engaged in this project in 1963 and 1964, I came clearly to visualize the economic accounts as an integrated whole and decided eventually to write a textbook on the subject. I am grateful to Raymond Goldsmith for providing this impetus to my work.

At the National Bureau, in 1965, Solomon Fabricant, while still Director of Research, offered me the opportunity to pursue my work in the economic accounts by developing exploratory estimates of imputed values for nonmarket activity and expanded saving-investment accounts, financed in part by grants from the National Science Foundation. Some preliminary results of this work are reported in the present volume, and I am grateful to Fabricant for initiating it and to John Meyer, now President of NBER, for continuing Bureau sponsorship. During my recent work at NBER, I was happy to have Nancy and Richard Ruggles as colleagues. Their major contribution, *The Design of Economic Accounts,* provides excellent collateral reading, at a somewhat more advanced level than the present volume.

My membership over the years in the Conference on Research in Income and Wealth and the International Association for Research in Income and Wealth has provided a continuing source of stimulation, and the proceedings of both organizations provide a rich collection of important literature in the field. Since 1956, I have taught a graduate course on the national income accounts at The George Washington University, and the interaction with graduate students in that seminar has been influential in shaping this volume, particularly its mode of presentation.

One of my ablest graduate students at George Washington University, Carol S. Carson, kindly consented to serve as my assistant in the latter stages of preparing this work. In order to help speed it to completion, Mrs. Carson, under my general guidance, wrote a number of the chapters (5, 9, 11, 12, 13, 15, and 16) and assisted generally in preparing the manuscript for the publisher, reading proof, and indexing. My debt to her is great, indeed. I am also much indebted to Prof. Richard Ruggles, who read the first draft of the manuscript and offered helpful suggestions for improvement. John Gorman of OBE read Chapter 13 on sources and methods behind the United States estimates, and was kind enough to offer a number of comments.

Like most authors, I am not entirely satisfied. But I am confident that continued rapid evolution of the field of economic accounts will in a few years provide the occasion to improve as well as update this work. In the meantime, I shall welcome suggestions for improvement. I only hope that students and teachers will agree with me on the basic utility of a course devoted exclusively to economic accounts along the lines of this volume.

JOHN W. KENDRICK

The Nature of
Economic Accounts

For at least three centuries, men have been trying to explain how the economy works. Until the last generation, however, economic theory was based largely on casual observation and fragmentary statistics covering selected variables and segments of the economy.

Over this same period, a growing band of economists has tried to provide an empirical counterpart of the economy which the theorists were trying to explain. They recognized that, like theory, a numerical description would have to be somewhat abstract, since the myriad details of daily economic transactions could scarcely be recorded, and even if they could, the record would be bewildering. Only by grouping transactors and transactions into significant categories would a set of "economic accounts," as one of the possible forms of numerical description, be both feasible and meaningful. Such a set of economic accounts, the statisticians of the past believed, would provide the means whereby economic theory could be tested and refined and, possibly, suggest new departures and developments of theory.

Since the time of Sir William Petty in seventeenth-century England, economists have sporadically attempted to estimate the national income of their countries and significant income categories or related variables. In the process of estimation and in the development of theory itself, concepts have been refined, data assembled, and estimating frameworks and methods developed.

The critical challenge posed to statesmen and their economic advisers by the Great Depression of the 1930s provided the impetus, and the prior work on national income provided the foundation, for the preparation of regular official national income estimates in the United States and a number of other countries. The further challenges of World War II and of postwar reconversion, reconstruction, and economic development resulted in major improvements and expansions of national income estimates to comprehend complete "social accounting" systems. After the war, the use of such estimates became almost universal.

From the outset, the national income and product estimates and the full panoply of economic accounts proved their utility for a variety of purposes. Thus the faith of early economic statisticians was confirmed, and the accounts were solidly established as valuable tools of analysis for advisers to government and business. It is the purpose of this volume to explain the economic accounts, as they are developing, and their uses. It is hoped that the student of economics will master the principles and contents of the accounts and use them confidently in quantitative economic analysis and projections as a basis for better-informed public and private policy formulation.

Despite the rapid strides in economic accounting since the 1930s, it must be emphasized that the economic accounts of the United States and other countries and of the United Nations (UN) are far from "finished." They are very much in a state of flux. Some changes are already planned, and work in progress may lead to still further modification. The changes reflect a growing understanding of economic accounts as well as insights into better modes of presentation to accommodate the known uses of the accounts (which themselves change). They also reflect dynamic changes within the economy itself, changes in concepts and definitions, changes in the quantity and quality of underlying data (usually, but not always, in the direction of improvement), and, sometimes, changes in the estimating methodology.

The "unfinished" nature of economic accounts explains the critical approach of this volume. It would be a mistake to teach the accounts as they are presently constituted in the United States, since, inevitably, they will be substantially altered. Rather, alternative and often better methods of treatment are pointed out, particularly with respect to the eventual integration of the various related types of accounts. The revised UN standard system of national accounts (1968) goes much further than its predecessor (1953) in outlining a comprehensive, integrated system. But there are flaws and deficiencies even in the new system, and the UN has left certain types of accounts, notably balance sheets, for detailed elaboration at a later time. Only by continuing constructive criticism will improvements be made in national accounts and in international systems designed to promote consistency and standardized reporting. Some of the students of this book may play a part in that improvement, and quite possibly in directions not envisaged by its author!

ECONOMIC ACCOUNTING

The economic accounts of a region, nation, or group of nations are a comprehensive and systematic presentation of economic transactions of various types among significant groups of transactors, during successive periods, and a presentation of the results of the transactions, in terms of balance sheets, at the ends of successive periods. The accounts show aggregates, but even more importantly, they show significant components of economic activity and balances, so that interrelationships and the structure of economic activity may be discerned. As in good theory, however, detail is kept within bounds so that important variables and relationships will not be obscured.

Economic accounting is similar to business accounting in that it is based on the double-entry system. Each account is a balancing statement, with total debits or outgoings (uses) on the left-hand side equal to total credits or incomings (sources) on the other side. Each entry in one account, say, that of the payer, must have an opposite and equal contra-entry in the account of the receiver. Even though each entry and its description must be written twice, this is useful in showing economic interrelationships and in promoting consistency, completeness, and accuracy. Other modes of presenting transactions are possible, as discussed below, but double-entry accounts have proved themselves in use as the basic framework for presenting economic statistics.

In some respects, economic accounting differs from business accounting. It is, for example, a closed system in that all parties to transactions are shown, whereas in business accounting, the books are kept from the point of view of the individual firm. Also, the economic accounts are synthetic; that is, the entries are contrived from statistical data according to useful economic concepts which do not necessarily correspond to those employed in business accounting.

Richard Stone, one of the pioneers in the development of the accounting approach, defines *social accounting* as "an orderly presentation of what is taking place in an economic system, expressed in terms of transactions between its various parts."[1] John P. Powelson states it this way:

> The accounting structure is more than a set of rules and definitions; it is a frame of reference. It enables the economist to sort out basic concepts, to visualize economic events in orderly sequence, and to keep in mind essential relationships so that none is forgotten. It provides no automatic solution to economic problems but helps chart the method of attack. In short, the accounting structure would be useful to economic analysis even if no data were available for the variables of which it is composed.[2]

In other words, the economic accounts involve a conceptual framework with significant cells which make up aggregates, and the accounting approach shows the relationships among groups of transactors: from-whom-to-whom relationships. This would be useful by itself even without data.

Since relationships and components are shown, influential economic theories obviously condition the design or structure of the accounts. As the Stones have written, "Social accounting is concerned with a comprehensive, orderly, consistent presentation of the facts of economic life, in which the concepts, definitions and classifications adopted lend themselves to actual measurement and, within this limitation, correspond to those which appear in economic theory and so can be used

---

[1] Richard Stone and Giovanna Croft-Murray, *Social Accounting and Economic Models* (London: Bowes & Bowes, Publishers, Ltd., 1959), p. 9.

[2] John P. Powelson, *National Income and Flow-of-funds Analysis* (New York: McGraw-Hill Book Company, 1960), p. 1.

for economic analysis."[3] It is economic theory that suggests which variables are significant and should be measured. On the other hand, the economic statistician must give operational definition to the theorists' concepts. Unless the concepts of the theorists can be given empirical content, there is no way to test the theories and they can hardly be said to pertain to the real world and observable phenomena. The national economic accounts specialist may also, on the basis of his institutional studies, suggest certain types of sectoring and categories of transactions which may be useful to the theorist. By making possible the testing and subsequent refining of theories, the economic statistician contributes to the development of theory, which, in time, provides further guidance for the structuring of economic accounts and the collection of data for the estimates required to fill the boxes of the accounting structure. In the interaction of theory and quantitative analysis, economic accounts play an important role, both in facilitating and benefiting from advances in tested theory.

Basic Constructs

In the accounts, economic transactors are grouped according to behavioral similarities; these groupings are called *sectors* of the economy. There are two main schemes of sectoring which may be used, depending on the analytical focus. Sectoring *by industry*, comprising establishments producing a given range of "primary" products in terms of which the industry is defined, is necessary for analysis of production functions and interindustry relationships. Sectoring *by institutional entities*, such as households, business enterprises, and governments, is necessary for studying decision-making processes relating to the acquisition and disposition of income, lending and borrowing, and the structuring of assets and liabilities.

Transactions are grouped according to major types of activities; these activity groupings are shown in a series of interrelated accounts: (1) production, or output, and cost (income); (2) appropriation, or income and outlay; (3) accumulation, or saving and investment; and (4) financing (flow of funds). Measures of stocks appear in (5) balance sheets and wealth statements and are related to the flows through the accumulation, or investment, accounts and the financing accounts.

Finally, there is the matter of identifying and defining the aggregates, significant components, and detailed classifications of the various types of economic flows and stocks presented. As will be amply demonstrated in the following chapters, there is room for controversy about the precise definitions, particularly the degree of inclusiveness, of major aggregates such as income and product, saving and investment, final and intermediate product, and so on. Decisions must be made about the types of classifications to use. For example, should national income be classified by legal forms or by functional shares? Then, there is the perennial question, How much detail should be included in the accounts and supporting tables? Decisions in these areas may be conditioned by the availability of data, but insofar as possible, criteria of usefulness for economic analysis are applied. At some point, the utility of additional detail must be weighed against the costs not only of collecting and presenting more detailed data, but also of the lessened comprehensibility associated with greater complexity.

[3] Richard Stone and Giovanna Stone, *National Income and Expenditure*, 6th ed., rev. (Chicago: Quadrangle Books, Inc., 1962), p. 112.

ECONOMIC ACCOUNTS AND THEIR USES

It must be said that the use of an accounting structure in presenting economic statistics is primarily an organizational and pedagogic device, rather than a framework for presenting time series. That is, in the United States national income publications, the interlocking sector accounts are only shown annually for the most recent year. The various components of these accounts are presented, frequently in much greater detail, for a series of years, quarters, and sometimes months in "supporting" tables. It would be awkward to show successive sets of accounts, and the time-series presentation facilitates use of the estimates. In addition, estimates may be shown which supplement the basic accounts or represent elaborations. The accounting structure is most helpful to the estimators in setting up the estimates or in modifying them; it makes clear the relationships of the various components; and it ensures completeness, provides checks, and makes possible estimates of some variables as residuals.

Alternative modes of presentation   An interrelated set of transaction accounts and balances for the nation and its sectors is the basic method of presentation used by the UN and most nations. For this reason, and because of its clarity and familiarity, it is the chief mode of presentation used in this volume. Yet it has some disadvantages, notably, that each transaction and its description must be written twice, once in the account of the payer as a debit and once in the account of the receiver as a credit. For some purposes, alternative methods of presentation may be preferable. There are at least four alternatives, which we now present briefly. A fuller discussion of each, together with numerical illustrations, may be found in chapter I of the UN report, *A System of National Accounts*.[4]

The first method is the use of diagrams, in which the various accounts may be depicted by boxes, with connecting arrows showing the flows among them. Numbers above the arrows may indicate the magnitude of the flows (as in diagrams 1.1 and 1.2 of the UN report). In the next section, we use a diagram, without numbers, to illustrate some of the basic flows in the economy. Diagrams are only appropriate for very simple systems or as a simplified introduction to more complex systems, since with increasing complexity a diagram can soon become confusing.

A second method of presentation is what the UN report calls "balance statements." These statements permit the use of only a single description of each entry on the vertical stub, with the debits and credits to the various accounts shown in the columns. For greater compactness and clarity, we make use of a balance statement in rearranging the United States national and sector accounts in Table 7-1.[5]

The matrix form is a third method of presentation. As stated succinctly in the UN report, "Matrices permit each transaction to be represented by a single entry and the nature of the transaction to be inferred from its position. In this form of presentation, each account is represented by a row and column pair and the convention is followed that incomings are shown in the rows and outgoings are shown in the columns."[6] The various categories may be subdivided, if desired, and each entry

---

[4] United Nations, Department of Economic and Social Affairs, Statistical Office, *A System of National Accounts*, Studies in Methods, ser. F, no. 2, rev. 3 (New York, 1968). (Hereafter referred to as UN, *SNA*, 1968.)

[5] A somewhat different form of the balance statement is shown in UN, *SNA*, 1968, p. 4, table 1.2.

[6] *Ibid.*, pp. 4-5.

interpreted as a submatrix. Thus, a small matrix can represent a big matrix, as an interaction on the small matrix shows the interaction of one set of categories with another.

An advantage of the matrix presentation is that it is much more concise than the accounts. The matrix form is commonly used in presenting interindustry relationships, and we discuss the input-output matrix in Chapter 5. The UN report uses matrices as well as accounts in explaining the revised system of national accounts (SNA). We reproduce the small matrix of the UN system in our summary, Chapter 14 (Table 14-2), and trace through the entries linking the opening and closing balance sheets. As collateral reading for Chapter 14, the student should work through the UN presentation of the revised system as a whole in terms of the matrix approach as well as in terms of the standard accounts and tables.[7] It would be premature to do so at this stage, since the very compactness of matrices can cause confusion until one has a thorough background in each of the various accounts that make up the system. Such a background is provided here in Chapters 3 through 10.

The fourth method of presentation is to use equations to represent the equalities of debits and credits. Most students are familiar, for example, with the Keynesian equations defining income and product, and the derived equality of saving and investment. However, except in that sort of highly aggregated case, the algebraic approach involves a large number of equations, unless matrix algebra is used. A more important disadvantage is that the equations relate to one account at a time, so this approach does not bring out the interaction of the various accounts. Consequently, we do not use this approach, although references are made to mathematical treatments.[8]

DIAGRAMMATIC INTRODUCTION TO THE ACCOUNTS

The structure of economic accounts can be illustrated by diagrams which picture the chief flows within an economy. We are all familiar with the simple (and oversimplified) two-sector diagram, which shows the provision of factor services by households to producing units, in return for factor compensation, and then the expenditure of that income by households for final goods and services. The solid lines in Diagram 1-1 below indicate the real flows, the dotted lines the monetary payments. This diagram is effective in showing the basic circular flow in an exchange economy—the sale of factor services for pay and the expenditure of money income for the goods and services produced by the factors in firms and other producing units. It is oversimplified, however, not only in assuming a closed economy and completely integrated firms (no intermediate products), but also in neglecting saving and investment.

A more realistic diagram of economic flows would have to be complicated. In addition to the household-enterprise transactions, it would bring in the government sector, showing tax payments to governments by the private sectors and the reverse flows of public services, as well as government purchases of services or goods from the other sectors. It should also open up the economy, showing transactions of the

[7] *Ibid.*, chaps. II and VIII.

[8] The UN report, *ibid.*, for example, has a mathematical discussion of input-output relationships in an annex to chap. III and symbolic representation of the entire system in the annex to chap. II.

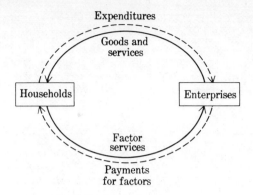

DIAGRAM 1-1
The circular flow of income and outlay, two-
sector model.

various sectors with the rest of the world, payments for imports, and receipts for exports of goods and services. Saving of the several sectors through financial inter- mediaries would also be shown, and the net lending by the intermediaries to finance investments. The enterprise account could also indicate interindustry transactions — which cancel out as far as intermediate goods used up in the current year's produc- tion are concerned. Only purchases of capital goods and additions to inventory would represent final products to be included in GNP.

THE INTEGRATED ACCOUNTING FRAMEWORK

In Diagram 1-2, we reproduce a schematic representation of an integrated system of national economic accounts from the recent monograph by Richard and Nancy Ruggles. This diagram also serves to indicate the structure of this volume, as references to succeeding chapters are shown in parentheses.

The first block in the upper left-hand corner, the national income and product account (Chapter 3), is indeed the cornerstone of a system of economic accounts. Much of the 300-year history of national income accounts (Chapter 2) has to do with this account, since it was only after 1940 that the concept of an interrelated set of sector accounts, as shown in the top tier, was developed. It was only after 1950 that the concept of a comprehensive integrated set of accounts, as shown in Diagram 1-2, gradually emerged.

The basic production account can be deconsolidated by industry in terms of value added, or industry product (Chapter 4), and further disaggregated into the input-output matrix (Chapter 5), as shown in the sixth box of the second tier. The subject of price deflation of the product accounts (Chapter 6) is not depicted on the diagram, since the boxes can refer to the accounts in either current or constant prices.

Across the top tier, the production account is related to sector income and outlay accounts, capital formation accounts, and an "external" rest-of-the-world account (Chapter 7). These are the basic income and production accounts. The United States accounts treat capital formation on a consolidated, national basis,

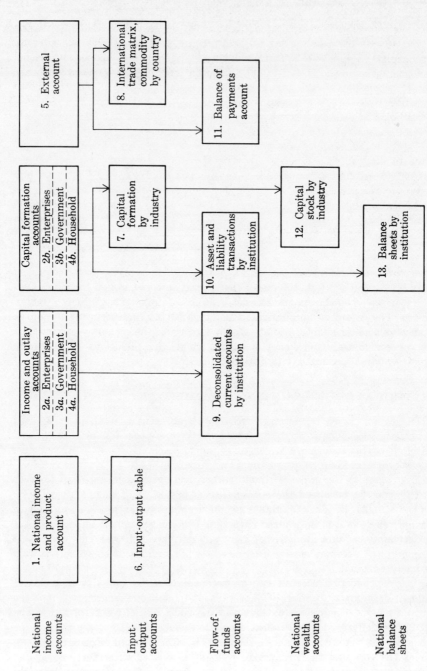

DIAGRAM 1-2

Components of the national economic accounts. Source: Richard Ruggles and Nancy Ruggles, *The Design of Economic Accounts* (New York: National Bureau of Economic Research, 1970).

but it is more informative to disaggregate by sector, as shown by the subdivisions 2b, 3b, and 4b relating to enterprises, governments, and households (Chapter 8). The sector capital accounts can be further elaborated to show net changes in financial assets and liabilities in the flow-of-funds accounts (Chapter 9), as depicted in boxes 9, 10, and 11, which provide the link to balance sheets, by sector (Chapter 10), shown in box 13. When sector balance sheets are consolidated, national wealth emerges, depicted in box 12 (also covered in Chapter 10), which can be viewed alternatively as the result of capital formation by industry, box 7. The entire system of national economic accounts is recapitulated in Chapter 14.

While the diagram is confined to a system of national accounts, the book covers other aspects: regional accounts (Chapter 11) and supranational accounts and international comparisons (Chapter 13). Throughout, we refer to uses of the accounts so that the student never loses sight of their practicality. The final three chapters (15 to 17) are devoted to a discussion of uses, with concrete illustrations of some of the more important.

REVIEW QUESTIONS

1 What is meant by economic accounting? Compare it with business accounting.
2 In economic accounting, groupings of transactors and transactions provide a system of ordering the detail of economic activity. What are the two main schemes of grouping transactors? What are the major types of activities into which transactions are grouped?
3 What are the alternative modes of presenting the major flows and balances of the economy?

SELECTED REFERENCES

POWELSON, JOHN P.: *National Income and Flow-of-funds Analysis* (New York: McGraw-Hill Book Company, 1960).
RUGGLES, RICHARD, and NANCY RUGGLES: *The Design of Economic Accounts* (New York: National Bureau of Economic Research, 1970).
UNITED NATIONS, DEPARTMENT OF ECONOMIC AND SOCIAL AFFAIRS, STATISTICAL OFFICE: *A System of National Accounts*, Studies in Methods, ser. F, no. 2, rev. 3 (New York, 1968).

The Development of National Income Estimation and Economic Accounting

2

The first national income estimate was made for England by Sir William Petty in 1665. Subsequent development of national income estimation may be divided roughly into two main phases.

The first phase was by far the longer, lasting through World War I. It was characterized by the preparation of national income estimates by a succession of individual investigators in a small number of relatively advanced countries. In addition to intellectual curiosity, the most frequent motivation of the individual scholars was nationalism—the desire to compare the economic performance of rival nations and the need to build a quantitative basis for formulation of tax and other policies to strengthen and reform national economies.

Data were often fragmentary, but they were gradually improved as the statistical requirements of governments for purposes of administration and regulation grew. Concepts of national income were clarified, with the *comprehensive* and *material product* concepts emerging as the two most popular, but with variants of each common. Estimating methodology was improved, and by the nineteenth century, income was estimated in terms of all three major approaches: factor income, final expenditure, and income originating (value added) by industry. But the idea of an interlocking set of sector accounts had been only dimly anticipated. Much of the potential usefulness of the estimates was lost because they were not continuing time series; nor did they generally have the degree of detail required for complex analysis. Most of the authors did not intend their estimates for general-purpose use; they were interested in specific analytical purposes of their own. But the groundwork was laid for the subsequent flowering of economic accounting.

Since World War I there has been a "takeoff" into self-sustaining institutional development of national income statistics; they have been transformed into economic accounts capable of elaboration in a variety of directions. Since World War II national income estimation has spread to virtually all the countries of the world, and governments have assumed responsibility for their preparation on a regular basis.

Given the foundation that was laid before 1919, progress in all the leading nations was accelerated by the need for a better quantitative background for devising countercyclical policies, heightened by the Great Depression of the 1930s; for waging total war, 1939 to 1945, and the cold war that followed; for carrying out reconstruction activities and aiding underdeveloped nations; and for meeting the statistical requirements of the United Nations and other international agencies that sprang up after World War II. Beginning in the 1930s, progress was also furthered by the development of macroeconomic theories of demand and employment. These theories required national income and product estimates for testing and implementation—especially in connection with the full-employment policies adopted by many nations after the war. Similarly, the spate of new theories concerning economic growth and development after the war increased the demand for national economic accounts and influenced the structure of the accounts. The invention of interlocking sets of sector accounts, the independent formulation of input-output and flow-of-funds accounts, and the development of sector balance sheets capable of integration with the basic production accounts were significant qualitative advances. Indeed, it may fairly be claimed that reasonably reliable economic accounts, together with the mathematics, statistics, and econometrics required to determine the relationships among the variables in the accounts, have become indispensable tools for the economist for improving theories and policy guidance.

DEVELOPMENTS BEFORE 1920

First, we shall look at the development of national income concepts, and then consider briefly the chief individuals in a few of the fourteen countries in which income estimates had been prepared by the end of World War I. In some cases, the estimators and theorists were the same persons; in others, individuals who contributed to the theory and concepts of national income did not attempt to prepare estimates.

Conceptual Strands

Sir William Petty and Gregory King in England, and the first French estimators, who followed their approach, adopted what Studenski calls the "comprehensive" income concept.[1] Petty defined the "income of the people" as the sum of the "annual value of the labor of the people" and the "annual proceeds of the stock or wealth of

[1] The first part of this chapter draws heavily upon Paul Studenski, *The Income of Nations* (New York: New York University Press, 1961), part I, "History." Quotations from original sources are found in Studenski on the pages cited unless otherwise noted.

the nation," the latter comprising rent, interest, and profits. On the other side of what was, in effect, a double-entry approach, he counted the "annual expense of the people," or consumption outlays, both private and collective, and the surplus remaining after current expenditures, which King called the "yearly increase of wealth." Since Petty estimated current consumption in terms of a per capita average times population, presumably he imputed a value to household production in addition to purchases through the market. The approach of the early estimators was quite similar to the present-day concept of national income and product at factor cost.

A far narrower concept of national income was advanced by the French physiocrats, led by François Quesnay, whose *Philosophie Rurale* was published in 1764. Quesnay and his followers identified national income with the income and product originating in agriculture, believing that only agriculture—still the mainstay of the French economy—produced a rent, or *produit net* over and above the costs of labor and capital. The narrow physiocratic concept had the useful by-product of forcing its authors to show the interrelationships between agriculture and the other sectors of the economy in terms of transfers of income and product. Quesnay's matrix, the *tableau economique,* was a forerunner of the modern national income sector accounts and of the input-output matrix. In two other respects the physiocrats were "modern": They stressed the importance of providing for the replacement and repair of capital goods (particularly in agriculture), in order to maintain the circular flow of income, and they emphasized the need for new investments to increase productivity. It was partly to meet this need, and partly to simplify the cumbersome French tax system, that the physiocrats advocated an *impôt unique* on the rent of landlords.

While agreeing with much of the physiocratic philosophy of economic liberalism, Adam Smith (1723-1790) disagreed with the physiocrats' concept of national income. He regarded both commodity production and the distributive trades as productive. Smith argued that manufacturing and distribution were as capable of returning a net income to producers, in the form of profit, as was agriculture, in the form of rent. Yet Smith's was also a restricted production concept in that he would exclude all services from the national income. He considered it significant that, in the production of goods, labor adds value to materials and "fixes itself" in vendible commodities that last beyond the production period, while direct services, as of servants, "generally perish in the very instant of their performance, and seldom leave any trace or value behind them, for which an equal quantity of service could afterwards be procured."[2]

According to Smith, the national product comprised commodities only, and the national income, a "neat revenue," consisted of wages, rent, and profit, including interest derived from the production of material goods, but not of services. In effect, he viewed expenditures on services, including government and dwelling rentals, as a redistribution of income, a transfer of neat revenue to the "unproductive" classes.

In light of the development of economic thought, Smith's definition of national income in terms of material product alone was an error and caused much confusion and controversy in succeeding decades. It is explainable in terms of Smith's concern with the expansion of material wealth as the basis of economic growth, for within his definition of growth he maintained that a nation becomes richer to the extent

[2] *Ibid.,* pp. 18-19.

that it spends more of its income on durable goods and less on perishables (and services), and thus increases its savings and capital accumulation.

The modern economist would point out that certain intangible service outlays also increase productive potential and that consumption of services yields utility, just as does consumption of commodities. But Smith's concept of national income was perpetuated by Ricardo and John Stuart Mill, in particular, and for almost a century held a prominent place in the mainstream of economic thought. Yet powerful opposition arose—particularly by Lauderdale, McCulloch, and Senior in Britain and by Storch, Say, Walras, and Hermann on the Continent. It was not until the writings of Alfred Marshall (1842-1924) that the comprehensive production and income concept was formally reestablished and clarified in Western thought.

Just as Smith's concept of national income was waning, it was given a different twist and a new lease on life by Karl Marx (1818-1883). Marx adopted Smith's distinction between productive and unproductive labor. Marx chose to associate productive labor with the creation of material goods alone, since he could thus more readily develop his theories of the materialization of surplus value into capital.

Marx did recognize the identity between income and product and the possibility of estimating their value from either side. In product terms, he defined value as comprising consumer goods and net investment. He saw income as comprising wages, rent, and profits (including interest). He designated the nonwage compensation as "surplus value," created by labor but appropriated by the owners of capital; thus, he refused to recognize the service rendered by the owners of capital. He included capital replacement in gross value, but not as a part of his "newly produced value," which we would call value added. Interestingly, he restricted the term "net income" to capital compensation (surplus value), and criticized Smith for including wages as well on the grounds that this was inconsistent with the philosophy of the capitalist system, which he interpreted as aiming for the production of a net income for the capitalist only.

Marx's concept is important because it was implemented subsequently by the Soviet Union and other Communist nations in the "material product system" of national accounts, as we shall see in the next section. In Western thought, however, the final *coup de grâce* was given Smith's income concept by Alfred Marshall in his *Economics of Industry* (1879) and later in his *Principles* (1890). By firmly identifying production with the creation of utility, and thus clearly comprehending direct services as well as commodities, Marshall pointed most Western economists back in the direction of the comprehensive production concept. He also distinguished clearly between gross and net income, as indicated in the following passage:

> The labour and capital of the country, acting on its national resources, produce annually a certain *net* aggregate of commodities, material and immaterial, including services of all kinds. The limiting word "net" is needed to provide for the using up of raw and half finished commodities, and for the wearing out and depreciation of plant which is involved in production: all such waste must of course be deducted from the gross produce before the true or net income can be found. And net income due on account of foreign investments must be added in. This is the true net annual income, or revenue, of the country; or, the national dividend: we may, of course, estimate it for a year or for any other period.[3]

[3] Alfred Marshall, *Principles of Economics*, 8th ed. (New York: The Macmillan Company, 1948), p. 523.

Country Developments

An interesting and detailed history of the early estimates of national income, with emphasis on Great Britain, France, and Russia, has been written by Studenski.[4] While recommended for the specialist, this history would be chiefly of antiquarian interest for most students of economic accounts. Nevertheless, to give some of the flavor of the early development, we summarize in Table 2-1 the pioneering estimators, their countries, the dates of the first estimates, and a few brief comments.[5] The important point to remember is that the work of the early individual investigators laid the groundwork for the subsequent rapid development of economic accounts under the auspices of the national governments, as described in the next section.

THE MODERN PERIOD: SINCE 1920

Owing to the institutional sponsorship of most of the work on national economic accounts since 1920, this section deals less with individuals than did the review of the earlier period. Here we shall describe national and international progress in more general terms. First, we shall summarize some of the theoretical and conceptual developments that influenced the evolution of the economic accounts.

Conceptual Developments

A. C. Pigou helped to give direction to the new era of institutional and government estimation when he defined national income as comprising goods and services that "can be brought directly or indirectly into relation with the measuring-rod of money."[6] Studenski refers to prevalence of the comprehensive production concept, but actually the official estimators, seeking objective rules to guide the estimation process, tended to confine national income and product to final goods entering organized markets, with imputations of value confined to those nonmarket transactions with important market counterparts from which values could be derived— thus conforming to Pigou's criterion. In the 1930s, the Polish economists Kalecki and Landau, and the Hungarians Matolcsy and Varga, advocated restricting production and income estimates entirely to market transactions, but so restricted a concept did not gain adherents. Rather, the tendency in recent years has been to expand imputations.

The economic theoretician with the most important influence in the 1930s was J. M. Keynes. Because his macroeconomic analysis was built around national income and outlay, attempts to test and apply his theory gave an impetus to estimation of these aggregates. By giving importance to both final outlays (particularly investments, as the strategic variable determining the level of income) and income (as the chief determinant of consumer outlay), as well as to government expenditures and receipts as a strategic policy variable, he encouraged the development of income and outlay accounts. Further, his distinctions among the several major sectors in

[4] See footnote 1.

[5] A more detailed summary of country developments to 1920 may be found in John W. Kendrick, "The Historical Development of National Income Accounts," *History of Political Economy*, vol. 2, pp. 284–315, Fall, 1970.

[6] A. C. Pigou, *The Economics of Welfare*, 4th ed. (London: Macmillan & Co., Ltd., 1932), pp. 11 and 31.

ECONOMIC ACCOUNTS AND THEIR USES

TABLE 2-1

Countries in Which National Income Estimates Were Prepared Prior to 1919

Country	First Estimator	Date of Preparation/ Publication	Comments
England	Sir William Petty	1665	Estimated "annual Income and Expense of the People"; further developed by Gregory King in 1696.
France	Pierre Bois-guillebert	1697	Equated income with consumption; more systematic estimates prepared in 1707 by Marshall Vauban.
Russia	B. F. J. Hermann (Austrian)	1790	Estimated per capita and total consumption, by type, of the Russian Empire in a statistical handbook.
	A. N. Radish-chev	1794	Estimate of "annually produced wealth of the country" —unpublished until 1811.
United States	George Tucker	1843	Included estimates of both wealth and income, by industry and state, in *Progress of the United States in Population and Wealth in Fifty Years* (expanded edition in 1855).
Austria	K. Czoernig	1861	Net output method based on Austria's first comprehensive census.
Germany	G. Rümelin A. Soetbeer R. E. May	1863–1899	Several estimates of private income distribution for individual German states; in 1899 May constructed a national total by blowing up state estimates.
Australia	T. Coughlan	1886	An officially prepared and published estimate for New South Wales by net output method; later estimates for all of Australia; first modern estimator to embrace net output, income-distributed, and final expenditure methods.
Norway	Unknown	1893	Unknown method.
Japan	K. Nakamura	1902	Net output method.
Switzerland	T. Geering & R. Hotz	1902	Income-distributed method, for selected years 1895–1899.
Netherlands	W. Bonger	1910	Income-distributed method, extended periodically until taken over by Central Statistical Office.
Italy	M. Santoro	1911	Net output method, for 1860-1910.
Bulgaria	K. Popoff	1915	Net output method.
Spain	A. Barthé (French)	1917	Net output method.

SOURCE: Paul Studenski, *The Income of Nations* (New York: New York University Press, 1961), part I,"History," chaps. 9 and 10, and especially tables 9-2, p. 141, and 10-5, p. 156.

terms of their motivations and behavior patterns suggested the development of interrelated sectoral accounts. Indeed, Keynes himself was influential in the statistical implementations of this approach in wartime Britain, as we shall see in the next section.

The emphasis which Keynes and other macroeconomic or cycle theorists put on the role of money and credit in economic fluctuations stimulated the development of financing, or flow-of-funds, accounts to reveal the changes in assets and liabilities, by type, in periods of expansion and contraction. Since World War II, there has been increased theoretical emphasis on the influence of asset holdings on expenditure decisions. This has led to attempts to estimate complete balance sheets for the various economic sectors and combined balance sheets for the economy as a whole.

Interest in real tangible assets, or wealth, and the role of such assets in economic growth goes back to Petty and the mercantilists. But the ground swell of renewed interest in economic growth and development after World War II, and in production functions especially, has led to many new attempts to define and measure real capital stocks more precisely. Of particular interest for the national income accountant has been the tendency to define investment and capital broadly to include all assets, tangible and intangible, owned by households, government, and business, which return a yield over a number of accounting periods. This broader view of investment for purposes of growth analysis is leading to a restructuring of the investment accounts, by sector, as compared with the narrower approach inherited from Keynes.

Finally, the increasing use of stock-flow relationships in both demand and supply analysis has spurred the attempt to integrate balance sheet and wealth estimates with the basic income and product accounts, by way of the sector investment and financing subaccounts.

The Spread of Economic Accounting

The number of countries for which national income estimates had been prepared increased from fourteen in 1919 to thirty-three in 1939. Beginning with Canada and the Soviet Union in 1925, nine countries had instituted continuing government estimates by 1939. Official work was undoubtedly stimulated by the Great Depression, the development of macroeconomic theory, and the prospect of using national income estimates as a background for more effective countercyclical policies.

Developments in the United States are perhaps illustrative. Early leadership in the national income field was exercised by the National Bureau of Economic Research. Shortly after the formation of the NBER in 1920, a study was undertaken to estimate national income by both the source of production and the income-received methods. The sources of data and statistical procedures were carefully set forth.[7] The estimates were extended from year to year, providing the only comprehensively estimated continuous estimates available.

The National Bureau estimates were produced, however, only with a considerable time lag. This fact was noted, for example, in a Senate hearing investigating the causes and consequences of the Depression. In 1932, at the depth of the depression. a Senate resolution was adopted calling for the Department of Commerce to prepare

---

[7] National Bureau of Economic Research Staff, *Income in the United States: Its Amount and Distribution, 1909–1919* (New York: Harcourt, Brace and Company, Inc., 1921 and 1922), vols. I and II.

estimates of national income, by industrial source and type of income, for the years 1929 to 1931. Simon Kuznets, who had taken over the National Bureau's work, cooperated with the Department of Commerce in preparing the estimates presented in 1934.[8] The estimates were continued on an annual basis. The document resulting from the original study, and another with estimates through 1935, prepared under the supervision of Robert R. Nathan, served as the basic frame for national income estimates for more than a decade. Within a relatively short time, the annual estimates were supplemented by income measures on a monthly basis (1938) and on a state by state basis (1939).[9]

In 1939, the League of Nations, in its annual *World Economic Survey,* for the first time published national income estimates, covering twenty-six countries for all or part of the period 1929 to 1938. Also in 1939, the League's Committee on Statistics first considered the problems of international comparability.[10] Unfortunately World War II slowed the spread of national income work among the nations of the world, but it stimulated some very important qualitative advances.

During the war, national income estimates were transformed into systems of national economic accounts; these systems were capable of elaboration in a number of directions in order fully to describe the chief transactions of an economy. Here, again, priority of development belongs to Great Britain. Parallel advances were taking place in Scandinavia, but these were not available to the outside world until after the war.

In the fall of 1939, the Chancellor of the Exchequer in Great Britain, under the influence of Keynes, authorized the preparation of national income estimates. Richard Stone and James Meade, with encouragement and detailed advice from Keynes, completed a set of national income and expenditure estimates for Great Britain which were published with the 1941 Budget. The formulation of government expenditures and revenues within the framework of national expenditure and income estimates was a departure which was to spread rapidly.

Methodologically, the British estimates were significant in that national product was grossed to include indirect business taxes, thus representing final output at market prices, and depreciation allowances, which are at least partially consumable over short periods if emergency requires. Of more importance, the British White Paper of April, 1941, stressed the "national income and outlay account" idea. That is, income (factor cost) and expenditure were viewed as the two sides of a double-entry production account for the entire national economy. National expenditure was thus firmly established as a coordinate variable, which together with income was necessary as background for budget formulation as well as projections and broader policy formulation.

Stone and his colleagues at the newly formed Central Statistical Office looked on the 1941 White Paper as merely a beginning. The idea of double-entry national production accounts led them to the related idea of constructing income and outlay

---

[8] *National Income, 1929–32,* 73d Cong., 2d Sess., Senate Doc. 124, 1934.

[9] A history of the United States income and product estimates has been prepared by Carol S. Carson in a doctoral dissertation at The George Washington University, Washington, D.C.

[10] See Introduction to *Problems in the International Comparison of Economic Accounts,* Conference on Research in Income and Wealth, Studies in Income and Wealth, vol. XX (Princeton, N.J.: Princeton University Press for the National Bureau of Economic Research, 1957), p. 4.

accounts for each major sector of the economy, connected with the national production account by appropriate credit and debit entries. Meade and Stone suggested four such sector accounts: households, business enterprises, governments, and rest of the world. Working along these lines, the British Treasury group brought out a White Paper in 1946 incorporating the social accounting approach.

Inspired by the British work, the National Income Division of the U.S. Department of Commerce began work on gross national product estimates in 1940 on a double-entry basis, and published a historical series in the *Survey of Current Business* in March, 1942, which was extended quarterly thereafter. By January, 1943, the new accounts were arranged to present a "Nation's Economic Budget," which in 1945 appeared in the official Budget document. The budget approach was also used for economic projections as a background for formulating postwar reconstruction plans (see Chapter 15).

In 1944, representatives of the British, United States, and Canadian national income agencies met in Washington to discuss concepts and modes of presentation to make their estimates comparable and more useful to their governments. These tripartite discussions resulted in the first international agreement in the field of national accounts. In 1947, the United States brought out an expanded set of income and product accounts by sector, and in 1948, the Canadians did likewise, incorporating the conventions developed in 1944.[11]

In the Netherlands, stimulated by Ed. Van Cleeff's articles on national bookkeeping, the Central Bureau of Statistics in 1941 attempted to construct a system of national accounts for the year 1938. Because of the war the results were not published. They were later incorporated in the first postwar publications on the national income accounts of the Netherlands. Similarly in Norway, during the German occupation, the Central Bureau of Statistics began work on national income estimates for the years 1935 to 1943, based on national accounting principles and paralleling the concepts of Stone and Meade in Great Britain. By the end of the war, the Norwegian income and product estimates were virtually completed; they were published in 1946.

Universalization of National Income Estimates

After World War II, the economic accounting approach spread rapidly. Richard Stone and other leaders published many articles on the subject, and in 1947 the League of Nations Committee of Statistical Experts published *Measurement of National Income and the Construction of Social Accounts.*[12] This report, and its appendix by Stone, set forth the basis for internationally comparable accounting systems.

About the same time, the International Association for Research in Income and Wealth was founded. This association was modeled after the Conference on Research in Income and Wealth in the United States established a decade earlier, and was intended as an international forum for scholarly papers in the national income field.

---

[11] See Edward F. Denison, "Report on Tripartite Discussions of National Income Measurement," in Conference on Research in Income and Wealth, Studies in Income and Wealth, vol. X (New York: National Bureau of Economic Research, 1947).

[12] Studies and Reports on Statistical Methods, no. 7 (Geneva: United Nations, 1947).

Its proceedings were published as the *Income and Wealth* series.[13] Regional meetings of the Association facilitate comparison of experience by researchers and estimators whose countries face similar situations.

With the organization of the United Nations, a research and statistics office, including a national income unit, was set up in the Economic and Social Council. The national income unit provided technical assistance to member countries for the development of economic accounts, since national income was used in a formula for assessment of dues. This promoted standardization of methods, as did development and subsequent revision of the system of national accounts (SNA). The same role was played by the national income group in the Organization for European Economic Cooperation (OEEC), which requested the submission of national income and product estimates from member countries compatible with the standards set forth in a standardized system of national accounts in 1953. The OEEC system was very similar to that of the UN; this is not surprising, since Richard Stone played a leading role in the formulation of both. The various regional economic commissions of the UN made extensive use of the national income estimates of constituent countries in reporting on economic developments and in preparing projections, or targets, for development (see Chapter 12).

Also, since World War II, the U.S. Department of Commerce has conducted training programs on the national income accounts for statisticians and economists from many other countries. This has helped to promote the spread of this type of work and has contributed to consistency of concept and method, although estimators have naturally tended to adapt their basic approach to the requirements and data systems of their own countries.

Between 1945 and 1955, the number of countries with national income estimates grew from 39 to 93, and by 1969 the total exceeded 130. In other words, economic accounts are now almost universal, and in most countries the estimates are prepared on a continuing basis. The thrust now is toward improving the quality of the estimates and elaborating the basic income and product accounts in useful directions.

Development of Other Kinds of Economic Accounts

The United States has been in the forefront of the development of economic accounts other than national income and product. The pioneering work of Wassily Leontief on input-output matrices, of Morris Copeland on flow of funds, and of Raymond Goldsmith on balance sheets and wealth estimates is referred to in the chapters discussing these accounts. In many countries, including the United States, the several kinds of accounts were developed independently of the income and product accounts. Although some countries have integrated two or more of the different sets of accounts, substantial work remains to be done in this area. The recent UN report on the revised SNA moves significantly in the direction of a fully integrated system. One of the main purposes of the present volume is to show how the various types of accounts relate to one another and may be integrated into a consistent whole, so we shall not pursue the subject further in this chapter.

---

[13] The first eleven of the series were published as books. Thereafter *Income and Wealth* has been a quarterly journal, *The Review of Income and Wealth*.

REVIEW QUESTIONS

1 Contrast the concepts of national income advanced by Petty and King, the physiocrats, and Adam Smith.

2 What are the relationships between Adam Smith's concept of income, the Marxian concept, and the present-day material product system?

3 What are some of the uses to which the pre-1920 estimates of national income were put?

4 What are the major post-1920 conceptual developments in national income work?

5 Suggest the theoretical relationship between Keynesian theory and the accounting approach to national income. Trace the development of this approach from 1939 to 1947.

SELECTED REFERENCES

LUNDBERG, ERIK, ed.: *Income and Wealth,* ser. I (London: Bowes & Bowes, Publishers, Ltd., 1951). See the modern developments in France, the United Kingdom, and the Netherlands.

NATIONAL ACCOUNTS REVIEW COMMITTEE: *The National Economic Accounts of the United States: Review, Appraisal, and Recommendations, Hearings before the Subcommittee on Economic Statistics of the Joint Economic Committee,* 85th Cong., 1st Sess., 1957. See especially chap. IV, for background of the United States estimates.

STUDENSKI, PAUL: *The Income of Nations* (New York: New York University Press, 1961), part I, "History."

The Production Account

3

The production account is the cornerstone of the economic accounting system, as indicated in Chapter 1. The production of goods and services that men want (i.e., the creation of utility) gives rise to the primary income flows which, together with income redistributions, provide the incomes that the various sectors spend or save and invest either directly or through financial intermediaries.

The value of production must equal the cost of production, when profit is counted as a cost from the social viewpoint. If interindustry sales and purchases are dropped from both the sources and uses sides of the production account (since they are equal), one is left with the national product or "final" expenditures on the sources (credit) side and factor costs and certain "nonfactor charges" on the uses (debit) side. We shall consider both national product and income in this chapter, but the former first. Priority is given production, since the creation of utility is the end of economic activity. (If activity were desired purely for its own sake, this would be play.) The boundaries given to productive activity automatically delimit the incomes to labor and property engaged in that production.

We defer until the next chapter the view of national product as the sum of value added by industry, since one cannot understand value added unless one knows that to which value is being added. Since value is added at successive stages of production, we must first probe the nature of final production and the associated costs, or income. The discussion in this chapter relates primarily to the United States income and product account (Appendix A, Table A-1), but we also refer to the UN revised SNA (Appendix B, Table B-I.1) when it differs significantly from the United States approach.

THE NATIONAL PRODUCT

Students in beginning economics courses are often taught the official Department of Commerce definition of national product: ". . . the market value of the output of [final] goods and services produced by the nation's economy." If it is the *gross* national product (GNP), the phrase ". . . before deduction of depreciation charges and other allowances for . . . consumption of durable capital goods" must be added. The beginning student does not generally realize the complexity of this deceptively simple definition. Much of the following discussion revolves around clarification and elaboration of the key words in the definition: final, gross, economy, market value, and nation. These will be taken up in turn.

Final versus Intermediate Products

The Commerce Department approach   The Department of Commerce has a relatively clean-cut operational or working definition of *final product* as "a purchase that is not resold," and of *intermediate product* as "one that is resold." Somewhat more precisely, one may refer to purchases "not charged to current cost . . . during the accounting period."[1] The criterion was established by reference to business practice, and is designed to prevent duplication in the national product estimates. That is, the value of raw materials or semifinished goods purchased by business for further processing is already included in the value of the final products into which the goods are incorporated, and their cost should not be added to the value of final product. By Commerce definition, final product is seen to comprise consumption expenditures, sales to business on capital account, net exports, and sales to general governments. (See Appendix A.)

Since expenditures by households and nonprofit institutions are considered to be incurred "largely to meet the needs of individuals, they consist in the main of goods and services that determine what is commonly regarded as the standard of living."[2] It is obvious that consumption goods purchased by households are not resold in the current period (if they are, the purchase is not really a consumption expenditure, but an intermediate purchase by an individual acting as a middleman). Eventually durable goods may be sold or traded in, but that is in a later accounting period, and the main purpose of the purchaser is to consume the services of the durable, and the resale or trade in is part of a new transaction. The Department, along with most other income estimators, regards people as the end, and not just a means of production. That is, no attempt is made to exclude expenditures for "maintenance" of (or "investment" in) human capital, since the daily living of people is taken as an end in itself.

Items sold to business on capital account, or "domestic investment," are not used up in the current period, but are added to stock and so are clearly final products.

---

[1] U.S. Department of Commerce, Office of Business Economics, *National Income* (1954), p. 30.
[2] *Ibid.*, p. 38.

The investment in durable capital goods is gradually recouped through depreciation allowances over time, but not in one accounting period. Strictly speaking, purchases of new capital goods out of depreciation allowances should not be included in final product in a net sense, although as we shall see later, there are reasons to measure gross investment and gross product in addition to the net magnitudes.

The goods sold to general government are not resold by government in any specific market sense. True, people as individuals or in organizations pay taxes to the government, but these are for the general support of government and do not represent payment for a particular good or service. In any case, the goods purchased by government from business are seldom if ever resold in the same form in the current accounting period; they are used by government employees to produce services, generally, which the population desires to obtain collectively and which "satisfy the needs of the members of the community."

Goods and services sold abroad are not resold domestically. But since the final purchases already enumerated include the value of imported goods, these must be subtracted from exports in order to arrive at *national* product. Also, net exports (except for the portion financed by grants or gifts) represent net additions to foreign claims, and thus enhance the future income of the nation just as domestic investment does.

Implicitly, the Department tends to associate final product with goods and services that satisfy human needs.[3] But the welfare criterion is not explicitly invoked, since it is recognized that some so-called final goods are "quasi-intermediate," whereas some purchases of intermediate products may promote economic welfare. "As a practical matter, one must generally deal with types of buyers and categories of goods and services . . . [and] any measure of total production must be somewhat conventional."[4] As the Department points out, its approach deals with actual trans-actors and transactions so as to show their interrelations in a realistic way, with a minimum of subjective adjustment by estimators.

For some purposes, it would even be desirable to show the value of total pro-duction, including sales of intermediate products—as, for example, in studies of the transactions velocity of money and in input-output studies, in which the production account is deconsolidated in order to show intermediate product transactions on an industry basis. But it is unlikely that a gross production measure would show the same movements as a final product measure or as a netter measure which was more welfare-oriented. Some business costs are not determined by technical production requirements, but are, within limits, discretionary. This is true, for example, of advertising and sales promotion, part of repair and maintenance, research and development engineering, and certain welfare-type outlays. Even those intermediate products which are technologically related to final output vary over time as a result of changing technology, particularly as it affects materials consumption per unit of output. The increasing proportion of GNP devoted to services has also tended to reduce intermediate production output relative to final output. So has the vertical integration of firms, at least as far as the sale (rather than the interplant transfer) of intermediate products is concerned.

[3] *Ibid.*, p. 38. It is asserted that the Department's criteria are "useful for segregating the major types of goods and services provided to satisfy the needs of individuals."
[4] *Ibid.*, p. 38.

Welfare-oriented measures Simon Kuznets is perhaps the best known of those economists who believe it undesirable to measure final product without explicit reference to the economic goals or ends of men and society. Kuznets has defined national product in terms of goods and services designed to satisfy the recognized needs of ultimate consumers, present and future.[5] The last phrase is added so that the definition includes both consumption goods and services and additions to capital stock. Net investment, like consumption, is a final product because it increases capacity to produce final goods in the future. In disposing of their incomes, people choose not only to spend for consumption but to maintain and expand their capital assets as well in order to provide for the future. Also, consider that net investment represents production which could be devoted to consumption purposes if people preferred. A disadvantage of the very restrictive view that final product is solely consumption output (once advocated by Irving Fisher) is that this magnitude would fluctuate, depending on people's choices between consumption and saving.

In accordance with his definition, Professor Kuznets considers national product as falling into two categories: (1) consumption expenditure, and here he would include both private expenditure and expenditure by government designed to satisfy consumer wants; and (2) investment, including private and government capital outlays. Kuznets's functional scheme has the advantage of focusing on two major purposes of the economy: consumption and additions to capital stock, regardless of whether privately or publicly financed. In contrast, the Commerce sectoral scheme is useful in showing final sector purchases, with government identified as a unit within the framework of the total economy.

Kuznets and the other welfare-oriented national income specialists would, in principle, examine the entire range of purchases in the economy to see which were truly final (including some business expenditures charged to current cost) and which were intermediate (including some purchases by consumers and government). In practice, Kuznets's estimates conform rather closely to those of the Commerce Department, with the principal exception of a portion of government purchases which Kuznets would classify as representing intermediate products, or "cost services to business." Examples of categories of purchases by the major sectors which might be classed as intermediate follow.

Certain "consumption expenditures" are clearly dictated by job requirements. Workers in some trades are still required to purchase their own uniforms, hand tools, and certain other producer goods. Transportation expense to and from work would appear to be a cost, and in some instances it is borne by employers. Less unambiguous examples have to do with elements in the general family budget which are employment-connected, such as certain entertainment expenses and even some aspects of the general "style of living."

There is little doubt that business capital outlays are final products, but certain categories of business purchases charged to current expense also might well be classed as final products. Research and development outlays may be charged to current expense under United States tax laws, but as a form of intangible investment, they qualify as final expenditure. The same is true of education and training

---

[5] Simon Kuznets, *National Income and Its Composition, 1919–1938* (New York: National Bureau of Economic Research, 1941), p. 57.

ECONOMIC ACCOUNTS AND THEIR USES

outlays by business which enhance income in future periods. Part of maintenance and repair expenses exceed the minimum level required for true maintenance and actually increase productive capacity; they also might be classed as investment if they could be quantified.

Another portion of business purchases charged to current expense might be classed as consumption goods and services. Some firms furnish welfare services directly to employees, as through medical and recreational facilities, or they subsidize portions of employee consumption, as through company cafeterias. One never knows, of course, whether the employee would choose the services furnished by the company if he had freedom of choice. Possibly more important is so-called expense account living, whereby certain classes of employees are reimbursed for costs incurred on company business, which may be so broadly construed as to cover significant amounts devoted to objects the employee would otherwise have purchased for himself.

The chief area of controversy regarding possible double counting, that is, counting as final product that which should be subtracted from the total as intermediate, is in the government sector. A few economists have contended that all government services are intermediate, since they "ensure only the maintenance of the present economic and social order and the maintenance of the present level of production."[6] This view seems to leave out both tangible and intangible public investment, not to mention consumer services.

Kuznets recognizes the final products rendered by governments. But he maintains that there are also important government services provided to business, which, since they facilitate production, are intermediate. In his early estimates, he made the convenient assumption that such cost services were equal to indirect business taxes paid (thus making national income and national product equal); later, he assumed government services to consumers to be equal to personal tax payments, government investment was estimated directly, and the remainder of government purchases was excluded from final product. In more recent writings, he advocated going down the list of government services and counting as final consumer products only those items which (1) are rendered gratis or for only a token payment, (2) are available to an individual only upon his initiative, and (3) have broad analogues in private markets.[7]

Studenski thinks Kuznets is too restrictive in his concept of final services, and points to national product estimates for Sweden and Germany, in which a much narrower set of government services is classed as intermediate. He also notes that Kuznets fails to develop criteria for allocating the services of joint-use facilities, such as public roads, which are used by both business and individuals as consumers.

During World War II, Kuznets revised his criteria to include national security outlays in final product. The justification was that, in wartime, national survival became an end of economic activity, along with the individualistic goal of want satisfaction. It would also have seemed anomalous to have GNP scarcely rise at all in a time when employment and most other production indexes were rising substan-

---

[6] A statement by the Hungarian economists Matolcsy and Varga, cited by Paul Studenski, *The Income of Nations* (New York: New York University Press, 1961), part II, "Theory and Methodology," p. 36. Studenski provides a review of the major points of this whole controversy.

[7] See "Government Product and National Income," in Erik Lundberg, ed., *Income and Wealth*, ser. I (London: Bowes & Bowes, Publishers, Ltd., 1951), pp. 192-197.

tially! Frederick Mills and the present writer extended Kuznets's reasoning to consider national security a social goal at *all* times and to include such expenditures continuously.[8] When this is done, national security outlays, together with consumer services and investment, absorb most of government output, and cost services become a relatively small category.

The Commerce Department counts *all* government purchases as final product. The Department economists claim that there are no clear-cut cases of direct services to business by government of any quantitative importance. The class of government intermediate products ". . . looms large only if the concrete notion of aid to business is stretched to cover the broad range of government services to the public which actually reflect a complexity of causes and purposes and cannot appropriately be classified under any such narrow head."[9] It is believed that under a narrow definition, the volume of such services would not be significant enough to distort the movement of total government purchases relative to a theoretically "purer" final output measure. In addition, the Department economists point to statistical difficulties in implementing an allocation, particularly as regards government services used jointly by business and individuals. Further, they maintain that elimination of intermediate services from government purchases "would obscure the national economic accounts in their capacity as records of actual transactions."[10]

In a subsequent elaboration of the Commerce Department position, George Jaszi pointed out that in measuring national product generally, we do not directly measure satisfactions as such, but rather the inputs (consumer purchases, including government purchases for collective consumption) which are used to produce satisfaction.[11] Most of the problems encountered in the government sector have analogues in the personal sector. Now, government cost services to business are part of input into final product, which are not included as such in the private sector. (Indirect business taxes are a price-increasing element to business, but they are not matched by corresponding services.) In current dollars, this would not be a drawback, since the private final goods would be counted at market price, even though certain government services in effect represented subsidies. But in the deflated product estimates, unless the government cost services showed the same movement as the final outputs, real product movements would be distorted unless the cost-service components of final product were separately measured and deflated for inclusion with the rest of the final product.

In connection with estimation of national product at factor cost, it is very clear that, to be consistent with the treatment of private industries, value added by government must include the factor costs associated with production of intermediate as well as final products. If the factor-cost approach were to be applied on a product as well as on an industry basis, it would be necessary to deduct indirect business taxes

[8] See John W. Kendrick, *Productivity Trends in the United States* (Princeton, N.J.: Princeton University Press for the National Bureau of Economic Research, 1961), appendix A, p. 236, and table A-I.

[9] U.S. Department of Commerce, *op. cit.*, p. 39.

[10] *Ibid.*

[11] "The Conceptual Basis of the Accounts: A Re-examination," in *A Critique of the United States Income and Product Accounts,* Conference on Research in Income and Wealth, Studies in Income and Wealth, vol. XXII (Princeton, N.J.: Princeton University Press for the National Bureau of Economic Research, 1958), pp. 70–72.

ECONOMIC ACCOUNTS AND THEIR USES

and add the value of government intermediate services on a product-group basis (i.e., adjust for the difference between indirect business taxes and subsidies, including government cost services which are a species of subsidy in kind). As pointed out in the next chapter, this approach is hardly feasible. But factor cost *is* estimated in total and on an industry basis and must include all compensation of government factors.

Conclusion It is obvious that the Commerce approach is simpler and more workable than the welfare approach. Counting all current purchases by households and non-profit institutions and by governments, and capital outlays by business, as final is cleaner than trying to run the whole gamut of individual purchases to determine which might be excluded as not contributing directly to satisfactions. It is also true that the official approach yields cruder welfare-type measures. But the proposed more refined measures (even assuming an adequate statistical base for the refinements) also would not be adequate welfare indicators. Theory teaches us that, to interpret welfare changes or differences, we would need much supplemental information relating to such factors as changes or differences in income distribution, in wants and technology, and in the portions of income required to offset "necessary evils"—as well as supplementary free goods.

Richard Ruggles clearly states the nonwelfare approach to income estimation:[12]

> The line separating intermediate from final services is too difficult to draw for either consumers or government, and as a consequence we must recognize that the aggregates of national income and product are not invariant measures of welfare. Even if government intermediate services were eliminated, we would still be left with many things that do not contribute to welfare but are rather regrettable necessities of our way of life. Elimination of government intermediate services would not solve the problem of measuring welfare, but it would leave much very valuable information out of the national accounts, and we would have less understanding of what was taking place in the economy, rather than more.

> We need to make gross national product even grosser than it is, and to recognize that it does not correspond to a measurement of welfare but rather provides a body of data useful to the economic analyst in understanding the behavior of the economy. The measurement of welfare and output in an economy is a complex task. National accounts may provide much of the necessary information for an analysis of changes in welfare over a period of time or for comparisons of welfare between countries, but it is asking too much to expect that any systematic collection of data on transactions in the economy, which do not and cannot reflect the changing pattern of institutions and needs, can itself be used as a thermometer yielding valid indications of changes in welfare.

As the Department economists themselves write, the national product is ". . . tied closely to the modern market-economy and is obtained, broadly speaking, by summing actual transactions of its major constituent economic groups." As such, it is part of an ". . . economic accounting system designed to facilitate an understanding of the functioning of the economy in terms of the interaction of these groups."[13]

---

[12] Richard Ruggles, "The Government Sector in National Accounts" (paper prepared for a joint session of the International Association for Research in Income and Wealth and a UN Seminar on National Accounts for Latin America, Rio de Janeiro, 1959).

[13] U.S. Department of Commerce, *op. cit.*, p. 39.

From this point of view, it would really be desirable for the Department to "gross up" the production account to show the value of total production, including all intermediate product sales. But most users would object if a net subtotal of national product were not also shown, since an overall production indicator is needed and is widely used. The Department seems to be satisfied with its net measure, agreeing, however, that a maximum of detail on purchases should be provided so that users may adjust it to suit their purposes.

The author's position is that estimates of gross flows, by transactor groups, and in considerable detail by type of transaction, are essential. If a net production estimate is given (GNP or, preferably, net national product (NNP)), and it should be, there is no objection to refining it further toward a true final product measure in the Kuznets sense—when further adjustments can be made based on adequate data and relatively clear-cut concepts. It is not true, as has been asserted by Commerce spokesmen, that further adjustments "would obscure the national economic accounts in their capacity as records of actual transactions."[14] Household purchases for business purposes, such as uniforms or tools, can be shown as a deduction from gross consumption expenditures and from personal income. Business purchases, such as research and development, charged to current cost—which are really investment— can be treated as an adjustment item in the same way that capital outlays charged to current expense were treated prior to 1965; and consumer-type services to employees can be shown as wages in kind. Government intermediate services can be treated in the same way as subsidies, being netted against government purchases on the credit side and indirect business taxes on the debit side. But all the gross flows would be kept in the record, with the adjustments clearly shown.

In practice, the adjustments that could be made in a clear-cut fashion would probably be quite limited. On balance, they might well increase the national product, since business intangible investment is relatively large, and this would be added. Probably it would not be wise for the Department to attempt to allocate mixed items if, as it argues, allocation formulas would have to be rough and imprecise. But it does not seem justified to make no adjustments in the direction of purer "final" product estimates in cases where the adjustments can be firmly based. After all, as we shall see below, substantial adjustments are made to the basic market-flow estimates in other areas, as imputations of value to nonmarket activities.

Even with all possible adjustments, the user of national product aggregates must realize that they are not precise welfare indicators, and more detailed and additional information is necessary to interpret them from this viewpoint. But they are, nonetheless, the most meaningful general-purpose indicators of production movements in the economy as a whole, and they should be improved where possible.

Gross versus Net

We have seen that the national product is basically a *net* concept—the value of production less the value of purchased intermediate products consumed in the production process. Yet, confusing as it sounds, there are both gross and net versions of national product. They relate to inclusion or exclusion of capital consumption allowances.

[14] *Ibid.*

This item consists primarily of reserves for depreciation of fixed durable capital goods (structures and equipment) plus accidental damage to fixed capital. The values of durable capital goods gradually decline because of physical wear and obsolescence due to technological improvements in successive models of the various types of durables; thus, the net income arising from the continued use of the capital goods declines until eventually their economic lives expire.

It seems clear that, like the consumption of intermediate products, the gradual consumption of durable capital assets over their lives (i.e., the reduction in their values) would be deducted from the value of production to arrive at a truly net national product estimate. That is, investment in new capital goods in a dollar volume equivalent to the decline in the value of existing capital assets (at current valuations) is necessary to maintain the future net income-producing ability of the stock of capital intact, and thus its value.

The official emphasis on the GNP, rather than the NNP, in the United States, as evidenced by the summation to GNP in the summary income and product account, is usually justified by two arguments. First, there are serious statistical difficulties in converting estimates of depreciation (and asset values) from the original (acquisition) costs at which they are carried on the books of companies to current (replacement) values. Perhaps these difficulties were insurmountable at the time of the first GNP estimates in 1942. But since then, a great deal of progress has been made in the estimation of wealth, including the conversion of original cost estimates into current replacement value estimates. Further progress is needed, but usable estimates of capital consumption at market prices are now feasible and should be prepared. Certainly the present NNP estimates, in which depreciation at original cost for all but farm durables is deducted from GNP at market price, are not useful, and the adjusted depreciation and NNP estimates could hardly help being far better despite remaining problems.

The second argument used to justify the official emphasis on GNP is that replacement of the capital values lost through depreciation can generally be deferred, so that, in effect, depreciation allowances can be consumed to a large degree in the short run. This was particularly relevant in 1942 when the chief use of the initial GNP estimates was to show the resources available for war and related purposes.

Yet, as we have seen, certain classes of intermediate product purchases, as for advertising and promotion, redesign, and maintenance, can also be deferred. The second argument could better be used to advocate a complete grossing of production value estimates, but with considerable detail on categories of intermediate products and capital consumed in production, as well as on final product.

It should be observed, before we begin a more extensive discussion of wealth estimates, that replacement of capital values may well increase the overall productive capacity of the nation. There are two reasons. First, if capital outlays are rising, which is the typical situation in a growing economy, depreciation allowances exceed physical replacement requirements, so the physical stock of capital goods (but not its value) is increased. Second, new capital goods usually produce a larger physical volume of final goods and services than the capital goods replaced, although their values in terms of expected contribution to net income may be the same. These matters, among the most difficult in economics, will be discussed further in Chapter 8.

The Economy: The Scope of "Economic" Activity

Both conceptually and in terms of operational statistical rules, it is very difficult to distinguish between economic and noneconomic activity. On the conceptual level, leisure-time pursuits, such as play or recreation, social activity, or rest, may be distinguished from economic activities in terms of their goals. The noneconomic activities are generally pursued for their own sake rather than because of the utility of a resulting product. Economic activities, on the other hand, result in end products with significant amounts of utility. This does not mean that work may not be very satisfying and rewarding in itself; one of the goals of economic progress is to decrease the disutility of work or to increase the satisfaction derived from work, as well as to increase the productivity of labor and other scarce resources in terms of the products of those resource inputs. But where there is a significant product, regardless of the degree of utility of the work itself, the activity may be called economic.

Irving B. Kravis was getting at the same thing when he offered the following rule to define economic activities: *The rule of sensitivity to rewards:* Within households, activities on which time spent is relatively responsive to changes in rewards for remunerated activities outside the household are economic. . . ." He might have added activities that would diminish (increase) if the price of such services performed by persons from outside the household decreased (increased). Activity pursued for its own sake would scarcely be affected by changes in prices or rates. Kravis also suggested: *The rule of remunerated activities:* The rendering of consumers' services to others in exchange for a *quid pro quo* is economic activity."[15] This would be a sort of exchange transaction in kind, although one would have to be careful to avoid classifying as economic the sort of exchange depicted by a critic of Kravis in the example of ". . . a man's playing of tennis with his inexpert wife in return for her babysitting later in the evening so that he can go out to have a drink of beer."

It is not incumbent upon us to solve the conceptual issues, even if we could. As a practical matter, in advanced countries economic activities are defined with reference to the market, or as A. C. Pigou put it, to what "can be brought directly or indirectly into relation with the measuring rod of money."[16] As the Commerce Department stated, "The basic criterion used for distinguishing an activity as economic production is whether it is reflected in the sales and purchase transactions of the market economy."[17] As it stands, this statement does not fully reflect what the Department does. Approximately 7 percent of the GNP consists of imputations of values to economic activities which either are not of a monetary nature or are not reflected in market transactions. But imputations are made only if the activities have significant market counterparts, which provide a basis for valuation. We shall examine these imputations shortly.

The concept of economic product used in the United States national income ac-

---

[15] "The Scope of Economic Activity in International Income Comparisons," in *Problems in the International Comparison of Economic Accounts,* Conference on Research in Income and Wealth, Studies in Income and Wealth, vol. XX (Princeton, N.J.: Princeton University Press for the National Bureau of Economic Research, 1957), pp. 349-350.

[16] A. C. Pigou, *The Economics of Welfare,* 4th ed. (London: Macmillan & Co., Ltd., 1932), p. 11.

[17] U.S. Department of Commerce, *op. cit.,* p. 30.

counts contrasts with some of the concepts described in Chapter 2. It contrasts with that of Communist countries, which relates to material production, that is, the output of goods and not of services, and also with the concept that includes both goods and services, but only those which pass through organized markets. Under the latter concept not only is all home production excluded; the services of government and nonprofit institutions, which are not sold in a market sense, are also excluded.

The comprehensive concept employed by the United States and other non-Communist countries seems preferable. First of all, as was stated earlier, services satisfy wants and thus are productive in the same way as goods. Also, the market criterion by itself is too restrictive, since there are certain significant categories of production that do not go through markets, but should be included in national product if trends are not to be seriously distorted. For example, over time there has been a marked shift of production from households to business enterprises such that if one were to count only marketed output, national product would appear to increase faster than it actually does as measured by the broader concept.

In the comprehensive measures, not all the nonmarket production is included, so there are still some distortions, but they are not as significant as they would be if the economy were defined as identical with the market. The main advantage of the market criterion is that prices are formed in markets, and thus a basis for evaluation exists. But if that nonmarket output which has market counterparts is included, market values can be imputed to it.

The chief imputations in the United States product estimates are:[18]

1 Food and fuel produced and consumed on the farm and space rental of owner-occupied farm dwellings (see 2 below). In primarily agricultural economies with many subsistence farms, outputs in this category may be over half the total. In the United States, the proportion of farm products consumed on the farms where produced has gradually declined as farmers have become more specialized; it now accounts for less than 10 percent of farm income.

2 Services of owner-occupied dwellings. The ownership of homes by the occupants has gradually increased as real income has increased. Now over 60 percent of dwelling units in the United States are owned by the occupants. The level and trends of national product would clearly be distorted if imputations were not made. The Commerce Department bases the imputation on rents paid in similar locations for similar types of houses. To get an estimate of the net income of the owner, which shows up in rental income of persons on the income side of the income and product account, the Department subtracts maintenance expense, real estate and other indirect taxes, interest, and depreciation from the gross rental value.

3 Payments in kind to domestic servants, farmhands, and members of the armed services. This imputation adds both to income and to the consumption side of product.

4 Services furnished without payment by financial intermediaries (see Chapter 4).

Certain other imputations have been suggested. A major example is the unpaid personal services of housewives and possibly other members of the family. This im-

[18] *Survey of Current Business,* vol. 49, p. 45, table 7.3, July, 1969.

putation has not been accepted in most countries, partly because of the difficulty of measuring the amount of work actually done. Yet its omission understates GNP and creates a trend bias. Increasing use of household equipment and the shifting of certain chores to commercial establishments enable more women to enter or reenter the labor force. Thus, unpaid household work is becoming a smaller proportion of GNP, but it still represents around 20 percent of the total. Another example is volunteer labor, which is of considerable consequence in the United States. Also, the opportunity cost of students of working age is an important component of educational costs.

A different type of imputation which should be made is for the services of capital or property owned by government, nonprofit institutions, and households. Capital assets owned by the nonbusiness sectors are productive, yielding valuable services, and as long as they are in use, they should be accorded a return rate that bears some relationship to the rate earned on property owned by private industry. Another reason for including them is that more and more governments and households, as well as businesses, are hiring equipment from rental and leasing concerns. The rents show up as part of income and product. Therefore, unless a service rate is imputed to this equipment, the trend toward increasing use of rental equipment tends to give an upward bias to national income and product.

This discussion leads to one criterion that has often been set forth as a rule for good social accounts: that estimates should be invariant to institutional changes. We have mentioned some institutional changes which would affect national income and product, e.g., the shift from households to outside product or the shift from owning equipment or property to renting it. By inclusive treatment of activities, they become invariant to institutional change. At best, however, imputations will be partial because of lack of data for some informal economic activities. So the rule of invariance to institutional change is an ideal which will be imperfectly realized in practice.

In connection with his work for the National Bureau of Economic Research, the author prepared some tentative estimates of the magnitude of the imputations mentioned above for the years 1929 and 1965.[19] First, it was pointed out that the imputations currently estimated by the Commerce Department came to 8.6 percent of the official GNP estimate for 1929, and 7.3 percent for 1965. The relative decline was due chiefly to the relative decline in agricultural activity. The proposed imputations in total amounted to 68.5 percent of official GNP in 1929, and 56.5 percent in 1965. The largest imputation is for the value of housewives' productive services, which has declined relative to GNP as an increasing proportion of women have entered the labor force and have less time for housework. Most of the other categories have increased relatively, but not enough to offset the relative decline in the imputed value of housewives' services. It is to be hoped that in the future, periodic sample household surveys of the use of time will permit more precise, and regular, estimates of the value of unpaid labor services. Better estimates of the stocks of nonbusiness capital goods will permit improved estimates of the rental value of these items, which is the second-largest area for which imputations are needed.

[19] "Studies in the National Income Accounts," in *Contributions to Economic Knowledge through Research*, Annual Report 47 (New York: National Bureau of Economic Research, 1967).

ECONOMIC ACCOUNTS AND THEIR USES

Market-price Valuation

The final products that make up the NNP are valued at market price if they pass through markets or have significant market counterparts; nonmarket products are generally valued at unit cost as a proxy for the market-price standard.

Valuation is obviously necessary for providing a common denominator to combine the heterogeneous collection of goods and services produced in the economy. Even when current values are converted back into physical volume estimates, unit values as of a base period are necessary as weights for purposes of aggregation.

Market prices are considered the appropriate values for purposes of welfare comparisons. Given rational behavior by purchasers, relative market prices reflect relative marginal utilities. In the absence of perfect markets, however, market prices do not necessarily reflect relative costs of production. First, there is the influence of government, which imposes indirect business taxes in differing proportions on different products or provides subsidies (monetary or in kind) with differing incidence. To mitigate the distorting influence of government on market prices, some analysts recommend unit factor-cost (factor-price) valuation for purposes of production and productivity comparisons (see next section). But even if government influences were corrected for, market imperfections could still distort relative prices as measures of relative input cost. This would be so if identical inputs commanded different prices or rates of numeration in different industries or locations. The influence of administered prices on profit rates is an example of distortion in certain markets. On the other hand, abnormal profits due to pioneering innovation are not necessarily distortions, since they may be regarded as an incentive cost of progress—so long as there are no artificial barriers to imitation, which, through competition, tends eventually to eliminate the "dynamic quasi-rents."

Since the national product is designed to measure the market value of current production, capital gains or losses are not included. This is the reason for valuation adjustments to eliminate the effect of changes in asset prices (inventories or depreciable capital) on profits. Later, in connection with balance sheets (Chapter 10), we shall discuss changes in asset values further.

Limits of the Nation

Since the national product is defined by Commerce as market value of all final goods and services produced by the *nation's* economy, we need to look at the concept of "the nation."

In United States economic accounts, the nation is taken to consist not of citizens of the country, but of residents. The earnings of anyone residing in the United States for more than six months are included in the national income figures. Conversely, United States citizens living abroad are not counted as part of the United States economy, except for employees of the United States government.

Income on foreign property owned by American residents is counted as part of national income and product. Portfolio earnings on foreign investments, for example, are counted as part of our national income and product, but earnings on equity and plants located in this country and owned by foreigners residing abroad are not counted as part of our national income.

In other words, there are two definitions: (1) domestic income—all the income arising in a geographic area; and (2) national income and product—domestic income plus income earned abroad by the work and property of United States residents, minus the income earned in the United States by the work and property of residents of other countries. Whereas the basic production account for the United States is cast in terms of *national* income and product, the UN standard system employs gross *domestic* product and expenditure (see Appendix B, Table B-I.1). In Appendix B, Table B-I.3, National Disposable Income and Its Appropriation, the UN system includes net factor income from the rest of the world (but excludes consumption of fixed capital). All in all, the UN treatment seems preferable, since production analysis can more readily be related to the geographic area, whereas analyses of national income and saving must take account of net income from abroad.

NATIONAL INCOME AND NONFACTOR CHARGES AGAINST PRODUCT

National income, as defined by the Department of Commerce, measures the total factor costs of the goods and services produced by the economy. Thus, the difference between national income and national product, both of which are measures of the goods and services produced, is the basis of valuation—market-price valuation for national product and factor-cost valuation for national income. The two methods of valuation and their usefulness for different purposes are discussed below. Also, although the term factor cost is used, this should not be taken to imply that the national income total is broken down into components according to the traditional triad of factors—land, labor, and capital. The operational categorization based on legal or institutional criteria is briefly described.

Factor-cost versus Market-price Valuation

Reference to Appendix A, Table A-1, will remind the reader of the items which make up the difference between national income and product. The chief item is indirect business taxes, from which subsidies may be deducted, since they can be viewed as negative taxes. The current surplus of government enterprises could as well be included in national income as a return on the capital invested in such enterprises (but is not, for consistency with the present treatment of capital owned by general government). The statistical discrepancy is added to national income as a reconciliation item merely because of the convenience of not having to assign or allocate it by product group.

The discussion of factor-cost versus market-price measures is related chiefly to the effect of indirect business taxes less subsidies. If there were no indirect taxes, and if we relied only on direct taxes on income of individuals and businesses, national income and net national product would be basically equal except for minor adjustments. Once the intermediate expenses have been taken out to avoid double counting, the cost of product is essentially the cost of basic factors of production. However, indirect taxes affect average and relative prices. Direct taxes may affect prices indirectly, but indirect taxes affect prices directly. The difference between national product and national income is purely a valuation difference; that is, both totals relate to the same collection of final goods and services, but the goods and services are valued differently. The difference is due to the price-increasing effect of indirect taxes.

34 ECONOMIC ACCOUNTS AND THEIR USES

The advantage of a market-price valuation is that the national product so valued can be allocated by type of product. This is why the national product concept was developed to supplement the basic national income concept—to see the total value of production by major types of product and by type of sector spending for final products. National product is generally a larger value than national income, since there are usually positive indirect taxes.

As noted earlier, market prices are the appropriate valuation for purposes of welfare comparisons, since consumers push their expenditures up to the point where the relative marginal utilities of different products equal relative prices. Unfortunately, the relative degrees of satisfaction are not equal to the relative volume of resources embodied in the different goods because of the distorting effect of indirect taxes and market imperfections.

In any case, market prices are not appropriate for production and productivity comparisons concerned with the relative volumes of basic resources embodied in different commodities. For the latter type of analysis, relative unit factor costs are the appropriate weights for outputs.[20] Take the case of cigarettes and bread as an illustration:

	Unit Price	Indirect Taxes	Factor Unit Cost
Bread	0.30	5	25
Cigarettes	0.30	20	10

Someone who both eats bread and smokes would push his expenditures on both commodities up to the point where he would get the same satisfaction from an additional pack of cigarettes as from an additional loaf of bread, since from a welfare point of view the unit prices are equal magnitudes. In comparing productivity, we would be quite misled by these unit price weights; they would be distorted by the heavy indirect tax on cigarettes. Instead, the factor costs of the two commodities would be used, giving bread 2-1/2 times more weight.

It would take an elaborate statistical project to estimate factor cost by product. This has not been done in the United States. It has been done, however, in Canada; the Canadians found that relative prices after adjustment for indirect taxes were generally not greatly different from those of the market. The difference was not enough to affect weighted aggregates significantly over time, so it probably is not worthwhile to adjust all national product down to factor cost by product. Even if we did, relative prices would still reflect the distorting effects of market imperfections, which it would be hopeless to attempt to adjust for. Fortunately, however, we can estimate factor cost on an industry basis (see Chapter 4), and this provides us with appropriate weights for purposes of combining industry production measures.

National Income by Type of Return

Given that national income is valued at factor cost, it would be very useful if the total could be distributed among the contributing factors. With that information it would be possible to discern the relative amounts of factors available for allocation

---

[20] This distinction was first made by J. R. Hicks, "The Valuation of the Social Income," *Economica*, n.s., vol. 7, pp. 105-124, May, 1940.

to various uses and to compare the relative importance of the several factors in the outputs of different industries. However, breakdowns closely following the factor divisions are not readily made. The data that are available follow the cost structure reported by business enterprises, and thus are institutional breakdowns. The following discussion of the United States institutional breakdowns brings out the divergence from a factor-return breakdown. (Further details on what each component comprises and methods of computation are contained in Chapter 13.)

Employee compensation consists of wages and salaries, plus "supplements to wages and salaries." This component can be associated approximately with the labor factor. In this component three imputations—for food furnished employees, standard clothing issued to military persons, and employees' lodging—help bring the component closer to factor return than if it were based purely on monetary wages. However, other types of income, especially entrepreneurial and rental income, also contain a probably substantial share of labor income.

Proprietors' income includes income of professional practitioners and other self-employed persons, as well as the net income of farm and nonfarm unincorporated business—whether individual proprietorships or partnerships. Proprietors' income is clearly mixed, consisting primarily of the compensation which could be imputed for the labor of proprietors and their unpaid family helpers, or of the return to their own invested capital, including imputations for interest and net rent, if one will, as well as "profit" in a residual sense. The inventory valuation adjustment and other possible adjustments to net income are discussed in connection with corporate profits.

Rental income of persons includes both monetary rents and imputed rents on owner-occupied dwellings. It includes the net rents received by persons who rent property as a sideline, as well as by those persons (not corporations) whose main business is real estate. It includes royalties on patents, trademarks, and copyrights, as well as on natural resource holdings. By no means does it represent the net return on the economic factor of land, since it includes rent on structures as well; portions of proprietors' income and corporate profits also represent (imputed) net rents on land and other natural resources owned by the business.

Net interest consists of monetary interest paid less monetary interest received in the private business sector plus monetary interest received from abroad less that paid out abroad. In addition, net *imputed* interest paid by financial intermediaries is included, estimated by methods explained in the next chapter. As noted earlier, there is no imputation of an interest income on the durable goods owned by households, institutions, and government. Interest paid by government and persons is excluded from factor cost altogether, although it is counted as a transfer payment. The rationale of the Department's treatment in the case of government is that the debt on which interest is paid was largely incurred for nonproductive purposes, i.e., war. This is only true of the federal government, however. Besides, it has nothing to do with whether an interest cost should not be imputed to the productive capital owned by government (or households), discussed further in Chapter 17.

Corporate profits before tax, as estimated by the Commerce Department, differ from profits reported by the same corporations to the Internal Revenue Service. The IRS definition is influenced heavily by institutional factors, such as the period over which capital goods may be written off, and thus it departs from a pure profit concept. The Commerce definition has similar problems. One that has been extensively debated relates to capital gains and losses, i.e., whether or not such gains and losses are really returns to a factor that should be included in national income. The decision has been made, in the United States and generally elsewhere, to exclude capital gains and losses. Thus an adjustment—the inventory valuation adjustment—is made to eliminate profits on losses of this type. A similar adjustment could and should be made for depreciation valuation—the difference between book depreciation and depreciation expressed in terms of current replacement values (see Chapter 10). Any other adjustments to business accounting practice would affect profit. For example, if research and development outlays were considered investment rather than current expense, profits and retained earnings (plowed back) would be correspondingly increased.

Estimating Returns to Labor and Nonhuman Capital

If a reasonable separation between the labor and property components of the net income of proprietors can be made, then factor cost (or national income) can be used to show return to the two broad factors of labor and property. Increasingly, economists merge the two categories, capital and land, to talk about two factors: labor and nonhuman capital, including land. This distinction accords with the legal distinction: We can dispose of our services, but not sell ourselves, whereas property can be bought and sold. Also, land and so-called reproducible capital have the same economic characteristics. Land can be produced for a cost, and the value of land, as of reproducible capital, is derived from the expected future income stream resulting from its use.

For practical statistical analysis of income distribution, we are interested in returns to labor and to nonhuman capital. One approach is to assume that a proprietor would earn, on the average, the same as an employee in his industry. Knowing the number of proprietors and imputing the average wage, one can estimate labor return and take the residual as the property return.[21] Other methods are possible, of course, but the described method gives reasonable results by comparison with corporate income distribution.

In the SNA gross domestic product and expenditure account (see Appendix B, Table B-I.1), it will be seen that factor incomes are reduced to two components: compensation of employees (line 1.3.1) and operating surplus (line 1.3.2). The latter category includes interest, rents and royalties, corporate profits, and net income of proprietors. If the labor income of proprietors were imputed and deducted, then operating surplus would equal property compensation, as we have discussed it above, although it would be confined to that originating domestically. In the companion Table B-I.3, Account 3, National Disposable Income and Its Application, net labor and property income from abroad is included, as in the United States national income. But the UN national disposable income, while net of capital consumption, includes indirect business taxes less subsidies. The UN accounts do not make use of the national income concept in the sense of aggregate factor cost, although it can be put together from the components.

---

[21] John W. Kendrick and Ryuzo Sato, "Factor Prices, Productivity, and Economic Growth," *American Economic Review*, vol. 53, pp. 974-1003, December, 1963.

REVIEW QUESTIONS

1 What are some of the areas in which a welfare approach would lead to a classification of final and intermediate goods different from that division now made by the Department of Commerce?
2 What two arguments were advanced in 1942 for the emphasis on a gross product concept? How well do these arguments stand up today?
3 What are the uses for which market-price and factor-cost valuations, respectively, are most advantageous?
4 What are some of the major exceptions now made to the basic criterion of distinguishing economic activity as being that reflected in the market? What additional imputations might be made?
5 Distinguish between gross *domestic* product and gross *national* product.
6 Suggest the major divergences between a factor-return breakdown of national income and the breakdown by type of return as presently prepared by the Department of Commerce.

SELECTED REFERENCES

KUZNETS, SIMON: *National Income: A Summary of Findings* (New York: National Bureau of Economic Research, 1946). See especially part IV, "Problems of Interpretation."

STUDENSKI, PAUL: *The Income of Nations* (New York: New York University Press, 1961), part II, "Theory and Methodology."

U.S. DEPARTMENT OF COMMERCE, OFFICE OF BUSINESS ECONOMICS: *National Income* (1954). The basic statement of the official position as represented in the United States accounts.

Income and Product by Industry of Origin: The Production or Value-added Approach

4

The production account presented in Chapter 3 is basic to aggregate economic analysis. In effect, it summarizes the expenditures for final product, by the major sectors, and shows the associated factor and nonfactor costs, or primary incomes, which are distributed to the major sectors of the economy. Before moving to the sector income and outlay accounts, however, we must first understand the contributions of the various sectors and industries to total national product in terms of the value added, or primary income produced, by each. This is really a third approach to the concept and estimation of national product. Studenski calls it the production approach, and we shall call it the value-added approach to emphasize its sectoral nature.

In a sense, it is the most basic approach, in that it views aggregate national production as a consolidation of the production statements (actual or constructed) of all the individual producing units of the economy, by significant groupings. Or in the terminology of the United States accounts, gross product originating, by sector, sums to gross national product.

The value-added approach was the last to be developed on a comprehensive basis, although national income, as opposed to gross national product, by industry of origin, had been developed much earlier. The first product estimates within the value-added framework were made in 1932 by the German Statistical Office. R. C.

39

Geary pioneered in statistical implementation of the concept, with estimates for Ireland in the early 1940s. In the United States, the value-added concept was developed with some precision by Solomon Fabricant in the late 1930s. The Bureau of the Census had been collecting data on a gross value-added basis for selected industries since the nineteenth century. The first estimates of income and product originating in an industry (agriculture) on a basis consistent with the national income and product estimates were made by the present author in 1951.[1] In 1962, the Commerce Department published its initial estimates for all industries on this basis, as described below. The UN revised SNA includes product, by kind of economic activity, which we review in the final section of the chapter.

THE BASIC CONCEPT

We shall start by considering the value-added approach generally, and then see how it is implemented in the various economic sectors. The main features of the concept are shown by the stubs in Table 4-1. Value added (column 3) may be estimated from two directions. First, in what may be called the production approach, one may begin with the value of total production in a sector, and then deduct the cost of intermediate products consumed in the production process. The estimate of intermediate products should be comprehensive of all materials and services purchased on current account. The Census Bureau's "value added by manufacture," for example, is net only of purchases of materials but not all services. Services such as advertising and communications, which are largely bought through central offices, are not included since the census is based on establishment reports.[2] This first estimating approach is parallel with the treatment for the economy as a whole. It will be recalled that only final products were included in national product; thus, in effect, although not in statistical practice, intermediate products were deducted from the value of production. Note that, for an industry, value added is not the same as the value of its final products, however. The mineral industry, for example, produces very little final product in relation to the value it adds (contributes) to the economy's final product.

Value added may also be estimated from the direction of summing factor and nonfactor costs (columns 4 and 5)—the income approach. In effect, this is a breakdown of national income and nonfactor charges against product by industry. But where feasible, it is desirable to estimate value added by both approaches. The production approach is necessary for purposes of price deflation on an industry basis (see Chapter 6), and it provides the starting point for the input-output matrix (Chapter 5). The income approach is desirable by industry in order to furnish a statistical check (the inevitable statistical discrepancy would be included in column 5), as well as for analysis of factor shares by industry and for deflation to obtain real factor cost. And in the nonbusiness sectors, as will be elaborated below, where outputs are not sold in markets, both value added and the value of total production must be estimated by summing costs.

[1] John W. Kendrick and Carl E. Jones, "Gross National Farm Product in Constant Dollars, 1910–50," *Survey of Current Business*, vol. 31, pp. 13–19, September, 1951.
[2] This is related to the problem of data collection by establishment as opposed to company, discussed below.

TABLE 4-1
Industry Value Added: Illustrative Framework

Industry	*(1)* Gross Value of Output	*(2)* Cost of Intermediate Purchases	*(3)* Value Added (1)−(2)= (3)+(4)	*(4)* Labor Compensation	*(5)* Property Income and Other Charges
A					
B					
.					
.					
.					
N					
Totals			(GNP)		

IMPLEMENTING THE BASIC CONCEPT

The Business Sector

It is in the business sector of the economy that the double-barrel value-added estimate is most relevant and is best supported by the financial statements of firms. In this section we shall develop the relationship of industry and business sector value added to the basic operating (income) statement of the firm. It should be clearly understood, however, that the Commerce Department does not prepare its estimates of business income and product by adjusting and then consolidating the statements of all the constituent firms in the various industries of the sector. Rather, as described in Chapter 13, the Department relies on aggregate data from the Census Bureau, Social Security Administration, Internal Revenue Service, and other sources, which it pieces together to show the various income and production flows. But in principle, nonfinancial business income and product could be obtained by adjusting and consolidating company statements, and it is the purpose of this section to explain the relationship. Most of the explanation will relate to the nonfinancial corporate part of the business sector, not only because it accounts for the preponderance of business sales, but also because the basic statements are much the same as in the unincorporated and financial part (the differences will be noted later).

We start in Table 4-2 with the operating statement of a hypothetical corporation, Mid-East Manufacturing. This statement is not unlike the income statements of most actual corporations. Current receipts come primarily from sales (net of discounts, refunds, etc.), but some revenue comes from interest on bulk accounts, notes, and bonds held in the corporate treasury. There might also be dividend receipts from

TABLE 4-2
Mid-East Manufacturing Corporation,
Operating Statement for the
Year Ending December 31, 1969
(Thousands of Dollars)

Total current receipts		
Total sales of products, net	$4,620	
Interest received	20	
Subsidies received	10	$4,650
Less: Cost of materials and services purchased	$1,800	
Depreciation of plant and equipment	210	
Taxes, other than corporate profits		
taxes, and licenses	120	
Bad debt expense	60	
Contributions to charity	40	
Social security contributions	75	
Wages and salaries	1,955	
Interest charges	45	−$4,305
Corporate profits before tax		
Corporate profits tax liability	$150	
Dividends paid	165	
Undistributed earnings	30	$345

holdings of equities. In addition, Mid-East received a modest subsidy from the federal government.

The chief costs of production are purchased materials and services and wages and salaries. The other costs are itemized in the table. The difference between receipts and costs is profits before tax, and the distribution of these profits is also shown, including the item of greatest interest to shareholders—dividend payments.

In Table 4-3 we merely rearrange the information from the operating statement into a T account to show sources and uses of income. The two sides of the account must balance, and they do, of course, since corporate profits is a residual item. We also break down sales by major customers, since in the consolidated statement for the sector it is important to be able to show sales outside the sector by major purchase groups. Also, for input-output tables, we would be interested in purchases and sales among firms in different industries.

In Table 4-4 the income statement has been converted to a production statement. The chief transformation was to add the estimated value of the net change in inventories of finished and in-process goods to sales receipts, since production is reflected in inventory accumulation as well as in sales, and sales can come out of inventories as well as from production. In the addendum, the direct costs (including an imputed profit) of the additions to inventory have been estimated by type, and these costs

TABLE 4-3
Mid-East Manufacturing Corporation,
Income Statement (Sources and Uses)
for the Year Ending December 31, 1969
(Thousands of Dollars)

Uses			Sources		
Cost of goods sold:			Sales:		
Purchased materials	$1,800		To Company A	$2,100	
and services			To Company B	750	
Depreciation	210		To Company C	1,125	
Taxes, other than on			Other sales	645	
corporate profits	120				
Bad debt expense	60		Interest received	20	
Charitable contributions	40		Subsidies received	10	
Wages and salaries	1,955				
Social security contributions	75				
Interest paid	45	$4,305			
Corporate profits before tax:		345			
Provision for tax	$150				
Dividends paid	165				
Undistributed profits	30				
Total uses		$4,650	Total sources	$4,650	

added to the appropriate cost categories on the uses side of the statement. Note also that costs have been grouped into categories of economic significance.

Finally, receipts from nonproduction sources were removed from the right-hand side of the account, so that only production revenue would be reflected there. Interest received was netted against interest paid on the uses side; dividends could be treated similarly. Subsidies are shown as a general deduction from cost.

In Table 4-5 the final stage of the transformation to a value-added (net production) statement is shown. Purchased intermediate products are removed from the uses side of the account and shown as a deduction from the value of gross production.

Value added in an industry can be obtained by consolidating the statements for each constituent firm. This would involve adding the various income and product items, except that both sales and purchased goods and services could be shown net of intermediate product sales and purchase transactions among the companies within the industry. Value added would be unaffected. The same is true of a consolidation for the entire corporate business. In the sector income and product statement, however, it is useful to break down sales by sector of destination, including sales to business on capital account, so that the flows among the sectors may be traced.

Unincorporated enterprise The treatment of unincorporated enterprise is much the same as that of corporations. The chief difference is that, for unincorporated

TABLE 4-4
Mid-East Manufacturing Corporation,
Production Statement for the
Year Ending December 31, 1969
(Thousands of Dollars)

Uses		Sources	
Purchased materials and			
services consumed	$1,920	Sales	
		To Company A	$2,100
Factor costs:		To Company B	750
Wages and salaries	2,085	To Company C	1,125
Social security contributions	80	Other sales	645
Net interest	25		
Corporate profits taxes	185		
Net dividends paid	165	Net inventory change	300
Undistributed profits	40		
Nonfactor charges:			
Depreciation	210		
Indirect business taxes	120		
Bad debt expense	60		
Charitable contributions	40		
	$4,930		
Less: Subsidies received	10		
Total uses	$4,920	Total sources	$4,920

ADDENDUM

Estimated cost of inventory accumulation:

Purchases from other firms	$120
Social security contributions	5
Wages and salaries	130
Corporate profits taxes	35
Undistributed earnings	10
	$300

NOTE: When consolidating for an industry, deduct sales and purchases among units within the industry.

enterprise, the residual on the uses side is net income, and instead of the corporate profits tax, there is the personal income tax. Another difference is that interest and dividends received by proprietors are counted as personal income and so do not need to be netted.

The main area of unincorporated business is agriculture. Table 4-6 shows the estimation of value added (gross product) for this sector. The sources side shows the imputed value of products consumed on the farm where they are produced, and also

TABLE 4-5
Mid-East Manufacturing Corporation,
Value-added Statement for the
Year Ending December 31, 1969
(Thousands of Dollars)

Income (Uses)			Product (Sources)		
Factor costs:			Sales		$4,620
Employee compensation		$2,165			
Net interest		25	Net inventory change		300
Corporate profits before tax		390	Value of gross		
Tax liability	$185		production		$4,920
Dividends	165				
Retained earnings	40	$2,580	Less: Purchased goods and		
			services consumed in		
			production process		1,920
Nonfactor charges:					
Depreciation		$210			
Indirect business taxes		120			
Transfers		100			
		$430			
Less: Subsidies received		10 420			
Total uses of value added		$3,000	Total gross value added		$3,000

the imputed value of farm homes, gross rental value of farm homes, in addition to the value of farm production as such (marketings plus inventory accumulation). Rental value of farm homes is included because the Department of Agriculture, which compiles the basic data, feels it is difficult to segregate farm homes from the farm business; however, there is some sentiment in favor of trying to split the rental value of homes between business and residence. On the uses side are shown the costs, including wages paid, in kind, along with money wages and salaries. Estimates of the major types of intermediate product purchases are made in some detail by the Department of Agriculture.

Another area of unincorporated enterprise is the real estate industry. In addition to the full-time proprietors in real estate, people who rent property as a sideline are, by convention, counted as proprietors. The operating statement is quite similar to that for other businesses, but with some differences: Income from production is gross rents; costs include purchases (mainly for maintenance), depreciation, indirect business taxes (mainly property taxes), and interest (mainly mortgage interest), with the residual net rent left as the net income of the proprietor.

The owner-occupant has to make these same outlays for maintenance, etc., so the estimate for the imputed rent is the same as for the actual rented property. Gross rents show up on the product side under consumption, the net rental income shows up on the income side, and intermediate expenses show up as value added in the various industries where the expenditures are made.

TABLE 4-6
Gross Farm Product, 1965–1968
(Millions of Dollars)

	1965	1966	1967	1968
Total value of farm output	**43,457**	**46,382**	**46,418**	**47,559**
Cash receipts from farm marketings and CCC loans	39,371	43,371	42,615	44,406
Farm products consumed directly in farm households	813	817	732	705
Change in farm inventories	973	−158	615	−131
Gross rental value of farm homes	2,300	2,352	2,456	2,579
Less: Value of intermediate products consumed, total	19,622	21,296	21,833	22,444
Intermediate products consumed, other than rents	17,598	19,164	19,732	20,310
Gross rents paid to nonfarm landlords (excluding operating expenses)	2,024	2,132	2,101	2,134
Plus: Other items	−169	−184	−196	−210
Equals: Gross farm product	**23,666**	**24,902**	**24,389**	**24,905**
Less: Capital consumption allowances	4,658	4,953	5,375	5,802
Indirect business taxes	1,589	1,720	1,861	1,978
Plus: Government payments to farm landlords	2,211	2,954	2,782	3,117
Equals: National income originating in farming	**19,630**	**21,183**	**19,935**	**20,242**

SOURCE: *Survey of Current Business,* vol. 49, p. 23, table 1.17. July, 1969.

Financial intermediaries   Banks, trusts, and other financial intermediaries require special treatment. In the case of banks, the main problem is that interest and dividends received by the banks from investment of funds deposited with them much exceed the interest and dividends paid out to bank depositors. This would give a negative net interest and dividends on the uses side. The reason for this is that in lieu of interest on demand deposits, commercial banks give customers a service: checking accounts. The Commerce Department's solution in the value-added statement for the banking sector is to impute a value for the financial services which are not charged for in whole, or in part, especially the checking account service.[3] Interest received is assumed to be paid to depositors, and then the depositor is assumed to pay back most of this to the bank for services. To show the reality of the situation, payments are imputed for services rendered, although no explicit charges are made (see Table 4-7). The imputed service charge is obtained by subtracting interest paid from actual interest received (100 − 95 = 5). Since this represents value of unpaid services performed by the bank, we add 95 to get the total value of production.

[3] U.S. Department of Commerce, Office of Business Economics, *National Income* (1954), pp. 46–47.

TABLE 4-7
Mid-East National Bank,
Production Statement for the
Year Ending December 31, 1969
(Thousands of Dollars)

Uses		Sources	
Purchases from other firms	$10,000	Interest received	$100,000
Usual other nonfactor items	20,000	Other receipts	10,000
Factor payments:		Actual service charges	5,000
Wages and salaries	50,000		
Actual interest paid out	5,000	Imputed service charges	95,000
Corporate profits taxes	10,000		
Dividends paid out	10,000		
Retained earnings	10,000		
Imputed interest paid	95,000		
Total	$210,000		$210,000

TABLE 4-8
Mid-East National Bank,
Value-added Statement
for the Year Ending December 31, 1969
(Thousands of Dollars)

Income (Uses)		Product (Sources)	
Usual other nonfactor items	$20,000	Actual service charges	$10,000
Factor payments:		Other receipts	5,000
Wages and salaries	50,000		
Net interest	0	Imputed service charges	95,000
Corporate profit taxes	10,000		$110,000
Dividends paid out	10,000	Less: Purchases from	
Retained earnings	10,000	other firms	10,000
Total Uses of Value Added	$100,000	Total Gross Value Added	$100,000

Two major modifications in the production statement are required to go to the value-added, or income and product, statement in Table 4-8. In the first place, purchases from other firms are shown as a deduction on the sources side, just as for any other type of firm. This leaves factor costs and nonfactor charges on the uses side. The other, more striking, adjustment is the netting of interest received against actual and imputed interest paid out, leaving zero net interest on the sources side.

Interest is netted out because interest is not produced by the bank's own property. Such treatment shows the bank's role as a financial intermediary in lending funds deposited with it. This interest is not part of the income produced by the bank; it is using funds which originated elsewhere. Interest is merely transferred from the industries in which it originates to depositors. Thus, it should not show up in value added in the banking sector, which reflects returns to the factors resident in the constituent enterprises. The imputed service charges become for other firms an intermediate product. The Commerce Department has to allocate these service charges to various industries and deduct them from the value of production in order to get value added in other industries.

In the case of life insurance companies (and similarly with mutual financial intermediaries), a problem arises because of the combined saving and insurance services performed, parallel to the checking account service of banks. The OBE treatment is also similar.[4] An imputed interest is calculated as equal to all property income received by these institutions less their "profit," called net gain from operations. Policyholders are assumed to make payments to life insurance companies to cover their operating expenses.

Government enterprise In the United States accounts, the choice was made to incorporate government enterprises—agencies of government whose operating costs are to a substantial extent covered by sales rather than taxes—along with business enterprises.[5] In several ways, however, there is a departure from the standard procedures used for business enterprises. First, profits of government enterprises are not treated as a factor cost, but as a nonfactor charge (see "Subsidies less current) surplus of government enterprises," in Appendix A, Table A-1). Second, capital formation is classified in government purchases of goods and services, rather than gross private domestic investment. Third, profits are calculated without deduction of net interest paid or depreciation, so that capital consumption allowances and net interest payments by business enterprises, respectively, do not include components attributable to government enterprises. These procedures are rationalized because of the difficulty of disentangling data from operations of government enterprises from those of general government. However, the treatment of government capital purchases and calculation of returns on them, as advocated by the author, would embrace modification of these procedures.

Nonbusiness Sectors

The nonbusiness sectors must be treated differently from the business sectors. Nonbusiness sectors do not sell their services on the market, so there is no total market value of production from which intermediate purchases may be deducted to obtain value added. Nevertheless, their value added may be estimated in terms of the factor costs in these sectors, plus nonfactor charges to the extent that these are recognized. When there are no nonfactor charges, product originating will be equal to income originating. For this, total value of production may be obtained by

[4] *Ibid.*, p. 48.
[5] *Ibid.*, p. 49.

TABLE 4-9
Production Statement,
All United States Governments, 1960
(Billions of Dollars)

Uses		Sources	
Purchases from nongovernment sellers	$52.8	Direct sales	$2.5
Compensation of government employees	47.3	Imputed value of product	97.6
Total	$100.1	Total	$100.1

SOURCE: Adapted from Sam Rosen, *National Income* (New York: Holt, Rinehart and Winston, Inc., 1963), p. 30, table 3.4.

adding the cost of intermediate goods and services consumed, and this is done in the case of general government.

In the following brief discussions, it will be noted that property income is generally not computed and credited to the nonbusiness sectors by the Commerce Department (except for depreciation on the fixed assets of private nonprofit institutions). We feel strongly that the underlying economic logic, as well as the desire for consistency among the nonbusiness sectors and with business, requires that in the nonbusiness sectors an imputed (interest) return on property and depreciation allowances for the gross estimates should be credited as factor cost, in addition to employee cost. While the principle of consistency would also be served by estimating the total cost of production in households and private nonprofit institutions, as well as in general government, it is less apparent that the resulting estimates would be useful.

General government   The value of government services is not taken to be measured by the dollar volume of taxes that taxpayers remit to the government; rather it is measured by the cost of those services.[6] It is assumed that the people's representatives reflect the desires of the people for collective goods and services and push government expenditures up to the point where the last dollar spent for government services gives the same satisfaction as the last dollar spent from their private incomes. Of course, this is only very approximately true, even in a democracy, and it is a particularly dubious assumption in a dictatorship. Nevertheless, it is the chief feasible statistical approach, and does have some theoretical basis.

Table 4-9 indicates how this approach, as implemented by the Commerce Department, can be formulated. This is analogous to the approach used for business, because the value of business output consists of the costs of intermediate products and the compensation of the factors. The only element left out is an imputed return to

[6] *Ibid.,* pp. 53–54.

property owned and used by governments. Note that the imputed value of government production is obtained by deducting the value of direct sales from the total cost of production.

Government value added is assumed to consist only of employee compensation. That is, purchases from nongovernment sellers is removed from the uses side and subtracted from the sources side, as in the other transformations. Yet the Wealth Inventory Planning Study found that the value of federal government property alone was $325 billion in 1963. Most of this is used for productive purposes. There is no imputed rental value for these billions of dollars worth of government property. There should be, however, for consistency with the business sector. In addition to estimating the current value of public property, one must determine an appropriate rate of return. One could use the average interest paid on government obligations.

Private nonprofit institutions   As in the case of governments (including public nonprofit institutions, such as state universities), private institutions generally cover only part of their operating costs with current contributions or fees. It seems more realistic to estimate the value of their services at cost. Income originating is estimated in terms of employee compensation, also without allowance for a net return on property.[7] Unlike in government, however, depreciation on the fixed assets of these institutions is counted in going from income to gross product originating.

Households   In households, income and product originating is estimated by the Commerce Department to consist of the compensation of servants and other household employees rendering personal services.[8] Services of housewives and other family members are not included, although some countries have attempted estimates of household production. Certainly, before such estimates are attempted, some objective data through surveys on the average hours spent per week and year should be obtained. This would still leave undetermined the appropriate average hourly compensation, presumably based on opportunity cost, to be imputed to the hours spent in productive activity. The boundary line between productive and nonproductive activity would also have to be drawn clearly, as discussed in Chapter 2. We would not recommend this major extension of income estimates before much more conceptual thought and exploratory statistical study were devoted to it.

Outlays for supplies, materials, and equipment rentals connected with household activities are included in personal consumption expenditures. No allowance is made for the value of the services of the stock of consumer durable goods owned and used by households, however. The work on gross and net consumer durable stocks has proceeded to the point where this might well be attempted. The imputed rate of return could be related to the average interest rate on consumer debt, but more thought must be given to this point. Certainly, the recent Commerce procedure of including the interest on consumer debt as a part of household income originating was inferior to the imputation of a net return on all consumer durables, whether financed by credit or not, since the financed portion has changed with time. Depreci-

---

[7] *Ibid.*, p. 52.

[8] *Ibid.*, p. 50. Later, in the 1965 revision, interest paid was excluded from income and product originating.

ation on consumer durables should be added to income originating to obtain gross household product.

Rest of the world   Income and product originating in the rest of the world is taken in the United States estimates to be net factor payments from the rest of the world.[9] This net factor income consists, first, of wages and salaries which are paid to United States residents who cross borders to work and come back to United States residences, plus wages and salaries paid to American employees of international institutions, less wages and salaries paid to foreigners who come here to work during the day, less wages and salaries paid by American organizations abroad. Then there is net interest: interest received by Americans on bonds or loans made to foreign residents less interest paid by Americans to foreigners who own United States bonds or other evidences of indebtedness. Finally, net dividends and retained earnings of branches of American companies abroad are included. In terms of United States statistics, net compensation of employees is a very minor item; most of product originating abroad consists of net property compensation, reflecting the large excess of foreign assets owned by United States residents over assets located in the United states but owned by residents of other countries.

THE PROBLEM OF INDUSTRIAL SECTORING AND THE UNITED STATES ESTIMATES BY INDUSTRY

Conceptually, a sector is a group of economic units that are homogeneous in their decision making with regard to the activity to be investigated. For the analysis of production, for example, the unit should be "homogeneous in respect of the character, cost-structure and technology of production."[10] The statistical unit which is most amenable to combination into sectors relevant for production analysis is the establishment. An establishment, as defined by the Census Bureau, is an economic unit which produces goods and services—a store, a plant, a farm. In most instances it is at one location. It is engaged predominantly in one type of activity, and it is classified and given a code number from the Standard Industrial Classification according to that activity. The statistical collection systems that provide data for the major portions of the national income classify economic units into industries on the basis of establishments.

For certain other components of national income, among them profits, interest, and inventory valuation adjustment, data are collected from companies, or firms, that is, because the data are taken from IRS statistics, the company, as a legal entity, is the reporting unit, and companies are classified by their major products. But companies may have several, diverse product lines. Companies may include several establishments, each producing a different kind of product. For example, a soft-coal mine owned by a corporation engaged primarily in the production of iron and steel would be classified with the iron and steel industry in a distribution by industries of companies, but with bituminous coal mining in a distribution by industries of establishments. Thus, because the establishment comes closer to being homogeneous in its productive activity, it is preferred for analysis in this field.

[9] *Ibid.*, p. 56.
[10] UN, *SNA*, 1968, p. 73.

This problem was confronted in estimating national income, by industry. National income, by industry, was one of the two ways that the first official estimates were presented, and such estimates have been available ever since. Because of statistical necessity, OBE used the company basis of industrial classification for corporate profits, inventory valuation adjustment, and interest.[11] This led to the cautionary statement that the comparability of distributive share estimates of some industries was impaired. It was believed that the industrial distribution of total national income was not seriously distorted, because the bulk of the total was on the preferred classification by industry of establishments, and the probable tendency for subsidiary activities to be offsetting.[12]

This problem was encountered to an even greater extent in estimating GNP by industry, since capital consumption allowances, also classified by industry of companies, had to be dealt with. As mentioned above, in 1962 OBE presented its initial estimates of GNP by industry. To do this, it reallocated profits and capital consumption allowances to industries of establishments, although with some admittedly arbitrary assumptions. This partly accounts for the broad industry divisions in which the estimates were prepared. They were much broader than suggested in the UN report, reviewed below, but further disaggregation would strain the reasonableness of the allocating procedures.

As implemented by OBE, the current-dollar estimates of an industry's gross product are derived by the income approach, that is, as the sum of its factor payments—OBE distinguishes employee compensation, net interest, and profit-type income—and nonfactor charges.[13] This is accomplished by adding to the national income originating in each industry its share of indirect business taxes, capital consumption allowances, and other nonfactor charges that reconcile national income and gross national product. In the case of the nonfactor charges, notably indirect business taxes, procedures had to be developed to allocate them by industry. Twelve major industries are shown, some with subdivisions. GNP by industry is only available annually, although OBE has sought funds to provide it on a quarterly basis.

The derivation of the constant-dollar estimates of GNP by industry is described in Chapter 6 (see also Table 6-1).

THE UNITED NATIONS SYSTEM

The conceptual discussion of value added by industry and sector can be summarized largely by reference to the UN revised *SNA* supporting table 1, Gross Domestic Product and Factor Incomes, by Kind of Economic Activity. (Refer to the UN report.) The UN approach is basically the same as the one we have described, with a few differentiations.

Part *a* of the table relates to industries, comprising the private domestic enterprise economy, including most government enterprises, and private nonprofit institutions servicing business. "The core of industries is made up of establishments

[11] U.S. Department of Commerce, *op. cit.*, p. 67.

[12] *Ibid.*

[13] Martin L. Marimont, "GNP by Major Industries," *Survey of Current Business*, vol. 42, pp. 6–18, October, 1962. The method has since been revised. For recent estimates, see *Survey of Current Business*, vol. 49, p. 25, table 1.22, July, 1969.

the activities of which are financed by producing goods and services for sale in the market at a price that is normally designed to cover the costs of production."[14] Industry divisions, according to the International Standard Industrial Classification (ISIC), are spelled out in the vertical stub. On the horizontal headings, we find gross domestic product (column 4), first obtained as the difference between gross output, at producers' values (column 2), and intermediate consumption (column 3). In turn, we see gross domestic product as the sum of domestic factor incomes (column 7), broken down between employee compensation and property compensation, or "operating surplus," plus consumption of fixed capital (column 6) and indirect taxes less subsidies (column 5). No explicit provision is made in the table for the inevitable statistical discrepancy.

As noted earlier, the provision of estimates of the dual streams of commodity flows, that is, gross output and intermediate consumption, permits the adjustment of gross product by industry for price changes by the double-deflation method to be described in Chapter 6. Factor incomes can likewise be adjusted for changes in factor prices, as we shall see, to provide measures of real factor services or inputs.

Part b of the table covers producers of government services, primarily general government agencies, plus some public enterprises that are not structured commercially. Part c covers producers of private nonprofit services to households, including domestic service (which OBE puts in the household sector proper). The services covered by parts b and c are also classified by kind of economic activity, according to ISIC codes.

The major difference between parts b and c and part a is that, since the non-business sectors do not produce commodities for sale in the market, they cannot be estimated in terms of market values, so value added likewise cannot be obtained by deducting intermediate costs from gross output values. But value added or gross product (column 4) *can* be obtained by summing factor costs and other charges against product—although property income would have to be imputed rather than obtained as a residual or "surplus." Similarly, gross output at cost can be obtained as a proxy for value by adding the costs of intermediate consumption to gross product. Obviously, the double-deflation approach cannot be applied to the nonbusiness sectors to correct for price changes; alternative approaches to estimating the physical volume of output and real product in these sectors are mentioned in Chapter 6.

Gross domestic product and factor incomes, by kind of economic activity, provide the link between the domestic production account and the input-output matrix. We turn to these matters in Chapter 5.

REVIEW QUESTIONS

1   Explain how value added by industry and sector provides a third approach to the estimation of national product.
2   Why are there two approaches to estimating income and product originating in the private domestic business sector, by industry, and only one approach in the non-business sectors?
3   What are the chief transformations necessary to convert a corporate income statement to a value-added basis?

[14] UN, *SNA*, 1968, p. 72.

4 How does the OBE estimate value added in the banking industry?

5 Define income and product originating in the rest of the world.

SELECTED REFERENCES

CONFERENCE ON RESEARCH IN INCOME AND WEALTH: *Output, Input, and Productivity Measurement,* Studies in Income and Wealth, vol. XXV (Princeton, N.J.: Princeton University Press for the National Bureau of Economic Research, 1961). See especially part II, "The Estimation of Real Product in the Economy by Industries."

GOTTSEGEN, JACK J.: "Revised Estimates of GNP by Major Industries," *Survey of Current Business,* vol. 47, pp. 18-24, April, 1967. Includes a brief description of statistical method of United States estimates.

MARIMONT, MARTIN L.: "GNP by Major Industries," *Survey of Current Business,* vol. 42, pp. 6-18, October, 1962. The "new set of accounts" is explained, and their use in analysis illustrated.

U.S. DEPARTMENT OF COMMERCE, Office of Business Economics: *National Income* (1954).

Deconsolidation of Industry Production Accounts: The Input-output Matrix

5

The last chapter showed that national production may be viewed as a consolidation of actual or constructed production statements of all individual producing units of the economy, grouped by sector. The present chapter will show how input-output matrices may be viewed as a deconsolidation by industry of these production statements, highlighting the intermediate flows among industries.

The usual square matrix form of an input-output table displays, down the column, for each industry, the debit side of a production account: purchases of materials and services from other industries plus purchases of factor services and nonfactor charges (value added). Across the row, for each industry, the table displays the credit side: sales to other industries plus sales to final users, including net inventory change. For each industry in the processing sectors, the sum of the column equals the sum of the row, or, in other words, total input equals total output. The industries are grouped to encompass all productive activity within the economy. Thus, the whole economic system appears on a from whom and a to whom basis.

The present chapter will treat briefly the conception and history of input-output, or interindustry, analysis. Until recently, input-output was developed in large part independently of the other types of economic accounts. A section below will demonstrate the relations between input-output matrices and the production accounts. Because, conceptually, the national income and product accounts are also built upon production statements, herein lies the key to the integration of the two accounting frameworks. The 1963 input-output study of the United States, prepared by the Department of Commerce, is integrated with the basic elements of the national income and product accounts. This study will be described in detail because it illustrates the structure of the matrices and the conventions and problems common to this type of study. The main features of the input-output data in the revised SNA will be outlined, showing some of the alternatives to the OBE procedure. Finally, work on some of the extensions of input-output will be mentioned.

HISTORICAL BACKGROUND

Input-output analysis is an economic application of general equilibrium theory. Its concern is the structural interdependence of economic activities. An early forerunner of input-output analysis can be found in the *Tableau Economique* by François Quesnay (1758). Indeed, the germinal work on the application of the technique begins: "The statistical study presented in the following pages may be best defined as an attempt to construct . . . a *Tableau Economique* of the United States for the year 1919."[1] In his *Tableau* Quesnay depicted the circular flow of economic goods among the three classes which made up his economy: Farmers, sole creators of economic surplus, transferred rent to the proprietors. Proprietors spent half of their rental income for agricultural products and half for industrial products purchased from artisans. Artisans purchased food and raw materials from farmers; farmers purchased industrial products from artisans.

A mathematical model of general equilibrium was developed by Leon Walras in his *Elements of Pure Economics* (1874).[2] His model is described as an idealized picture of the economic system, solvable in principle but not operational. The core of his purely and perfectly competitive model is four sets of equations.[3] First, for each consumer good an equation relates the quantity consumed to its price, the price of all other consumer goods, and the prices of productive services (i.e., incomes). Second, for each productive service there is an equation allocating it among the commodities which it helps to produce; in each case the amount of the resource used is equal to the number of units of each commodity multiplied by the input coefficient. Third, a set of equations stipulates that the price of each commodity equals its cost per unit. Fourth, for each productive service, an equation relates the quantity supplied to its price, the prices of all other productive services, and the price of all commodities. Since the price of one of the commodities is set as the *numeraire,* there are as many independent equations as there are unknowns. In general equilibrium, the prices of productive services make each demand equal each supply, and each compatible with all others; and the commodity prices make each demand equal each

[1] Wassily Leontief, "Quantitative Input and Output Relations in the Economic System of the United States," *Review of Economics and Statistics*, vol. 18, p. 105, August, 1936.

[2] Translated by William Jaffe (Homewood, Ill.: Richard D. Irwin, Inc., for the American Economic Association and the Royal Economic Society, 1954).

[3] See the explanation in Mark Blaug, *Economic Theory in Retrospect* (Homewood, Ill.: Richard D. Irwin, Inc., 1962), pp. 523-526, and Donald S. Watson, *Price Theory and Its Uses* (Boston: Houghton Mifflin Company, 1963), pp. 287-289.

supply, and each compatible with all others. Because the resource and commodity markets are doubly connected, there is one grand general equilibrium. Following Walras's lead, Gustav Cassel and Vilfredo Pareto, among others, have elaborated this theory.

More than any other person, Wassily Leontief is responsible for the modern input-output tables and analysis—essentially a modified and limited solution of the general equilibrium system. His work during the 1930s culminated in publication in 1941 of the input-output tables for 1919 and 1929 for the United States.[4] During World War II the input-output technique was considered for use in war production planning, but it was not employed. Rather, concern with postwar employment readjustment led to official support for Leontief's research. In 1941 the Bureau of Labor Statistics (BLS) of the Department of Labor initiated work under Leontief's direction on a table for 1939. This table contained ninety-six sectors, but was aggregated to forty-two and used mainly in that form.[5]

Preparation of a comprehensive table for the year 1947 was begun in 1949. The table covered 450 to 500 American industries, consolidated to 200. It was begun under the sponsorship of a number of government agencies and private research organizations, but government support was terminated in 1953.[6] Although theoretical work continued in private organizations, no other government-sponsored, economy-wide table was published until 1964. At that time the Department of Commerce made available results of the 1958 study. This was followed in 1969 with the publication of the results of the study for 1963 (see discussion below).

By the early 1960s, input-output methods had been used in over forty nations. After World War II, the technique was used for reconstruction planning in Norway, the Netherlands, and Italy. Several nations in Africa, Asia, and Latin America used input-output methods in their development programs. By the time of the third international conference on interindustry relations in 1961, papers reported on a wide range of experience. The 100 active participants came from 41 countries, capitalist as well as Communist, developed as well as less developed.

CONCEPTUAL METHODOLOGY OF AN INPUT-OUTPUT MATRIX

A static input-output matrix for an economy may be built up by combining production statements for the economy's component producing units. The emphasis in input-output analysis is on the interrelations of these producing units. Therefore, compared with the data in other types of accounts discussed so far, the data in the production statement must break out in greater detail the other industries from whom purchases are made and to whom sales are made.

---

[4] Wassily Leontief, *The Structure of the American Economy, 1919-1939*, 2d ed. (New York: Oxford University Press, 1951).

[5] Some of the literature, particularly the early literature, uses "sector" to refer to aggregates of firms producing similar products. That meaning is best reserved for "industry"; "sector" then refers to the kind of market that industries serve.

[6] A description of this work is in W. Duane Evans and Marvin Hoffenberg, "The Interindustry Relations Study for 1947," *Review of Economics and Statistics*, vol. 34, pp. 97-142, May, 1952. The study was a focal point for the Conference on Research in Income and Wealth, *Input-Output Analysis: An Appraisal*, Studies in Income and Wealth, vol. XVIII (Princeton, N.J.: Princeton University Press for the National Bureau of Economic Research, 1955).

TABLE 5-1
Production Statement for the Economy, 1969
(Thousands of Dollars)

INDUSTRY I. MID-EAST MANUFACTURING CORPORATION

Purchased materials and services consumed in the production process	$1,920	Sales to other industries	$3,975
		Sales to industry II	2,030
		Sales to industry III	1,945
Purchased from industry II	820		
Purchased from industry III	1,100	Other sales (including net inventory change)	945
Employee compensation	2,165		
		Sales to persons	600
Other factor and nonfactor charges	835	Other sales	345
Total uses	$4,920	Total sources	$4,920

INDUSTRY II. MID-WEST REFINING CORPORATION

Purchased materials and services consumed in the production process	$2,430	Sales to other industries	$1,320
		Sales to industry I	820
		Sales to industry III	500
Purchased from industry I	2,030		
Purchased from industry III	400	Other sales (including net inventory change)	1,680
Employee compensation	500		
		Sales to persons	1,300
Other factor and nonfactor charges	70	Other sales	380
Total uses	$3,000	Total sources	$3,000

INDUSTRY III. MID-SOUTH SERVICES CORPORATION

Purchased materials and services consumed in the production process	$2,445	Sales to other industries	$1,500
		Sales to industry I	1,100
		Sales to industry II	400
Purchased from industry I	1,945		
Purchased from industry II	500	Other sales (including net inventory change)	2,000
Employee compensation	700		
		Sales to persons	1,700
Other factor and nonfactor charges	355	Other sales	300
Total uses	$3,500	Total sources	$3,500

For the construction of a general-purpose, static input-output table, assume that the productive activity of the economy is carried out by three industries and that each industry consists of only one corporation. The production statement for the economy is given in Table 5-1. The table has three parts, corresponding to the economy's three industries. The first part is recognizable as a rearrangement of Table 4-4, the gross production statement of the Mid-East Manufacturing Corporation, industry I. On the uses side, the purchased materials and services have been broken down into purchases from the other two industries. Because their detail is not essential in this context, factor costs and nonfactor charges have been simplified into two items: employee compensation, and other factor costs and nonfactor charges. On the sources side, sales to what in Table 4-4 were designated as several companies have been arbitrarily divided between the two other industries. Net inventory change and the item previously titled other sales have been combined; sales to persons are shown as a separate category, illustrative of what may be viewed as the components of final expenditure in the income and product accounts. Similarly rearranged production statements have been drawn up for industries II and III.

Transformation of Production Statements

Table 5-2 shows this information from the production statements arrayed in an input-output matrix. As is customary, sales of output of an industry are shown across the row; purchases of inputs are shown down the column. For example, industry II sells to industry I a quantity of its product valued at $820,000 and to industry III a quantity valued at $500,000. Further, $1.68 million worth of its product is sold to final demand sectors. In its operations during this period, industry II purchased $2.03 million worth of materials and services from industry I and $400,000 worth from industry III. It paid its employees $500,000; its other factor costs and nonfactor charges came to $70,000.

The Four Quadrants

The matrix has four quadrants, which conceptually distinguish inputs—classified as intermediate and primary—and output or uses—classified as intermediate and final. Quadrant I shows both purchases of intermediate inputs and sales of intermediate outputs among the producing industries. It is these interrelationships that are uniquely highlighted by input-output tables. Accordingly, in empirically based tables, this quadrant is shown in detail, with ten to fifty, or in a few cases as many as several hundred, industries. Quadrant II shows sales by the producing industries to final demand. Quadrants I and II together allocate the total output of each industry in the economy. Quadrant III shows the primary factor inputs (and nonfactor charges) that are required by each producing industry, thus constituting the value added by, or gross product originating in, each industry. Quadrants I and III together show the total inputs used in production by each industry in the economy. Quadrant IV shows significant accounting totals. The totals at the foot of the final demand columns conceptually may represent the familiar gross national product expenditure components, as illustrated by the personal consumption expenditure column. The column total for total final demand represents gross national product. Similarly, the totals at the end of rows originating in the value-added quadrant

TABLE 5-2
An Input-Output Matrix for the Economy, 1969
(Thousands of Dollars)

		I Manufacturing	II Refining	III Services	Intermediate Inputs, Total	Personal Consumption Exp.	Other	Total Final Demand	Total
Intermediate Inputs	I Manufacturing		2,030	1,945	3,975	600	345	945	4,920
	II Refining	820		500	1,320	1,300	380	1,680	3,000
	III Services	1,100	400		1,500	1,700	300	2,000	3,500
	Intermediate inputs, total	1,920	2,430	2,445					
Primary Inputs	Employee compensation	2,165	500	700					3,365
	Other	835	70	355					1,260
	Total, value added	3,000	570	1,055					4,625
	Total	4,920	3,000	3,500		3,600	1,025	4,625	

I   II

III   IV
Intermediate Uses   Final Uses

conceptually may represent national income and nonfactor charge categories, as illustrated by employee compensation. The row total for value added exhibits the necessary equality with the column total representing gross national product.

For contrast, a national income and product statement developed from these same production statements is shown as Table 5-3. Note that in the consolidation the intermediate flows between industries cancel.

THE 1963 INPUT-OUTPUT STUDY

The Office of Business Economics (OBE) has undertaken the periodic presentation of a set of input-output tables as part of an integrated system of national

TABLE 5-3
National Income and Product, 1969
(Thousands of Dollars)

Employee compensation	$3,365	Personal consumption expenditure	$3,600
Other	1,260	Other	1,025
Charges against Gross National Product	$4,625	Gross National Product	$4,625

SOURCE: Derived from Table 5-2.

ECONOMIC ACCOUNTS AND THEIR USES

economic accounts. The input-output tables prepared by Leontief and the BLS, in contrast, had not been conceptually and statistically integrated with the national income and product accounts. A principal, if not the most important, recommendation of the National Accounts Review Committee was that the various types of economic accounts, including input-output tables, be integrated. Another recommendation was that advantage be taken of the data from the 1958 business censuses to prepare the tables. The results of the ensuing 1958 study were made available, beginning in 1964.[7] A table for 1961 was developed largely by summary adjustments to the 1958 table.

Late in 1969 the results of the study for 1963 were published, showing detail for about 370 industries. The industry categories have been aggregated to the 86 industries provided for the 1958 table.[8] It is this aggregated form which will be the basis of the discussion below.[9] The basic table, titled Interindustry Transactions, 1963, is reproduced as Table 5-4. It shows the value of the flow during that year of current account goods and services among each of the industries and to final users, as well as the value added of each industry. The table's basic structure is depicted in Table 5-5, emphasizing its conformance with the conceptual scheme discussed above.

A first thing to notice about Table 5-4 is that the valuation is in producers' prices. Such prices exclude the distribution costs which make up the difference between producers' and purchasers' prices (but include excise taxes collected and paid by the producers). Alternatively stated, producers' prices are equivalent to values f.o.b. the shipper's plant. This basis of valuation, rather than purchasers' prices, is customary for the construction of input-output tables in the United States and in most other nations. The distribution costs appear as a separate "purchase" from the trade and transport industries. For example, if one unit of a product has an actual delivered price of $6, of which $5 is production cost and $1 is cost of dealer's markup and freight, the table would show $5 as output of the producing industry and $1 as output of the trade and transportation industries.

It is helpful to examine the structure of Table 5-4 from the point of view of the quadrants discussed in the preceding section. In quadrant I, all productive activities have been grouped into eighty-six industries.[10] An important objective of grouping

[7] The following are among the principal documents released: Morris R. Goldman, Martin L. Marimont, and Beatrice N. Vaccara, "The Interindustry Structure of the United States: A Report on the 1958 Input-Output Study," *Survey of Current Business*, vol. 44, pp. 10–29, November, 1964; "The Transactions Table of the 1958 Input-Output Study and Revised Direct and Total Requirements Data," *Survey of Current Business*, vol. 45, pp. 33–56, September, 1965. A discussion of technical and conceptual aspects is in U.S. Department of Commerce, Office of Business Economics, National Economics Division, "The 1958 Interindustry Relations Study" (1964). (Mimeographed.)

[8] The 1947 table prepared by BLS was also made consistent with the OBE tables, facilitating analysis of change in structure over time.

[9] See National Economics Division, "Input-Output Structure of the United States Economy: 1963," *Survey of Current Business*, vol. 49, pp. 16–47, November, 1969. With regard to definitions and conventions there were only minor differences between the 1958 and 1963 studies, except for the fourfold expansion in industry detail.

[10] The number 87 is assigned to inventory valuation adjustment, the means by which nonfarm business inventories are converted from book values to average prices during the year. This inventory valuation adjustment has been calculated for the totals only and not for individual industries.

TABLE 5-4

The Office of Business Economics Interindustry Transactions Table, 1963
(Millions of Dollars at Producers' Prices)

For the distribution of output of an industry, read the row for that industry.

For the composition of inputs to an industry, read the column for that industry.

Industry No.	Industry	1 Livestock and live-stock products	2 Other agricultural products	3 Forestry and fishery products	4 Agricultural, forestry and fishery services	5 Iron and ferroalloy ores mining	6 Nonferrous metal ores mining	7 Coal mining	8 Crude petroleum and natural gas	9 Stone and clay mining and quarrying	10 Chemical and fertilizer mineral mining	11 New construction	12 Maintenance and repair construction	13 Ordnance and accessories
1	Livestock & Livestock Products	4,750	1,819	117	192							328	(*)	
2	Other Agricultural Products	7,897	769	117	550							3	(*)	
3	Forestry & Fishery Products		1,053	35										1
4	Agricultural, Forestry & Fishery Services	445		74										
5	Iron & Ferroalloy Ores Mining					55	263							
6	Nonferrous Metal Ores Mining	6	1			25	1	410	297	5	1	478	259	1
7	Coal Mining					5	6	1		5	1			
8	Crude Petroleum & Natural Gas	1	85		(*)		7	14	379	17	5	17	7	6
9	Stone and Clay Mining and Quarrying	1	35			1				1	31		3	161
10	Chemical & Fertilizer Mineral Mining									11	3	26		
11	New Construction	200	367	44	34				2			31	3	(*)
12	Maintenance & Repair Construction		2		41		10	17				124	13	4
13	Ordnance & Accessories					2			2		2	29	723	16
14	Food & Kindred Products	3,554										3,553		5
15	Tobacco Manufactures													
16	Broad & Narrow Fabrics, Yarn & Thread Mills	9	9	62	14					6		342	4	2
17	Miscellaneous Textile Goods & Floor Coverings	17	29	1					101	34	20	184	71	3
18	Apparel	2	43									208	2	7
19	Miscellaneous Fabricated Textile Products		2			21	56	38		52	6	2	1	16
20	Lumber & Wood Products, Except Containers		97		86							201	64	1
21	Wooden Containers				1							2		
22	Household Furniture			2										
23	Other Furniture & Fixtures	12										308	859	13
24	Paper & Allied Products, Except Containers	2	3	4			7	23	64	70	6	1,119	540	103
25	Paperboard Containers & Boxes	5	9	34	3	11	10	33	16		2	487	139	
26	Printing & Publishing	57		1		7								
27	Chemicals & Selected Chemical Products		1,424		3									
28	Plastics & Synthetic Materials	83												
29	Drugs, Cleaning & Toilet Preparations				3				5					
30	Paints & Allied Products	170	3			4		39	41	116	14	81	93	149
31	Paving, Roofing & Related Industries	29	9	34		21	27		30	28	2	5,813	410	193
32	Rubber & Miscellaneous Plastics Products			1		1	2			2		2,125	317	
33	Leather Tanning & Industrial Leather Products	7		1								1,244	209	
34	Footwear & Other Leather Products	5												
35	Glass & Glass Products	1												
36	Stone & Clay Products		39											
37	Primary Iron & Steel Manufacturing													
38	Primary Nonferrous Metal Manufacturing	1	13											
39	Metal Containers	8		21										

62

40	Heating, Plumbing & Structural Metal Products					(*)	2		18	2	1	6, 159	569	10
41	Stampings, Screw Machine Products & Bolts	25										112	19	35
42	Other Fabricated Metal Products	21	31	15	132	1	4	12	13	4	1	975	269	35
43	Engines & Turbines					8	11	36	16	37	5	26		3
44	Farm Machinery & Equipment	5	229									2	1	(*)
45	Construction, Mining & Oil Field Machinery					24	30	85	25	48	16	238	71	3
46	Materials Handling Machinery & Equipment					(*)	3	1		16	4	257	96	1
47	Metalworking Machinery & Equipment					1	1	5				11	(*)	22
48	Special Industry Machinery & Equipment													1
49	General Industrial Machinery & Equipment			(*)		(*)	1	2	25	23	2	210	43	20
50	Machine Shop Products	3	7	(*)	(*)	(*)	32	11	(*)	8	2	12	1	13
51	Office, Computing & Accounting Machines													(*)
52	Service Industry Machines											404	116	10
53	Electric Industrial Equipment & Apparatus					(*)	1	7	82	7	5	337	56	25
54	Household Appliances											184	99	5
55	Electric Lighting & Wiring Equipment	1	1	36	(*)	(*)	1	11	(*)	1	1	1, 123	183	46
56	Radio, Television & Communication Equipment					(*)	(*)		4			79	20	281
57	Electronic Components & Accessories						(*)		15			1	1	106
58	Miscellaneous Electrical Machinery, Equipment & Supplies	6	25	2	(*)	(*)	(*)	1	1	1	(*)	37	10	18
59	Motor Vehicles & Equipment	7	14	(*)	(*)	2	2	8	3	15	1	36	14	1
60	Aircraft & Parts				(*)									1, 868
61	Other Transportation Equipment	(*)	4	21		(*)	2	9		(*)	(*)	4	(*)	17
62	Scientific & Controlling Instruments			1		(*)	1		4			208	70	40
63	Optical, Ophthalmic & Photographic Equipment											4	(*)	53
64	Miscellaneous Manufacturing	2	2	(*)	(*)	(*)	1	(*)	(*)	(*)	(*)	89	77	1
65	Transportation & Warehousing	606	308	44	26	126	30	46	281	34	39	2, 143	490	28
66	Communications; Except Radio & TV Broadcasting	52	83			1	2	4	9	1	3	180	79	52
67	Radio & TV Broadcasting													
68	Electric, Gas, Water & Sanitary Services	96	204	(*)	1	27	41	65	141	62	36	205	90	26
69	Wholesale & Retail Trade	870	843	56	42	21	28	58	145	54	14	5, 453	1, 702	93
70	Finance & Insurance	156	315	3	6	7	25	28	94	29	6	401	161	27
71	Real Estate & Rental	289	2, 020		41	111	42	73	2, 246	45	11	307	134	30
72	Hotels; Personal & Repair Services exc. Auto													10
73	Business Services	139	836	1	(*)	33	14	28	108	22	6	2, 959	281	110
75	Automobile Repair & Services	76	161	7	1	1	2	8	42	19	1	235	101	9
76	Amusements													
77	Medical, Educational Services & Nonprofit Organizations	181	13			1	1	2	5	(*)	2	57	24	8
78	Federal Government Enterprises	4	4	(*)	(*)	1	1	2	5	1	2	18	8	10
79	State & Local Government Enterprises	(*)	1	(*)	(*)	1	1	1	3	2	1	28	10	(*)
80A	Directly Allocated Imports	2	214		(*)									
80B	Transferred Imports	174	221	428		423	213	2	1, 046	108	88			18
81	Business Travel, Entertainment & Gifts	18	32	18	16	3	7	11	67	11	2	359	154	49
82	Office Supplies	1	1	(*)	(*)	(*)	(*)	1	5	1	(*)	17	7	10
83	Scrap, Used & Secondhand Goods			5		1	5	1		5	1	38		
84	Government Industry													
85	Rest of the World Industry													
86	Household Industry													
87	Inventory Valuation Adjustment													
I.	Intermediate Inputs, Total	19, 992	12, 437	1, 153	1, 190	954	893	1, 097	5, 338	901	336	39, 629	8, 663	3, 777
VA.	Value Added	6, 692	14, 830	598	582	475	625	1, 540	6, 926	1, 123	360	25, 890	11, 132	2, 525
T.	**Total**	**26,684**	**27,266**	**1,751**	**1,772**	**1,429**	**1,519**	**2,637**	**12,265**	**2,024**	**696**	**65,519**	**19,794**	**6,302**
TR.	*Transfers* [1]	*210*	*261*	*709*	*550*	*555*	*237*	*3*	*1,365*	*258*	*116*			*1,589*

*Less than $500,000.

1. Entry in each column represents the sum of the value of transferred imports at domestic port value and the value of the secondary output of other industries which has been transferred to the industry named at the head of the column. See text for further discussion.

2. The detailed entries reflect gross exports of goods and services from each producing industry. Imports in total are shown as negative entries in this column on rows 80A and 80B. Therefore, the sum of the column equals the GNP component "net exports of goods and services."

TABLE 5-4 (Continued)

Industry No.	Food and kindred products (14)	Tobacco manufactures (15)	Broad and narrow fabrics, yarn and thread mills (16)	Miscellaneous textile goods and floor coverings (17)	Apparel (18)	Miscellaneous fabricated textile products (19)	Lumber and wood products, except containers (20)	Wooden containers (21)	Household furniture (22)	Other furniture and fixtures (23)	Paper and allied products, except containers (24)	Paperboard containers and boxes (25)	Printing and publishing (26)	Chemicals and selected chemical products (27)	Plastics and synthetic materials (28)	Drugs, cleaning, and toilet preparations (29)	Paints and allied products (30)	Petroleum refining and related industries (31)	Rubber and miscellaneous plastics products (32)
1	16,305	1,125	47	181			170							17		2			
2	6,093		1,328	29			916							28		8			
3	304															1			
4																			
5		2		1	115	(*)	2	(*)	1	1	76	1	1	83	24	4	(*)	9	9
6			13				(*)				56			85		3		9,813	
7	39		(*)		2		(*)				12			68		2	5	79	10
8	7	7												32				1	
9	5		29	9	15	4	36	1	5	3	45	12	26	33	24	25	6	349	27
10			32	21		(*)	1	(*)		(*)	123	(*)	4	470	20	322	100	(*)	(*)
11	148	1,764											14					25	(*)
12							14	1	214	2	71	5	4	81	1	1	1		181
13	12,888	1		3		1,245	3,172	157	105	35	31	(*)	23	(*)	3	(*)	(*)	3	394
14		5				315	24	13	2	1	10	(*)	28	241	3	3			22
15	15		53	47	11	61	19		1	150	19			2	212	12	1	4	6
16	3		69	29	127	272	26	2	568	39	800	2	18	7	41	2	19	102	28
17	50	35	345	15	2	8	18		72	42	1		2,630	15	2,322	74	499	61	4
18	95	91	1,091	557	14		16	1	24		2,260	5	1,808	42	100	214	228	581	3
19	3	57	7	8	349	2	94		3	32	392	(*)	34	4	22	32	21	66	53
20		78	22	73	10	23	2		(*)	1	104	(*)	384	201	22	966	1	20	161
21	88	6	29			28	51	2	(*)		458	4	2	90	111	27	105	1,622	2
22			1	(*)	17	1	14		7	36	183	2	24	2,983	104	516	10	2	383
23	(*)	(*)		5	28	28	1	(*)	7	4	15	35	43	346	1	58	(*)	2	1,790
24	902	(*)	42		40	1	14	1	91	90	106	12	72	230	(*)	289	(*)	(*)	5
25	1,138	(*)	1	(*)	16	3	54		6	2	184			65	1		1		10
26	450		(*)	5		3	46	1	253	181	2	7		28		163	11	55	21
27	244						7		4	20	(*)			4		19	6	1	445
28	102					5	1		(*)		49	18	2	10	3		23	50	5
29	216	9			(*)	1	14	34	27	40	2	33	6	36	14	180	148	134	13
30	210					3	54		92	15	13		1	227					24
31	254					3	46		32	181	(*)			213					74
32	3						7		(*)	20				156					50
33	(*)																		24
34	776																		2

64

NOTE.—Detail may not add due to rounding.

3. Entry in each row represents the value of the secondary output of the industry named at the beginning of the row which has been transferred to the primary producing industries.

ᵃ text for further discussion.

TABLE 5-4 (Continued)

For the distribution of output of an industry, read the row for that industry.

For the composition of inputs to an industry, read the column for that industry.

Industry No.		33 Leather tanning and industrial leather products	34 Footwear and other leather products	35 Glass and glass products	36 Stone and clay products	37 Primary iron and steel manufacturing	38 Primary nonferrous metal manufacturing	39 Metal containers	40 Heating, plumbing and structural metal products	41 Stampings, screw machine products and bolts	42 Other fabricated metal products	43 Engines and turbines	44 Farm machinery and equipment	45 Construction, mining and oil field machinery
1	Livestock & Livestock Products	57			7									
2	Other Agricultural Products													
3	Forestry & Fishery Products													
4	Agricultural, Forestry & Fishery Services													
5	Iron & Ferroalloy Ores Mining					1,168	15							
6	Nonferrous Metal Ores Mining					4	891							
7	Coal Mining	2		(*)	17	470	13				1	2	2	2
8	Crude Petroleum & Natural Gas	(*)		3	82		18				2	(*)	(*)	(*)
9	Stone and Clay Mining and Quarrying			37	797	70	(*)							
10	Chemical & Fertilizer Mineral Mining			1	24	12								
11	New Construction	1	4	13	43	173	44	3	15	6	13	4	3	6
12	Maintenance & Repair Construction				4	(*)5	(*)6	4	18	20	5	12		
13	Ordnance & Accessories								15					
14	Food & Kindred Products	240	1	(*)		(*)	12		18		1			
15	Tobacco Manufactures						13							
16	Broad & Narrow Fabrics, Yarn & Thread Mills		99	4	14		7	(*)2	2	(*)5	44	(*)2	(*)3	(*)3
17	Miscellaneous Textile Goods & Floor Coverings		107		17	20			9		9	2	7	3
18	Apparel		33		10			2	1	36	57	1	2	1
19	Miscellaneous Fabricated Textile Products		30		20				21					
20	Lumber & Wood Products, Except Containers	1	39	58	29	35	22	(*)		3	5	1	1	
21	Wooden Containers	(*)	3	11	(*)2	3	2	2	9	6	13			
22	Household Furniture		(*)	14			(*)		2	18	7			
23	Other Furniture & Fixtures	3	15	2	147	7	21	1	11	55	61	1	1	2
24	Paper & Allied Products, Except Containers		55	134	41	16	12	44	15	1	88	8	9	6
25	Paperboard Containers & Boxes	32	(*)	130	1	2	148	88	42	36	4	4	8	6
26	Printing & Publishing		8	1	172	411	128	8	1	24	123			
27	Chemicals & Selected Chemical Products	39	7	5	71	(*)2	1	3	38	3		1	16	1
28	Plastics & Synthetic Materials				25			78		27	5	10	7	12
29	Drugs, Cleaning & Toilet Preparations			1	2				6		66	5	58	10
30	Paints & Allied Products			5				4	90	18			14	80
31	Petroleum Refining & Related Industries	3	3	8	112	157	82	7	26	65	32	18		
32	Rubber & Miscellaneous Plastics Products	8	315	62	100	15	16	(*)	13	(*)	124	5	9	14
33	Leather Tanning & Industrial Leather Products	179	607	(*)3	(*)2	5	(*)1		(*)	1	(*)			
34	Footwear & Other Leather Products	2	100				1		74	19	10			
35	Glass & Glass Products			190	2		35	5	21		10	18		
36	Stone & Clay Products	1	(*)	78	1,065	45					72	(*)		

37	Primary Iron & Steel Manufacturing	----	6	7	111	4,897	136	993	2,154	1,047	1,543	235	424	639
38	Primary Nonferrous Metal Manufacturing	----	1	16	23	528	4,883	35	671	287	742	92	22	46
39	Metal Containers	----	----	----	----	1	----	1	11	18	1	----	----	----
40	Heating, Plumbing & Structural Metal Products	----	----	11	16	8	4	3	183	30	68	4	6	40
41	Stampings, Screw Machine Products & Bolts	(*)	(*)	2	2	149	43	48	165	100	141	57	87	47
42	Other Fabricated Metal Products	1	31	1	101	424	67	5	339	71	338	25	51	91
43	Engines & Turbines	----	----	----	1	2	11	----	15	16	4	195	139	121
44	Farm Machinery & Equipment	----	(*)	----	(*)	32	(*)	----	2	20	4	25	147	88
45	Construction, Mining & Oil Field Machinery	----	----	----	46	20	(*)	(*)	38	(*)	24	23	20	164
46	Materials Handling Machinery & Equipment	(*)	1	1	13	13	4	(*)	15	1	16	8	2	30
47	Metalworking Machinery & Equipment	----	----	3	27	80	73	3	34	51	114	62	42	131
48	Special Industry Machinery & Equipment	----	----	(*)	1	47	7	----	13	7	23	8	4	7
49	General Industrial Machinery & Equipment	(*)	(*)	(*)	11	126	42	(*)	85	29	55	92	262	268
50	Machine Shop Products	(*)	(*)	(*)	1	172	109	(*)	8	(*)	(*)	82	83	16
51	Office, Computing & Accounting Machines	----	----	----	(*)	----	----	----	1	(*)	14	----	(*)	7
52	Service Industry Machines	(*)	----	----	5	15	3	----	137	1	20	(*)	1	2
53	Electric Industrial Equipment & Apparatus	----	----	10	11	139	27	2	122	3	48	26	8	49
54	Household Appliances	----	----	(*)	(*)	5	6	----	18	5	31	----	4	(*)
55	Electric Lighting & Wiring Equipment	(*)	(*)	(*)	14	5	31	(*)	(*)	1	6	(*)	11	(*)
56	Radio, Television & Communication Equipment	(*)	(*)	1	1	(*)	22	----	6	15	13	45	9	1
57	Electronic Components & Accessories	----	----	(*)	1	(*)	1	(*)	3	2	5	(*)	3	2
58	Miscellaneous Electrical Machinery, Equipment & Supplies	(*)	(*)	(*)	1	5	50	(*)	2	1	13	53	29	5
59	Motor Vehicles & Equipment	(*)	(*)	(*)	8	77	70	(*)	12	122	53	24	43	95
60	Aircraft & Parts	----	----	(*)	(*)	(*)	----	11	25	2	41	76	(*)	17
61	Other Transportation Equipment	----	----	----	----	1	(*)	----	75	(*)	11	32	14	21
62	Scientific & Controlling Instruments	(*)	12	2	2	22	6	(*)	59	17	37	7	4	8
63	Optical, Ophthalmic & Photographic Equipment	(*)	11	1	1	2	1	(*)	3	1	1	(*)	1	(*)
64	Miscellaneous Manufacturing	(*)	67	6	26	31	9	(*)	3	10	35	(*)	13	(*)
65	Transportation & Warehousing	14	34	65	527	1,146	330	57	142	71	105	25	55	49
66	Communications; Except Radio & TV Broadcasting	2	15	10	47	103	45	4	55	25	35	10	11	16
67	Radio & TV Broadcasting	----	----	----	----	----	----	----	----	----	----	----	----	----
68	Electric, Gas, Water & Sanitary Services	9	13	113	308	624	325	17	63	44	82	13	18	27
69	Wholesale & Retail Trade	35	112	108	244	737	425	73	280	112	251	74	118	132
70	Finance & Insurance	6	22	21	77	214	72	18	54	35	59	8	24	39
71	Real Estate & Rental	10	28	24	61	55	56	17	110	52	85	3	13	23
72	Hotels; Personal & Repair Services exc. Auto	(*)	1	2	4	12	3	1	27	3	5	2	3	3
73	Business Services	8	86	66	197	328	144	47	146	79	163	38	79	56
75	Automobile Repair & Services	(*)	3	3	28	19	7	1	10	3	8	3	3	4
76	Amusements	----	----	----	----	----	----	----	----	----	----	----	----	----
77	Medical, Educational Services & Nonprofit Organizations	(*)	2	1	6	9	4	1	6	3	5	2	2	3
78	Federal Government Enterprises	1	12	4	9	16	7	1	9	5	9	3	4	5
79	State & Local Government Enterprises	(*)	(*)	1	10	8	3	(*)	1	1	1	1	(*)	1
80A	Directly Allocated Imports	4	1	----	13	----	6	----	----	----	----	----	----	----
80B	Transferred Imports	50	4	59	108	715	1,103	8	4	44	161	24	131	22
81	Business Travel, Entertainment & Gifts	3	22	20	70	83	47	12	82	31	78	17	21	29
82	Office Supplies	1	5	3	8	15	6	1	9	4	8	2	3	4
83	Scrap, Used & Secondhand Goods	----	----	14	2	661	610	----	14	----	12	----	9	2
84	Government Industry	----	----	----	----	----	----	----	----	----	----	----	----	----
85	Rest of the World Industry	----	----	----	----	----	----	----	----	----	----	----	----	----
86	Household Industry	----	----	----	----	----	----	----	----	----	----	----	----	----
87	Inventory Valuation Adjustment	----	----	----	----	----	----	----	----	----	----	----	----	----
I.	Intermediate Inputs, Total	716	1,921	1,325	4,953	14,166	10,292	1,610	5,625	2,718	5,220	1,467,	2,068	2,455
V.A.	Value Added	251	1,505	1,607	4,594	10,453	3,980	835	3,371	2,237	3,743	931	1,013	1,607
T.	**Total**	**967**	**3,427**	**2,932**	**9,548**	**24,618**	**14,272**	**2,445**	**8,996**	**4,955**	**8,963**	**2,398**	**3,080**	**4,062**
TR.	*Transfers* [1]	*69*	*75*	*134*	*383*	*1,264*	*1,530*	*76*	*778*	*535*	*1,557*	*334*	*267*	*389*

TABLE 5-4 (Continued)

Industry No.	46 Materials handling machinery and equipment	47 Metalworking machinery and equipment	48 Special industry machinery and equipment	49 General industrial machinery and equipment	50 Machine shop products	51 Office, computing and accounting machines	52 Service industry machines	53 Electric industrial equipment and apparatus	54 Household appliances	55 Electric lighting and wiring equipment	56 Radio, television and communication equipment	57 Electronic components and accessories	58 Miscellaneous electrical machinery, equipment and supplies	59 Motor vehicles and equipment	60 Aircraft and parts	61 Other transportation equipment	62 Scientific and controlling instruments	63 Optical, ophthalmic and photographic equipment	64 Miscellaneous manufacturing
1																	4		11
2																			4
3																			
4																		3	
5																			
6										5									
7		1																	1
8														15					
9	(*)				7							(*)					(*)		(*)
10	2	1	1	1	(*)	1	1		2	1	1	(*)	1	2	2	2	(*)		2
11																		4	15
12	2	11	5	9	2	9	5	2	4	3	11		2	71	22	7	7	9	(*)
13	1	1	6	5	3			31	(*)		108	10		16	207	(*)	9	2	12
14							3										14	2	102
15	3		3	5	2														51
16	1	6	1	9	1	1	5	10	7	3	1	6	2	15	6	1	65	1	16
17		1	4	2		3	2	3		8			2	129	8	35	9		6
18	2	6						4	3	3	10	2		17	11	6	14		
19	3	1	15			1	7	6		3			1	397	2	18	65		186
20		1				1	10	3	11		10		1	27	12	151	22		
21				6	1	8	3	6	8	3	1	62	1	7		29	7	54	21
22	(*)	11	2	14	9	13	4	6	3	1	10	25	18	(*)	3	(*)	1	15	141
23	3	1	4	1	5	4	21	3	5	1	3	1	47	1	4	6	5	(*)	126
24	(*)	14	1	19		2	1	40	63	54	6	75	10	10	39	12	2	154	44
25	5		11			7	19	21	31	17	193	23	47	13	8	5	4	22	59
26	45	(*)	5	1	1	1		10	20	30		1	(*)	42	11	13	(*)		186
27		1	2	3		2	21	45	8	16	25	5		2	4	1			19
28		3	2	(*)				21	41	1	101			194	35	23			55
29														11	18	1			
30								1						2	2				
31	2	20	24	30	5	2	8	22	(*)	16	18	11	3	366	15	12	20	3	23
32		43	50	28	9	7	69	32	239	31	30	82	91	69	49	64	24	34	308
33				3		47		88		79	29			893	95		27		17
34	(*)	(*)	4	(*)			4	(*)	3		15	135	(*)		(*)	(*)	17	(*)	31
35			1			1			13	110	46	29			1		9	39	33
36	2	84	10	46	27	14	23	59	54	32	38		15	79	36	20	114	6	23

TABLE 5-4 (Continued)

For the distribution of output of an industry, read the row for that industry.

For the composition of inputs to an industry, read the column for that industry.

Industry No.	Industry	Transportation and warehousing (65)	Communications; except radio and TV broadcasting (66)	Radio and TV broadcasting (67)	Electric gas, water and sanitary services (68)	Wholesale and retail trade (69)	Finance and insurance (70)	Real estate and rental (71)	Hotels; personal and repair services except auto (72)	Business services (73)	Automobile repair and services (75)	Amusements (76)	Medical, educational services and non-profit organizations (77)	Federal Government enterprises (78)
1	Livestock & Livestock Products	2						960				18	6	
2	Other Agricultural Products	88						1,583					36	636
3	Forestry & Fishery Products							17						
4	Agricultural, Forestry & Fishery Services					169		7						(*)
5	Iron & Ferroalloy Ores Mining					(*)		6						
6	Nonferrous Metal Ores Mining					1		10						
7	Coal Mining	9			3	2		80	1				11	67
8	Crude Petroleum & Natural Gas	21			636	7		15	1	(*)				
9	Stone and Clay Mining and Quarrying					4		4		(*)				(*)
10	Chemical & Fertilizer Mineral Mining	1			1,948					1				
11	New Construction	1,159	386	(*)	889	397	112	7,215	150	31	23	81	669	42
12	Maintenance & Repair Construction					19		1	1	(*)				
13	Ordnance & Accessories					732		107	2	1	6	(*)	302	214
14	Food & Kindred Products	132			2	4	(*)	6			6			
15	Tobacco Manufactures													
16	Broad & Narrow Fabrics, Yarn & Thread Mills													
17	Miscellaneous Textile Goods & Floor Coverings	17	4	1	2	14		18	44	3				18
18	Apparel	15				20		3	6				3	4
19	Miscellaneous Fabricated Textile Products				7	105		36	64				16	
20	Lumber & Wood Products, Except Containers	3			2	42		1	87					6
21	Wooden Containers					86		27						
22	Household Furniture					51		2						
23	Other Furniture & Fixtures		9			23		5						
24	Paper & Allied Products, Except Containers	10			22	20	195	28	48	89	3	1	51	14
25	Paperboard Containers & Boxes	10			1	782		7	24	13			2	1
26	Printing & Publishing	47	1		2	580	300	85	8	7,057	5			16
27	Chemicals & Selected Chemical Products	40	2		55	236	1	237	59	113		47	456	3
28	Plastics & Synthetic Materials				2	151		33				61	47	2
29	Drugs, Cleaning & Toilet Preparations	4				44		54	251	118	74		599	5
30	Paints & Allied Products	5				215		8	7	10	120			
31	Petroleum Refining & Related Industries	1,544	86	1	223	32	84	490	145	116	234	18	146	17
32	Rubber & Miscellaneous Plastics Products	197	15		6	1,358	8	67	58	17	(*)	2	43	9
33	Leather Tanning & Industrial Leather Products					322		2	12					
34	Footwear & Other Leather Products	(*)	(*)			2		8	150			5	4	(*)
35	Glass & Glass Products	3				38		12	(*)		73		3	(*)
36	Stone & Clay Products	8	(*)		1	154		30	62	11	108	(*)		1

70

	C1	C2	C3	C4	C5	C6	C7	C8	C9	C10	C11	C12	C13
37 Primary Iron & Steel Manufacturing	225			58	46		26	5					(*)
38 Primary Nonferrous Metal Manufacturing	20	7		17	39		14					2	2
39 Metal Containers					5		6						
40 Heating, Plumbing & Structural Metal Products				(*)	119		48						(*)
41 Stampings, Screw Machine Products & Bolts	7				51		11	53	122			2	
42 Other Fabricated Metal Products	103			2	112		14		83			2	(*)
43 Engines & Turbines	56			1	15		1		33				
44 Farm Machinery & Equipment					18		6						
45 Construction, Mining & Oil Field Machinery	1				46		14		86				(*)
46 Materials Handling Machinery & Equipment	20				18		6		14				
47 Metalworking Machinery & Equipment					32		14		19				
48 Special Industry Machinery & Equipment	13	1			53		79			1			(*)
49 General Industrial Machinery & Equipment	10				53		14		19				(*)
50 Machine Shop Products					17		6						1
51 Office, Computing & Accounting Machines	1				47		47	2	2	109	(*)	1	(*)
52 Service Industry Machines					36		3		302				(*)
53 Electric Industrial Equipment & Apparatus	28	172		(*)	42		27	32	102				(*)
54 Household Appliances					49		16	146	116	16			1
55 Electric Lighting & Wiring Equipment	13	(*)	(*)	24	63	(*)	1	8				(*)	
56 Radio, Television & Communication Equipment		7	7	1	40		13		5	13	(*)	1	(*)
57 Electronic Components & Accessories	34				33	45	14	404	28			3	1
58 Miscellaneous Electrical Machinery, Equipment & Supplies	83	3		2	90	848	8	5	4	193	3	4	(*)
59 Motor Vehicles & Equipment	110		2	2	99		36	5	5	846	4	5	8
60 Aircraft & Parts	204	4	3	3	107	2	16				1	1	
61 Other Transportation Equipment	255	146		(*)	17	2	17	9	15		84	236	(*)
62 Scientific & Controlling Instruments		124			67	595	67	3	6	(*)	7	62	(*)
63 Optical, Ophthalmic & Photographic Equipment	1	113	1	(*)	60	390	60	130	167		111	47	1
64 Miscellaneous Manufacturing	1	252	17		189	6,063	13	319	376	84	34	116	
65 Transportation & Warehousing	3,168	4	99	570	907	1,625	302	102	76	70	17	403	1,290
66 Communications; Except Radio & TV Broadcasting	370	235	102	80	1,267		177	128	854		54	17	9
67 Radio & TV Broadcasting	250	104	13		10		10	224	2,224	71	84	950	64
68 Electric, Gas, Water & Sanitary Services	1,044	2	23	5,529	2,071	2,519	1,255	430	454	1,274	132	589	64
69 Wholesale & Retail Trade	654	12	27	166	2,159	78	2,611	220	699	165	105	192	15
70 Finance & Insurance		65	24	216	1,897	1			244		721		
71 Real Estate & Rental	890	7	52	167	6,416	358	2,769	861	1,356	303	7	2,694	137
72 Hotels; Personal & Repair Services exc. Auto	13	39			258	653	210	395	197	8	343	147	3
73 Business Services	692		93	493	5,687	93	1,687	413	1,362	116	19	662	108
75 Automobile Repair & Services	608		1	44	87	130	127	127		37	1,481	151	16
76 Amusements	46	2	606	8	120	15	131	2	114		19	31	(*)
77 Medical, Educational Services & Nonprofit Organizations	91			520	1,186		76	42	51	6		311	1
78 Federal Government Enterprises	993		3		1,449		328	42	673	6	28	249	2
79 State & Local Government Enterprises	758	7		3,841	26		636	9	15	154	23	23	244
80A Directly Allocated Imports	1,017										133		
80B Transferred Imports				105									
81 Business Travel, Entertainment & Gifts	182	96	57	113	1,189	455	85	218	879	49	201	556	60
82 Office Supplies	63	56	3	25	266	578	44	28	66	5	11	130	5
83 Scrap, Used & Secondhand Goods					7					24			
84 Government Industry													
85 Rest of the World Industry													
86 Household Industry													
87 Inventory Valuation Adjustment													
I. Intermediate Inputs, Total	15,342	2,062	1,019	15,787	32,165	15,153	22,298	5,542	18,382	4,439	3,736	9,980	3,090
V.A. Value Added	23,873	11,433	1,289	13,874	88,448	18,548	61,589	9,828	17,563	6,427	3,961	23,180	2,774
T. Total	39,215	13,495	2,308	29,660	120,613	33,700	83,887	15,370	35,945	10,866	7,697	33,160	5,864
TR. Transfers [1]	2,058			4,632	4,229	121	8,293	2	10,415	149	17		

71

TABLE 5-4 (Continued)

State and local government enterprises (79)	Gross imports of goods and services (80A & 80B)	Business travel, entertainment and gifts (81)	Office supplies (82)	Scrap, used and secondhand goods (83)	Government industry (84)	Rest of the world industry (85)	Household industry (86)	Inventory valuation adjustment (87)	Intermediate outputs, total	Final Demand: Personal consumption expenditures	Final Demand: Gross private fixed capital formation	Final Demand: Net inventory change	Final Demand: Net exports [2]	Final Demand: Federal Government purchases	Final Demand: State and local government purchases	Final Demand: Total final demand	Total	Transfers [3]	Industry No.
		36							24,492	1,762		374	38	5	12	2,193	26,684	2,026	1
2		107							20,901	2,868		584	2,917	−92	88	6,365	27,266	2,681	2
(*)		7							1,411	420		44	46	−172	2	340	1,751	7	3
1									1,762	15			11	17	−33	9	1,772	7	4
									1,357			−55	118	9		72	1,429	14	5
									1,279			−3	1	242		239	1,519	40	6
81									2,117	165		(*)	305	35	14	520	2,637	16	7
39									12,237			16	12			27	12,265	622	8
									1,998	15		1	38	3	−30	26	2,024	87	9
2									609	2		−1	62	(*)	24	88	696	217	10
											46,151		2	4,010	15,356	65,519	65,519		11
1,307									14,871					1,414	3,510	4,924	19,794		12
(*)		8							648	181		−26	197	5,300	2	5,654	6,302	454	13
		2,069							21,306	49,921		583	1,648	317	488	52,957	74,263	3,099	14
		166		9					1,950	4,943		23	508		1	5,474	7,425	187	15
				92					12,141	630		33	281	33	14	990	13,131	832	16
(*)									2,471	1,011	63	83	29	12	(*)	1,197	3,668	210	17
1		8		8					3,974	13,697		67	147	69	75	14,055	18,029	264	18
2				3					1,541	1,482		40	35	69	8	1,634	3,174	160	19
(*)		3	(*)						10,152	230	5	63	194	6	3	502	10,654	229	20
									412			1	2	4		7	420	34	21
									800	3,025	124	73	10	17	18	3,267	4,067	142	22
									382	133	1,127	14	19	42	205	1,540	1,923	103	23
22		4	421	23					11,248	1,241		90	449	47	45	1,872	13,119	841	24
				36					4,550	74		33	23	10	59	199	4,748	159	25
4		10	1,208	78					12,285	3,160		109	163	117	450	3,999	16,283	8,406	26
79		1	10						14,009	394		88	1,160	1,036	206	2,885	16,893	1,303	27
									5,708	12		25	553	42	(*)	633	6,341	649	28
3		52							2,702	5,428		160	335	73	355	6,351	9,053	649	29
(*)									2,363	23		39	31	3	3	99	2,462	147	30
55				10					11,737	8,232		177	678	711	301	10,100	21,837	1,651	31
7		3	10	12					7,357	1,863	18	105	276	171	101	2,534	9,891	696	32
				8					933			−8	41	1		34	967	23	33
(*)		30		1					420	3,032		−48	18	4	1	3,007	3,427	113	34
(*)		3	(*)						2,484	238		68	96	12	33	448	2,932	61	35
19		2							9,097	217		71	128	23	13	450	9,548	556	36

Row																		
37	1,526	24,618	653	3	45	493	102	22	10	23,965				135	4			12
38	886	14,272	636	(*)	-11	491	122	9	12	13,635				135		(*)		(*)
39	86	2,445	68	(*)	7	25	28	9		2,377				9	(*)			1
40	627	8,996	1,021		58	252	86	536	88	7,975				26	7	7	5	
41	559	4,955	405	11	28	44	56	242	266	4,551				45				1
42	713	8,963	1,222	8	40	259	93	388	580	7,742				24				
43	295	2,398	1,022	15	179	303	27	1,902	125	1,376				3				
44	341	3,080	2,270	33	11	285	46	1,760	10	810				10				
45	407	4,062	887	1	105	936	52	665		1,175				13	9	9		
46	180	1,617	844	22	70	96	12	1,670	77	773								1
47	384	5,144	2,334	7	86	423	56	2,025	21	2,810				9				
48	421	3,716	2,656	12	17	561	25	1,386		1,061				18	(*)			(*)
49	608	5,354	2,055	43	236	378	43	6	2	3,299				30	(*)			2
50	194	2,257	109		49		9			2,148				19				6
51	543	3,925	2,619	111	448	317	41	1,615	88	1,305				1			10	5
52	363	3,391	1,828	73	47	209	52	1,112	336	1,563				4			18	
53	739	6,495	2,733	61	423	343	23	682	22	3,762				13	9		53	20
54	848	3,673	3,280	64	10	132	211	120	2,793	1,393				7			3,186	2
55	301	3,081	653	116	13	81	27	55	422	2,428						37		
56	1,201	12,440	9,332	5	4,686	366	151	1,924	2,089	3,108				72	(*)			
57	379	4,512	865	13	398	199	-9	96	176	3,647				11	141			
58	275	2,256	793	644	110	75	28	198	368	1,464				2	294	51		
59	1,230	40,031	24,357	(*)	663	1,386	611	5,671	15,381	15,674				161				
60	2,019	14,317	9,226	644	7,532	857	342	446	49	5,091				17				2
61	372	4,894	3,811	30	1,124	165	46	1,465	980	1,084				22				5
62	603	4,280	2,028	118	405	373	56	673	403	2,252				10	(*)	10		1
63	385	2,534	1,327	65	147	157	14	340	604	1,207				12	141	18	82	
64	1,084	7,152	4,170	102	8	186	49	497	3,327	2,983				17	294	53	247	
65	4,493	39,215	14,715	682	1,320	3,040	152	574	8,946	24,500				73			3,186	32
66	553	13,495	6,755	344	341	43		485	5,542	6,740								
67	2,234	2,308	44	17		28				2,264								
68	132	29,660	12,513	860	264	30			11,358	17,148								
69	2,342	120,613	85,551	114	728	1,735	325	4,858	80,791	32,063				5	(*)	450		701
70	1,124	33,700	17,222	268	37	37		1	16,879	16,478								39
71	14	83,887	56,140	478	162	397			53,878	27,747						1,008		103
72	1,414	15,370	12,603	163	361	4		1,224	12,074	7,767								50
73	672	35,945	6,108	962	1,981	199			2,967	29,837								2
74	96	10,866	6,813	99	21				6,693	4,054						163		247
75	403	7,697	5,085	-53	107	313	6		4,712	2,612						52		13
76	112	33,160	31,506	723	1,416	32			29,335	1,654								(*)
77	1,214	5,864	1,276	182	1,115	90			888	4,588								8
78	6,011	7,236	858	21	198			166	638	6,378								7
79			-3,477	3	2,649	-12,320	21		6,064	3,477			924	336		251		3
80A	14,318	7,793	-14,318			-14,318				14,318								
80B		2,106																
81		1,518	385	243	143	329	106		-250	7,793								10
82		55,029	-334	506	-53			-972		1,721								12
83		4,183	55,029	30,581	24,449	6,208			-1,382	1,852								
84		3,824	4,183		-643				3,824									
85		-502	3,824				-502				-502							
86			-502								-502							
87																		
I.		590,389	590,389	59,082	64,115	5,812	5,329	80,510	375,540			924	55,029	1,518	2,106	7,793	2,986	
V.A.											-502	3,259	55,029	1,518	2,106	7,793	4,250	
T.		590,389	590,389								-502	4,183		1,518	2,106	7,793	7,236	
TR.												924						

SOURCE: *Survey of Current Business*, vol. 49, table 1, pp. 30–35, November, 1969.

TABLE 5-5
Schematic Presentation of the Structure of the Table of Interindustry Transactions, 1963*

Input \ Output	1-4	5-10	11-12	13-64	65-68	69	70-71	72-77	78-79	80	81-83	84-86	87	Inter. Outputs, Total	Personal Cons. Expenditure	Gross Priv. Fixed Capital Form	Net Inventory Change	Net Exports	Gov. Purchases	Total Final demand	Total	Transfers
1-4 Ag., for., & fish.	X	—	X	X	X	X	X	X	X	—	X	—	—	X	X	—	X	X	X	X	X	X
5-10 Mining	X	X	X	X	X	X	X	X	X	—	X	—	—	X	X	—	—	X	X	X	X	X
11-12 Construction	X	X	X	X	X	X	X	X	X	—	X	—	—	X	—	X	—	X	—	X	X	—
13-64 Manufacturing	X	X	X	X	X	X	X	X	X	—	X	—	—	X	X	X	X	X	X	X	X	X
65-68 Trans. & util.	X	X	X	X	X	X	X	X	X	—	X	—	—	X	X	X	X	X	X	X	X	X
69 Wls. & rtl. trade	X	X	X	X	X	X	X	X	X	—	X	—	—	X	X	X	X	X	X	X	X	X
70-71 Fin., insur., & r. est	X	X	X	X	X	X	X	X	X	—	X	—	—	X	X	X	—	X	X	X	X	X
72-77 Services	X	X	X	X	X	X	X	X	X	—	X	—	—	X	X	—	X	X	X	X	X	X
78-79 Gov. enterprises	X	X	X	X	X	—	X	X	X	—	X	—	—	X	X	—	—	X	X	X	X	X
80 Imports A	—	—	—	—	—	X	—	X	—	—	—	—	—	X	—	X	X	X	—	X	—	—
80 Imports B	X	X	—	X	X	—	X	—	X	—	X	X	—	—	X	—	—	X	X	X	—	X
81-83 Dummy industries	—	—	—	—	—	—	—	X	—	—	—	—	—	—	—	X	X	X	—	X	X	—
84-86 Special industries	—	—	—	—	—	—	—	—	—	—	—	—	—	—	—	—	—	X	—	X	X	—
87 Inventory val. adj.	X	X	X	X	X	X	X	X	X	—	X	X	—	—	X	X	X	—	X	—	X	—
Intermediate inputs, total	X	X	X	X	X	X	X	X	X	—	X	X	X	—	X	X	X	—	X	—	—	—
Value added	X	X	X	X	X	X	X	X	X	—	X	X	X	—	X	X	X	X	X	X	X	—
Total	X	X	X	X	X	X	X	X	X	—	X	X	X	—	X	X	X	X	X	X	—	—
Transfers	X	X	—	X	X	X	X	X	X	—	X	X	—	—	X	X	X	X	X	X	—	—

* X indicates an entry in the aggregated 1963 table; — indicates no entry in the aggregated 1963 table. Source: See OBE table reproduced as Table 5-4.

the industries is homogeneity in terms of input patterns. A difficult grouping problem is posed by "secondary products," or products of an establishment (the basic unit in collecting the statistics) other than that establishment's primary output. Secondary products may introduce elements of heterogeneity in two ways: First, if the input patterns of the primary and secondary products differ, a change in the establishment's product mix will alter the overall input pattern. Second, a product may be produced as a primary product of one industry and a secondary product of another, so that a consumer may purchase from either supplier, although the statistics, which usually show only total usage of a product, would not indicate which. In the industry groupings, the secondary products of the trade, construction, and service sectors were handled by "redefinition." That means that the output and inputs attributable to the secondary product were subtracted from the industry's totals and added to the industry to which it was a primary product. In the mining and manufacturing sectors, an alternative procedure referred to as "transfer" was used. Secondary production is left where it occurs, but is treated as if it were sold to the primary industry, where it becomes part of the output available for distribution.

Industries 80 through 86 in Table 5-4 call for special comment. The row for industry 80, imports, is shown in two parts. Imports used for production which are substitutes for domestically produced goods and services are treated similarly to transferred secondary products. The domestic industry is shown as making fictitious purchases from the import row 80B, and as distributing these imports along with their own product. (The sum of these transferred imports plus secondary products is shown in the last row of the table as the italicized item *transfers*.) Row 80A shows imports used in production for which there are no domestic substitutes, plus imports purchased directly by the final demand sectors in substantially unaltered form. The distinction made between parts A and B helps to maintain technological homogeneity.[11]

Industries 81, 82, and 83 are "dummy" or synthetic industries. The business travel, entertainment and gift, office supplies, and scrap industries are each a synthesis of numerous commodities and services, originating in different industries, whose use is related to a common activity and for which statistical information on consumption is generally limited to the group as a whole. The use of such dummy industries simplifies the analytical picture without sacrificing very much detail critical to general use of the table.[12]

The "special" industries (84 to 86) are the government, rest of the world, and household industries. Entries for these industries measure income and product originating in them. For example, for the household industry, the product or row entry reflects personal consumption expenditure by households for domestic services, valued (in 1963) at $3.824 billion. The income or column entry reflects the employee

[11] The intersection of parts A and B of row 80 with the final demand category net exports shows negative entries equal to the import totals (and thus the final total at the end of the row shows the entries canceling out). These negative entries for imports combined with that column's gross exports by industry sum to equal the gross national product component, net exports of goods and services. Note that column 80, gross imports, has no entry at all.

[12] The dummy industries have no entry for value added. Thus, in each case their total intermediate inputs equal their total inputs. That the transfers item in each case equals total output reinforces the idea of their composition as a synthesis of goods and services originating in different industries.

compensation of the domestic workers; this $3.824 billion entry appears in the value-added quadrant.[13]

In quadrant II, the final demand quadrant, the final markets—households, capital formation, net exports, government—are the same final markets as in the national income accounts. This means that if one cross-checks, the column total of personal consumption expenditure in the input-output table would be identical to personal consumption expenditures as a component of the 1963 GNP (in 1963 dollars, as yet in process of revision), and similarly for the other columns. From the column for gross private fixed investment, it is seen that the inputs recorded in the table represent transactions on current account only. All private capital purchases by producing industries are aggregated into this final demand column. As an extreme but illustrative case, industry 11, new construction, produces no intermediate, i.e., current account, output; its output goes to gross private fixed capital formation and also to government purchases and net exports.

The value-added quadrant in Table 5-4 consists of a single row. Unlike the national income accounts, which show separately the different types of payments (compensation of employees, proprietors' income, rental income of persons, etc.), the value added by each industry, in whatever form, is aggregated into this one row.

Other Tables

In addition to the basic transactions table, OBE presented tables of direct and total requirements. The direct requirements table (Table 5-6) shows for each column the inputs required of other industries to produce one dollar's worth of the given industry's output. For example, the livestock and livestock products industry requires 18 cents of its own product; 30 cents of other agricultural products; 2 cents of agricultural, forestry, and fisheries services; and so on to produce one dollar's worth of its own product. Thus, each column shows input coefficients. In each column, after adjustment for scrap and by-products, the coefficients for intermediate inputs plus primary inputs (value added) add up to 1.00000.

Table 5-7 shows the direct and indirect, or total, requirements per dollar of delivery to final demand.[14] Thus, when there is an increase in the final demand for the products of the livestock industry, there will be a direct increase in purchases by the livestock industry from industries producing other agricultural products, agricultural services, and so on, as we saw above. But further, when output in these industries is increased, this will in turn increase the demand for the output of all industries that supply their inputs, including the livestock industry. It is the total impact of these wavelike effects of demand throughout the economy that is captured in the total requirements table. Note that, unlike the direct requirements table, there are no empty cells (excluding the special case of new construction); this emphasizes the interdependence of all industries. Note also that Table 5-7 relates only to

---

[13] In tables not using these special industries, these activities are found in the primary inputs quadrant. See, for example, Hollis B. Chenery and Paul G. Clark, *Interindustry Economics* (New York: John Wiley & Sons, Inc., 1959), pp. 14-17; and William H. Miernyk, *The Elements of Input-Output Analysis* (New York: Random House, Inc., 1965), pp. 11-16.

[14] This table is also called the inverse coefficient table, after the mathematical procedure of its calculation. For an explanation of this method, see texts such as those of Chenery and Clark, *ibid.*, and Miernyk, *ibid.*

ECONOMIC ACCOUNTS AND THEIR USES

the output of industries; i.e., there is no value-added row. This table is the form in which input-output data are used to calculate the impact on the various industries which results from stipulated changes in final demand.

INPUT-OUTPUT DATA IN THE SNA

One of the major purposes of the revision of the *SNA* was the elaboration of the system to include data for input-output analysis. [15] This was accomplished by setting forth standard tables to encompass the data found at the intersection of the production rows and columns as depicted in the overall matrix of the system (see Table 14-2). The major classifications of the production accounts are by kind of activity (industries, producers of government services, and producers of private nonprofit services for households) and by kind of commodity. In setting forth the data structure for a commodity X commodity matrix, as well as an industry X industry matrix, the *SNA* goes beyond the input-output work described so far.

Two standard tables (and their constant-dollar counterparts), together with information on net final demand, provide the basic data for input-output analysis. Standard table 2, Supply and Disposition of Commodities, arrays, horizontally, the various commodities, and vertically, the sources of supplies (activities, elaborating industries) and disposition of supplies (intermediate consumption, final consumption, increase in inventories, gross fixed capital formation, and exports). Standard table 3, Gross Output and Input of Industries, arrays, horizontally, the various industries, and vertically, gross output and gross input, including intermediate consumption of commodities. Schematic presentations of these tables are reproduced from the *SNA*'s explanatory chapter as Tables 5-8 and 5-9. In Table 5-8, the square submatrix within the heavy lines, showing supply of commodities by industry, can be interpreted as an *output matrix*. In it, each row shows the distribution by commodity of the *output of an industry;* each column shows the distribution by industry of the *output of a commodity*. In Table 5-9, the square submatrix within the heavy lines, showing intermediate consumption of commodities, can be interpreted as an *input matrix*. In it, each row shows the distribution by industry of the *input of a commodity;* each column shows the distribution by commodity of the *input of an industry*. [16]

Given the data to fill the cells of the separate input and output tables, the construction of an input-output matrix involves transfer of inputs and outputs between categories. These transfers make it possible to show either (1) inputs of commodities into the production of commodities, producing a commodity X commodity matrix, or (2) inputs from industries into industries, producing the familiar industry X industry matrix. There are several procedures for accomplishing these transfers. [17] Output alone can be transferred, or both inputs and outputs can be transferred. There are mechanical procedures available, based on different assumptions about

[15] This section draws upon chap. III, "The System as a Basis for Input-Output Analysis," UN, *SNA*, 1968, pp. 35–51.

[16] The above relates to the competitive commodities, defined as those for which there is some domestic production. See the next paragraph on the treatment of complementary commodities, which are imports.

[17] See UN, *SNA*, 1968, pp. 37–40, for details.

TABLE 5-6

The Office of Business Economics Direct Requirements Table, 1963: Industries 1–14
(Direct Requirements per Dollar of Gross Output; Producers' Prices)

For the composition of inputs to an industry, read the column for that industry.

Industry No.	Industry	1. Livestock and livestock products	2. Other agricultural products	3. Forestry and fishery products	4. Agricultural, forestry and fishery services	5. Iron and ferroalloy ores mining	6. Nonferrous metal ores mining	7. Coal mining	8. Crude petroleum and natural gas	9. Stone and clay mining and quarrying	10. Chemical and fertilizer mineral mining	11. New construction
1	Livestock & Livestock Products	0.17800	0.06673	0.06687	0.10823							0.00493
2	Other Agricultural Products	.29596	.02819	.06665	.31040							
3	Forestry & Fishery Products	.01667	.03863	.01392								.00005
4	Agricultural, Forestry & Fishery Services			.04243							.00215	
5	Iron & Ferroalloy Ores Mining					.03846	.00089	.00004		.00002		
6	Nonferrous Metal Ores Mining	.00021	.00002			.01782	.17332	.00010	.00002	.00225	.00013	
7	Coal Mining					.00361	.00090	.15561	(*)	.00227	.00087	
8	Crude Petroleum & Natural Gas	.00006							.02418			.00729
9	Stone and Clay Mining and Quarrying		.00311			.00339	.00029	.00026		.00860	.00772	
10	Chemical & Fertilizer Mineral Mining		.00129				.00408	.00001		.00072	.04442	
11	New Construction	.00750				.00060	.00491	.00549	.03093	.00543	.00394	.00027
12	Maintenance & Repair Construction		.01344	.02529	.01933							.00008
13	Ordnance & Accessories		.00008								.00010	.00040
14	Food & Kindred Products	.13319										
15	Tobacco Manufactures											
16	Broad & Narrow Fabrics, Yarn & Thread Mills	.00035	.00034	.03536	.02296	.00001	.00019	(*)		.00006	.00043	.00047
17	Miscellaneous Textile Goods & Floor Coverings		.00106			(*)	.00010		.00017			.00189
18	Apparel	.00065	.00158				.00001					.00044
19	Miscellaneous Fabricated Textile Products	.00008	.00008	.00072								.00011
20	Lumber & Wood Products, Except Containers				.00798	.00169	.00651	.00636	.00001	.00002		.05424
21	Wooden Containers											.00523
22	Household Furniture	.00044	.00004	.00022	.00003							.00281
23	Other Furniture & Fixtures	.00006	.00011			.00015	.00026	.00038	.00014	.00287	.00289	.00317
24	Paper & Allied Products, Except Containers				.04877							.00007
25	Paperboard Containers & Boxes											
26	Printing & Publishing	.00018	.00032	.00020	.00001	.00002	.00005	.00002	.00003	.00004	.00005	.00003
27	Chemicals & Selected Chemical Products	.00213	.05224	.00091	.00051	.01487	.03669	.01443	.00822	.01688	.02871	.00307
28	Plastics & Synthetic Materials						.00009			.00011	.00025	.00002
29	Drugs, Cleaning & Toilet Preparations	.00310		(*) .00252	(*)	(*)	.00001	(*)	.00037	.00001	.00002	.00003
30	Paints & Allied Products						.00001			.00001		.00469
31	Petroleum Refining & Related Industries	.00636	.03499	.01959	.00195	.00737	.00462	.00868	.00524	.02550	.00823	.01709
32	Rubber & Miscellaneous Plastics Products	.00109	.00419	.00059	.00004	.00473	.00641	.01233	.00128	.03455	.00250	.00743
33	Leather Tanning & Industrial Leather Products											.00001
34	Footwear & Other Leather Products	.00027		(*)	.00156	(*)	.00001	(*)		.00001	.00001	
35	Glass & Glass Products	.00020								.00123		.00123

36	Stone & Clay Products	.00005	.00143	.00028	(*)	.00251	.00112	.00119	.00333	.05715	.00065	.08872
37	Primary Iron & Steel Manufacturing					.01493	.01777	.01486	.00243	.01362	.01974	.03244
38	Primary Nonferrous Metal Manufacturing	.00003	.00003			.00102	.00025	.00003		.00116	.00287	.01898
39	Metal Containers	.00029	.00046	.01216								
40	Heating, Plumbing & Structural Metal Products					.00022	.00099		.00150	.00084	.00080	.09400
41	Stampings, Screw Machine Products & Bolts	.00093										.00171
42	Other Fabricated Metal Products	.00077	.00115	.00861	.07439	.00091	.00249	.00466	.00107	.00220	.00099	.01488
43	Engines & Turbines					.00585	.00719	.01355	.00129	.01838	.00663	.00040
44	Farm Machinery & Equipment	.00020	.00840									.00002
45	Construction, Mining & Oil Field Machinery					.01674	.01954	.03210	.00200	.02354	.02341	.00364
46	Materials Handling Machinery & Equipment					.00015	.00228	.00022		.00792	.00636	.00393
47	Metalworking Machinery & Equipment					.00083	.00037	.00172				.00017
48	Special Industry Machinery & Equipment											
49	General Industrial Machinery & Equipment			.00025		.00016	.00048	.00079	.00200	.01130	.00240	.00320
50	Machine Shop Products	.00011	.00024	.00011	.00001	.00014	.02082	.00425	.00003	.00378	.00248	.00018
51	Office, Computing & Accounting Machines											
52	Service Industry Machines											.00617
53	Electric Industrial Equipment & Apparatus					.00004	.00043	.00279	.00666	.00367	.00693	.00515
54	Household Appliances											.00280
55	Electric Lighting & Wiring Equipment	.00003	.00005	.02045	.00001	.00013	.00040	.00419	.00002	.00051	.00137	.01715
56	Radio, Television & Communication Equipment					.00004	.00013		.00033			.00121
57	Electronic Components & Accessories						(*)		.00119			.00002
58	Miscellaneous Electrical Machinery, Equipment & Supplies	.00022	.00093	.00105	.00001	.00017	.00018	.00030	.00007	.00069	.00020	.00056
59	Motor Vehicles & Equipment	.00025	.00051	.00022	.00003	.00156	.00155	.00301	.00027	.00724	.00143	.00056
60	Aircraft & Parts				.00022							
61	Other Transportation Equipment	(*)	.00016	.01184		.00006	.00122	.00337		.00006	.00044	.00007
62	Scientific & Controlling Instruments			.00040		.00025	.00033		.00036			.00317
63	Optical, Ophthalmic & Photographic Equipment											.00007
64	Miscellaneous Manufacturing	.00006	.00007	.00012	(*)	.00001	.00067	(*)	(*)	.00002	.00003	.00136
65	Transportation & Warehousing	.02272	.01131	.02517	.01445	.08811	.01947	.01760	.02293	.01661	.05592	.03271
66	Communications; Except Radio & TV Broadcasting	.00196	.00303			.00091	.00115	.00134	.00070	.00030	.00402	.00275
67	Radio & TV Broadcasting											
68	Electric, Gas, Water & Sanitary Services	.00360	.00749	.00009	.00045	.01868	.02687	.02469	.01148	.03054	.05155	.00313
69	Wholesale & Retail Trade	.03260	.03090	.03215	.02382	.01502	.01827	.02199	.01180	.02669	.02059	.08323
70	Finance & Insurance	.00583	.01155	.00188	.00322	.00476	.01637	.01076	.00763	.01423	.00832	.00612
71	Real Estate & Rental	.01082	.07407		.02324	.07753	.02748	.02769	.18312	.02212	.01622	.00469
72	Hotels; Personal & Repair Services exc. Auto											
73	Business Services	.00519	.03068	.00038	.00002	.02282	.00923	.01080	.00881	.01076	.00882	.04516
75	Automobile Repair & Services	.00285	.00589	.00387	.00051	.00073	.00151	.00293	.00343	.00932	.00137	.00358
76	Amusements											
77	Medical, Educational Services & Nonprofit Organizations	.00677	.00047			.00054	.00068	.00077	.00039	.00019	.00262	.00087
78	Federal Government Enterprises	.00015	.00015	.00018	.00017	.00080	.00082	.00068	.00043	.00050	.00230	.00028
79	State & Local Government Enterprises	.00002	.00003	.00017	.00003	.00040	.00057	.00024	.00026	.00112	.00122	.00043
80	Gross Imports of Goods & Services	.00659	.01594	.24437	.00006	.29580	.14007	.00083	.08531	.05336	.12564	
81	Business Travel, Entertainment & Gifts	.00066	.00117	.01002	.00904	.00231	.00453	.00409	.00544	.00533	.00274	.00547
82	Office Supplies	.00003	.00003	.00025	.00023	.00023	.00030	.00041	.00041	.00041	.00032	.00026
83	Scrap, Used & Secondhand Goods			.00309		.00037	.00344	.00033		.00233	.00145	.00059
V.A.	Value Added	.25080	.54388	.34163	.32835	.33257	.41171	.58412	.56475	.55470	.51735	.39516
T.	Total	1.00000	1.00000	1.00000	1.00000	1.00000	1.00000	1.00000	1.00000	1.00000	1.00000	1.00000

*Less than 0.000005. NOTE.—Detail may not add due to rounding.

SOURCE: *Survey of Current Business*, vol. 49, p. 36, table 2, November, 1969.

TABLE 5-7

The Office of Business Economics Total Requirements Table, 1963: Industries 1–14 (Total Requirements per Dollar of Delivery to Final Demand; Producers' Prices)

Each entry represents the output required, directly and indirectly, from the industry named at the beginning of the row for each dollar of delivery to final demand by the industry named at the head of the column.

Industry No.	Industry	1 Livestock and livestock products	2 Other agricultural products	3 Forestry and fishery products	4 Agricultural, forestry and fishery services	5 Iron and ferroalloy ores mining	6 Nonferrous metal ores mining	7 Coal mining	8 Crude petroleum and natural gas	9 Stone and clay mining and quarrying	10 Chemical and fertilizer mineral mining
1	Livestock & Livestock Products	1.31963	0.10112	0.11907	0.18536	0.00291	0.00268	0.00239	0.00483	0.00253	0.00193
2	Other Agricultural Products	.43481	1.07832	.12999	.39019	.00381	.00314	.00285	.00639	.00296	.00222
3	Forestry & Fishery Products	.00141	.00073	1.02090	.00130	.00048	.00134	.00124	.00038	.00038	.00037
4	Agricultural, Forestry & Fishery Services	.03898	.04347	.05041	1.01832	.00028	.00029	.00027	.00042	.00024	.00019
5	Iron & Ferroalloy Ores Mining	.00074	.00090	.00111	.00153	1.04173	.00375	.00242	.00063	.00233	.00470
6	Nonferrous Metal Ores Mining	.00063	.00091	.00083	.00143	.02314	1.21088	.00113	.00051	.00396	.00151
7	Coal Mining	.00182	.00156	.00120	.00187	.00653	.00433	1.18698	.00113	.00630	.00472
8	Crude Petroleum & Natural Gas	.01799	.02576	.01660	.01405	.01088	.01089	.01162	1.03246	.02066	.01430
9	Stone and Clay Mining and Quarrying	.00245	.00460	.00167	.00225	.00447	.00135	.00120	.00142	1.01508	.00900
10	Chemical & Fertilizer Mineral Mining	.00180	.00373	.00081	.00174	.00090	.00701	.00090	.00050	.00202	1.04780
11	New Construction	.02803	.02957	.00064	.01835	.01665	.01670	.01643	.05321	.01650	.01616
12	Maintenance & Repair Construction	.00008	.00007	.00009	.00015	.00012	.00016	.00023	.00011	.00009	.00018
13	Ordnance & Accessories	.21689	.02195	.05810	.06081	.00406	.00560	.00466	.00484	.00550	.00442
14	Food & Kindred Products	.00021	.00020	.00042	.00043	.00019	.00029	.00026	.00027	.00040	.00020
15	Tobacco Manufactures										
16	Broad & Narrow Fabrics, Yarn & Thread Mills	.00313	.00340	.01341	.00975	.00084	.00152	.00139	.00068	.00279	.00149
17	Miscellaneous Textile Goods & Floor Coverings	.00290	.00326	.04164	.02729	.00062	.00095	.00119	.00055	.00239	.00056
18	Apparel	.00064	.00047	.00091	.00099	.00035	.00048	.00047	.00034	.00064	.00039
19	Miscellaneous Fabricated Textile Products	.00228	.00227	.00261	.00195	.00019	.00026	.00028	.00015	.00056	.00021
20	Lumber & Wood Products, Except Containers	.00485	.00562	.00319	.01094	.00468	.01367	.01318	.00365	.00326	.00304
21	Wooden Containers	.00229	.00444	.00106	.01007	.00009	.00016	.00015	.00009	.00016	.00010
22	Household Furniture	.00010	.00010	.00021	.00027	.00006	.00010	.00012	.00006	.00009	.00006
23	Other Furniture & Fixtures	.00006	.00006	.00006	.00012	.00004	.00005	.00005	.00004	.00007	.00005
24	Paper & Allied Products, Except Containers	.01327	.00861	.00356	.03399	.00466	.00571	.00540	.00384	.01086	.00812
25	Paperboard Containers & Boxes	.00776	.00459	.00615	.05617	.00119	.00181	.00183	.00097	.00280	.00152
26	Printing & Publishing	.01370	.01342	.00678	.01021	.00976	.00764	.00753	.00646	.00814	.00669
27	Chemicals & Selected Chemical Products	.03981	.07668	.02055	.03908	.02566	.06130	.02855	.01544	.03461	.04297
28	Plastics & Synthetic Materials	.00390	.00448	.01021	.00877	.00263	.00428	.00494	.00176	.01020	.00281
29	Drugs, Cleaning & Toilet Preparations	.00646	.00227	.00164	.00225	.00090	.00143	.00095	.00078	.00136	.00140
30	Paints & Allied Products	.00197	.00207	.00412	.00200	.00117	.00147	.00145	.00305	.00154	.00132
31	Petroleum Refining & Related Industries	.03544	.05210	.03428	.02758	.01822	.01563	.01827	.01308	.03688	.01929
32	Rubber & Miscellaneous Plastics Products	.00706	.00757	.00553	.00694	.00797	.01105	.01863	.00343	.04126	.00608
33	Leather Tanning & Industrial Leather Products	.00020	.00016	.00012	.00052	.00007	.00010	.00010	.00006	.00008	.00008
34	Footwear & Other Leather Products	.00054	.00020	.00026	.00193	.00009	.00012	.00012	.00010	.00017	.00009
35	Glass & Glass Products	.00328	.00078	.00195	.00135	.00040	.00053	.00073	.00064	.00076	.00050

No.	Industry										
36	Stone & Clay Products	.00270	.00389	.00223	.00309	.00460	.00370	.00375	.00593	.06772	.00302
37	Primary Iron & Steel Manufacturing	.01035	.00951	.01917	.02613	.03139	.04617	.04418	.01031	.04014	.04263
38	Primary Nonferrous Metal Manufacturing	.00471	.00535	.00891	.01509	.06072	.01011	.00983	.00470	.01212	.01258
39	Metal Containers	.00620	.00228	.01458	.00271	.00057	.00097	.00065	.00058	.00087	.00076
40	Heating, Plumbing & Structural Metal Products	.00122	.00128	.00137	.00154	.00131	.00262	.00165	.00354	.00258	.00216
41	Stampings, Screw Machine Products & Bolts	.00299	.00134	.00231	.00294	.00143	.00224	.00285	.00097	.00319	.00201
42	Other Fabricated Metal Products	.00759	.00730	.01625	.08295	.00404	.00779	.01049	.00358	.00817	.00514
43	Engines & Turbines	.00072	.00104	.00083	.00370	.00816	.01101	.01956	.00195	.02223	.00945
44	Farm Machinery & Equipment	.00433	.00078	.00139	.00073	.00075	.00095	.00139	.00027	.00113	.00094
45	Construction, Mining & Oil Field Machinery	.00052	.00070	.00039	.00074	.01941	.02570	.04052	.02567	.02871	.02984
46	Materials Handling Machinery & Equipment	.00032	.00037	.00022	.00045	.00065	.00352	.00094	.00042	.00934	.00770
47	Metalworking Machinery & Equipment	.00068	.00078	.00104	.00187	.00260	.00394	.00559	.00076	.00364	.00252
48	Special Industry Machinery & Equipment	.00063	.00111	.00076	.00130	.00065	.00116	.00090	.00053	.00118	.00094
49	General Industrial Machinery & Equipment	.00118	.00180	.00173	.00186	.00296	.00462	.00627	.00322	.01734	.00690
50	Machine Shop Products	.00087	.00107	.00082	.00094	.00177	.02967	.00750	.00050	.00666	.00443
51	Office, Computing & Accounting Machines	.00058	.00067	.00034	.00062	.00058	.00050	.00057	.00044	.00061	.00046
52	Service Industry Machines	.00045	.00049	.00035	.00056	.00039	.00046	.00051	.00062	.00072	.00051
53	Electric Industrial Equipment & Apparatus	.00109	.00129	.00212	.00164	.00159	.00296	.00613	.00845	.00701	.01005
54	Household Appliances	.00041	.00043	.00058	.00071	.00035	.00048	.00062	.00069	.00072	.00056
55	Electric Lighting & Wiring Equipment	.00052	.00062	.02199	.00057	.00060	.00102	.00588	.00084	.00126	.00209
56	Radio, Television & Communication Equipment	.00052	.00052	.00061	.00070	.00066	.00099	.00106	.00102	.00125	.00084
57	Electronic Components & Accessories	.00042	.00041	.00072	.00053	.00048	.00079	.00076	.00193	.00089	.00080
58	Miscellaneous Electrical Machinery, Equipment & Supplies	.00137	.00168	.00249	.00111	.00097	.00115	.00160	.00053	.00213	.00111
59	Motor Vehicles & Equipment	.00311	.00302	.00285	.00301	.00304	.00585	.00921	.00204	.01567	.00552
60	Aircraft & Parts	.00071	.00051	.00081	.00132	.00134	.00135	.00166	.00058	.00186	.00131
61	Other Transportation Equipment	.00067	.00062	.01371	.00069	.00126	.00248	.00535	.00051	.00110	.00157
62	Scientific & Controlling Instruments	.00059	.00049	.00102	.00091	.00077	.00139	.00087	.00103	.00104	.00075
63	Optical, Ophthalmic & Photographic Equipment	.00061	.00061	.00040	.00058	.00048	.00046	.00046	.00040	.00053	.00040
64	Miscellaneous Manufacturing	.00159	.00158	.00169	.00208	.00112	.00209	.00124	.00104	.00167	.00102
65	Transportation & Warehousing	.05962	.03203	.05176	.04894	.11195	.04261	.03795	.03689	.04034	.07874
66	Communications; Except Radio & TV Broadcasting	.00910	.00793	.00390	.00621	.00504	.00544	.00531	.00384	.00479	.00601
67	Radio & TV Broadcasting	.00271	.00316	.00117	.00199	.00234	.00163	.00165	.00139	.00176	.00143
68	Electric, Gas, Water & Sanitary Services	.02165	.02173	.01031	.01695	.03317	.03121	.04521	.02354	.03182	.07696
69	Wholesale & Retail Trade	.08091	.05503	.05991	.04494	.03059	.03814	.04167	.02735	.04712	.03670
70	Finance & Insurance	.02567	.02563	.01168	.02038	.01610	.03172	.02278	.02097	.02611	.01822
71	Real Estate & Rental	.06725	.10152	.02556	.07187	.09630	.04684	.04565	.20300	.03873	.03058
72	Hotels; Personal & Repair Services exc. Auto	.00236	.00182	.00263	.00305	.00157	.00194	.00181	.00200	.00212	.00146
73	Business Services	.04330	.05064	.01877	.03180	.03737	.02606	.02645	.02192	.02814	.02288
74	Automobile Repair & Services										
75		.00951	.00885	.00715	.00682	.00375	.00382	.00539	.00643	.00180	.00396
76	Amusements	.00145	.00164	.00094	.00136	.00128	.00101	.00100	.00117	.00107	.00083
77	Medical, Educational Services & Nonprofit Organizations	.01012	.00200	.00147	.00231	.00129	.00168	.00164	.00118	.00106	.00344
78	Federal Government Enterprises [1]	.00384	.00358	.00224	.00323	.00375	.00417	.00367	.00303	.00376	.00067
79	State & Local Government Enterprises	.00555	.00497	.00348	.00455	.00859	.00917	.00785	.00571	.00977	.01383
80	Gross Imports of Goods & Services	.03454	.03137	.27063	.02899	.32309	.18303	.01298	.09393	.06975	.14571
81	Business Travel, Entertainment & Gifts	.00727	.00658	.01470	.01505	.00638	.00998	.00905	.00868	.01066	.00695
82	Office Supplies	.00134	.00113	.00103	.00136	.00114	.00151	.00145	.00123	.00157	.00129

*Less than 0.000005.

1. To remove a source of instability in the measurement of total requirements per dollar of delivery to final demand, the Commodity Credit Corporation has been excluded from this industry. The excluded inputs to the CCC from the specified industries are: Industry 2, $836 million; Industry 14, $214 million; Industry 16, $15 million; Industry 65, $642 million; Industry 69, $24 million; and value added, -$1,531 million.

SOURCE: *Survey of Current Business*, vol. 49, p. 42, table 3, November, 1969.

TABLE 5-8
Schematic Presentation of the SNA Standard Table: "Supply and Disposition of Commodities"

					Competitive commodities		
	(1) Agriculture, Forestry, Fishing	(2) Mining	(3) Food, Beverages, Tobacco	(4) Textiles, Wearing Apparel, Leather	(5) Rubber, Chemicals, Petroleum Products	(6) Basic Metal Industries	(7) Metal Products, Machinery, Equipment
Sources of supply							
Agriculture, forestry, fishing . 1	1,695						
Mining 2		974	3				
Food, beverages, tobacco . . . 3			3,637		21		1
Textiles, wearing apparel, leather 4				2,907	5		2
Rubber, chemicals, petroleum products 5		1	69	8	2,917	1	9
Basic metal industries 6					12	2,639	58
Metal products, machinery, equipment 7				3	8	85	7,929
Manufacturing n.e.c. 8		4		6	7	1	18
Gas, electricity, water 9					109		
Construction 10						1	6
Transport and communication .11						1	3
Distribution 12			27	28			
Services 13							5
Producers of government services							
Producers of private non-profit services							
Import duties	25	1	26	21	17	3	41
Imports, c.i.f.	741	129	592	200	423	151	382
TOTAL	2,461	1,109	4,354	3,173	3,519	2,882	8,454
Destinations of supply							
Intermediate consumption, industries	942	867	819	1,463	2,495	2,478	3,336
Intermediate consumption, producers of government services	15	20	26	20	137		534
Intermediate consumption, producers of private non-profit services							
Final consumption in domestic market, households	1,434	192	3,266	1,257	333		796
Increase in inventories	28	– 81	48	46	62	116	204
Gross fixed capital formation . .		19					1,865
Exports	42	29	195	387	492	288	1,719
TOTAL	2,461	1,109	4,354	3,173	3,519	2,882	8,454

SOURCE: UN, *SNA*, 1968, p. 36, table 3.1.

ECONOMIC ACCOUNTS AND THEIR USES

	(8) Manufacturing, n.e.c.	(9) Gas, Electricity, Water	(10) Construction	(11) Transport and Communication	(12) Distribution	(13) Services	Complementary commodities (14) Agriculture, Forestry, Fishing	(15) Mining	(16) Food, Beverages Tobacco	(17) Basic Metal Industries	(18) Manufacturing, n.e.c.	Commodity Taxes, Net
	16											−147
	3	3	1									8
	1	1										353
	5	1			7							105
	20	61	1									63
	6	54	1									7
	21	3	38									329
	2,983	8	17									85
		1,187										37
	13		3,151									3
				3,313								33
					3,818							77
				1		4,920						583
	20											1,288
	419			558		291	457	423	130	204	116	
	3,507	1,318	3,209	3,872	3,825	5,211	457	423	130	204	116	2,824
	2,352	707	1,000	1,668	845	1,340	316	423		204	116	1,613
	112	66	197	81	41	385						72
	621	459	312	981	2,800	2,862	141		130			1,159
	77	− 1			29							
	88	86	1,698	110	11	169						59
	257	1	2	1,032	99	455						− 79
	3,507	1,318	3,209	3,872	3,825	5,211	457	423	130	204	116	2,824

TABLE 5-9

Schematic Presentation of the SNA Standard Table: "Gross Output and Input of Industries"

		(1) Agriculture, Forestry, Fishing	(2) Mining	(3) Food, Beverages, Tobacco	(4) Textiles, Wearing Apparel, Leather
	Gross output at basic values	1,711	984	3,661	2,927
	Commodity taxes, net............	−147	8	353	105
	Gross output at producers' prices ...	1,564	992	4,014	3,032
Competitive intermediate inputs	Agriculture, forestry, fishing.... *1*	76		641	211
	Mining *2*	3	19	18	25
	Food, beverages, tobacco *3*	281		473	4
	Textiles, wearing apparel, leather *4*	8	6	12	1,116
	Rubber, chemicals, petroleum products................. *5*	175	33	143	213
	Basic metal industries *6*		28	7	2
	Metal products, machinery, equipment *7*	73	44	90	62
	Manufacturing n.e.c........... *8*	12	30	126	40
	Gas, electricity, water........ *9*	12	21	26	28
	Construction................*10*	51	46	11	18
	Transport and communication ..*11*	69	36	81	62
	Distribution *12*	54	20	53	57
	Services....................*13*	56	19	100	78
Complementary intermediate inputs	Agriculture, forestry, fishing....*14*			149	73
	Mining *15*				
	Food, beverages, tobacco *16*				
	Basic metals *17*				
	Manufacturing n.e.c. *18*				
	Commodity taxes, net..........	13	12	891	21
Primary inputs	Compensation of employees......	341	570	436	675
	Operating surplus	367	50	343	172
	Consumption of fixed capital	120	50	61	70
	Indirect taxes, net.............	−147	8	353	105
	TOTAL COSTS	1,564	992	4,014	3,032

SOURCE: UN, *SNA*, 1968, p. 38, table 3.2.

	Industries								
	(5)	*(6)*	*(7)*	*(8)*	*(9)*	*(10)*	*(11)*	*(12)*	*(13)*
	Rubber, Chemicals, Petroleum Products	*Basic Metal Industries*	*Metal Products, Machinery, Equipment*	*Manufacturing, n.e.c.*	*Gas, Electricity, Water*	*Construction*	*Transport and Communication*	*Distribution*	*Services*
	3,087	2,770	8,087	3,044	1,296	3,171	3,317	3,873	4,926
	63	7	329	85	37	3	33	77	583
	3,150	2,777	8,416	3,129	1,333	3,174	3,350	3,950	5,509
	14								
	197	120	24	102	271	34	41	7	6
	18			4			32	7	
	64	4	59	69	1	8	16	84	16
	784	164	290	174	93	95	133	121	75
	24	812	1,353	17	14	202	15	3	1
	104	101	2,091	111	57	165	217	78	143
	90	30	253	747	17	466	33	203	305
	88	119	98	59	85	7	7	84	71
	16	15	35	16	3	553	58	114	63
	117	117	159	98	47	79	670	98	36
	57	120	120	100	23	54	55	89	43
	117	109	303	155	17	122	76	121	57
	94								
	333	73	17						
		204							
	19			97					
	22	10	38	24	41	27	116	142	256
	464	475	2,493	895	295	1,061	1,353	1,616	2,073
	370	232	592	305	105	256	151	984	1,369
	95	65	162	71	217	42	344	122	412
	63	7	329	85	37	3	33	77	583
	3,150	2,777	8,416	3,129	1,333	3,174	3,350	3,950	5,509

input structure. These mechanical procedures may be supplemented with manual methods based on available input structure data.

The *SNA* makes the distinction between commodities and the industries in which they are produced because there is not a one-to-one correspondence between the two. As was mentioned in regard to the problem of defining an industry, a product may be produced in more than one industry. Statistically, data on sales (output) structure usually relate to commodities, and data on cost (input) structure usually relate to industries. The *SNA* document suggests that if both kinds of tables cannot be prepared, a commodity X commodity table is preferred. Most applications begin with a given final demand for commodities and work out the corresponding levels of commodity output needed to fulfill direct and indirect requirements. For this purpose a commodity X commodity table is most appropriate. Other applications examine primary inputs into industries. This can be done by transforming commodity output into industry output, eliminating the need for the industry X industry table for this purpose. Unfortunately, a commodity X commodity table is difficult to implement statistically.

The *SNA* document made recommendations on several other points. Whereas the 1958 OBE table, and many others, were expressed in producers' prices, as distinguished from purchasers' prices, which include trade and transport charges, the recommended valuation is in "basic values." Basic values are producers' values less commodity taxes on output. Basic values are preferred, because these taxes not only vary between types of buyers but between types of product within a commodity class. Notes to the tables indicate that valuation in these terms may be difficult to implement statistically.

It is also proposed that competitive imports be distinguished from complementary imports (see the intersection, in Table 5-8, of the row "imports, c.i.f.," with the various columns, where competitive and complementary commodities are separated). The SNA method, which distributes total supply (domestic production plus competitive imports) to users, is preferred to the routing of imports directly to users. The preference is based on the fact that the SNA method does not call for as much information; specifically, it does not require data on the source of supply as between domestic and imported commodities for individual user industries. The OBE procedure for the 1958 tables was to distribute the total supply of goods used in production, for which there were competitive imports, among the user industries.

The *SNA* document concludes the discussion of input-output analysis with the question, "Is there an ideal input-output table?" For most purposes for most countries, the answer given is:

> The table should be of medium size, with around fifty branches, based on rectangular input and output tables [more commodity subdivisions than industry subdivisions]. Basic values provide a suitable means of valuation and, if only one table is to be constructed, a commodity X commodity table is to be preferred to an industry X industry table. Inputs should be transferred as well as outputs and, while special information should be used as far as possible in doing this, the mechanical methods, which in most countries will have to do nearly all the work, should be based on a mixture of assumptions, the precise mixture varying with the nature of industrial connexions in different countries.[18]

[18] *Ibid.*, p. 48.

APPLICATION OF INPUT-OUTPUT TABLES

Thus far we have described input-output tables in terms of an economic accounting framework, as an alternative and supplement to the more familiar income and product accounts. However, utilization of the statistical data assembled means moving from an accounting framework to an economic model. This section will discuss the main assumptions implied when this transition is made.

A transactions table, with its accompanying direct and total requirements tables, such as those presented by OBE, is most readily and commonly adapted to a static, open model. The model is static in the sense that capital requirements are explicitly excluded from intermediate inputs and instead aggregated as final demand purchases. It is open in the sense that not all of its variables are mutually and simultaneously determined by operation of the model. Usually the final demand sectors are the ones which are not so determined; the model allows final demand, or a bill of goods, to be autonomously specified, and then the solution is sought in terms of the levels of output of the producing industries.

Many of the uses involve the simplifying assumption that input coefficients established by the empirical study are stable over time and through a range of output levels. This latter assumption is also called the "proportionality" or "constant returns to scale" assumption. These assumptions, static, open, and stability, imply that the industries have been successfully grouped so that changes in output mix do not alter input relations, and that substitution due to input price changes or availability and technological changes can be ignored.[19] Acceptance of these assumptions does not rest on a belief in their theoretical validity, but in a belief that they are sufficiently close to reality to make useful work possible within their confines. However, not all economists are ready to go even that far, and input-output techniques still have vocal critics. The difficulties of these assumptions have led to considerable developmental work on models which use more sophisticated relationships between inputs and outputs.

EXTENSIONS OF INPUT-OUTPUT ANALYSIS

Efforts to expand the size of input-output tables and further refine the data contained in them are expected to reach limits. The major area of work is thus in supplementing and giving greater analytical power to the models utilizing the tables. This is a wide field. Two examples of this work will be mentioned: projection of input-output relationships and preparation of capital flow tables.

Projection of Input-Output Tables

The necessity of assuming stability of input-output relationships when a given table is applied to a time period other than that for which the data were collected has limited the usefulness of input-output models. One way to expand their usefulness is to project the relationships in such a way as to take into account changes in tech-

---

[19] Chenery and Clark, *op. cit.* pp. 157–158; and Carl F. Christ, "A Review of Input-Output Analysis," in Conference on Research in Income and Wealth, *Input-Output Analysis: An Appraisal*, pp. 139–141.

nology and product mix, substitution of materials, and other factors. The Bureau of Labor Statistics worked out a technique to do this for *Projections, 1970.*[20] The problem was to project the input coefficients as found in the OBE table for 1958 to the year 1970, the target year of the study. A combination of analyses of specific industries and of general methods applicable to all industries was used. As an example of the former, a study of the agricultural sector indicated that selected purchased inputs, such as fertilizer and seed, were rising relative to output. The sectors supplying these inputs were identified. Since this long-term trend was expected to continue, the appropriate adjustments were made in the coefficients relating the agricultural sector to the supplying industries. The Harvard Research Project under Leontief investigated the more important input relations in a number of industries and made similar adjustments. One of the general approaches used was to compare the 1947 table with the 1958 table to ascertain major changes in coefficients. These and other methods were used to compile a table that, for each of the eighty-six industries in the 1958 table, gave an index of coefficient change in terms of the weighted average change in use of an industry's output by intermediate users.

Capital Flow Tables

The extension of input-output by preparation of a capital flow matrix was also done by BLS. As explained above, static tables show only the interindustry flows of current outputs and inputs; capital expenditures are aggregated into the gross private fixed capital formation column in the final demand quadrant. A capital flow matrix takes capital formation as a control total and shows, across the rows, sales of capital-producing industries, and down the column, purchases of capital-consuming industries. The Bureau prepared capital flow tables to supplement the 1958 input-output table.[21] Capital purchases and industries were defined the same way as in the 1958 input-output table. A set of three tables was prepared: the dollar values of capital production and consumption, capital coefficients by consuming industry (calculated by finding the percentage distribution of each column), and capital distribution by producing industry (calculated by finding the percentage distribution of each row). The procedure followed in allocating capital production to the consuming industries varied according to the information available. In the case of equipment, the distribution of existing stock, distributions of closely connected occupations, and distributions of an industry's output were among the methods used. In the case of plant, in many instances the distribution could be based on end use of the construction; hospital construction, e.g., was allocated to the medical sector. For industrial construction, the Census of Manufactures provided a distribution of plant expenditure by industry. The capital flow matrix was used by BLS to determine a distribution of capital by producing industry consistent with the relative industry growth rates that were projected over the period to 1970. This distribution of capital was then used to modify the initial estimates of the 1970 final demand for plant and equipment. Another possible use is to analyze marketing patterns of capital goods, similar to the analysis of current production that is made possible

[20] U.S. Department of Labor, Bureau of Labor Statistics, *Projections, 1970: Interindustry Relationships, Potential Demand, Employment,* Bulletin no. 1536 (1966).
[21] U.S. Department of Labor, Bureau of Labor Statistics, *Capital Flow Matrix, 1958,* Bulletin no. 1601 (October, 1968).

by input-output tables. The usefulness of the present tables will be enhanced by improvements in data upon which to construct the tables and by development of better techniques for projecting change in input patterns.

REVIEW QUESTIONS

1 A static input-output matrix may be built by combining production statements for component producing units. What rearrangements of the statements are necessary to do this?
2 Sketch out the four quadrants of an input-output matrix. What is the economic significance of the entries in each of these quadrants?
3 Briefly comment on the role of the following items in the 1963 OBE study: producers' prices, secondary product, "dummy" industries, and "special" industries.
4 Distinguish between the three major kinds of input-output tables: transactions table, direct requirements table, and total requirements table.
5 Discuss the assumptions implied by use of an input-output model.
6 What major recommendations for input-output tables were incorporated in the *SNA*?
7 Work to extend the analytical power of input-output tables is underway. Describe recent efforts to project input-output relationships and to prepare a capital flow table.

SELECTED REFERENCES

CHENERY, HOLLIS B., and PAUL G. CLARK: *Interindustry Economics* (New York: John Wiley & Sons, Inc., 1959).
> A comprehensive text.

CONFERENCE ON RESEARCH IN INCOME AND WEALTH: *Input-Output Analysis: An Appraisal,* Studies in Income and Wealth, vol. XVIII (Princeton, N.J.: Princeton University Press for the National Bureau of Economic Research, 1955).
> An introduction, seven papers dealing with general problems and evaluations of methods and results, and a report of the Puerto Rico study. The papers were presented in 1952.

GOLDMAN, MORRIS R., MARTIN L. MARIMONT, and BEATRICE N. VACCARA: "The Interindustry Structure of the United States: A Report on the 1958 Input-Output Study," *Survey of Current Business,* vol. 44, pp. 10–29, November, 1964.

MIERNYK, WILLIAM H.: *The Elements of Input-Output Analysis* (New York: Random House, Inc., 1965).
> An introductory text. References to recent literature.

NATIONAL ECONOMICS DIVISION: "Input-Output Structure of the United States Economy: 1963," *Survey of Current Business,* vol. 49, pp. 16–47, November, 1969.

UNITED NATIONS, DEPARTMENT OF ECONOMIC AND SOCIAL AFFAIRS, STATISTICAL OFFICE: *A System of National Accounts,* Studies in Methods, ser. F, no. 2, rev. 3 (New York, 1968).
> See especially, chap. III, "The System as a Basis for Input-Output Analysis."

U.S. DEPARTMENT OF LABOR, BUREAU OF LABOR STATISTICS: *Projections, 1970: Interindustry Relationships, Potential Demand, Employment,* Bulletin no. 1536 (1966).
> This study is being updated and extended to 1975 and 1980.

Deflating Income and Product for Price Change

6

The accounts as we have presented them thus far are expressed in current prices. But in a dynamic world in which neither the general price level nor relative prices stand still, changes in the values or costs of the various goods and services entering the accounts are due not only to changes in the physical volume of flows (or stocks), but also to changes in the prices at which they are sold—or might be sold, in the case of imputations. As we all know, value is the product of quantity and price ($V = Q \times P$); the task of price deflation in the economic accounts is to disentangle the Q's from the P's. The result is a set of accounts showing real flows (and stocks) in constant prices, together with supplementary tables showing the associated price indexes.

The task sounds quite simple, yet it involves difficult conceptual and statistical problems. The results are worth the pains that must be taken, however, since we would be unable to analyze many aspects of economic growth, and changes in economic structure by type of product and industry, without possession of the real (deflated) income, product, and wealth estimates and the associated price series.

Economic growth itself is usually defined in terms of the rate of increase in real national product, in absolute or per capita terms. The physical volume of production in the economy, and its industrial divisions, is usually regarded as a function of the physical volume of related inputs and as a technological and organizational variable which reflects the "state of the arts" and other factors affecting productive efficiency. Changes in productive efficiency, or "productivity" of the factors of production, may be measured in terms of the relationship between real product and real factor input. This relationship may be expressed as the ratio between the two variables or as a technological "scalar" in the statistically fitted production function (see Chapter 17). But note that, from our point of view, factor input can be measured as real (deflated) factor cost on the income side of production accounts, and related to real product. Thus, total factor productivity, a crucial element in economic growth, may be analyzed within an economic accounting framework.[1] Further, the overall output and input price indexes provide essential elements for quantitative analysis of changes in the general price level. Also, quantity and price estimates for both labor and property inputs make possible the calculation of elasticities of factor substitution, and analysis of the changing functional distribution of national income.

Deflation of product by type and by industry enables the analyst to observe the differential relative changes. These may be related to relative changes in the associated prices to calculate price elasticities which, along with income elasticities and shifts in tastes, explain the changes in relative demands and outputs. By means of input-output matrices, changes in the composition of final demand may, of course, be linked to changes in the industrial structure of national product.[2] Eventually, the sets of input and output quantity and price data embraced by economic accounts may be used in comprehensive structural models of the economy, to complement the demand models which have been developed in recent years.

BASIC APPROACHES

The objective of adjusting the national product for price changes is to obtain a constant-price–weighted quantity aggregate for a succession of time periods. If Q stands for quantities of final goods and P for their prices, and if subscript o indicates the base period and subscript x any given period, then $\sum_{i=1}^{n} Q_x P_o$ indicates the constant-dollar national product consisting of n final goods and services. Or instead of referring to quantities of final outputs, if Q indicated quantities of inputs and P the corresponding input prices, then the expression would refer to constant-dollar national income in the sense of real factor cost.

The constant-price–weighted quantity aggregate can be obtained directly by

---

[1] This view of the national economic accounts as a framework for productivity analysis was first developed systematically by John W. Kendrick in his Introduction to *Output, Input, and Productivity Measurement,* Conference on Research in Income and Wealth, Studies in Income and Wealth, vol. XXV (Princeton, N.J.: Princeton University Press for National Bureau of Economic Research, 1961), pp. 3–20.

[2] Introduction, in John W. Kendrick, ed., *The Industrial Composition of Income and Product,* Studies in Income and Wealth, vol. XXXII (New York: Columbia University Press for the National Bureau of Economic Research, 1968), pp. 3–16.

multiplying given period quantities by base-period prices. It can also be obtained indirectly by deflating current values by a composite price index. Thus:

$$\Sigma Q_x P_o = \Sigma Q_x P_x \div \frac{\Sigma P_x Q_x}{\Sigma P_o Q_x}$$

Note that the composite price index has changing—that is, given year—quantity weights for the component prices. This so-called Paasche-type price index (with given year weights) is consistent with the Laspeyres-type quantity aggregate (with base-period weights). Actually, most general price indexes have fixed-quantity weights, reflecting the fact that expenditures surveys or censuses are required to provide weights. They are therefore not directly applicable as deflators of GNP.

Deflating Final Expenditures

Since 1951, OBE has presented, at first, annual and then quarterly, constant-dollar estimates in increasing component detail. The technique used is to apply appropriate component prices indexes compiled by BLS, the Department of Agriculture, and other sources to the finest subdivision of GNP by final expenditures category. For the quarterly estimates, 142 components of GNP are separately deflated, and more detail is incorporated in the annual estimates. The deflated expenditures categories are summed and divided into current-dollar expenditure groupings, and total GNP, by sector, in order to obtain the "implicit price deflator."[3] Ideally the result should be three sets of data: (1) current-dollar GNP, (2) constant-dollar GNP, and (3) implicit price deflators, all at the same level of detail.[4]

The implicit price deflators incorporate, in effect, current-period weighting among the component price indexes and fixed weighting within the components. As a result, when an implicit price deflator is used to compare two years, neither of which is the base year of the price index, the deflator will measure a combination of the difference in the weights of the two years and the change in price of the fixed group of goods and services. A comparison of the deflator with two specially constructed fixed weighted price indexes, 1965 to 1968, showed that the implicit deflator for total GNP increased at the same annual rate—3-1/2 percent—as fixed weighted indexes, although for the shorter periods within the time span, the measures did on occasion move differently. The deviations reflect the shifting composition of expenditures in the implicit deflator. For example, a shift toward components showing above-average price increases would increase the implicit deflator more than a fixed weighted index.[5]

The formula given above indicates that either price deflation or direct weighting of quantities may be used. The choice depends on the relative availability of relevant data. Price deflation recommends itself for much of the accounts, since the value estimates are at hand and price data are relatively abundant. Generally, only a representative sample of goods in a product "family" need be priced in order to obtain

[3] This procedure is described in U.S. Department of Commerce, Office of Business Economics, *National Income*, (1954), part IV, "Gross National Product in Constant Dollars, 1929-53."

[4] See the presentation each month in the *Survey of Current Business*, "National Income and Product Tables," tables 1 and 16, 2 and 17, and 3 and 18.

[5] Allan H. Young and Claudia Harkins, "Alternative Measures of Price Change for GNP," *Survey of Current Business*, vol. 49, pp. 47-52, March, 1969.

ECONOMIC ACCOUNTS AND THEIR USES

a measure of price changes for the entire family. This is not true of output data; one cannot assume that uncovered outputs show the same movements as those covered by the data. Yet for some industries, output data are plentiful enough to permit direct physical production measures, and thus are amenable to direct weighting. The Federal Reserve Board index of industrial production covering manufacturing, mining, and utilities is a prime example. Even though the FRB index uses Census Bureau value-added weights for the industry components, i.e., the P's in $\sum\limits_{i=1}^{n} Q_x P_o$ are unit value added, the Q's are gross output measures, so the indexes are not true net output measures.

Deflating GNP by Industry

Real industry product estimates are generally prepared by the double-deflation method: deflating gross value of output and deducting deflated intermediate costs. If the price indexes used to deflate the final outputs of each industry are the same as those used to deflate GNP (final expenditures), and if the same price indexes are used to deflate the intermediate outputs and inputs, then the sum of real industry products should equal the real GNP obtained as the sum of deflated final expenditures. This statement assumes that the current-dollar estimates are the same by both approaches; actually, there is usually a small statistical discrepancy which would carry over to the deflated estimates.

The OBE uses the double-deflation method for only about one-half of industry product; for the rest, it directly deflates product in current prices or extrapolates base-period industry product by gross output measures, assuming no change in the gross-net ratios. Despite such deviations from preferred methodology, the sum of the OBE real industry product estimates is close to deflated final product in most years. Estimates by both approaches for selected years, with the indicated statistical discrepancy, are shown in Table 6-1.

At this point it will be noted that the deflation procedures described relate only to two of the three sets of income and product measures—those which deal with commodity flows. Generally it is considered undesirable to deflate income flows. Some income flows, e.g., disposable personal income, may be deflated on an ad hoc basis, but deflating income usually involves an arbitrary determination of the items for which the income is believed spent. Only by coincidence could it be expected that these deflated flows would balance with real product.

WEIGHTING PROBLEMS

In macroeconomic measurement and theory, one inevitably runs into the problem of weights by means of which component variables are combined into aggregates. Apples and oranges, or horses and tractors, cannot be added together meaningfully unless the physical counts of each are weighted (multiplied) by measures of their relative economic importance. This section discusses the two major questions that arise in this connection: What indicators of relative importance should be used? From what period or periods should the weights be drawn?

TABLE 6-1

Gross Private Domestic Business Product by Industrial Division, Selected Years, 1948–1966
(Billions of 1958 Dollars)

	1948	1953	1957	1960	1966
Private domestic					
business economy[a]	285.1	359.6	396.1	428.0	581.4
Agriculture, forestry,					
and fisheries[b]	21.5	22.8	23.0	24.7	25.5
Farms[b]	20.5	21.6	21.8	23.5	24.2
Mining	10.7	12.0	13.6	13.1	15.5
Contract construction	14.1	18.9	21.1	21.7	24.4
Manufacturing	96.3	128.6	134.6	140.9	205.7
Nondurable goods					
industries	41.3	49.5	54.9	59.9	80.8
Durable goods					
industries	55.0	79.1	79.6	81.0	124.9
Transportation	20.7	21.2	22.5	22.5	31.2
Railroads	10.5	9.9	9.5	8.7	11.7
Communications	4.7	6.7	8.5	10.0	15.9
Telephone & telegraph	4.4	6.1	7.7	9.1	14.8
Electric, gas, and					
sanitary services	5.0	7.8	10.3	12.4	17.3
Wholesale and retail trade	54.2	64.9	75.1	82.3	111.7
Finance, insurance, and					
real estate[c]	35.0	45.2	55.5	62.5	85.2
Finance and insurance	9.9	11.9	14.1	14.9	16.4
Services and government					
enterprises	27.6	30.5	34.5	38.5	50.9
Residual[d]	−4.7	1.0	−2.6	−0.6	−1.9

NOTE: Detail may not add to total because of rounding.

[a]Obtained by deflating final expenditures.

[b]Includes gross rents paid to nonfarm landlords by farmers.

[c]Excludes gross rents paid to nonfarm landlords by farmers.

[d]Residual differs slightly from OBE number in several years because of rounding. It is the difference between the aggregate of real industry product and real GNP deflated by final expenditure categories.

SOURCE: Adapted from Jack J. Gottsegen, "Revised Estimates of GNP by Major Industries," *Survey of Current Business,* vol. 47, April, 1967.

Types of Weights

The chief general alternative weights for goods and services are market prices and unit factor cost—the difference being indirect business taxes less subsidies per unit of output. As discussed in Chapter 3, for purposes of welfare comparisons, market price weights are indicated. For production and productivity analysis, unit factor-cost weights are more appropriate. This is so because relative unit factor costs indicate relative resource absorption (direct and indirect), assuming perfect competition. In any case, it is obvious that indirect taxes distort market prices as an approximation to unit cost.

Actually, tests indicate that, in economies such as those of the United States and Canada, real national product valued at market price shows much the same movement as real national product valued at factor cost. Since most price indexes are based on market price, it would take much work to recast them in terms of unit factor costs. So real product at constant market prices is usually taken as a proxy for the preferred measure in production analysis.

When one's interest is in unit requirements for particular inputs, such as man-hours or kilowatthours, then outputs may be weighted by the unit requirements for the particular inputs in the base period. This ensures that the aggregate is an internal weighted mean of the components. Such special-purpose partial input weights have been compiled in Census Bureau–Federal Reserve Board indexes of manufacturing production.[6]

The Weight Base

To state the problem in general terms at the outset, if relative changes in prices (or other weighting values) are significantly correlated with relative changes in quantities, then the movements of weighted quantity aggregates will vary depending on the period(s) from which the weights are chosen. This ubiquitous situation is sometimes referred to as the aggregation problem, or the index number problem.

The problem can be illustrated simply for two commodities, A and B, in time periods I and II. As is not untypical in an expanding economy, A is a rapidly growing output whose relative price falls, and B is a slow-growing commodity whose relative price increases. As can be seen from the numerical example in Table 6-2, use of period I prices as weights results in a larger growth of the output aggregate, since the relative price of the rapidly growing output A is greater in the earlier period.

The results presented in the table are representative of a dynamic economy, in which relative increases in productivity are associated with relative decreases in price and thus with relative increases in output. Since both producers and consumers tend to shift to goods which show relative price declines, these enjoy relative sales increases. So the more recent the weight base, the less the apparent increase in the quantity aggregate. The analogous effect shows up in price indexes: the more recent the quantity weights, the less the apparent rise in the general price level.

The aggregation problem is important in interpreting macroeconomic estimates. For example, for many years the Soviet industrial production index was based on weights drawn from the mid-1920s. This produced a much larger rise than would have been apparent if later weights had been used.

Unfortunately, there is no unique solution to the index number problem. Fisher's "ideal" index number, which employs a geometric mean of the weights from both periods in a binary comparison, is neat, but it has no more fundamental economic rationale than using either first or last period weights! Some economists like weights chosen from a recent year or group of years, on the grounds that we view the past through the eyes of the present and that recent economic structure is most relevant. The federal government statistical agencies periodically update the weight bases underlying the "official" index numbers. But even here, there is a difference in the

[6] U.S. Bureau of the Census and Board of Governors of the Federal Reserve System, *Census of Manufactures, 1963*, vol. IV, *Indexes of Production* (1968), pp. 13-15.

TABLE 6-2

The Effect of Alternative Weight Bases on Movement of Aggregates

Line no.		Periods I	Periods II	Link Relative (II/I X 100)
	Commodity A			
1	Quantity	100	400	400
2	Price	$2.00	$3.00	150
3	Value: Current prices (1 X 2)	200	1,200	600
4	I prices (1 X 2 I)	200	800	400
5	II prices (1 X 2 II)	300	1,200	400
	Commodity B			
6	Quantity	200	300	150
7	Price	$1.00	$4.00	400
8	Value: Current prices (6 X 7)	200	1,200	600
9	I prices (6 X 7 I)	200	300	150
10	II prices (6 X 7 II)	800	1,200	150
	Aggregate			
11	Current dollars (3 + 8)	400	2,400	600
	Constant dollars:			
12	I price base (4 + 9)	400	1,100	275
13	II price base (5 + 10)	1,100	2,400	218
	Implicit price deflator:			
14	Period I = 100 (11/12 X 100)	100	218	218
15	Period II = 100 (11/13 X 100)	36.4	100	275

procedures used. When OBE shifts to a more recent base, as it did in changing from 1939 to 1954 to 1958, the entire real product series is reweighted. In contrast, when weights are updated in the FRB index of industrial production, the old weights remain incorporated in the index, which is linked to the ongoing segment incorporating new weights. The National Bureau of Economic Research also employs the system of changing weights for successive segments of production indexes.

Ideally, in making binary comparisons, one should use weights from both years in order to bracket the difference in movement of the index. This is hardly feasible

ECONOMIC ACCOUNTS AND THEIR USES

in time series, but occasional sensitivity analyses to show the difference in movements occasioned by use of alternative weight bases are quite instructive.

Thus, it is a sad fact of quantitative macroeconomics that most aggregate time series are not unique constructs. Most of them incorporate conventional procedures, and their movements differ, depending on the particular conventions, including weighting procedure. Fortunately, sensitivity to alternative weight bases is frequently not very great.

But in using aggregates, the analyst is well advised to know how they are constructed and, in general terms, how much difference plausible alternative methods would make.

OUTPUT MEASUREMENT

If the physical units of output of each commodity or service were homogeneous and standardized over time, the problems of economic statisticians would be fewer. But dynamic economies, particularly that of the United States, are characterized by frequent improvements (or at least changes) in the quality of many kinds of products; new products are invented and old ones drop out; and some products are not standardized at all, but are custom-built. Also, the list prices that underlie many price series may fail to reflect changes in discounts and other terms of sale that affect the realized revenues per unit of output. Methods of coping with these problems are discussed in this section;[7] analogous problems that beset input measurement will be dealt with in the next section.

Nonstandard Products

In some industries, portions or all of the output may be custom-built, nonstandardized goods, the units of which can obviously not be added together and compared over successive time periods. This is notably true in the construction industry, the shipbuilding and aircraft manufacturing industries, and certain service industries, particularly those of a professional nature.

If custom goods are only a portion of total output, the value of this portion may be deflated by indexes of the prices of the standardized part of the industry's output. This is done for the output of the machinery industry and some of the service industries, for example. The procedure assumes that productivity advances are as great for the custom-built as for the standardized portion of output. To the extent that productivity goes up less and thus implicit prices rise more in the custom portion, real product increases would tend to be overstated.

In an industry such as building construction, virtually none of the output is standardized. There are various "construction cost" indexes, compiled as a weighted average of wage rates in the building trades and the prices of construction materials. Such indexes are inadequate deflators because they do not allow for changing overhead and profit margins or for changes in productivity. The latter defect is

---

[7] A more extended discussion of these problems is found in John W. Kendrick, "Measurement of Real Product," and in George Jaszi, "Comment," *A Critique of the United States Income and Product Accounts*, Conference on Research in Income and Wealth, Studies in Income and Wealth, vol. XXII (Princeton, N.J.: Princeton University Press for the National Bureau of Economic Research, 1958), pp. 405–428.

particularly serious from a long-run standpoint and probably results in a cumulative upward bias in the deflators and a corresponding downward bias in the real product series.

A preferable procedure is to take periodic "bids" or estimates from a sample of contractors on a hypothetical structure whose specifications are held constant in adjacent periods. The contractors allow for changes: a modified structure can be specified, and the new sets of bids can be linked to the old in an overlap period. Thus, in effect, one has a true price index, which, while hypothetical, reflects actual conditions in the industry. An index of this type is prepared by the Associated General Contractors and appears each month in the *Survey of Current Business*.

An alternative procedure is to take a common denominator, such as square feet or cubic feet, within relatively homogeneous categories of construction, as defined by price ranges or types of construction, and calculate cost per square or cubic foot within each. The several unit-cost indexes can then be weighted together to provide a deflator. While this is still a "unit-value" rather than a true price index, it tends to minimize the influence of shifts among price classes that may distort the movement of gross unit-value indexes relative to true price indexes, which are based on the pricing of homogeneous products in successive time periods.

In actual practice, in some areas, particularly in the services sector, OBE uses cost indexes, often the relevant average wage-salary index, as deflator. This tends to impart a downward bias to real product estimates, but fortunately the areas so treated constitute but a small portion of the total GNP.

New and Old Products

Occasionally, new products are introduced subsequent to a base period, or old products drop out prior to a recent base period. In order to assign weights, one must hypothesize what the price movement would have been during the intervening period. The conventional procedure is to extrapolate the price of a particular product by the average price of the commodity grouping to which it belongs. Thereby, one is assuming that the product has the same relative price during the intervening period as it had in the first (or last) year in which it was explicitly priced. Declining products would probably show a relative price rise and new products a relative price decline, reflecting the "learning curve" experience. But since there is little or no production of these products during the period in question, distortions arising from the conventional treatment would be minor.

Quality changes   For a long time, economists have been exercised over the problem of changes in product quality. Such changes occur with considerable regularity in a dynamic economy. The conventional procedure in preparing price indexes, and in adjusting quantities, is to allow for those quality changes reflected in the real unit costs of production and to ignore the others. Thus, if a new model of a particular make and type of automobile is priced 5 percent higher than the old model, but costs 3 percent more to manufacture because of added or improved features, the pure price increase would be estimated at 2 percent. Thus, the rise in physical volume per car due to quality improvement is estimated at the 3 percent rise in unit real cost.[8]

[8] See Ethel D. Hoover, "The CPI and Problems of Quality Change," *Monthly Labor Review*, vol. 84, pp. 1175–1185, November, 1961.

The trouble is that quality improvement may entail no increase in cost or may even be associated with a decline in cost. After all, quality has many dimensions, involving durability, safety, comfort, maintenance costs, efficiency, style, and so on. Unless differences in these aspects are associated with price or cost differences (either cross-sectionally or intertemporally),[9] it is not possible to assign weights to them, and the attempt to quantify quality differentials would perforce be subjective.

Hence, it has become standard procedure when discussing price and volume indexes to qualify the results by statements to the effect that the price indexes tend to have an upward bias, and the physical volume indexes a downward bias, to the extent that there have been net quality improvements. We like to think that most quality changes are improvements, yet we should not forget that quality deterioration also occurs—as in a shift from handicraft to mass production. Also, many style changes may not reflect quality change in any functional sense. There is, further, the comforting idea that utility is a relative matter and that, for example, owners of Cadillacs in 1929 may have derived as much satisfaction from them as Cadillac owners did in 1969, although the automobile has doubtless been improved. Yet these arguments can be pushed too far, and we should probably continue to attach qualifications to price and volume movements on the score of quality, admitting that not everything, even in the material sphere, can be quantified.

Cyclical Biases

The price data underlying deflation are frequently based on list prices less standard discounts for quantity and so on. Yet it is well known that the actual terms of sale of many goods, particularly durables and intermediate products at wholesale, may be considerably more variable and may be difficult to measure. Discounts may be reflected in deviations of trade-in values from resale values; in special services, such as installation, which may or may not be part of the terms of sale; or in credit terms. Sometimes discounts from list may frankly be granted "under the table" in order not to excite competitors or suppliers.

The important point is that the discount margin will vary, depending on the state of the market. In general, one would expect larger discounts in slack periods than in boom time. Under some conditions of very tight supply, as in wartime or postwar shortages, customers may even pay premiums. This means that in recessions the realized prices tend to fall more or rise less than list prices and that in expansions they tend to rise more. Thus, the amplitude of fluctuations in real product over the cycle may be exaggerated by the typical price deflators. When physical volume data are used, to the extent that there are shifts within categories to lower priced lines in contractions, and vice versa in expansions, amplitudes may be understated.

In recent years, the Price Division of BLS has attempted to approximate more closely the movements of realized prices for a growing list of commodities. If this worthwhile effort continues, the cyclical bias in deflated series due to inadequate price data would tend to diminish.

[9] See Zvi Griliches, "Notes on the Measurement of Price and Quality Change," and George Jaszi, "Comment," in *Models of Income Determination*, Conference on Research in Income and Wealth, Studies in Income and Wealth, vol. XXVIII (Princeton, N.J.: Princeton University Press for the National Bureau of Economic Research, 1964), pp. 381-409.

INPUT MEASUREMENT

To the extent that inputs of certain industries are outputs of others—i.e., intermediate products—the problems of measurement are those discussed in the preceding section. In this section, we consider factor inputs—the real services of the human and nonhuman resource stocks, known to economists as the factors of production. In the current-dollar accounts, as we know, the costs of the factor services constitute the national income and may be built up or broken down by industry.

Before we can aggregate units of factor inputs or deflate factor costs by appropriate factor-price indexes, we must be clear about what the input units are. In general, it is this author's approach that, to be most useful for production and productivity analysis, the factor inputs should be viewed as the time rate of use of the various factors employed in the production process, weighted by the base-period compensation per unit as an approximation to marginal value productivity. The time rate of use is best seen in terms of hours—man-hours, machine-hours, and so on. By using fixed hourly compensation rates, one obtains real factor-cost measures in which productivity is held constant. By comparing rates of change in real factor costs with those of real product, one obtains a measure of the rates of change in average factor productivity. That is, changes in the ratio of real product to real factor cost indicate, for a given period, changes in the actual output obtained from the factors compared with what the factors *would* have produced at base-period efficiency.

This is a superior procedure to deflating income by the deflator for national product (at factor cost), since this would merely yield a measure of real purchasing power, a measure which would be equal to real product and therefore of no interest. As in the case of national income and product in current prices, the ratio of the two measures would be unity over time (abstracting from the statistical discrepancy). But if factor cost is deflated by factor (not product) price, the resultant real factor-cost measure diverges from the real product measure over time in an interesting way. In fact, an increasing number of economists in recent years have been trying to explain the reasons for the increases in the total factor productivity ratio, or the "residual" which has been challengingly called a "measure of our ignorance."

Labor Input

Rather than deflate labor compensation, including imputations for the labor services of proprietors, by an index of average wage-salary rates with changing weights, it is simpler to weight man-hours worked, by categories, by base-period average hourly compensation. The compensation figure should include fringe benefits, as well as payments in kind if these are included in product. It should represent compensation per hour worked rather than per hour paid for, since changes in time paid for but not worked really represent changes in pay rates, because employers are buying working time. The time of all workers, including management personnel and proprietors, should be included. There are alternative ways of imputing labor income to proprietors; one common method is to assign their working hours the same rate of compensation as that received by employees in that industry.

One possibly controversial aspect of measuring labor input relates to the degree of detail in which man-hours should be classified and weighted. Measuring and

ECONOMIC ACCOUNTS AND THEIR USES

weighting man-hours on an industry basis recommends itself, since national productivity indexes will thereby be an internal mean of the component industry measures. Otherwise, shift of workers from lower- to higher-paying industries would show up as an increase in productivity rather than an increase in labor input. The desirable procedure is less clear with respect to measuring and weighting man-hours by occupational groupings. In this case, a quality element is introduced, since relative shifts to higher-paying occupations will presumably involve investments in education and training, which may better be treated as an explanation of productivity advance.

We may recapitulate by pointing out that weighted man-hours (L) represent the stock of human resources available for production, i.e., the labor force (LF) adjusted by the rate of employment (E), for average annual hours worked (MN/E) and the ratio of man-hours weighted by average hourly earnings to unweighted man-hours (L/MH). In algebraic form: $L = LF \times E/LF \times MH/E \times L/MH$.

Capital Input

The real stock of nonhuman capital consists of land and other natural resources, structures, machinery and equipment, and inventories. Thus, there is no physical common denominator in the same sense that "man" is in the employed labor force, which represents the productive stock of human resources. However, the constant dollar can play the same role, so we start by estimating the real stock of capital (see Chapter 10). The real capital stock may then be adjusted for changes in the rate of utilization, although the author would argue that, in a private enterprise economy, capital carries a charge and represents a real cost regardless of the intensity of use. Then, the real capital stock (adjusted or unadjusted for rate of utilization) should be multiplied by the base-period rate of return in order to reduce it to a real capital cost or input basis.

This procedure is more direct than trying to deflate property compensation by the appropriate price index. It should be noted, however, that the implicit price deflator is really the product of the average price of the underlying physical capital goods and the rate of return on the asset values they represent. This can be seen in the following formulation in which K is the real capital stock, P the average price of the capital goods, π the rate of return on the capital stock in current prices ($= KP$), and C the current-dollar compensation of capital: $C/K = \pi KP/K = \pi P$.

In effect, the price of capital is equivalent to a rental cost per real capital-hour used or available for use in production. [10]

In real dollar terms, capital plus labor input in the base period equals the national income, which equals the real NNP at factor cost. Or instead of summing real factor costs, one can obtain index numbers of total factor input showing the same movements by weighting the index numbers of real labor input and capital input by their respective shares (percentages) in the base-period national income.

This same approach can be used for each of the component industries of the economy. For symmetry with the weighted man-hour series, it is desirable that the

---

[10] See a somewhat different formulation by Z. Griliches and D. W. Jorgensen, "The Explanation of Productivity Change," *The Review of Economic Studies*, vol. 34, pp. 249–283, July, 1967, reprinted (with corrections) in *Survey of Current Business*, vol. 49, part II, pp. 29–64, May, 1969.

real capital stock be measured for each of the industries for which man-hours are obtained, and then aggregated by weighting the real industry capital stocks by the base-period rate of return in each. Thus, the capital input series reflects shifts among industries with different rates of return in the same way that the labor input does. Total factor input for the economy is then an internal mean of the industry components.

One final issue concerns the relative desirability of using real gross or net stocks in the case of fixed depreciable capital goods. Gross stocks reflect retirements of capital goods but not depreciation over their lifetimes as in the case of net stocks. Since the output-producing capacity of fixed capital goods probably does not decline much with age, assuming adequate repair and maintenance, the real gross stocks may be preferable for production analysis. The property income weights should also be gross of depreciation allowances, as should the output or real product series to which the inputs are related. However, if one is interested in real product from a welfare standpoint, it seems clear that NNP is the correct measure and that the corresponding capital input measure should be net of accumulated depreciation.

THE UN DISCUSSION

Most of the problems discussed in this chapter, and some others, have been treated in the UN report, in a chapter entitled "The System as a Basis for Quantity and Price Comparisons." The UN discussion, while generally more condensed, covers much the same ground that we have, and suggests many of the same approaches.

In a summary paragraph the report states: "It cannot be claimed that this formulation of the problems, and the examples which illustrate it, provide definite answers to particular questions. The answers reached in practice must depend to some extent on the data available and to some extent on the importance attached to improving these data in specific cases."[11]

Unfortunately, the coverage and quality of basic price and quantity data, and the conventions used to meet the problems posed in difficult areas such as quality change, nonstandard outputs, and nonenterprise outputs, may differ widely among countries. Such conceptual and statistical differences undoubtedly affect comparative rates of growth in real product and productivity, by industry. This is merely one more of the many problems encountered in international comparisons, discussed in Chapter 12.

Yet the UN is probably right not to try to provide rigid guidelines in areas in which concepts and methodology are far from definitive and experimentation is still proceeding. Since there is an international demonstration effect in the realm of statistics as well as consumption, best practices presumably tend to spread. In the meantime, we must be even more circumspect in interpreting comparative rates of growth in real product than in interpreting the intertemporal comparison in the same country. In either case, there is no substitute for knowledge of the underlying concepts, data, and methods and the probable effects on the estimates in relation to alternatives.

[11] UN, *SNA.*, 1968, p. 62.

REVIEW QUESTIONS

1 What is the essence of the index number problem? Why does a recent weight base for United States output measures result in less apparent growth than an earlier weight base?

2 What are some of the chief problems involved in measuring output units (or their prices) over time?

3 Explain the double-deflation approach to measuring the real product of an industry.

4 How may real capital input be measured? Is it symmetrical with the usual type of labor input measure?

5 What are some of the chief uses of real income and product measures?

SELECTED REFERENCES

KENDRICK, JOHN W.: "Measurement of Real Product," *A Critique of the United States Income and Product Accounts,* Conference on Research in Income and Wealth, Studies in Income and Wealth, vol. XXII (Princeton, N.J.: Princeton University Press for the National Bureau of Economic Research, 1958).

PRICE STATISTICS REVIEW COMMITTEE OF THE NATIONAL BUREAU OF ECONOMIC RESEARCH: *The Price Statistics of the Federal Government: Review, Appraisal, and Recommendations* (New York: 1961).
    Background on price statistics, upon which deflation rests.

UNITED NATIONS, DEPARTMENT OF ECONOMIC AND SOCIAL AFFAIRS, STATISTICAL OFFICE: *A System of National Accounts,* Studies in Methods, ser. F, no. 2, rev. 3 (New York: 1968).
    See chap. IV, "The System as a Basis for Quantity and Price Comparisons."

The Appropriation
Accounts by Sector

Current production is the source of "primary" income for the various sectors of the economy, and sector outlays for final products compose aggregate demand. Separate accounts must be set up to study the important process of distribution of current income and its disposition. Appropriation or "income and outlay" accounts are necessary to study demand. For two reasons, the receipt of income by a sector will always differ, and may differ markedly, from its generation of primary income, described in Chapter 4.

In the first place, the services of the factors which "reside" in a given sector may be used for productive activity in a different sector. Thus, most factor services provided by the household sector are used for production in the other sectors, particularly in private business, but their compensation is credited to the household sector. Conversely, while the bulk of production takes place in private firms, most of the factor income originating is paid out to households, and only gross profits are retained in the business sector for its disposition.

Second, primary income is redistributed among the sectors through tax and transfer payments, which we call "secondary" income flows. These flows differ from primary income distributions in that they do not represent payments for specific current services. This is obviously true of gifts and other transfer payments by all sectors, particularly governments. Some of the transfers, such as veterans benefits, are in recognition of past services, not a payment for current productive contributions. Tax payments by the nongovernment sectors support the public establishment and thus the provision of current government services, but they are not a purchase of specified amounts of particular services selected by the taxpayer, as is true of market transactions. Most government income comes from tax receipts, just as much income of private nonprofit organizations comes from gifts or membership dues.

It is the distribution of primary income from the consolidated production account (gross national income and product) to the major sectors, its further redistribution among sectors, and the final purchases (credited back to the production account) and saving of each sector that the basic income and outlay accounts are designed to show. The sector accounts and supporting tables are an indispensable basis for analyzing the behavior of the several sectors. The final purchases of each are influenced by current income. This is particularly so in the personal sector. But even here, credit flows and asset holdings also have an important bearing, given the basic psychological propensities and expectations. The latter forces are much more significant in the business sector. In the government sector, the narrow economic factors are generally overshadowed by both noneconomic and economic goals of the community as a whole, as reflected in political processes.

So the appropriation accounts are only a beginning of the study of sector behavior. Even in terms of economic forces alone, it is clear that capital accounts and balance sheets are necessary supplements, which is why we spend some time in the next several chapters showing how these may be developed as part of an integrated structure by elaborating the sector income and outlay accounts.

In the following sections, we shall discuss the notion of the institutional sector, compare the United States and the UN sectoring, and note alternative methods of sectoring that have been proposed. Then we shall review first the United States and the revised UN income and outlay accounts, as reproduced in Appendixes A and B, respectively.

INSTITUTIONAL SECTORING

In contrast to the industry sectoring of the economy, which is used for disaggregation of the production account, an institutional sectoring is used for the study of flows of income, outlay, saving, investment, borrowing, lending, and the associated balances. That is, those decision-making units which react similarly to given stimuli with regard to receiving and disbursing and owning property are classed together.

Perhaps the simplest, most basic system of sectoring is that employed by the U.S. Department of Commerce. There are three main sectors: the personal sector, including private nonprofit institutions as well as households; business; and general governments. A separate account is shown for the rest of the world, although this is not, strictly speaking, a sector. Actually, an account for the business sector is only implicit in the OBE system, although we make it explicit in the following section.

The revised UN system distinguishes two business sectors: nonfinancial enterprises, corporate and quasi-corporate, and financial institutions. The general governments sector is the same as in the OBE system. However, the UN system breaks out private nonprofit institutions serving households as a separate sector. The household sector includes private unincorporated nonfinancial enterprises not included with the corporate or quasi-corporate. (See Appendix B, Tables B-III.A through B-III.E.

All things considered, it would have been preferable if the UN system had kept all the enterprises together. It is true that it is often difficult to separate household and proprietorship accounts in the case of small unincorporated business, especially agriculture. But the business and household functions are so different that it would seem worthwhile to try to divide the accounts even if prorating or arbitrary allocation of certain transactions were necessary.

Having said this, we must commend the UN for breaking out the financial institutions sector, since this is essential for the capital finance account, particularly the flow-of-funds elaboration, as we shall see in Chapter 9. If the United States income and product accounts are eventually to be integrated with sector capital finance accounts, financial and nonfinancial enterprise sectors will likewise have to be distinguished. It is also commendable that private nonprofit institutions were broken out of households in the UN system, although some would argue that this is such a small sector that it should be combined with nonfinancial enterprises.

The chief additional comment on sectoring is that further subdivision of the basic sectors would be desirable for more precise analysis. In particular, the nonfinancial enterprises sector could be divided between farm and nonfarm, and the latter among several of the chief industry groupings. The industry groupings would comprise firms rather than establishments, since investment and financing decisions are made at a company level. In the case of financial institutions, further desirable subdivisions are set forth in Chapter 9. General governments might well be divided into central (federal), state, and local government. The personal or household sector could also be split according to a variety of socioeconomic criteria, such as urban-rural, employees-proprietors-retired, income-size classes, and so on.

At some point, the statistical burden of additional detail outweighs the further analytical advantages. Near this border, perhaps occasional rather than regular tabulations of detail would serve the purposes of most users.

THE INTERRELATIONSHIPS OF THE SECTOR ACCOUNTS

In order better to demonstrate the accounting interrelationships among the production account and the several sector accounts, in Table 7-1, we set up the United States accounts side by side. In this presentation, two basic accounting principles are observed. For each credit (debit) to one account, there is a corresponding debit (credit) to the other relevant account. Transactions *within* each account are generally netted. But *within* each account, *total* debits and credits must balance, that is, equal each other. If sector saving is estimated as a residual, the balance is exact. If not, a statistical discrepancy entry provides the balance, as in the production account.

In the vertical stub, we first show the primary income flows which are debited to the production account and credited to the sector account. Then we show the secondary income flows which redistribute income among the sectors. Next come the final purchases, debited to the sector accounts and credited to the production account.

ECONOMIC ACCOUNTS AND THEIR USES

Finally, the saving by each sector is shown as the residual, or balancing, item in each sector account. Since the Commerce Department shows only one consolidated saving-investment (capital) account, the saving of each sector (a debit, or use of funds) is credited to the saving-investment account, and the tangible domestic investment and net foreign investments are summarized as a debit to this capital account.

In Table 7-1, we follow the Commerce Department numbers and structure with one exception: We present a separate account for the business sector. Prior to the 1958 revision, the Department showed a separate business sector. This was eliminated in 1958, with business production included in the consolidated production account, its income distributions credited to the sector accounts (and retained corporate earnings to the saving-investment account). Since only business was conceived of as engaging in tangible investment, this credit to the production account was debited to the saving-investment account.

We have reintroduced a business sector account partly for reasons of symmetry and completeness. It is useful to see the current income and disposition of current income by business, with saving here, too, a balancing item. Actually, in this table only corporate saving is shown, since we follow the Federal Reserve Board convention that all net income of proprietors is credited to the household sector and merged with other personal income for disposition there.

Since in the next chapter we shall deconsolidate the saving-investment account by sector, there is a second reason why it is essential to set up the business account separately: Business is a major investor even when investment is more broadly defined than it is by the Department. Further, when we proceed to the financing activity subaccounts, the financial portion of the business account must be broken out separately, so that the important role of financial intermediaries may be traced.

THE SECTOR CURRENT ACCOUNTS

Table 7-1, which was set up to show the debit-credit relationships among the producing, appropriation, and saving-investment accounts, does not show in compact form each of the sector T accounts. We shall run over each of these briefly and refer to the major supporting tables prepared by OBE which relate to the several accounts other than that for production, which we have already examined. We shall defer until the next chapter the examination of the saving-investment account, since this is not coordinate with the sector accounts, but represents a consolidated activity subaccount, distinct from the appropriation subaccounts which relate to current income and purchases of currently consumed final products. In the sections that follow, the number given in parentheses, in this case 1.9, refers to the table so designated in the latest national income supplement to the *Survey of Current Business* and the July issues of that publication.[1] In Chapter 3, we questioned the Commerce classification of some household and government purchases as representing current consumption, and some business purchases as being intermediate instead of current income and investment. In this chapter, however, we explain the Commerce framework, with reference in the final section to the *SNA*.

[1] U.S. Department of Commerce, Office of Business Economics, *The National Income and Product Accounts of the United States, 1929–65: Statistical Tables* (1966).

TABLE 7-1
United States National Income and Product Accounts by Sector, 1968 (Billions of Dollars)

Item	National Product		Households		Government		Business		Rest of the World		Saving & Investment	
	Dr	Cr	Dr	Cr	Dr	Cr	Dr	Cr	Dr	Cr	Dr	Cr
Primary income flows												
Factor cost (national income):												
Compensation of employees	513.6			513.6								
Wages and salaries	465.0			465.0								
Employer contributions for social insurance	24.4					24.4						
Other labor income	24.2			24.2								
Proprietors' income	63.8			63.8								
Rental income of persons	21.2			21.2								
Net interest	28.0			28.0			63.8	63.8				
Corporate profits and inventory valuation adjustment	87.9							87.9				
Inventory valuation adjustment							−3.2					−3.2
Corporate profits tax						41.3	41.3					
Dividends				23.1			23.1					
Undistributed profits							26.7					26.7
Nonfactor charges:												
Indirect business taxes	77.9					77.9						
Current surplus of government enterprises, less subsidies	0.8				0.8							
Capital consumption allowances	73.3						73.3	73.3				73.3
Business transfer payments	3.4			3.4								
Statistical discrepancy	−2.5											−2.5

Secondary income flows

Secondary income flows												
Nonbusiness taxes and transfers												
Personal tax and nontax payments				97.9		97.9						
Personal contributions for social insurance			-22.6			22.6						
Net interest paid by government			11.9		11.9							
Interest paid by consumers		14.2		14.2								
Government transfer payments												
To persons			55.8		55.8							
To foreigners (net)					2.1				2.1			
Personal transfer payments to foreigners (net)				0.8					0.8			
Final purchases												
Government purchases	200.3				200.3							
Personal consumption	536.6			536.6								
Gross private domestic investment	126.3										126.3	
Exports	50.6									50.6		
Imports	-48.1								48.1			
Balancing items												
Personal saving				38.4								38.4
Government surplus					-6.7							-6.7
Net foreign investment									-0.3		-0.3	
Totals	865.7	865.7	687.9	687.9	264.2	264.2	225.0	225.0	50.6	50.6	126.0	126.0

NOTE: Detail may not add to totals because of rounding.
SOURCE: Adapted from *Survey of Current Business*, vol. 49, pp. 14-15, table A, "Summary National Income and Product Accounts, 1968," July, 1969.

The Household Account

The bulk of personal income represents payments by the producing sectors for factor services furnished by households. Note, however, that some portions of national income (as well, of course, as the nonfactor charges against gross product) which accrue to the factors are not paid out to them: employer contributions for social insurance, the excess of wage accruals over disbursements (as a result, for example, of retroactive wage increases), and all of corporate profits except the dividend portion. Contrariwise, certain payments made to households are transfers in that they do not represent payments for current services: net interest paid by government and by consumers, and the transfer payments by business and, more importantly, by government. Personal contributions for social insurance are shown as a deduction from the sources side (since the social insurance benefits are a credit). These relationships are summarized conveniently in the table, Relation of Gross National Product, National Income, and Personal Income (1.9, and see our Table 16-1). This table provides a convenient framework for summarizing the derivation of personal income from gross product over time without duplicating the T-account structure for successive years.

On the debit side of the personal account (see Appendix A, Table A-2) are the three major uses of personal income: personal tax and nontax payments (credited to government), personal outlays, and personal saving, which is the residual, on the definition that saving equals disposable (after-tax) income less current outlays. Of the personal outlays, personal consumption expenditures are credited to final demand in the production account, interest paid by consumers is credited to the same sector as part of personal interest income, and transfers to foreigners are credited to the rest-of-the-world account.

Stanley J. Sigel has suggested that separate appropriation and current purchase subaccounts might be useful. In this arrangement, personal tax and nontax payments (possibly together with gifts sent abroad, which are really transfers but are now counted as part of personal outlays) would be the only debit against personal income. Thus, the appropriation account would show only the distributions and redistributions of income. The balancing item on the debit side, disposable personal income (DPI), would be carried down as a credit to the current purchase account, against which personal consumption expenditures would be debited. Personal saving is again the balancing item to be entered internally as a credit to the capital account.[2]

It is, however, easy to compute DPI from the Commerce personal income and outlay account. Indeed, the Department carries this as a line, obtained as total personal income less personal tax and nontax payments, in the table, Personal Income and Its Disposition (2.1). In addition, personal outlays are shown, as a deduction from DPI, to obtain personal saving.

Part 2 of the national income numbers (usually the July issues) and supplements to the *Survey of Current Business* carry the detailed supporting tables for the personal sector. The various types of personal income are shown on an annual,

---

[2] Stanley J. Sigel, "An Approach to the Integration of Income and Product and Flow-of-funds National Accounting Systems: A Progress Report," in *The Flow-of-funds Approach to Social Accounting*, Conference on Research in Income and Wealth, Studies in Income and Wealth, vol. XXVI (Princeton, N.J.: Princeton University Press for the National Bureau of Economic Research, 1962), pp. 29–38.

quarterly, and monthly basis (2.1 and 2.2), as well as its disposition (annual and quarterly). These tables summarize in time-series form all the material in the basic household sector T account.

The remaining tables in Part 2 present the detail on personal consumption expenditures by twelve major groups of goods and services and eighty-three types of products under these groupings. The eighty-three types are then rearranged in the three familiar categories of durable commodities, nondurable commodities, and services. Durable commodities are those whose lives normally extend beyond three years. Formerly, the Department segregated semidurable commodities, whose life-times normally fall between one and three years. Prior to the 1954 revisions, the Department published almost twice as much detail on types of products, but many of the figures were believed to be significantly less reliable than the combined categories.

Most of the consumption categories are self-explanatory. Note that under personal business, services furnished by financial intermediaries are estimated in terms of their costs, as explained in Chapter 3. Most of the services of private nonprofit institutions, estimated at cost, come under group XI, religious and welfare activities, but a few, such as clubs and fraternal organizations except insurance, come under group IX, recreation. Note that both foreign travel and remittances, group XII, are net estimates. Both expenditures abroad by United States residents and government personnel, and the deduction item, expenditures in the United States by foreigners, are shown separately. Another deduction is presented for personal remittances in kind to foreigners (noncash remittances); these are listed separately as a component of personal outlays. Personal consumption expenditures in constant dollars by ten major types and three major categories are also shown on an annual basis (2.6).

The Government Account

The appropriation account for all government is shown in Appendix A, Table A-3. It is a combination of federal and state and local governments, but separate accounts could be shown for each (but with grants-in-aid as a debit to federal and a credit to state and local governments in addition to the items shown here). State and local governments are shown separately in the supporting tables (3.3 to 3.6).

The government receipts and expenditures (appropriation) account is set up much as budgets of the component governments might be set up, with receipts on the credit side, and expenditures plus surplus or deficit on the debit side as the balancing items. Actually, the federal government budget on income and product account differs from the unified budget published in the official budget document in coverage, netting, and timing. The relationship of the two statements is detailed in a reconciliation table (see also Chapter 16).[3]

Commerce estimates of state and local government receipts and expenditures are not derived by assembling all relevant underlying budget documents. Rather they are based on data collected by the Governments Division of the Census Bureau. Prior to July, 1969, a reconciliation table was provided, but at that time it was dis-

---

[3] This reconciliation table appears in the national income numbers of the *Survey of Current Business* as table 3.12. It replaces a table similarly numbered, which appeared in the 1966 supplement, showing the relation to the now outmoded budget concepts.

continued until it could be reworked. Primarily, receipts and expenditures of utilities, liquor stores, and other commercial activities are taken out; sales and purchases of land and existing assets are also excluded.

The supporting tables give annual estimates of receipts and expenditures in considerable detail for the federal government and for state and local government, respectively (3.1 and 3.3), and quarterly receipts and expenditure estimates, both seasonally adjusted and unadjusted, for the broad categories of the basic account (3.2 and 3.5 for the federal government, 3.4 and 3.6 for state and local government).

A group of three tables contains information on social insurance and other government transfers. Accounts for both federal and state and local government insurance funds, showing contributions, their disposition, and the surplus or deficit position of the funds are presented (3.7). The next table shows the contributions of employers, employees, and self-employed persons for social insurance by type of fund (3.8). The third table details federal and state-local transfer payments to persons—benefits from social insurance funds, by type, and other transfers (3.9).

A very important presentation is contained in the table, Government Expenditures by Type of Function. This table shows both federal and state and local expenditures, horizontally arrayed by type of spending (purchases, transfers, etc.), and vertically arrayed by type of function. Ten major functions are distinguished: national defense; space research and technology; general government; international affairs and finance; education; health, labor, and welfare; veterans benefits and services; commerce, transportation, and housing; agricultural resources; and natural resources. Under these headings, fifty more-detailed functions are listed.

Unfortunately, this very informative kind of presentation only goes back to 1952. It became available as a result of budget reform and the post-World War II trend toward functional budgeting, which makes possible more rational legislative spending decisions as compared with straight agency requests by object of expenditure. A related trend toward "performance budgeting" has resulted in an increasing amount of information on units of work performed in pursuit of the various functions of agencies. These measures are most important in trying to make estimates of the physical volume of output, or "real product," discussed in Chapter 6.

A partial object breakdown of government purchases has also been available since 1952 (3.11). Compensation of employees, structures, and other purchases of goods and services are shown for classifications of national defense and other, in the case of the federal government, and education and other, in the case of state and local governments.

Foreign Transactions Account

The current account of transactions between United States residents and foreigners is quite simple. Although it is not really a sector account, since it combines the external transactions of all sectors, it is convenient to treat it here. This account is set up from the viewpoint of the rest of the world, so imports of goods and services and other sources of funds for foreigners are shown on the right-hand side, and United States receipts from exports which represent foreign payments, a use of funds, are shown on the left-hand side. Transfer payments from the United States government and persons to foreigners are shown on a net basis on the credit side. The difference between exports and imports plus unrequited net transfer payments gives rise to net foreign investment. Net foreign investment is equal to the acquisition of foreign assets by United States residents less the acquisition of United States assets by foreign residents, as detailed in the balance-of-payments statistics (see Chapter 9). The foreign capital finance account has an errors and omissions item, necessary to reconcile net foreign investment as a balancing item in the current account, as just described, with the difference between direct measures of the acquisition of claims against foreigners and their acquisition of claims against United States residents. Conceptually, the two numbers should be equal, since an excess of United States exports over imports, to the extent that it is not financed by transfers, must give rise to an increase in net claims against foreigners. But since the statistics are generally neither complete nor completely accurate, there is usually a statistical discrepancy, which is included in the capital finance account because the current transactions statistics are considered more accurate.

The UN external transactions account (Appendix B, Table B-I.6) is identical with that of the United States except that factor incomes paid to and received from the rest of the world are shown separately, instead of being included in imports and exports of goods and services.

THE UN INCOME AND OUTLAY ACCOUNTS

The income and outlay accounts of the revised *SNA* are shown in Appendix B, Section III, Account 3, for the five sectors (A through E) referred to earlier. One general comment is in order before we briefly review each sector account. The UN system counts as investment the outlays of the nonbusiness, as well as of the business, sectors for inventory accumulation, fixed capital, and net purchases of land and intangible assets, and includes these in a separate capital finance account for each sector (discussed in Chapter 8). Thus, the saving of the nonbusiness sectors would be substantially higher in income and outlay accounts drawn up according to UN as compared with United States concepts. The net lending of each sector would be the same, however, if both sets of accounts comprised the same items of income and of current plus investment outlays.

Enterprise Sectors

The entries for the two enterprise sectors, nonfinancial and financial (A and B), as well as for the unincorporated nonfinancial enterprise portion of the household sector E, are virtually the same and can be discussed together. Perhaps the chief terminological difference between the UN and the implicit United States business accounts is the UN item of operating surplus. This is defined as the excess of value added by resident producers during the period of account over the sum of the costs of employee compensation, capital accumulation, and indirect taxes less subsidies. In the case of corporations, it gives rise on the debit side to direct taxes on income, property income including interest and rent paid, as well as dividend disbursements, and the retained earnings which are part of the residual saving.

The operating surplus of the unincorporated business enterprises, included with households, may be subdivided into entrepreneurial income and property income. Entrepreneurial income equals the excess of operating surplus over the property income paid or due in connection with the firm's productive activities. The entrepreneurial income of quasi-corporate (and corporate) enterprises would equal the sum of operating surplus *and* the property income received less property income, except dividends, paid. In the case of corporations, the dividends represent the owners' withdrawals, of course. In the case of quasi-corporate enterprises, withdrawals from entrepreneurial income—shown both as receipts of owners and as disbursement of the enterprises—would in principle be the actual payment made to proprietors out of the sum of operating surplus and net property income of the enterprises. In practice, owing to accounting data limitations, it will generally be necessary to equate the withdrawals to net incomes, after tax. Thus, it is quite possible to have negative withdrawals, implying that owners of quasi-corporate enterprises furnish funds to compensate for negative entrepreneurial net income.

On the credit side of the enterprise accounts, in addition to operating surplus, entrepreneurial withdrawals, and property income receipts, there are casualty insurance claims and an imputation for unfunded employee welfare contributions.

On the debit side, in addition to entrepreneurial withdrawals from the quasi-corporate enterprises in the sector, property incomes paid (interest, dividends, rents, and royalties), there are direct taxes, fines and penalties, net current transfers, net casualty insurance premiums (also shown as a credit for the financial institutions sector), and unfunded employee welfare benefits. As in the United States accounts, saving is computed as the difference between the receipts and disbursements, and shown as the balancing item on the debit side of the account. As we shall see in the next chapter, the saving of each sector is the link to its capital account, where it is entered as a credit.

General Government Sector

According to the revised *SNA,* government transactions are to be recorded on a gross basis, so many of the same categories are shown on both sides of the accounts to provide for transactions among units of the same sector. But in the case of general government, it is recommended that transactions among various levels and types of government organizations should be consolidated in order to delineate sharply the transactions between the public (nonenterprise) sector and the enterprise and other private sectors.

Since there are usually production-type activities even in the general government, the income and outlay account for this sector (Appendix B, Table B-III.C.3) shows the same entries described above for enterprises. In addition, on the credit side, there are revenues from various types of taxes; compulsory fees, fines, and penalties; subsidies; social security benefits and social assistance grants; and other current transfers. It should be noted that property income is limited to interest on public debt and rents paid, since dividends are not a relevant disbursement for the public sector.

Final "consumption" expenditure is roughly equivalent to the OBE category of government purchases of goods and services, less capital formation. As stated in the UN report: "The final consumption expenditure of government services and private non-profit services to households is equivalent to the value of the services and goods which they produce for their own use on current account."[4] Since the products

---

[4] UN, *SNA,* 1968, p. 109.

are not sold, they are valued at cost. Although the UN report uses the term "consumption," it is clear that the product represents collective consumption on behalf of households and the community generally. The UN classification of government "purposes" is given in a supplementary table and is similar to the function breakdown in the United States accounts.

The balancing item on the debit side, saving, represents the general government surplus or deficit on income account. Since the revised *SNA* puts purchases of capital goods, own-account construction, and inventory accumulation in the capital finance account, it is clear that general government saving, by UN concepts, is larger by this amount than it would be by present United States concepts.

Households and Private Nonprofit Institutions

Based on the foregoing discussion, the UN account for private nonprofit institutions serving households is self-explanatory (Table B-III.D.3). The chief source of income is current transfers to the sector from households. As in the government sector, final consumption expenditure represents the costs incurred by the institutions in providing services to households. A special classification of purpose of these services is suggested. The UN report recognizes that some countries may have to combine this account with the household account, as is done by the United States.

Since the household account (Table B-III.E.3) includes private unincorporated nonfinancial enterprises, it includes all the entries noted above in connection with the enterprise accounts. The chief advantage of this consolidation is that proprietors' incomes and financial transactions do not have to be allocated between enterprises and households. But on balance, a segregation would be analytically useful, even if it involved arbitrary allocations of certain entries.

In addition to the property incomes, the chief receipts are employee compensation and transfers. The chief outlays, in addition to the enterprise-type disbursements, are final consumption expenditure and current transfers to private nonprofit institutions, other residents, and the rest of the world. A classification of household outlays on goods and services is provided, according to the purpose for which the acquisition is made. It is designed also to separate goods from services and to draw distinctions between durable, semidurable, and nondurable goods. The breakdown is designed to facilitate demand and welfare study, and also studies of household stocks of goods and cyclical variation in demand.[5]

Interest on consumer debt is included under property income payments. Income and other direct tax payments comprise the total amounts levied on both proprietors' and household incomes. As in all the other income and outlay accounts, saving is the balancing item at the bottom of the debit side, providing the link to the capital accounts discussed in the next chapter.

REVIEW QUESTIONS

1   How are sector income and outlay accounts related to the basic national income and product account?
2   Define secondary income flows and give some examples.

---

[5] UN, *SNA*, 1968, pp. 105–109, including table 6.1.

3   What are the chief differences between the United States and the revised UN income and outlay accounts with respect to sectoring and definition?

4   What is the operating surplus of an enterprise?

5   What is the role of saving in the sector accounts?

SELECTED REFERENCES

The basic references for this chapter are the appropriations accounts themselves, as found in the United States and the UN systems. They are reproduced in Appendixes A and B. Beyond the reproduced tables, the reader is referred to the original sources.

UNITED NATIONS, DEPARTMENT OF ECONOMIC AND SOCIAL AFFAIRS, STATISTICAL OFFICE: *A System of National Accounts*, Studies in Methods, ser. F, no. 2, rev. 3 (New York: 1968).

See especially the notes accompanying the standard accounts, the glossary, and chap. V, "The Transactors of the System."

U.S. DEPARTMENT OF COMMERCE, OFFICE OF BUSINESS ECONOMICS: *National Income* (1954).

A supplement to the *Survey of Current Business*. See part II, "The Conceptual Framework of National Income Statistics," where the sector accounts are described. It should be kept in mind, however, that in 1958 the accounting structure was revised: the business account was eliminated, and information on the institutional structure of productive activity was relegated to statistical tables.

The Saving-investment Account and Its Deconsolidation by Sector

8

Investment occupies a key position in the thought of economists. It has long been recognized that abstinence from current consumption, and the use of the diverted resources for capital outlays, is necessary to increase the productive stock and capacity of an economy. More recently, business-cycle theorists have credited variability in investment with chief responsibility for economic fluctuations. Business investment was raised by J. M. Keynes to the status of a major determinant of the general level of income and employment. Due to Keynes's influence on the budding national income and product accounts of Western countries, investment was defined in terms of tangible business investment (plus net foreign investment), and as equal to saving, ex post. These definitions underlie the Commerce Department accounts, which we examine in the first section of this chapter.

The United States saving-investment account is presented by the Department for the total economy only. In effect, it represents a combination of the saving and investment of each component sector. The UN capital finance accounts, which we look at after the United States accounts, deconsolidate the national saving-investment account by sector. Also, the UN system defines investment more broadly than does the Commerce Department, including government as well as business purchases of durable goods and inventory accumulation.

117

In recent years, with the revival of interest in economic growth, there has been a tendency to define investment still more broadly to include *all* outlays designed to increase future income- and output-producing capacity. By this definition, research and development, education and training, and other intangible investment outlays as well as tangible capital outlays would be included as investment if they met the test of producing a payoff in the future. In the final section of the chapter, we shall develop this approach further and present our own set of current and capital accounts for the United States economy, by major sector, embodying this definition. With the heightened recent interest in investment, the sector deconsolidation of an expanded capital account is useful in showing the sources of saving and the undertakers of all forms of investment in as much detail as can be built into the accounting structure.

THE OFFICIAL UNITED STATES SAVING-INVESTMENT ACCOUNT

The gross saving and investment account of the Commerce Department is reproduced in Appendix A, Table A-5. Personal saving and government saving (surplus or deficit on income and product account) are credited to this account from the household and government appropriation accounts, respectively, where they were balancing items on the debit side (the difference between income and outlay). In the Commerce table, all the gross corporate saving items are credited from the national production account, bypassing a business account. In our rearrangement of the Commerce estimates to include a business account, capital consumption allowances, corporate saving (and proprietors' saving, if it can be measured), and the inventory valuation adjustment are all credited from the current account of the business sector. The statistical discrepancy is still entered from the production account, since it is always added to the gross national income rather than product, and thus affects saving, which is defined as a residual. Gross private domestic investment is debited from the production account, and net foreign investment from the rest-of-the-world account. By OBE definition, there is no household or government tangible investment.

Within the limits of its definition, the Department provides considerable detail on saving and investment in the supporting tables of Section 5 of *The National Income and Product Accounts of the United States, 1929–1965: Statistical Tables.* Table 5-1 shows all the items of the capital account in time-series form. Tables 5-2 and 5-3 show new construction by eighteen types of private activity and eleven types of public, in current and constant dollars. Purchases of producers' durable equipment, by twenty-two types, are given in current and constant dollars in tables 5-4 and 5-5. It is also possible to obtain a breakdown of business expenditures on new plant and equipment by industry. This is the same series for which the Department and SEC, obtain businessmen's expenditure plans for the quarter and (once a year) the year ahead. Table 5-6 shows a breakdown of the net change in business inventories by major industry groups and legal forms of organization. Table 5-7 compares the Commerce residual estimates of personal saving with direct estimates prepared by SEC.

Critique of the OBE Treatment of Investment

Despite the considerable amount of useful information presented in the United States national saving-investment account and the related supporting tables, the Commerce Department treatment may be criticized on two main grounds. In the first place, there are strong arguments for counting as investment the outlays for structures and equipment and the inventory accumulation of *all* domestic sectors, not just private business. After all, there is strong substitutability between the purchase of capital goods by the nonbusiness sectors and the leasing of goods or the direct purchase of services of the durables from the business sector by households and government. Thus, an increasing trend toward purchasing rather than leasing equipment would impart a downward bias to investment as measured by OBE in contrast to the broader definition. This is recognized by OBE with respect to residential structures, all purchases of which are counted as investment whether intended for owner occupancy or for lease by rental firms to tenants. But the same argument applies to structures which may be purchased or leased by government agencies and to durable goods, such as automobiles, which may be purchased or leased by the nonbusiness sectors. In brief, if the basic definition of investment as "adding to stock" is followed, and all purchases of durable goods defined as those lasting more than a year are included in gross investment, then durable purchases and inventory accumulation of households and government must be counted along with business investment. This is quite apart from including intangible investments, the case for which will be argued after we review the SNA treatment which, like the United States accounts, excludes intangibles.

The Commerce Department does go beyond the definition of investment as business capital outlays in one major instance: residential construction. The Department counts *all* new residential construction as business investment, including that intended for owner occupancy and purchased by households. A rental value is imputed to the latter, based on rentals received for comparable properties owned by the real estate industry. The fiction is maintained that the homeowner is in the business of renting his property to himself, but obviously the same fiction could be used to cover all nonbusiness capital expenditures.

Owing to the clear substitutability between homeownership and rental, the Commerce procedure is desirable. If purchases of new houses by individuals for purposes of occupancy were not counted, investment in new residential structures would vary according to the proportion intended for rental. Likewise, consumer outlays for housing would vary according to the proportion of the stock that was owner-occupied if rental imputations were not made.

But does not the same argument apply to all other nonbusiness durables? Although rentals are not as widespread for durables other than houses, organized leasing arrangements exist for automobiles, certain major household durables, and, in the case of government, office buildings and equipment. Even if one cannot lease the good directly, one can purchase the service, as with laundromats vis-à-vis household washers and dryers, freezer lockers vis-à-vis home freezers, etc. Although furniture is not generally leased, one can rent a furnished house or office building. These examples help to document the fact that there is a considerable degree of substitutability between business and household equipment, and also between privately and publicly owned capital goods.

The chief problem in including nonbusiness durables in investment, and their services in product, is finding an appropriate rental rate to apply to the estimated stocks. The indicated solution appears to be to break down the gross rental into its chief components: depreciation, interest on the net capital stock, and maintenance and repair outlays. The last item is already included in final product and would only have to be segregated. Depreciation on consumer durables poses the same problem as that on fixed business capital—determination of average lives and mortality curves and the pattern of depreciation—and the required data are as good, if not better.

The more knotty problem is determination of an appropriate rate of return, or interest. In the household sector, the average borrowing rate for consumer credit seems reasonable for the portion of stock financed by debt, and the average lending rate seems reasonable for the residual equity. In the case of governments, again the average borrowing rate could be used. These are the rates toward which the rates of return on new investment would tend to be pushed, given economic rationality.

The second major criticism of the present United States accounts flows from the first. Once investment by all sectors is recognized, the case becomes very strong for splitting the several sector accounts into current and capital accounts. That is, only noninvestment purchases (including imputed rental values of nonbusiness assets) and other current outgoings would be shown in the current account, with net saving the difference between income and outlay so defined. The saving, carried in the debit side of the current account would be entered as a credit on the capital account and, together with capital consumption allowances and possible net capital transfers from other sectors, would provide the source of funds for investments, which would be detailed on the debit side of the capital account. This is, indeed, the scheme followed in the revised *SNA*. Although the *SNA* does not go all the way in reclassifying all durable purchases as investment, nor does it include intangibles in our sense, its accounting framework would accommodate further expansion of the capital or "accumulation" account, as we shall see below.

THE UN CAPITAL FINANCE ACCOUNTS

The chief advance of the revised *SNA* over the OBE accounts with respect to saving-investment is the UN deconsolidation of the national accumulation account by sector, providing a link to flow-of-funds or financing subaccounts. Before looking at the sector accounts, however, we shall refer to the UN national capital finance account (Appendix B, Table B-I.5), which differs in several respects from the United States saving-investment account for the nation.

First, note that the capital finance account for the nation, as for the sectors, is subdivided between accumulation, equivalent to the OBE saving-investment account, and finance, which is treated in the next chapter. In the accumulation subaccount, sources of funds are shown in terms of the three major categories of saving, consumption of fixed capital, and net capital transfers. For the national economy, the net capital transfers would have to come from (or go to) the rest of the world, although any one sector could receive net capital transfers, plus or minus, from other sectors. The Commerce Department does not show capital transfers, since these tend to be small and difficult to distinguish from current transfers. But, at least conceptually, it is desirable to distinguish this source of capital.

On the debit side, there are four major categories of uses of capital funds. The first three are the increase in stocks (inventory accumulation), gross fixed capital formation (structures and equipment), and net purchases of intangible assets n.e.c., (such as rights to patents, trademarks, copyrights, and natural resources). For the national economy, the last item relates to net purchases from the rest of the world. The fourth category is net lending, which for the nation must be to the rest of the world. Net lending in the accumulation subaccount is a balancing item. That is, to the extent that capital funds provided by saving, capital consumption allowances, and net capital transfers are not fully used for tangible capital outlays and net purchases of intangible assets, funds are available for lending, on net balance.

The balancing item of net lending also provides the link to the financing (flow-of-funds) subaccount, where it is entered on the credit side. The financing accounts will be explained in the next chapter, but here we may note that net lending plus net incurrence of liabilities of various types equals the net acquisition of financial assets of various types.

Looking at the capital finance accounts for each sector, we see that the gross accumulation subaccount is virtually the same for each sector and that it differs in only a couple of respects from the national gross accumulation account. One difference is that net capital transfers and net purchases of intangible assets are not just in relation to the rest of the world, but also in relation to other sectors. The other difference is that the sector subaccounts also include purchases of land, net. Since land purchases and sales are considered to take place between resident institutions only, they cancel in the national capital account. The same sales value of the land is entered in the accounts of both seller and buyer. Sales are netted against purchases for members of each sector shown. Transfer costs of the transaction, such as brokers' commissions, are recorded in the fixed capital formation of the buyer and seller in proportion to the transfer costs borne by each.

The gross saving of each sector is equal to investment only if net lending is included with the tangible investments. For the nation as a whole, net domestic lending cancels, and only net lending to the rest of the world remains in addition to tangible investment, as we have seen. As in the national capital finance account, net lending provides the link to the financing subaccount of each sector. In the sector accounts, however, the net acquisition of assets and the net incurrence of liabilities are spelled out in some detail. The detail differs for each sector, however, depending on the particular structure of each sector's flow of funds, as we shall see in Chapter 9.

Like the present United States system, the revised *SNA* does not count consumer durable outlays, or other household tangibles other than residential structures, as investment. However, since the UN account III E also includes private unincorporated nonfinancial enterprises, provision is made in the gross accumulation account for all forms of tangible investment. In other words, the structure of the UN accounts would accommodate inclusion of nonbusiness outlays for durable goods and other tangible investments. Specific provision for such investments is made in accounts III C and III D covering general government and private nonprofit institutions serving households—although in the latter no provision is made for inventory accumulation because of its presumed small magnitude.

THE EXPANDED INVESTMENT CONCEPT

We have argued above that purchases of durable goods and inventory accumulation by all sectors should be classed as investment, an objective realized only partially in the revised *SNA* and to an even lesser extent in the United States accounts. Our approach is based on the definition of (net) investment as outlays designed to enhance the output- and income-producing capacity of the economy in future periods (years), regardless of whether the income stream is monetized or not. In addition to nonbusiness and business tangible investments, this definition may be construed to cover various types of intangible and human investments as well. These investments contribute to the human and nonhuman capital stocks which yield productive services over a period of years and which are, or may be, valued in terms of their discounted future net income streams.

Chief Types of Intangible and Human Investments

A brief discussion of the five chief types of intangible and human investments that we would include in the investment concept follows.[1] Thereafter, we indicate specifically how these investments may be treated in the sector and national accounts.

1 Research and development (R&D) expenditures are directed toward the uncovering of new knowledge and the commercial application of new ideas in the form of new products, processes, or methods of production. The resulting technological advances are a major factor in growth of income and product through increasing productivity and increased quality and variety of goods.

Basic and even applied research does not always result in new knowledge applicable for commercial use. But we count the costs of all research and the related development and engineering as investments to be amortized from the increased income resulting from successful inventions and innovation. The analogy is with the petroleum industry, in which the cost of drilling dry holes as well as successful wells is counted as investment.

In line with OBE practice, we attribute R&D investment to the financing sectors. But we then transfer the resulting capital to the sector of primary benefit, which in the case of R&D we assume to be business. Even though the bulk of R&D is financed by the federal government, private firms perform most of it. This and most of the rest of R&D become available to private business for use in devising new products and cost-reducing methods, which enhance business net income.

2 Education and training, which disseminate knowledge and know-how, increase the income-producing capacity of their recipients, as demonstrated in the studies of Schultz, Becker, Mincer, and others.[2] Education conduces to psychic as well as monetary income, of course, through increased capacity for enjoying cultural activities. But most of this relates to future activities—which underlines the nature of education as an investment. We disregard as relatively unimportant the satis-

---

[1] A more extended discussion of concepts, sources, and methods of estimation may be found in John W. Kendrick, "Restructuring the National Income Accounts for Investment and Growth Analysis," *Statistisk Tidskrift*, Stockholm, 1966: 5; also, the *Forty-seventh Annual Report* of National Bureau of Economic Research (New York: 1968), pp. 9–15.

[2] See "Investment in Human Beings," *Journal of Political Economy*, vol. 70, Supplement, October, 1962; and Gary Becker, *Human Capital* (New York: National Bureau of Economic Research, 1964).

factions obtained from the educational process, which, if monetized, would augment consumption.

Formal education includes mainly the current costs of institutions, imputed rental values of assets used by public and private nonprofit educational institutions, and opportunity costs of students of working age—the largest component of educational investment. Informal education includes the cost of educational programs on radio and TV and relevant parts of expenditures for newspapers and periodicals, libraries and museums, and teaching aids in nonschool use. [3] Under training costs, we include formal programs and informal on-the-job training. Costs of the latter include the time of supervisors and any production losses incurred during the breaking-in period for new employees.

Education and training, and the other human investments discussed below, are financed by all sectors, but the value of the services of the resulting human capital is reflected in labor compensation, which is credited to the personal sector. So for consistency, we transfer human capital formation out of the government and business sectors to the personal sector.

3   Medical and health expenditures, like those on education, frequently increase monetary and psychic incomes over a number of years. A part of health outlays is in the nature of current consumption, representing short-term maintenance. But a substantial portion (which we estimate at half of the total) has long-term benefits in terms of reduced mortality, disability, and debility. Increases in income as a result of prolongation of working life and reduction of time lost from illness have been estimated in part. [4] It is more difficult to estimate the monetary returns from heightened vitality, but the benefits in this area, as from elimination of certain chronic diseases, are real and further strengthen the case for counting a substantial portion of health outlays as investment.

4   Mobility investments comprise the costs required to shift human resources in response to dynamic changes in technology and other forces affecting the economy. Income and efficiency are increased as resources are shifted among occupations, industries, and regions in response to relative changes in their marginal productivity. Costs involved in transferring nonhuman capital are already included in tangible investment. But special calculations must be made of the costs of human mobility resulting from economic considerations.

In this category, we include the costs of job search and hiring, moving expenses of migrants who seek or assume jobs in other counties or states, and the opportunity cost of the frictionally unemployed less subsidies. Frictional unemployment, as distinguished from that arising from cyclical insufficiency of aggregate demand, may not improve the lot of individual workers, but it is a necessary concomitant of dynamic economic changes, particularly technological advances, which raise productivity and thus the real income of the community. We use 3 percent of the labor force (or the actual rate, if below 3 percent) as the frictional norm, and the average compensation per full-time equivalent employee, in imputing the forgone earnings.

5   Tangible human investment comprises the costs of rearing children to work-

[3] See Fritz Machlup, *The Production and Distribution of Knowledge in the United States* (Princeton, N.J.: Princeton University Press, 1962), chap. 6.

[4] See Selma J. Muskin, "Health as an Investment," *Journal of Political Economy*, vol. 70, Supplement, October, 1962.

ing age. This is a basic aspect of creating human capital, although intangible investments in improving the productive efficiency of human beings (excluded from this component) are quantitatively even more important. The return to the tangible and the intangible human capital is reflected in the labor compensation component of national income—and in the psychic income from nonmarket activities not included in the estimates. The motivation for having children is, of course, more for psychic return to the parents than for monetary return, most of which accrues to the children when they enter the labor force. But even though the decision to incur rearing costs is not based on a narrow economic rationale, these outlays are nonetheless investment, as we view it.

This view may be somewhat controversial, but we believe that it permits a deeper analysis of the saving and investment processes. While there is some abstinence effect on parents, rearing costs compete to a significant extent with other forms of investment, including education and other intangible human investments, for the limited resources provided by saving. This is particularly true in low-income countries with high birthrates, where it seems clear that lower rearing expenditures would release more funds for education, equipping the existing labor force with more capital goods, and so on.

The tangible human capital stock is replenished and augmented not only by natural increase within the country, but also by net immigration. The estimated value of the human capital acquired through net immigration is treated as a capital transfer from abroad to persons. This is shown in Annex Table V (at end of chapter) as a credit to the foreign sector capital account (line 8), where it augments net foreign investment as a component of accumulation.

This leads to the final topic of this section—estimation of the stocks and consumption of human capital. We do not need to estimate human capital stocks for purposes of imputing a return, since we argue that returns to human capital are already included in labor compensation. But we do need stock estimates to compute human capital consumption and thus to distinguish more clearly between gross and net income and saving. Basically, our procedure with respect to human investments is to estimate the cumulative amounts (in real terms) for each population cohort per capita, and then for each year multiply the cumulative investments for each age class per capita by the number of persons in that class. Each year's new investment for each age class is then depreciated on a straight-line basis up to age seventy-five, taking account of mortality experience along the way. The constant-dollar stock and depreciation estimates can then be converted to current prices by means of the same price indexes used to deflate the current-dollar investment estimates. In the case of applied R&D, average lives of the product and process innovations were obtained from a survey, and stock and depreciation estimates obtained by the perpetual inventory method, using flat distributions of mortality around the mean lives (see Chapter 10 for a more detailed discussion of stock estimates).

A Diagrammatic Presentation

To recapitulate the preceding discussions of total investment and capital, it may be helpful to refer to Diagram 8-1. The two large blocks at the bottom of the diagram represent the stocks of human and nonhuman capital at the beginning of a period. On the left, the nonhuman capital consists not only of a given quantum of

ECONOMIC ACCOUNTS AND THEIR USES

material, natural (as developed by man) or man-made, but also a certain level of embodied technology, or "state of the arts." Similarly, on the right, human capital consists not only of a certain number of members of a labor force, but also the productive knowledge, or know-how, with which they have been equipped. The services of the two major factor classes merge to produce a stream of final production. The stream of consumer goods and services flows down and back to the labor force. Its character as a sort of maintenance for human capital is brought out by a small

DIAGRAM 8-1
Total investment and the growth process

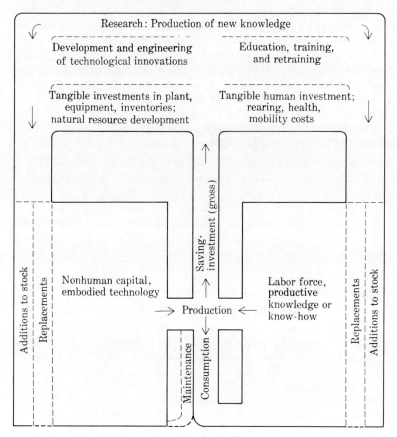

stream of output of goods and services required for maintenance and repair of the nonhuman capital—but this stream is indicated by a dashed line: It is not part of final product, as are consumer products, since man is the end as well as a means of production.

The stream of investment goods flows back and augments the initial stocks of capital. The investment flows subdivide into several channels before rejoining each of the capital stocks. At the top is the flow of investment funds into basic research.

This is the fountainhead of production of new technology and know-how which enhances the productivity of both human and nonhuman factors when embodied in the existing capital stock or additions to it. Specifically, on the left of the diagram further investment funds go into the development and engineering of technological innovations. Together with tangible investment in new capital goods, or in the discovery and development of natural resources, these investment flows go to augment the nonhuman capital stocks.

In parallel fashion on the right-hand side, investments in education, training, and health, in conjunction with the rearing of human beings to working age, the financing of immigrants of labor-force age, and other mobility costs, flow back to enhance the quantity and quality of human capital.

Note that part of each of the gross investment flows is needed to offset the retirements during the period of labor-force members or of items of nonhuman capital. Only the remainder goes to increase the capital stocks (expansion between beginning and end of period shown in dashed lines). Instead of retirements, depreciation and other capital consumption could be shown if net investment were conceived as additions to the real income-producing power of the capital stocks.

EXPANSION OF THE NATIONAL AND SECTOR SAVING-INVESTMENT ACCOUNTS

In order to summarize and make concrete our suggestions for deconsolidation and expansion of the saving-investment (accumulation) account by sector, the author, with major assistance from Jennifer Rowley, has prepared a dummy set of national and sector accounts as shown in the Annex to this chapter. For several of the imputations suggested in Chapter 3, we have entered the item descriptions in parentheses, with no numbers. A full set of estimates and a description of the sources and methods used in obtaining the estimates which supplement or modify the Commerce estimates are contained in a report for the National Bureau of Economic Research.[5]

The Expanded National Production Account

To obtain an overall picture of the chief changes in our suggested accounts, in contrast to the United States and, to a lesser extent, the UN systems, turn first to the proposed national income and product account, Annex Table I. On the product side, note first the importance of the investment categories which here comprise more than one-half of expanded GNP, contrasted with about one-sixth according to the more restrictive OBE concepts.

Gross tangible nonhuman investment (line 31) includes not only the gross private domestic business investment of OBE plus minor tangible durable goods charged to current expense by private firms, but also the purchases of new structures, equipment and other durable goods, and inventory accumulation by households and general governments. Our total is a bit more than twice OBE's $121.4 billion gross private domestic business investment figure for the year 1966.

Gross tangible human investment (line 37), it will be recalled, is the cost of rearing children to working age. Although this category amounts to about $55

[5] John W. Kendrick, assisted by Jennifer A. Rowley, *Total Investment, Capital, and Economic Growth in the United States* (New York: National Bureau of Economic Research, in process).

billion, only a little more than 10 percent of total investment in the United States, it would be much more important in relation to total saving and investment in many less developed countries with high birthrates.

Gross intangible human investment (line 38), at almost $200 billion in 1966, has grown relatively over the years to a magnitude about two-thirds that of tangible investment. By far the largest part of this total is expenditures for education and training (line 39), and the largest part of educational outlays is the opportunity cost of students of working age (see Table 8-1 below), an addition to official GNP. Together with health and mobility outlays (lines 40 and 41), education and training represent investments embodied in human beings. Most of research and development expenditures (line 42) are embodied in nonhuman capital goods.

Net exports of goods and services of $5.3 billion in 1966 is the OBE estimate. As shown in the foreign sector accounts, Annex Table V, it comprises $2.4 billion net foreign investment and $2.9 billion net personal and government transfer payments to foreigners.

Consistent with our expanded definition of investment, personal consumption (line 29) and government consumption (line 30) exclude the tangible and intangible investments of these two nonbusiness sectors. Partially offsetting these exclusions from the OBE estimates are the imputed rental values of household and government tangible capital assets that result from the nonbusiness outlays we include now as investment. The repair and maintenance portion of gross rental values of the nonbusiness sectors is already included in official GNP, but the imputed net interest charge and depreciation allowance represent additions. No imputations of rental values are made for human capital, since insofar as this is used for productive purposes, the return is already included in labor compensation and thus reflected in market prices of final products. To the extent that human capital gives rise to psychic income from noneconomic activities, we do not value this, since we are confining our imputations to nonmarket economic activity.

Turning now to the income side, to the official factor-cost estimates we add our imputations for labor income of proprietors (line 6), nonmarket labor services (line 7), and imputed net rental income on the productive assets of consumers and governments (lines 8 and 12). The latter items are exclusive of monetary interest paid by the two nonbusiness sectors, which is thus considered productive and included in net interest income (line 13), unless it exceeds the imputed net rental of the sector or subsector, in which case it is deducted as nonproductive (lines 15 and 17).

A noteworthy innovation in this table is the adjustment in line 18 whereby we deduct our imputation for human capital consumption allowances in order to arrive at net national income. It is often not realized by users of the accounts that the official national income estimates are asymmetrical in that property income is net of capital consumption allowances, whereas labor compensation is gross. In our table, we thus allow for the decline in value of human capital, tangible and intangible, as it ages. Note, however, that in the other charges, we add back in the capital consumption allowances on human capital, together with the capital consumption allowances on nonhuman capital assets of persons and governments as well as business (lines 19-24). Thus, GNP is not affected by this treatment, but it does provide a more comprehensive and informative set of capital consumption allowance estimates. We do not carry symmetry in treatment of labor and capital income to the point of excluding estimated "maintenance" of human capital. Here we follow the classic argument that, even though much of personal consumption represents maintenance, man is the end of economic activity and such consumption is desired for its own sake and thus represents final product.

It was noted earlier that when the GNP estimates are adjusted for consistency with the total investment concept, they are significantly higher—by 32 percent in 1966, to be precise. The adjustment items are shown in Table 8-1 below. Business investments charged to current expense include small tools, formerly included in GNP by OBE, but primarily they represent research and development, training, and other intangible investments financed by private business. The intangible investments of the other sectors, while not classed as investment, are already part of official GNP. Student compensation and frictional unemployment costs represent the opportunity costs of students of working age and of the frictionally unemployed, considered to be part of investments in education and mobility, respectively. If we included imputations for the other unpaid labor services suggested in Chapter 3, total GNP would be raised by at least another 25 percent. These items are shown in parentheses in Annex Table II, part A, but no figures are entered since they are not required for present purposes.

The final category in Table 8-1 is the imputed gross rental values on nonbusiness capital goods over and above the components in official GNP, primarily repair and maintenance and relevant indirect business taxes. In other words, the item represents primarily imputed net interest and depreciation, which accords nonbusiness capital assets a treatment symmetrical to that now given private business assets and owner-occupied residences in the United States accounts.

The Sector Accounts

The three major domestic sector accounts, current and capital, shown in Annex Tables II to IV, reflect the expanded definition of investment and the associated imputations. We follow OBE in distinguishing three major sectors: persons (including private nonprofit institutions), government, and business (which is implicit in the OBE accounts), plus a foreign transactions account. Obviously, the OBE sector accounts could be further disaggregated, but the basic principle we develop would apply to the subaccounts. In particular, it would be desirable to have a separate financial sector account, whose role is examined in the next chapter.

Personal sector account   To start with the personal sector account (Annex Table II), note that the credits on current account include imputed labor compensation (lines 15 and 16) and net rentals on owner-used capital goods (line 22), in addition to the items included by OBE. Also, in order to be able to enter human capital consumption, along with other capital consumption allowances, as a source of funds on capital accounts, we have deducted it from personal income, so that personal income and the balancing saving item on the debit side are truly "net."

On the debit side, under personal consumption (line 2), we have deducted from the OBE estimate consumer durables, estimated inventory change, and the estimated consumption of children under working age (rearing costs). We then added the imputed rentals on the sector's assets (line 3), less that which was allocated as invest-

TABLE 8-1

Imputations in Gross National Product and Selected Additional Imputations
Consistent with Total Investment Concept, 1966

	Billions of Dollars	Percentage of Official GNP
Market GNP	695.9	92.8
Plus: official imputations	54.0	7.2
Official GNP	749.9	100.0
Plus: additional imputations for consistency with total investments, of which:	240.6	32.1
Business investments charged to current expense	28.9	3.9
Student compensation	70.5	9.4
Frictional unemployment cost	13.7	1.8
Rentals on capital additional to components in official GNP	127.5	17.0
Consumer durables and inventories	75.1	10.1
Institutional plant and equipment	3.2	0.4
Government structures, equipment, and inventories	49.2	6.6
GNP consistent with total investment concept	990.5	132.1

SOURCES: Official GNP and market and imputed components from *Survey of Current Business*, vol. 49, p. 45, table 7.3, July, 1969. All other estimates from John W. Kendrick, assisted by Jennifer A. Rowley, *Total Investment, Capital, and Economic Growth in the United States* (New York: National Bureau of Economic Research, in process).

ment costs (line 8), such as the implicit rental value of private nonprofit educational and research institutions. Unproductive interest (line 11) is that paid on security credit.

Net personal saving (line 12) is carried down as the initial entry on the credit side of the sector's capital account (line 54). Even more important as a source of investment funds are the personal capital consumption allowances (line 55), which are entered in some detail under the human and nonhuman headings. It is important to realize that as far as households are concerned, accounting estimates of depreciation are seldom made on tangible assets, let alone on human capital. Yet, in an economic sense, the implicit capital consumption allowances, which are an implicit part of personal income, help in the financing of new investments. According to our estimates for 1966, $159.6 billion worth of the $262 billion gross personal investment (line 34 on the debit side of the capital account) was plowed back out of that portion of personal income estimated to represent capital consumption.

In addition to gross saving, the personal sector in 1966 was the recipient of $70 billion worth of transfers of capital from other sectors (line 66). This represents the education and other human investment financed by government and business where benefits accrue to individuals through enhanced compensation, and possibly also through increased psychic income not included in our estimates. There is a small offset of $0.3 billion representing research and development outlays of private non-profit institutions, where we assume that benefits accrue largely to business.

On the debit side of the capital account, there is an equivalent amount of net capital transfers (line 47) shown by major types, which augments the gross investment (line 34) directly undertaken and financed by the personal sector. Net financial investment (line 53) is the balancing item representing the difference between gross saving and gross tangible and intangible investment, as we define the terms. As noted earlier, this item provides the link to the sector's financial account.

Government sector account   The accounts for government (Annex Table IV) are similar in principle to those for persons. On the credit side of the current account, in addition to the usual tax sources and interest, we add the net rental income on general government assets (line 20). On the debit side, to government consumption (line 7 — purchases less investment), transfer payments, and subsidies less enterprise surplus, we add the imputed gross rentals on public assets (line 2) less that portion included in intangible investments (line 6) and less unproductive interest payments (line 11), which is the difference between actual interest payments of the federal government and the imputed net rental (interest) on productive assets. The balancing item, surplus or deficit on current account (line 13), is the difference between government revenues and outlays.

The surplus is carried down to the credit side of the capital account (line 38). To this is added the estimated capital consumption allowances on fixed reproducible capital assets (line 39). Here, again, we must note that federal and state and local general governments do not prepare capital budgets in which depreciation charges are entered. But in an economic sense, such allowances are appropriate. The deduction for capital transfers (line 42) is an attempt to shift investments to the sectors which are benefited by public intangible investment — business in the case of research and development, and persons in the case of the other intangibles, primarily education.

On the debit side of the capital account, gross public investments (line 22) are shown in broad detail. The capital transfer offsets (line 32) indicate that all the intangible investments are assumed to result in capital of primary value to other sectors. Net financial investment (line 37) is the balancing item and the link to the sector's financial account.

Business sector account   The accounts of the business sector (Annex Table III) are different from the others in that business does not purchase final goods on current account. As we have set it up, the current disposable income of business is composed of corporate profits before income taxes (line 13), profits of proprietors (line 12), and net rental income as an auxiliary activity of persons (line 10). It would be possible, as in the *SNA*, to cut into business income at an earlier stage and credit revenues from current production, with intermediate product purchases and labor costs, as well as the disposition of profits, shown on the debit side. But we follow the OBE approach of consolidating all production activities in the national income and product account, and then crediting the various sectors with their shares of factor incomes and nonfactor charges, which are disposable for transfers, final purchases, and saving.

The net income of enterprises, gross of capital consumption allowances and income taxes, is adjusted in several ways. First, there is the familiar inventory valuation adjustment, designed to eliminate profits due to price appreciation of inventories (line 17). A similar depreciation valuation adjustment should be made to correct the depreciation charges on tangible capital from acquisition costs as usually carried on the books to current replacement cost, and to add back in the tangible capital outlays charged to current cost (line 15). One further adjustment is needed to comport with our expanded definition of investments. Now that we class as investment the outlays for R&D and the other intangibles shown under line 24, which are charged to current expenses under present tax laws, this item must be added back to profits, less any capital consumption allowances on the intangible capital commanded by the sector as a result of the intangible investments. As with government, we transfer the human investments financed by business to the personal sector. But business is assumed to be the beneficiary of the R&D of the economy, which is capitalized and depreciated. Thus, the entry on line 16 represents total business intangible investment (line 24) less capital consumption allowances on R&D (line 41).

With regard to debits on business current account, net rental income (line 1) and the profits of proprietors (line 2) are assumed to be wholly withdrawn by the owners in their capacity as consumers and members of the household sector. Actually, some of these incomes are saved, but because of the difficulty of estimation, we follow the OBE procedure of allocating all these incomes and the associated saving to the personal sector. In the case of corporate profits, the allocations are known, and we can separately debit profits, tax liabilities (line 3), dividends (line 4), and the residual net saving on "retained earnings" after adjustments (line 5).

Net business saving is carried down to the credit side of the accumulation account (line 35). Of even greater size are business capital consumption allowances (line 36), consisting primarily of depreciation on tangible capital (line 37), but also including depreciation on the accumulated stock of productive knowledge resulting from applied research and development outlays (line 41).

Net capital transfers (line 42) are negative, reflecting larger transfers out to households in the form of intangible investments in human beings than transfers in from the other sectors of research and development outlays.

On the debit side of the capital account, gross private domestic investment of the business sector (line 18) is detailed by major types of tangible and intangible investment. The accumulation through net capital transfers (line 29), which on balance provides a small deduction from sector gross investment as discussed above, is also detailed by type. The balancing item, net financial investment (line 34), as in the case of the other sectors, provides the link to the financing accounts.

Foreign sector account   The foreign sector current account (Annex Table V) is the same as that of OBE except that under credits we follow the *SNA* in calling the balancing item "surplus of the nation" (line 5). This item provides the link to the capital account, where it appears as a debit, since the foreign sector account is set up from the viewpoint of the rest of the world in order to provide the appropriate contra-entries to the domestic production and sector accounts.

Our estimate of net capital transfers from abroad (line 8) is confined to human capital, because in its estimates OBE counts all financial and tangible nonhuman transfers as current (lines 3 and 4). It augments net foreign investment as a channel of accumulation on foreign account. The human capital acquired from abroad does not affect the size of gross national product, since it is a transfer.

Annex Table VI is the consolidated capital formation account. On the credit side, we find gross investment, by sector (lines 6 to 9). It is of interest that, by the expanded definition, gross investment of the personal sector is well over half the total and government investment approaches that of business.

Also on the credit side, the accumulation of capital transfers by sector is offsetting as far as domestic transfers are concerned, and the net balance (line 10) represents net transfers from abroad (line 4), which in our estimates are confined to human capital.

The same is true of net financial investment, and the net balance (line 14) represents the surplus of the nation on foreign account (which equals net foreign investment, line 5, less the statistical discrepancy, line 18). The discrepancy shows up in net financial investment, since that is the ultimate residual of the system.

On the debit side, we find the five major categories of investment. The detail is not shown in this summary table, since it may be found in the production and sector accounts.

The estimates contained in these accounts and the associated balance sheets should be of great value in time-series form for dynamic economic analysis. The national and sector saving and investment functions would look quite different from those based on the conventional accounts to which we are accustomed. Further, the associated real total capital stocks should be of major importance in explaining economic growth. We demonstrate these uses in the final chapter of the book.

REVIEW QUESTIONS

1 Describe and criticize the official United States saving-investment account.
2 What are the main features of the capital finance accounts in the *SNA*? How could they be improved?
3 Name the chief types of intangible investments.
4 On what basis is it feasible to impute gross rental values to the services of stocks of nonbusiness tangible capital assets? Why are such imputations desirable?
5 In what way is national income as conventionally measured asymmetric and not truly "net"?
6 Explain the dual significance of the net financial investment item in sector, and national, capital accounts.

SELECTED REFERENCES

"Investment in Human Beings," *Journal of Political Economy*, vol. 70, Supplement, October, 1962.

KENDRICK, JOHN W.: "Restructuring the National Income Accounts for Investment and Growth Analysis," *Statistisk Tidskrift,* Stockholm, 1966:5.

—— assisted by JENNIFER A. ROWLEY: *Total Investment, Capital, and Economic Growth in the United States,* New York: National Bureau of Economic Research, in process. For a preliminary brief summary, see *Forty-seventh Annual Report* of the National Bureau of Economic Research (New York: June, 1968).

UNITED NATIONS, DEPARTMENT OF ECONOMIC AND SOCIAL AFFAIRS, STATISTICAL OFFICE: *A System of National Accounts,* Studies in Methods, ser. F, no. 2, rev. 3 (New York: 1968).

Annex to Chapter 8
National and Sector Income and Product Accounts

TABLE I
Expanded National Income and Product Account
(Billions of Current Dollars)

*Line
No.*

DEBITS

1. Labor compensation
2.   Wage and salary disbursements [IIA-13.]
3.   Wage accruals less disbursements [IIB-71.]
4.   Employer contributions for social insurance [IVA-19.]
5.   Other labor income [IIA-14.]
6.   Imputed compensation of proprietors [IIA-15.]
7.   Additional labor compensation imputations [IIA-16.]

8. Net rental income of persons and institutions
9.   From auxiliary business activities [IIIA-10.]
10.   From owner-used capital [IIA-22.]

11. Profits of business enterprises [IIIA-11.]

12. Net rental income of government [IVA-20.]

13. Net interest
14.   Personal interest income [IIA-28.]
15.   Less: Unproductive interest paid by consumers [IIA-11.]
16.   Government interest income [IVA-21.]
17.   Less: Unproductive interest paid by government [IVA-11.]
        NATIONAL INCOME

18. Less: Human capital consumption [IIA-33.]
        NET NATIONAL INCOME

19. Capital consumption allowances
20.   Personal [IIB-55.]
21.   Nonhuman
22.   Human
23.   Business [IIIB-36.]
24.   Government [IVB-39.]
        GROSS NATIONAL INCOME

25. Current business transfer payments [IIA-30.]
26. Indirect tax and nontax charges [IVA-16.]
27. Less: Subsidies less current surplus of government enterprises [IVA-12.]
28. Statistical discrepancy [VI-18.]

CHARGES AGAINST GROSS NATIONAL PRODUCT

CREDITS

29. Personal consumption [IIA-2.]
30. Government consumption [IVA-1.]
31. Gross tangible nonhuman investment [VI-1.]
32.   Structures
33.   Residential
34.   Nonresidential
35.   Durable goods
36.   Change in inventories
37. Gross tangible human investment [VI-2.]

38. Gross intangible human investment [VI-3.]
39.   Education and training
40.   Health
41.   Mobility
42.   Research and development

43. Net export of goods and services
44.   Exports [VA-1.]
45.   Less: Imports [VA-2.]

GROSS NATIONAL PRODUCT

TABLE II
Personal Sector Accounts
(Billions of Current Dollars)

Line
No.   A – CURRENT ACCOUNT (cash basis)

DEBITS

1. Personal tax and nontax payments [IVA-14.]

2. Personal consumption [I-29.]
3.   Imputed rentals for services of capital
4.   Owner-occupied residences
5.   Institutional plant
6.   Consumer durable goods and inventories
7.   Institutional equipment
8.   Less: Imputed rentals allocated to intangible and human investment
        (Consumption provided by business to employees)
        (Current consumption transfers from business to general public)
9.   Other consumption expenditures

TABLE II (Continued)

10. Personal transfer payments to foreigners (net) [VA-3.]

11. Unproductive interest paid by consumers [I-15.]

12. Net personal saving [IIB-54.]
    DISPOSAL OF PERSONAL INCOME

CREDITS

13. Wage and salary disbursements [I-2.]

14. Other labor income [I-5.]

15. Imputed labor compensation of proprietors [I-6.]

16. Additional labor compensation imputations [I-7.]
17.   Students
18.   Frictionally unemployed
        (Household members)
        (Volunteers)
        (Employees for business provided consumption)

19. Withdrawals of proprietors' profits [IIIA-2.]

20. Net rental income
21.   From auxiliary business activities [IIIA-1.]
22.   From owner-used capital [I-10.]
23.   Residences
24.   Institutional plant
25.   Consumer durable goods and inventories
26.   Institutional equipment

27. Dividends [IIIA-4.]

28. Personal interest income [I-14.]

29. Current transfers to persons
30.   From business [I-25.]
        Cash
        (Consumption provided to general public)
31.   From government [IVA-9.]

32. Less: Personal contributions for social insurance [IVA-18.]
    PERSONAL INCOME

33. Less: Human capital consumption [I-18.]
    NET PERSONAL INCOME

B – CAPITAL ACCOUNT (accrual basis)

DEBITS

34. Gross personal investment [VI-7.]
35.   Tangible nonhuman investment
36.   Residential structures
37.   Institutional plant
38.   Consumer durable goods
39.   Institutional equipment
40.   Change in household inventories
41.   Tangible human investment
42.   Intangible investment
43.   Education and training
44.   Health
45.   Mobility
46.   Research and development

47. Accumulation through capital transfers [VI-11.]
48.   Tangible human capital
49.   Education and training
50.   Health
51.   Mobility
52.   Research and development

53. Net financial investment [VI-15.]
      GROSS ACCUMULATION

CREDITS

54. Net personal saving [IIA-12.]

55. Personal capital consumption allowances [I-20.]
56.   Tangible nonhuman capital
57.   Residential structures
58.   Institutional plant
59.   Consumer durable goods
60.   Institutional equipment
61.   Tangible human capital
62.   Intangible capital
63.   Education and training
64.   Health
65.   Mobility

66. Net capital transfers
67.   Capital transfers from business [IIIB-45.]
68.   Capital transfers from government [IVB-43.]
69.   Capital transfers from abroad [VB-7.]
70.   Less: Capital transfers to business [IIIB-43.]

71. Wage accruals less disbursements [I-3.]
      FINANCE OF GROSS ACCUMULATION

TABLE III
Business Sector Accounts
(Billions of Current Dollars)

Line
No.   A – CURRENT ACCOUNT

DEBITS

1.   Withdrawals of net rental income from auxiliary business activities [IIA-21.]

2.   Withdrawals of proprietors' profits [IIA-19.]

3.   Corporate profits tax liability [IVA-15.]

4.   Dividends [IIA-27.]

5.   Net business saving [IIIB-35.]
6.   Unincorporated business nonwithdrawn profits before adjustment
7.   Corporate undistributed profits before adjustment
8.   Amortization adjustment
9.   Inventory valuation adjustment
         DISPOSAL OF NET BUSINESS INCOME

CREDITS

10. Net rental income from auxiliary business activities [I-9.]

11. Profits of business enterprises [I-11.]
12.   Unincorporated business profits before adjustment
13.   Gross corporate profits before adjustment
14.   Amortization adjustment
15.   Tangible capital
16.   Intangible capital
17.   Inventory valuation adjustment
         NET BUSINESS INCOME (BEFORE INCOME TAX)

B – CAPITAL ACCOUNT

DEBITS

18. Gross business investment [VI-8.]
19.   Tangible investment
20.   Residential structures
21.   Nonresidential structures
22.   Producers' durable equipment
23.   Change in inventories
24.   Intangible investment
25.   Education and training
26.   Health
27.   Mobility
28.   Research and development

29.   Accumulation through capital transfers [VI-12.]
30.   Education and training
31.   Health
32.   Mobility
33.   Research and development

34.   Net financial investment [VI-16]
         GROSS ACCUMULATION

CREDITS

35.   Net business saving [IIIA-5.]

36.   Business capital consumption allowances [I-23.]
37.   Tangible capital
38.   Residential structures
39.   Nonresidential structures
40.   Producers' durable equipment
41.   Intangible capital, research and development

42.   Net capital transfers
43.   Capital transfers from persons and institutions [IIB-70.]
44.   Capital transfers from government [IVB-44.]
45.   Less: Capital transfers to persons [IIB-67.]
         FINANCE OF GROSS ACCUMULATION

TABLE IV
Government Sector Accounts
(Billions of Current Dollars)

Line
No.   A – CURRENT ACCOUNT

DEBITS

1.   General government consumption [I-30.]
2.   Imputed rentals for services of capital
3.   Public land
4.   Structures
5.   Equipment and inventories
6.   Less: Imputed rentals allocated to intangible investment
7.   Other consumption expenditures

8.   Government transfer payments
9.   To persons [IIA-31.]
10.   To foreigners (net) [VA-4.]

11.   Unproductive interest paid by government [I-17.]

12.   Subsidies less current surplus of government enterprises [I-27.]

TABLE IV (Continued)

13. Surplus or deficit (−) on current account [IVB-38.]
    DISPOSAL OF GOVERNMENT INCOME

CREDITS

14. Personal tax and nontax receipts [IIA-1.]

15. Corporate profits tax accruals [IIIA-3.]

16. Indirect tax and nontax charges [I-26.]

17. Contributions for social insurance
18.   Personal [IIA-32.]
19.   Employer [I-4.]

20. Net rental income of government [I-12.]

21. Government interest income [I-16.]
    GOVERNMENT INCOME

B − CAPITAL ACCOUNT

DEBITS

22. Gross government investment [VI-9.]
23.   Tangible investment
24.   Structures
25.   Equipment
26.   Change in inventories
27.   Intangible investment
28.   Education and training
29.   Health
30.   Mobility
31.   Research and development

32. Accumulation of capital transfers [VI-13.]
33.   Education and training
34.   Health
35.   Mobility
36.   Research and development

37. Net financial investment [VI-17.]
    GROSS ACCUMULATION

CREDITS

38. Surplus or deficit (−) on current account [IVA-13.]

39. Government capital consumption allowances [I-24.]
40.   Structures
41.   Equipment

140

42. Less: Capital transfers by government
43.   To persons [IIB-68.]
44.   To business [IIIB-44.]
          FINANCE OF GROSS ACCUMULATION

TABLE V
Foreign Sector Accounts
(Billions of Current Dollars)

*Line
No.*   A – CURRENT ACCOUNT

DEBITS

1. Exports of goods and services [I-44.]
        RECEIPTS FROM FOREIGNERS

CREDITS

2. Imports of goods and services [I-45.]

3. Personal transfer payments to foreigners (net) [IIA-10.]

4. United States government transfer payments to foreigners (net) [IVA-10.]

5. Surplus of the nation on current foreign account [VB-6.]
        CURRENT DISBURSEMENTS AND SURPLUS ON FOREIGN ACCOUNT

B – CAPITAL ACCOUNT

DEBITS

6. Surplus of the nation on current foreign account [VA-5]

7. Capital transfers from abroad to persons (human, net) [IIB-68.]
        SOURCE OF ACCUMULATION

CREDITS

8. Accumulation through net (human) capital transfers from abroad [VI-4.]

9. Net foreign investment [VI-5.]
        ACCUMULATION ON FOREIGN ACCOUNT

TABLE VI
Consolidated Capital Formation Account
(Billions of Current Dollars)

Line
No.   **DEBITS**

1.   Gross tangible nonhuman investment [I-31.]

2.   Gross tangible human investment [I-37.]

3.   Gross intangible investment [I-38.]

4.   Accumulation through net (human) capital transfers from abroad [VB-8.]

5.   Net foreign investment [VB-9.]
        GROSS ACCUMULATION

                                              CREDITS

6.   Gross investment
7.   By persons and institutions [IIB-34.]
8.   By business [IIIB-18.]
9.   By government [IVB-22.]

10. Accumulation through net capital transfers
11.   By persons [IIB-47.]
12.   By business [IIIB-29.]
13.   By government [IVB-32.]

14. Net financial investment
15.   By persons and institutions [IIB-53.]
16.   By business [IIIB-34.]
17.   By government [IVB-37.]

18. Statistical discrepancy [I-28.]
        SOURCE OF GROSS ACCUMULATION

Financing Accounts by Sector

Chapter 8 carried the development of an integrated set of accounts to the gross saving-investment accounts, by sector. In those accounts net saving and capital consumption were placed on the credit side, and gross tangible investment on the debit side. Net borrowing was the balancing item on the credit side; alternatively, net lending might have appeared on the debit side. It is with this net borrowing (or lending) that the financing accounts are concerned. In the financing accounts, net borrowing represents the difference between the net changes in financial liabilities and financial assets.

The main topic of this chapter is the financing, or flow-of-funds (FOF), accounts. The discussion will focus on the accounts prepared by the Board of Governors of the Federal Reserve System, since they are the form which the financing accounts have taken in the United States. The independent development of these financing accounts, the structure of the accounts matrix, certain conventions used in constructing the accounts, and supporting tables will be discussed. Alternative presentations of financing accounts, in particular the Canadian national transactions accounts and the revised *SNA,* will be mentioned more briefly. A chief objective of this chapter is to show the place of financing accounts in an integrated economic accounting system.

THE FLOW-OF-FUNDS ACCOUNTS

The initial work on what has evolved into the FOF accounts was done by Morris A. Copeland.[1] Following up on a memorandum prepared by Wesley Mitchell in 1944, Copeland's exploratory work, providing annual flow estimates for the years 1936 to 1942, demonstrated the feasibility of a national accounting of the economy's flow of funds by major sectors and by significant categories. The flows that Copeland attempted to record were all money flows arising from "transactions in goods and services, purchases for resale as well as purchases that appear in the national income and product accounts; all transfer payment money flows—grants, benefits, etc.— that pass from one sector of the economy to another; and the net money flows through financial channels from one sector to another."[2] The resulting accounts, and the early FOF accounts prepared at the Federal Reserve, were essentially a separate self-contained system of economic accounts. Their purpose was different from that of other sets of accounts, and accordingly, in the process of construction, differences arose between the national income and product and the FOF accounts: Different categories of transactions were selected; transactions were grouped differently with respect to types of transaction or classification of transactor; entries were based on different values or different points of time; and transactions were recorded with different degrees of netting.[3] Reconciliation tables were provided, but their complexity made simultaneous use of the two systems difficult.

Since the Federal Reserve's initial publication of the FOF accounts in 1955, the accounts have been considerably modified, extended, and improved.[4] One important aspect of the changes is that by 1968 the Federal Reserve could report, "The flow of funds accounts can in fact be viewed as a direct extension of the Commerce income and product structure into the financial markets of the economy."[5] The FOF accounts have moved in the direction of showing only a minimum of information on income, saving, and capital investment rather than duplicating other measures of these flows, and they primarily record changes in financial assets and liabilities.

The Structure of the Flow-of-funds Accounts

Viewed as a direct extension of the income and product structure into the financial markets of the economy, the FOF accounts link the data in the OBE saving and

---

[1] Morris A. Copeland, *A Study of Money Flows in the United States* (New York: National Bureau of Economic Research, 1952).

[2] *Ibid.*, p. 11.

[3] The contrast between the FOF accounts and input-output tables is great. The former stress financial flows, which the latter omit. Data for the former are on an enterprise basis, for the latter on an establishment or process basis.

[4] The initial publication was *Flow of Funds in the United States, 1939-1953* (Washington, D.C.: Board of Governors of the Federal Reserve System, 1955). Important revisions were reported in the *Federal Reserve Bulletin*, vol. 45, pp. 828-859, August, 1959, beginning quarterly presentations; vol. 48, pp. 1393-1407, November, 1962, beginning seasonal adjustment; vol. 51, pp. 1533-1538, November, 1965, incorporating statistical revisions and changes in structure that were part of the revised income and product data published by OBE in that year. See also footnote 6.

[5] *Flow of Funds Accounts, 1945-1967* (Washington, D.C.: Board of Governors of the Federal Reserve System, 1968), p. I.8.

investment account with the lending and borrowing that are associated with it.[6] The FOF accounts in effect deconsolidate the OBE saving-investment account among the domestic sectors and explicitly record the financial flows among sectors, indicating the routes by which sectors that have excess saving over tangible investment lend to sectors that have an excess of tangible investment over saving. That is, the OBE Gross Saving and Investment Account, which is reproduced as Appendix A, Table A-5, shows for the economy as a whole gross saving equal to gross tangible investment plus net foreign investment. Transactions in financial assets and liabilities cancel out in the process of consolidation that results in the national saving-investment totals. However, while gross saving equals investment for the economy as a whole, this is not usually so for the individual sector. In households, for example, saving exceeds tangible investment, and some saving then takes the form of financial investment. On the other hand, saving of a sector may be augmented by borrowing if a sector's gross tangible investment exceeds that sector's own saving. In a complete capital account for a sector, the sources of funds (saving plus net borrowing) equal the uses of funds (tangible investment plus net lending or financial investment).

The summary sector-by-transactions matrix, which is basic to the flow-of-funds presentation, demonstrates these relationships. The matrix has been reproduced as Table 9-1. The table shows columns for nine sectors of the economy. Each of the columns is a sector account, where entries opposite the transactions categories are debits or uses of funds (U), or credits or sources of funds (S). The nonfinancial items appear in rows 1 through 9, where, ignoring for the moment certain definitional problems, gross saving appears as a credit and net private capital expenditures as a debit. Net financial investment (row 10) is the balancing item. This net financial investment is struck as the difference, for each sector, of all the categories of transactions which use funds and all those which are a source of funds. It is a measure of net funds advanced by each sector to all other sectors. The various entries in the financial transactions categories which give rise to the final net financial investment are the data unique to the FOF accounts. These entries show the routes by which gross saving is equated to gross investment—routes that may shift secularly and cyclically with the composition of capital expenditures, or have other significance for economic analysis.

Presentation of the data in matrix form enforces consistency of analysis in a setting where the interreactions of all transactions of the economy are to be posted. In the matrix this consistency is enforced by the requirement, first, that, for each sector, total investment (capital outlays plus net financial investment) equal saving. For example, in Table 9-1, for the business sector, private capital expenditures, net, of $99.2 billion plus net financial investment of − $25.4 billion plus the discrepancy of $7 billion equals gross saving of $80.8 billion. Because the net financial investment

---

[6] This discussion of structure uses as its main source the comprehensive survey of the FOF accounts found in *ibid*. The November, 1969, issue of the *Federal Reserve Bulletin* published estimates that reflected changes in structure, statistical procedure, and table form. *See Flow-of-Funds Accounts, 1945-1968* (Washington, D.C.: Board of Governors of the Federal Reserve System, 1970). As far as possible, on the basis of present information, these structural changes have been incorporated in the discussion below.

TABLE 9-1

Summary of Flow-of-funds Accounts, 1968

(Billions of Dollars)

Transaction Category / Sector	Households U	Households S	Business U	Business S	State and Local Govts. U	State and Local Govts. S	Total U	Total S	U.S. Govt. U	U.S. Govt. S	Total U	Total S
1 Gross saving	....	139.3	....	80.8	....	−5.6	....	214.6	....	−6.5	....	3.6
2 Capital consumption	....	76.2	....	62.3	....	....	....	138.5	....	....	....	1.3
3 Net saving (1−2)	....	63.2	....	18.5	....	−5.6	....	76.1	....	−6.5	....	2.3
4 Gross investment (5 + 10)	136.4	....	73.8	....	−4.9	....	205.3	....	−6.3	....	3.5	....
5 Pvt. capital expenditures	109.1	....	99.2	....	....	....	208.3	....	....	....	1.3	....
6 Consumer durables	83.3	....	....	....	....	....	83.3	....	....	....	....	....
7 Residential construction	21.2	....	9.0	....	....	....	30.2	....	....	....	....	....
8 Plant and equipment	4.6	....	82.9	....	....	....	87.5	....	....	....	1.3	....
9 Inventory change	....	....	7.3	....	....	....	7.3	....	....	....	....	....
10 Net financial invest. (11−12)	27.3	....	−25.4	....	−4.9	....	−3.1	....	−6.3	....	2.1	....
11 Financial uses	61.9	....	28.2	....	5.8	....	95.9	....	9.3	....	99.1	....
12 Financial sources	....	34.6	....	53.6	....	10.7	....	98.9	....	15.6	....	96.9
13 Gold & off. fgn. exch.	....	....	....	....	....	....	....	....	20	....	−1.2	....
14 Treasury currency	....	....	....	....	....	....	....	....	....	0.4	0.2	....
15 Demand dep. and currency	10.7	....	1.3	....	1.3	....	13.2	....	−1.7	....	0.8	14.7
16 Private domestic	10.7	....	1.3	....	1.3	....	13.2	....	....	....	0.8	15.9
17 U.S. govt	....	....	....	....	....	....	....	....	−1.7	....	....	−1.3
18 Foreign	....	....	....	....	....	....	....	....	....	....	....	0.1
19 Time and svgs. accounts	27.7	....	2.2	....	3.2	....	33.1	....	....	....	−.2	33.0
20 At coml. banks	15.1	....	2.2	....	3.2	....	20.5	....	0.1	....	0.1	20.6
21 At svgs. instit	12.6	....	....	....	....	....	12.6	....	....	....	−0.2	12.4
22 Life insurance reserves	4.5	....	....	....	....	....	4.5	....	....	*	....	4.6
23 Pension fund reserves	14.8	....	....	....	....	....	14.8	....	....	1.3	....	13.4
24 Interbank items	....	....	....	....	....	....	....	....	....	....	3.2	3.2
25 Credit mkt. insts.	4.8	31.8	9.0	39.1	1.2	10.2	15.1	81.1	5.2	13.4	89.9	15.1
26 Corporate shares	−7.7	....	....	−0.8	....	....	−7.7	−0.8	....	....	9.7	4.7
27 U.S. govt. securities	7.1	....	1.8	....	−0.1	....	8.8	....	.1	13.4	8.2	3.2
28 State and local oblig.	−0.2	....	0.4	....	*	9.9	0.2	9.9	....	....	9.7	....
29 Corp. and foreign bonds	4.0	....	....	12.9	1.1	....	5.1	12.9	....	....	9.7	1.1
30 Home mortgages	.6	14.9	....	0.3	0.2	....	0.8	15.2	0.8	−0.1	13.7	0.2
31 Other mortgages	1.0	1.1	....	11.0	....	....	1.0	12.1	0.3	....	10.8	....
32 Consumer credit	....	11.1	2.4	....	....	....	2.4	11.1	....	....	8.7	....
33 Bank loans n.e.c.	....	3.0	....	10.6	....	....	....	13.7	....	....	15.7	2.3
34 Other loans	....	1.6	4.5	5.1	....	0.3	4.5	7.1	3.9	....	3.7	3.6
35 Security credit	0.7	2.1	....	....	....	....	0.7	2.1	....	....	3.3	2.0
36 To brkrs. and dealers	0.7	....	....	....	....	....	0.7	....	....	....	1.0	2.0
37 To others	....	2.1	....	....	....	....	....	2.1	....	....	2.3	....
38 Taxes payable	....	....	....	3.7	0.1	....	0.1	3.7	3.3	....	....	−0.2
39 Trade credit	....	0.4	14.8	7.0	....	0.5	14.8	7.9	0.6	*	0.3	....
40 Equity in noncorp. business	−3.1	....	....	−3.1	....	....	−3.1	−3.1	....	....	....	....
41 Miscellaneous claims	1.8	0.4	0.9	6.9	....	....	2.6	7.3	−0.3	0.5	2.7	11.1
42 Sector discrepancies (1−4)	3.0	....	7.0	....	−0.7	....	9.3	....	−0.2	....	0.1	....

SOURCE: *Federal Reserve Bulletin*, vol. 55, A-70, November, 1969

	Financial Sectors								Rest of the World		All Sectors		Discrepancy	Natl. Savings and Investment	
	Sponsored Credit Agencies		Monetary Auth.		Coml. Banks		Pvt. Nonbank Finance								
	U	S	U	S	U	S	U	S	U	S	U	S	U		
....	0.1	....	*	....	3.3	....	0.1	....	0.3	....	212.0	....	211.6	1
....	....	....	....	....	0.7	....	0.6	....	....	....	139.7	....	139.7	2
....	0.1	....	*	....	2.7	....	-0.5	....	0.3	....	72.2	....	71.9	3
*	....	*	....	2.4	....	1.0	....	1.2	....	203.6	....	8.4	208.4	4
....	....	....	....	0.6	....	0.7	....	....	....	209.6	....	2.3	209.6	5
....	....	....	....	....	....	....	....	....	....	83.3	....	....	83.3	6
....	....	....	....	....	....	....	....	....	....	30.2	....	....	30.2	7
....	....	....	....	0.6	....	0.7	....	....	....	88.8	....	....	88.8	8
....	....	....	....	....	....	....	....	....	....	7.3	....	....	7.3	9
*	....	*	....	1.8	....	0.3	....	1.2	....	-6.0	....	6.0	-1.2	10
3.2	....	3.8	....	43.2	....	48.8	....	8.3	....	212.6	....	....	7.1	11
....	3.2	....	3.8	....	41.4	....	48.5	....	7.1	....	218.6	....	8.3	12
....	....	-1.2	....	....	....	....	....	1.2	2.1	....	2.1	....	....	13
....	....	0.2	....	....	....	....	....	....	....	0.2	0.4	0.2	....	14
*	....	....	1.4	....	13.3	0.8	....	0.1	....	12.4	14.7	2.3	....	15
*	....	....	2.4	....	13.5	0.8	....	....	....	14.1	15.9	1.9	....	16
....	....	....	-1.1	....	0.2	....	....	....	....	-1.7	-1.3	0.4	....	17
....	....	....	0.1	....	*	....	....	0.1	....	....	0.1	....	....	18
....	....	....	....	....	20.6	-0.2	12.4	*	....	....	33.0	....	....	19
....	....	....	....	....	20.6	.1	....	*	....	....	20.6	....	....	20
....	....	....	....	....	....	-0.2	12.4	....	....	....	12.4	....	....	21
....	....	....	....	....	....	....	4.6	....	....	....	4.5	....	....	22
....	....	....	....	....	....	....	13.4	....	....	....	14.8	....	....	23
....	....	1.0	2.1	2.1	1.0	....	....	....	....	....	3.2	....	....	24
3.2	3.5	3.7	....	38.0	0.2	45.0	11.4	2.3	3.0	112.5	112.5	....	....	25
....	....	....	....	....	-0.1	9.7	4.7	2.0	0.2	....	4.0	....	....	26
-0.1	3.2	3.8	....	2.8	....	1.7	....	-0.5	....	....	16.7	....	....	27
....	....	....	....	8.7	....	1.0	....	....	....	....	9.9	....	....	28
....	....	....	....	0.3	0.3	9.4	0.8	0.3	1.1	....	15.1	....	....	29
1.6	....	....	....	3.5	....	8.6	0.2	....	....	....	15.3	....	....	30
0.5	....	....	....	3.2	....	7.1	....	....	....	....	12.1	....	....	31
....	....	....	....	4.9	....	3.8	....	....	....	....	11.1	....	....	32
....	....	....	....	15.7	....	....	2.3	....	-0.3	....	15.7	....	....	33
1.2	0.2	-0.1	....	-1.1	....	3.7	3.3	0.6	2.0	....	12.7	....	....	34
....	....	....	....	1.3	....	2.0	2.0	0.3	0.2	....	4.4	....	....	35
....	....	....	....	1.0	....	....	2.0	0.3	....	....	2.0	....	....	36
....	....	....	....	0.3	....	2.0	....	....	0.2	....	2.3	....	....	37
....	....	....	....	....	-0.2	....	*	....	....	3.4	3.5	0.1	....	38
....	....	....	....	....	....	0.3	....	0.9	0.7	16.6	8.6	-8.0	....	39
....	....	....	....	....	....	....	....	....	....	....	....	....	....	40
*	-0.1	....	0.2	1.9	6.5	0.8	4.6	3.6	1.1	8.0	20.1	11.4	....	41
....	....	....	....	0.9	....	0.9	....	-0.9	....	-0.9	....	8.4	3.2	42

item is the difference struck between the source of funds entries and the use of funds entries, this means that the whole column is balanced vertically. The second way consistency is enforced is that, across any row, the sum of all uses of funds is equal to the sum of all sources of funds. For example, in row 36, security credit to brokers and dealers, the sum of uses is $2 billion ($0.7 plus $1 plus $0.3), and the sum of the sources is likewise $2 billion. (Row 1, gross saving, and row 5, private capital expenditures, can be seen as the sources and uses entries, respectively, for a single row representing nonfinancial transactions.) This means that there is balance horizontally between payments and receipts.

Thus, the relations among the columns, among the rows, and between columns and rows express the interlocking nature of the accounting system. No one cell of the matrix can be altered without changing at least three others: one in the same sector column (since each use of funds must have a source within the same sector), one in the same row (since each payment is also a receipt), and at least one other for the corresponding column and second row (since a receipt is a source for that column for which there must be a use in another transactions row; the same holds if the reaction is started by a change in a source item).

Conventions Used In Constructing the Accounts

Having in mind the structure of the summary FOF matrix, we can now note some of the problems that arise in its construction and the solutions or conventions adopted. These include differences in definition and allocation between the FOF accounts and the national income and product accounts, sectorization, itemization of transactions, degree of netness and grossness, and float.

Since the FOF accounts were first officially published, progress has been made in harmonizing them conceptually and statistically with the national income and product accounts, especially in conjunction with the 1965 revision of the latter accounts. The link between the two systems was emphasized above, but some differences remain. The major difference lies in the definition of investment, and thus of saving. The FOF accounts move partway toward the definition of investment that was advocated in Chapter 8, i.e., durable goods and new construction purchased by households and governments as well as by business. The FOF accounts include as investment the purchases of durable goods by consumers (see Table 9-4). However, the capital expenditures of government are not included in FOF investment. Thus, with consumer durables treated as capital rather than current outlays, the FOF accounts show a smaller amount of current outlays and a larger amount of saving than the official national income and product estimates. Table 9-2 shows this in a reconciliation of the two sets of accounts for the year 1968.

There is also a difference between the two sets of accounts in the distribution between public and private saving. The FOF accounts treat government life insurance and pension claims by households as assets in the capital account, whereas the OBE accounts treat them as social insurance contributions and transfer payments in the current account. The one other difference stems from the fact that the FOF accounts measure net foreign investment as the residual in the capital account of the balance of payments. The OBE accounts measure net foreign investment as the residual in the current account. The net capital balance and net current balance may differ by the amount of the errors and omissions in the balance-of-payments statement; the

TABLE 9-2
Reconciliation of the National Income and Product Accounts and Flow-of-funds Accounts, 1968
(Billions of Dollars)

	(1) Income and Product	(2) Flow of Funds	(3) Difference (2) − (1)	Source of Difference
A Gross private saving	$135.2	$223.7	$88.5	Lines B and C
B Government surplus	−6.7	−12.1	−5.4	Insurance and pensions, etc.
C GROSS NATIONAL SAVING	$128.5	$211.6	$83.3	Consumer durables
D Gross private domestic investment	$126.3	$209.6	$83.3	Consumer durables
E Net foreign investment	−0.3	−1.2	−0.9	Errors and omissions in balance of payments
F GROSS NATIONAL INVESTMENT	$126.0	$208.4	$82.4	Lines D and E
Statistical discrepancy (C−F)	−2.5	−3.2	−0.9	Line E

SOURCE: *Survey of Current Business*, vol. 49, p. 15, July, 1969, and *Federal Reserve Bulletin*, vol. 55, A-70, November, 1969.
NOTE: Detail may not add to totals because of rounding.

149

amount of the errors and omissions will appear as the difference between the two net foreign investment totals.

Reference to the summary matrix of the FOF accounts shows that the sectoring of the economy is different from that found in the United States production and appropriation accounts. The chief difference is the separation of financial sectors. Sectors are groupings of transactions similar in economic motivation and behavior. Since the FOF accounts have the special purpose of bringing financial activities into explicit relation with one another and linking financial and nonfinancial activities, those transactors whose motivation revolves about liquidity creation and financial intermediation must be separated to make this possible. Table 9-3 shows the sector structure of the FOF accounts. This detailing of the sector structure indicates that in the FOF accounts the sectors are institutional (for example, the business sectors and the household sector) rather than functional (for example, the producing sector and the consuming sector).

A recent survey of statistics on business financial claims conducted for the Wealth Inventory Planning Study suggested that important information for analysis could be obtained by further breakdown of the business sectors by industry.[7] In the nonfinancial business sector, industries (of companies) are not homogeneous in their financing patterns. As illustrations, the aircraft and aircraft parts industries have unique financial relations with the federal government; railroads have distinctive methods of financing acquisitions of tangible assets; utilities have special long-term financing requirements. The study group recommended data collection by broad industry groupings, that is, at the two-digit Standard Industrial Classification (SIC) level or combinations thereof for most nonfinancial industries. For finance (including insurance) a three- or four-digit coding was strongly recommended. The latter would provide an expanded and somewhat altered sector structure from that now available at the most detailed level in the FOF accounts: Finance companies would be sub-sectored into five types, investment companies would be further subdivided, and a personal trusts category established.

Transactions in the FOF accounts are arranged in three major transaction groups: current nonfinancial (which in the summary matrix, Table 9-1, is not detailed but netted into gross saving), capital nonfinancial, and financial. Itemization of the financial transactions, in rows 13 through 41, makes up the bulk of the table. The relevant breakdown of claims should reflect the financial structure of the economy to which it is to be applied. It was recommended that more detailed classifications be made of certain items, primarily to take into account post-World War II shifts in the financial structure.[8] An important recommendation was for greater detail on maturity of the instrument. Among the other suggestions applicable to the FOF accounts, it was recommended that cash be separated from deposits; separate totals be obtained for state and local securities; stocks be further divided into those publicly traded and those for which no public market exists; and subtotals be obtained for bonds, notes, and debentures publicly offered and privately placed.

Several conventions of netting should be noted. First, for each financial trans-

---

[7] Eleanor J. Stockwell, "Nonfarm Business Financial Claims," a report of the Working Group on Nonfarm Business Financial Claims, appendix II-O, *Measuring the Nation's Wealth*, by the Wealth Inventory Planning Study, Joint Committee Print (1964), p. 812.

[8] *Ibid.*, pp. 799, 801–804.

TABLE 9-3
Sector Structure of the Flow-of-funds Accounts

Households

Farm business ⎫
Nonfarm noncorporate business ⎬ Noncorporate business ⎫
Corporate nonfinancial business   ⎬ Nonfinancial business ⎫
State & local governments, general funds   ⎬ Private domestic nonfinancial ⎫
U.S. government   ⎬ Nonfinancial
Rest of world

Monetary authorities ⎫
Commercial banks ⎬ Banking system ⎫
Federally sponsored credit agencies   ⎪
                                                           ⎪
Savings and loan associations ⎫   ⎪
Mutual savings banks ⎬ Savings institutions ⎫   ⎪
Credit unions   ⎪   ⎬ Finance
                                            ⎪   ⎪
Life insurance companies ⎫   ⎬ Nonbank   ⎪
Other insurance companies ⎬ Insurance   ⎪   finance   ⎪
                                            ⎪   ⎪
State & local government retirement funds ⎫ ⎪   ⎪
Private pension funds   ⎪ ⎪   ⎪
Finance companies   ⎪ ⎪   ⎪
Security brokers & dealers   ⎬ Finance   ⎪
Open-end investment companies   ⎪   not elsewhere⎪
Agencies of foreign banks   ⎪   classified   ⎪
Banks in U.S. territories & possessions   ⎭   ⎭

SOURCE: Board of Governors of the Federal Reserve System, *Flow-of-funds Accounts*, 1945-67 (1968), p. I.33, as revised according to Board of Governors of the Federal Reserve System, Division of Research and Statistics. "Flow of Funds, Seasonally Adjusted, 3rd Quarter, Preliminary," Nov. 12, 1969, p. 3 (Mimeographed.)

151

actions category the asset entry represents funds used to acquire assets of that type less funds realized from the disposition of such assets, and the liability entry represents funds raised by borrowing less funds used in repayments. Statistics on a gross, rather than on this net, basis are limited in availability. Presentation of transactions on a gross basis, particularly for some types of securities which would show separately issues and retirement by issuers and purchases and sales by sector, would provide useful information for some purposes. There have been recommendations, including the one by the National Economic Accounts Review Committee, that more information be secured about these gross flows. Second, liabilities of a type are not netted against assets of a type. This means, for example, that the business sector may be shown both using and supplying trade credit or that households may be shown both using and supplying funds for home mortgages. Third, within the general structure of the accounts, a liability incurred to purchase an asset is not netted against that asset. As an illustrative case, the household sector's security credit is not deducted from its security holdings.

In social accounting, empirical estimates are derived from a variety of sources and based on assumptions and conventions. One of the resulting problems is that of float, where records of the two parties to a transaction do not agree, either because the transaction is not recorded by the two parties simultaneously or because different sources of information are used for recording the two sides of the transaction.[9] Flow data relating to transactions in real as well as financial assets may occasion some float because of time consumed in shipping goods and in mailing and processing checks, securities, and other documents. This problem may take two forms: *Duplicating float* occurs when an asset is not debited at the same time that the account acquiring the asset is credited; *vanishing float* occurs when the asset is removed from one account before it is credited to the other. An example of duplicating float is bank float, where checks deposited in the payee's account are not deducted from the payer's account until the check is returned to the latter's bank. An example of vanishing float is some kinds of physical inventories in transit, where the goods are already removed from the seller's books but not yet received and entered by the buyer. In the accounts, it may not be possible to balance both sector and transaction accounts without float items. Although statistically most of these floats cannot be estimated, those which can will appear in the discrepancy column of the summary matrix. One of these appears in the discrepancy of demand deposits and currency, where differences between liabilities recorded in bank records and assets recorded in holder-sector records are mail float. The largest volume of transactions generating float is in trade credit; here also the float is in the discrepancy (along with statistical inconsistencies of the estimates).

Other Flow-of-funds Tables

In addition to the summary matrix of the accounts, most FOF presentations include several sets of supporting tables. A table entitled Saving, Investment, and Financial Flows summarizes in time-series form the national saving and investment

[9] George Garvy, "The Float in Flow-of-funds Accounts," *The Flow-of-funds Approach to Social Accounting: Appraisal, Analysis, and Applications,* Conference on Research in Income and Wealth, Studies in Income and Wealth, vol. XXVI (Princeton, N.J.: Princeton University Press for the National Bureau of Economic Research, 1962), pp. 431-455.

TABLE 9-4

Sector Statement of Sources and Uses of Funds: Households,[a] 1964-1968
(Billions of Dollars)

			1964	1965	1966	1967	1968
1	Personal income		497.5	538.9	587.2	629.4	687.9
2	Less:	Personal taxes & nontaxes	59.4	65.7	75.4	82.7	97.9
3		Personal outlays	411.9	444.8	479.3	506.2	551.6
4	Equals:	Personal saving, NIA basis	26.2	28.4	32.5	40.5	38.4
5	Plus:	Credits from govt. insur.[b]	4.2	4.8	5.3	6.0	5.4
6		Capital gains dividends[c]	0.6	0.9	1.3	1.7	2.5
7		Net durables in consumpt	11.2	14.8	15.2	12.4	16.9
8	Equals:	Net saving	42.1	49.0	54.3	60.7	63.2
9	Plus:	Capital consumption	55.9	59.9	64.3	69.8	76.2
10		On owner-occ. homes	6.8	7.1	7.4	7.8	8.2
11		On nonprofit pl. and eq. ...:......	1.1	1.2	1.3	1.4	1.5
12		On consumer durables	48.0	51.5	55.6	60.6	66.5
13	Equals:	Gross savings	98.0	108.8	118.6	103.5	139.3
14	**Gross investment**		**101.3**	**112.4**	**118.8**	**131.6**	**136.4**
15	Capital expend. (net of sales)		82.2	89.6	94.2	94.4	109.1
16	Residential construction		19.3	19.1	18.9	16.9	21.2
17	Consumer durable goods		59.2	66.3	70.8	73.0	83.3
18	Plant and equip. (nonprofit)		3.7	4.1	4.5	4.5	4.6
19	**Net finan. investment**		**19.0**	**22.8**	**24.6**	**37.2**	**27.3**
20	*Net acquis. of finan. assets*		*47.2*	*53.0*	*48.2*	*60.9*	*61.9*
21	Total deposits and curr		30.2	33.6	22.2	42.6	38.4
22	Demand dep. and curr		63.	7.2	3.1	10.1	10.7
23	Savings accounts		23.9	26.4	19.1	32.5	27.7
24	At commercial banks		8.2	13.3	11.9	15.8	15.1
25	At savings institutions		15.7	13.1	7.2	16.7	12.6
26	Life insurance reserves		4.3	4.8	4.6	4.8	4.5
27	Pension fund reserves		10.9	12.3	13.4	15.3	14.8
28	Credit mkt. instruments		4.0	2.5	10.3	*	4.8
29	U.S. govt. securities		2.2	2.1	5.7	1.4	7.1
30	State and local oblig.		2.0	2.3	2.1	−2.1	−0.2
31	Corporate and fgn. bonds		−0.5	0.8	2.0	4.6	4.0
32	Investment co. shares		1.9	3.1	3.7	2.6	4.7
33	Other corp. shares		−1.9	−5.0	−4.7	−7.4	−12.4
34	Mortgages		.3	−.8	1.4	1.0	1.6
35	Net invest. in noncorp. bus		−3.1	−1.9	−3.5	−4.6	−3.1
36	Security credit		−0.1	0.5	*	1.1	0.7
37	Miscellaneous		.9	1.3	1.2	1.7	1.8

TABLE 9-4 (Continued)

		1964	1965	1966	1967	1968
38	*Net increase in liabilities*	*28.1*	*30.2*	*23.6*	*23.7*	*34.6*
39	Credit mkt. instruments	27.9	28.8	23.2	19.7	31.8
40	Home mortgages	16.0	15.2	12.3	10.5	14.9
41	Other mortgages	1.0	1.2	1.3	1.2	1.1
42	Installment cons. cr	7.2	8.6	6.2	3.4	9.0
43	Other consumer credit	1.3	1.4	1.0	1.2	2.1
44	Bank loans n.e.c.	1.5	1.4	.4	2.1	3.0
45	Other loans^d	.9	.9	2.0	1.3	1.6
46	Security credit	−0.2	0.8	−0.2	3.3	2.1
47	Trade debt	0.3	0.2	0.3	0.4	0.4
48	Miscellaneous	0.2	0.3	0.4	0.3	0.4
49	Discrepancy (13-14)	−3.2	−3.6	−.1	−1.1	3.0

^aIncludes personal trusts and nonprofit organizations.
^bImputed saving associated with growth of government life insurance and retirement reserves.
^cFrom open-end investment companies.
^dPolicy loans, hypothetical deposits and United States govt. loans to nonprofit organizations.
  SOURCE: *Federal Reserve Bulletin,* vol. 55, A-71.3 and A-71-11, November, 1969.

totals and breaks out certain flows that illuminate the extent of the basic credit flow and of intermediation, i.e., borrowing for the purpose of lending rather than to make nonfinancial outlays.

The table, Principal Financial Transactions, in effect treats a row as a single account and, in time-series form, shows significant market data. Items relevant to a given transactions category, and thus not necessarily the same items for each category, are presented. Sector Statements of Sources and Uses of Funds treats each column as a separate account and presents relevant data in time-series form for each. As an example, the statement for the household sector is shown in Table 9-4. More nonfinancial transactions detail is often presented in these statements than in the summary matrix in order to bring out the link between nonfinancial and financial activities. The household sector statement is of particular interest because it involves the treatment of consumer durables as capital rather than as current expenditures, as was mentioned above.

The sector statement for the rest of the world is shown in Table 9-5. It is of special interest because it is statistically consistent with the United States balance-of-payments statement, although the items are arranged to reflect the FOF purposes and uses. For comparison, the balance of payments, prepared by a division of OBE in the Department of Commerce, is shown in Table 9-6. Purchases of goods and services and sales of goods and services in the FOF sector statement are, respectively, exports and imports in the balance of payments. What is in effect the opposite sign attached to the numbers reflects the fact that, although the rest-of-the-world sector

TABLE 9-5

Sector Statement of Sources and Uses of Funds: The Rest of the World, 1964–1968
(Billions of Dollars)

		1964	1965	1966	1967	1968
1	**Net U.S. exports**	**8.5**	**6.9**	**5.3**	**5.2**	**2.5**
2	U.S. exports	37.1	39.2	43.4	46.2	50.6
3	U.S. imports	28.6	32.3	38.1	41.0	48.1
4	Transfer receipts from U.S.	2.8	2.8	2.8	3.0	2.9
5	Current account balance	−5.7	−4.1	−2.4	−2.2	0.3
6	**Net financial investment**	**−4.8**	**−3.7**	**−2.0**	**−1.1**	**1.2**
7	*Net acquis. of financial assets*	3.4	1.9	3.3	7.6	8.3
8	Gold	0.1	1.7	0.6	1.2	1.2
9	U.S. dem. dep. and currency	0.5	0.3	−1.0	0.9	0.1
10	Time deposits	1.4	0.6	0.8	1.4	*
11	U.S. govt. securities	0.5	−0.2	−2.4	2.1	−0.5
12	Other credit market instr.[a]	0.1	−0.1	0.6	0.8	2.8
13	Other financial assets[b]	0.9	−0.3	4.7	1.3	4.8
14	*Net increase in liabilities*	8.2	5.6	5.3	8.7	7.1
15	Official U.S. fgn. exchange[c]	*	0.4	*	1.1	2.1
16	Securities	0.7	0.8	0.5	1.3	1.3
17	Loans[d]	4.3	1.9	1.1	2.8	1.7
18	Other liabilities[e]	3.3	2.5	3.8	3.5	2.1
19	Discrepancy[f]	−0.9	−0.3	−0.4	−1.0	−0.9
	U.S. gold & net fgn. exchg. held by:					
20	Monetary auth	*	−1.3	−0.3	−0.5	−1.2
21	U.S. Treasury	−0.2	0.1	−0.2	0.4	2.0

[a]Corporate securities and acceptances.
[b]Trade credit, direct investment in the United States, bank liabilities to foreign branches, deposits at agencies of foreign banks, security credit, and unallocated items.
[c]Includes net IMF position.
[d]Bank loans, acceptances, and loans from United States government.
[e]Trade debt, direct investment abroad, foreign currencies other than in line 15, subscriptions to international organizations except IMF, and unidentified liabilities.
[f]Errors and omissions in United States balance-of-payments statement.
 SOURCE: *Federal Reserve Bulletin,* vol. 55, A-71.11, November, 1969.

is defined to include the same transactors and transactions in both statements, the FOF data are entered into that statement from the point of view of the rest of the world, whereas in the balance of payments the data are entered as foreign transactions of the domestic sectors.

It is with regard to the financial items that the divergence in categorization between the two statements appears. The FOF categories are the same as those used

TABLE 9-6
United States International Transactions, Balance of Payments,
and Reserve Position, 1964-1968.
(Millions of Dollars)

A. INTERNATIONAL TRANSACTIONS

Line		1964	1965	1966	1967	1968
1	**Exports of goods and services**	**38,611**	**41,027**	**44,362**	**47,093**	**51,432**
2	**Excluding transfers under military grants**	**37,271**	**39,399**	**43,360**	**46,188**	**50,594**
3	Merchandise, adjusted, excluding military[1]	25,478	26,447	29,389	30,681	33,598
4	Transfers under military sales contracts	747	830	829	1,240	1,427
5	Transfers under military grants, net	1,340	1,628	1,002	905	838
6	Transportation	2,317	2,414	2,608	2,775	2,924
7	Travel	1,207	1,380	1,590	1,646	1,770
8	Fees and royalties from direct investments	756	924	1,030	1,136	1,279
9	Other private services	1,114	1,227	1,337	1,502	1,546
10	Other U.S. government services	265	285	326	335	352
	Income on U.S. investments abroad:					
11	Direct investments[2]	3,674	3,963	4,045	4,517	4,985
12	Other private assets	1,256	1,421	1,614	1,717	1,949
13	U.S. government assets	456	509	593	638	765
14	**Imports of goods and services**	**−28,691**	**−32,278**	**−38,081**	**−41,011**	**−48,078**
15	Merchandise, adjusted, excluding military[1]	−18,647	−21,496	−25,463	−26,821	−32,972
16	Military expenditures	−2,880	−2,952	−3,764	−4,378	−4,530
17	Transportation	−2,462	−2,675	−2,922	−2,990	−3,248
18	Travel	−2,211	−2,438	−2,657	−3,195	−3,022
19	Private payments for other services	−500	−439	−491	−579	−625
20	U.S. government payments for other services	−535	−550	−642	−687	−749

Line		1	2	3	4	5
	Income on foreign investments in the United States:					
21	Private payments[2]	−1,003	−1,241	−1,593	−1,764	−2,231
22	U.S. government payments	−453	−488	−549	−598	−702
23	**Balance on goods and services (lines 1 and 14)**	9,920	8,749	6,281	6,082	3,354
24	**Excluding transfers under military grants (lines 2 and 14)**	8,580	7,121	5,279	5,177	2,516
25	**Unilateral transfers, net; transfers to foreigners (−)**	−4,037	−4,386	−3,835	−3,903	−3,703
26	**Excluding military grants**	−2,697	−2,758	−2,833	−2,998	−2,865
27	Private remittances	−530	−581	−556	−755	−753
28	Military grants of goods and services[1]	−1,340	−1,628	−1,002	−905	−838
29	Other U.S. government grants[1]	−1,888	−1,808	−1,910	−1,802	−1,706
30	U.S. government pensions and other transfers	−279	−369	−367	−441	−406
31	**Balance on goods, services, and unilateral transfers (lines 23 and 25, or 24 and 26)[3]**	5,883	4,364	2,446	2,179	−349
32	**Transactions in U.S. private assets, net; increase in assets (−)**	−6,578	−3,794	−4,310	−5,655	−5,157
33	Direct investments[2]	−2,328	−3,468	−3,639	−3,154	−3,025
34	Foreign securities newly issued in the United States	−1,063	−1,206	−1,210	−1,619	−1,659
35	Redemptions	192	222	406	469	495
36	Other transactions in foreign securities	194	225	323	−116	−102
	Claims reported by U.S. banks:[1]					
37	Long term	−941	−232	337	255	358
38	Short term	−1,524	325	−84	−730	−89
	Claims reported by U.S. residents other than banks:[1]					
39	Long term	−485	−88	−112	−281	−174
40	Short term	−623	428	−331	−479	−960
41	**Transactions in U.S. government assets, excluding official reserve assets, net; increase in assets (−)**	−1,676	−1,598	−1,534	−2,421	−2,249

TABLE 9-6 (Continued)

Line		1964	1965	1966	1967	1968
42	Loans and other long-term assets[1]	-2,375	-2,454	-2,501	-3,634	-3,713
43	Foreign currencies and other assets[1]	-19	-16	-265	209	72
	Repayments on credits:					
44	Scheduled	594	651	803	997	1,123
45	Nonscheduled (including sales of foreign obligations to foreigners)	123	221	429	6	269
46	Transactions in U.S. official reserve assets, net; increase in assets (−)	171	1,222	568	52	-880
47	Gold[4]	125	1,665	571	1,170	1,173
48	Convertible currencies	-220	-349	-540	-1,024	-1,183
49	Gold tranche position in IMF[4]	266	-94	537	-94	-870
50	Transactions in foreign assets in the United States, net; increase in foreign assets (U.S. liabilities) (+).	3,318	383	3,320	6,852	9,352
51	Direct investments[2]	-5	57	86	258	319
52	U.S. securities other than Treasury issues	-84	-357	909	1,016	4,360
53	Long-term liabilities reported by U.S. banks	237	203	981	1,052	590
	Other liabilities reported by U.S. private residents other than banks:					
54	Long term	-38	29	180	85	673
55	Short term	113	149	296	499	750
	Nonmarketable liabilities of U.S. government, including medium-term securities payable prior to maturity only under special conditions:[1]					
56	Associated with specific transactions	489	197	129	-19	-138
57	Other medium-term securities	-23	-7	-49	469	2,010

Line		1964	1965	1966	1967	1968
58	U.S. Treasury marketable or convertible bonds and notes[1]	39	46	-1,561	412	-500
59	Deposits and money market paper held in the United States[1]	2,590	67	2,350	3,080	1,287
60	Errors and omissions, net	-1,118	-576	-489	-1,007	-717

B. BALANCE OF PAYMENTS AND RESERVE POSITION

Line		1964	1965	1966	1967	1968
	Balance on liquidity basis — measured by increase in U.S. official reserve assets and decrease in liquid liabilities to all foreigners:					
1	Seasonally adjusted; decrease in net assets (−)	-----	-----	-----	-----	-----
2	*Less* seasonal adjustment	-----	-----	-----	-----	-----
3	Before seasonal adjustment (lines 4 and 8, with sign reversed)	-2,800	-1,335	-1,357	-3,544	93
4	U.S. official reserve assets (part A, line 46); increase (−)	171	1,222	568	52	-880
5	Gold[1]	125	1,665	571	1,170	1,173
6	Convertible currencies	-220	-349	-540	-1,024	-1,183
7	IMF gold tranche position[1]	266	-94	537	-94	-870
8	Liquid liabilities to all foreigners (part A, lines 58 and 59); decrease (−)	2,629	113	789	3,492	787
9	To official agencies	1,075	-18	-1,595	2,020	-3,100
10	To commercial banks[2]	1,454	116	2,697	1,272	3,450
11	To other foreign residents and unallocated[3]	343	306	212	414	374
12	To internal and regional organizations	-243	-291	-525	-214	63
	Balance on official reserve transactions basis — measured by increase in U.S. official reserve assets and decrease in liquid and certain nonliquid liabilities to foreign official agencies:					
13	Seasonally adjusted; decrease in net assets (−)	-----	-----	-----	-----	-----
14	*Less* seasonal adjustment	-----	-----	-----	-----	-----

TABLE 9-6 (Continued)

Line		1964	1965	1966	1967	1968
15	**Before seasonal adjustment** (lines 16 through 18, with sign reversed)	**-1,564**	**-1,289**	**266**	**-3,418**	**1,639**
16	U.S. official reserve assets (line 4); increase (−)	171	1,222	568	52	-880
17	Liquid liabilities to foreign official agencies (line 9); decrease (−)	1,075	-18	-1,595	2,020	-3,100
18	Certain nonliquid liabilities to foreign official agencies; decrease (−)	318	85	761	1,346	2,341
19	Liabilities reported by U.S. private residents (part A, portion of line 53)	149	-38	793	894	535
20	Liabilities reported by U.S. government (part A, portions of lines 56 and 57)	169	123	-32	452	1,806

p: preliminary.
[1] Reflects $259 million payment of gold portion of increased U.S. subscription to the IMF in the second quarter of 1965.
[2] Includes deposits of foreign branches of U.S. banks and of foreign commercial banks, associated with their U.S.-dollar denominated liabilities to foreign official agencies. Includes liabilities payable in foreign currencies to foreigners other than official agencies.
[3] Many include U.S. government bonds and notes held by foreign commercial banks.
SOURCE: *Survey of Current Business*, vol. 49, pp. 26-27, 31, tables 1 and 3, June, 1969.

in the statements for the other sectors. For the balance of payments, the major categories distinguish transactions in foreign-held versus domestically held assets, private versus official, and long-term versus short-term assets, which have greater relevance to analysis of international payments developments and liquidity. The balances indicate how the "regular," or "above-the-line," transactions on current and capital accounts are financed. At present, two balances are shown, providing two evaluations of balance-of-payments performance according to two alternative accounting definitions. The balance on liquidity basis provides a measure of surplus or deficit that includes United States reserve assets and changes in all liquid liabilities to any foreigner, as private individuals or organizations or as official agencies. The official reserve transactions basis counts claims on the United States held by foreign official agencies.

Flow-of-funds presentations also include data on year-end levels of financial assets and liabilities on a basis parallel to the tables on flows, that is, a matrix of assets and liabilities and time-series compilations for individual rows and columns. These tables are thus partial balance sheets; they are partial in that they exclude physical assets and, therefore, exclude any measure of net worth. Except in the case of corporate stocks, which are valued at market prices, the levels of assets and liabilities are at year-end book values.[10] Thus, the annual changes in asset and liability levels are equal to the corresponding flows. Indeed, some of the flows are obtained as the difference between levels at the beginning of the period and at the end of the period. This method, however, is only a substitute for the more informative and accurate method of separately determining the volume of acquisitions and sales.

ALTERNATIVE PRESENTATIONS OF FINANCING ACCOUNTS

A survey of presentations of financing accounts alternative to the American flow-of-funds accounts shows that financing accounts have been developed by relatively few other countries.[11] Flow-of-funds-type data continue to be published in Japan. Canada's efforts, published in 1959, have now been followed up. In the mid-1960s the National Bank of Yugoslavia developed a set of flow-of-funds accounts to be used in the process of monetary planning for that country.[12] Six countries provide measures of total lending and borrowing that are essentially flow of funds. Also, eight countries carry their estimates to the point of providing sector surpluses or deficits.

The Canadian National Transactions Accounts are sketched out in this section to illustrate an alternative form of financing accounts. Furthermore, the document describing the revision of the SNA states that the purpose of that system is to provide guidance for the development of statistics in individual countries and a basis

[10] By valuation at book values, except on corporate stock, revaluation of the instrument due to price change is not encountered in these partial balance sheets. Revaluation is treated in Chap. 10.

[11] A survey of financial accounting, in a broad sense, in various countries is found in Graeme S. Dorrance, "Financial Accounting: Its Present State and Prospects," *International Monetary Fund Staff Papers*, vol. 13, pp. 198–228, July, 1966.

[12] See the interesting article by Dimitrije Dimitrijevic, "The Use of Flow-of-funds Accounts in Monetary Planning in Yugoslavia," *The Review of Income and Wealth*, ser. XV, pp. 101–115, March, 1969.

for country reporting. Thus it is appropriate to survey the form of financing accounts in that system as a probable line of development for the future financing accounts in individual countries.

The Canadian National Transactions Accounts

An explicit initial decision made financing accounts in Canada consonant with the national income and expenditure accounts prepared by the Dominion Bureau of Statistics.[13] Thus they are an example of how financing accounts fit into at least the flow portion of an integrated system of economic accounts. In 1955 a study of the feasibility of constructing flow-of-funds accounts was undertaken by the Bank of Canada. Subsequently an interest developed in the possibility of constructing the transactions (nonfinancial and financial) accounts as a basis for the study of financial aspects of economic growth. The result was the cooperative responsibility for the estimates that appeared in *Financing Economic Activity in Canada.*[14]

Conceptually, the transactions accounts embrace all transactions in the economy. There are three main accounts in the matrix. (1) A current transactions account enters current income (by type of service rendered) and current outlays, balanced by gross saving. Gross saving is carried to the (2) investment transactions account, which shows investment in fixed capital and inventories. The balancing entry is saving minus investment; it is carried to the (3) financial transactions account. Saving minus investment is recognized as the measure of resources each sector is making available to or obtaining from other sectors, comparable to net financial investment in the American FOF accounts. The object of the financial transactions account is to demonstrate the actual financial channels through which the intersector exchanges take place.

A condensed version of the financial transactions account appears as Table 9-7. The year shown is 1954. The eleven sectors, arranged vertically, are the same in the financial transactions account as in the other accounts. For each sector there is a row for credit entries and a row for debit entries. Credits, or sources of funds, represent changes in liabilities; debits, or uses of funds, represent changes in assets. Since both gains and losses of an asset item are posted as debits, a gain is posted with a plus sign and a loss with a minus sign. Transactions of the various types are arranged horizontally. The total debits must balance total credits of a sector when other transactions and errors (a residual summed into a single column) are included; this is demonstrated in the last column of the table. The last row in the table shows that, for each transactions category, the change in that item as an asset must equal the change in that item as a liability.

---

[13] This discussion relies on S. J. Handfield-Jones, "The Canadian National Transactions Accounts," *The Flow-of-funds Approach to Social Accounting: Appraisal, Analysis, and Applications, op. cit.,* pp. 103–132. Also see L. M. Read, "The Development of National Transactions Accounts: Canada's Version of or Substitute for Money Flows Accounts," *Canadian Journal of Economics and Political Science,* vol. 23, pp. 42–56, February, 1957.

[14] L. M. Read, S. J. Handfield-Jones, and F. W. Emerson, "A Presentation of National Transactions Accounts for Canada, 1946–54," in W. C. Hood, *Financing Economic Activity in Canada* (Ottawa: Royal Commission on Canada's Economic Prospects, 1959). See reference at end of chapter to recently developed official series.

Financing Accounts in the Revised SNA

The United Nations document describing the original SNA states: "No further classification of these [lending and borrowing] flows is undertaken in the system since, to produce meaningful results this would require a greater number of sectors including, in particular, a separate sector for banks and other financial intermediaries. These are now consolidated with other corporations . . . and the present flows of lending and borrowing have therefore relatively little analytical significance."[15] A major purpose of the revision was to develop the required sector elaboration and other modifications necessary to bring financial flows (as well as flows of goods and services and of stocks) into the system. Development of a system that encompasses financing accounts has not been an easy task. To an even greater extent than for standardized national income or balance-of-payments accounts, a minimum financial accounting system must describe underlying phenomena that differ markedly from country to country.[16] Even after a system for international use is formulated, it may be some time before countries have the necessary data to fill in all the detail.

The revised *SNA* includes consolidated accounts designed to summarize the transactions which take place in the economy.[17] Of these consolidated accounts, capital finance is the principal concern of this chapter. In two separate panels it shows (1) gross accumulation equal to finance of gross accumulation and (2) net acquisition of financial assets equal to net incurrence of liabilities plus net lending to the rest of the world. The three entries in the second panel are the three aggregates mentioned in the equality; there is no detail.

Paramount interest centers on the deconsolidation by sector of this consolidated capital finance account. The SNA provides separate accounts for the following institutional sectors: nonfinancial enterprises, corporate and quasi-corporate; financial institutions; general government; private nonprofit institutions serving households; and households, including private unincorporated nonfinancial enterprises (see Appendix B, Tables B-III.A.5, B-III.B.5, B-III.C.5, B-III.D.5, and B-III.E.5). Parallel to the consolidated account, the sector accounts have two panels. The lower panel, detailing the items of net acquisition of financial assets as equal to net incurrence of liabilities plus net lending, is recognizable as what we have called financing accounts. These sector accounts differ in the detail shown in the case of financial items. The capital finance account (as well as the income and outlay account) can also be contrasted with the sector statement for households drawn from the United States FOF accounts, which was shown in Table 9-4.

A standard table (table 24 of the UN report) supports the lower panels of the sector capital finance accounts. It exhibits financial transactions of subsectors and detail by type of transaction. It can be viewed as summarizing the financial transactions in the same sense that the basic sector-by-transactions matrix in the United States FOF accounts summarizes. Financial transactions are classified by type of instrument, degree of liquidity, the circumstances in which the transaction took place, and for some categories of asset, by institutional sector of debtor. As executed, these

[15] United Nations, Department of Economic and Social Affairs, Statistical Office, *A System of National Accounts and Supporting Tables*, Studies in Methods, ser. F, no. 2, rev. 2 (New York: 1964) p. 37.

[16] Graeme S. Dorrance, *op. cit.*, pp. 203–204.

[17] UN, *SNA*, 1968, especially pp. 132–134, 152–153, 159–163, 199–200.

TABLE 9-7

The Financial Transactions Account of the Canadian National
Transactions Accounts, 1954
(Millions of Dollars)

		Savings Minus Investment	Currency & Deposits	Charge & Installment Credit	Loans	Claims on Associated Enterprises
Consumers	D		921.0			85.2
	C	809.0		37.0	97.9	
Unincorporated business	D			21.4		
	C	-828.0		-19.6	36.8	85.2
Nonfinancial corporations	D		181.8	40.8		355.7
	C	68.2			42.2	656.4
Government enterprises	D		-2.3		0.6	7.3
	C	-383.0			32.1	-70.9
Banking	D		-20.7		60.3	66.8
	C	14.2	487.5			119.4
Life insurance	D		-7.4		15.4	-31.2
	C	-8.2			-1.2	
Other finance	D		38.4	-44.8	71.6	-0.2
	C	31.8	304.7		-51.7	97.9
Government: Federal	D		-265.4		-52.4	-67.1
	C	-100.0	2.4			
Government: Provincial	D		24.2		38.5	136.3
	C	155.0			-6.9	
Government: Municipal	D		14.7		-3.0	58.1
	C	-186.0			36.9	2.2
Rest of world	D		65.9			392.0
	C	427.0	155.6		-55.1	112.8
TOTAL	D		950.2	17.4	131.0	1,003.0
	C		950.2	17.4	131.0	1,003.0

SOURCE: S.J. Handfield-Jones, "The Canadian National Transactions Accounts," in Conference
Analysis, and Applications, Studies in Income and Wealth, vol. XXVI (Princeton, N.J.: Princeton
rections made).

Mort-gages	Bonds	Stocks	Insur-ance & Pensions	Foreign Inheri-tances & Migrants' Funds	Other Trans-actions & Errors	Total
436.4	-213.1		416.2	94.0	9.3	1,748.0
				89.0	715.1	1,748.0
						21.4
747.0						21.4
8.2	131.0				659.3	1,376.8
186.0	400.3	99.2			- 75.5	1,376.8
-0.1	62.5				40.8	108.8
-0.6	565.5		0.2		-34.5	108.8
74.0	508.2				5.4	694.1
		42.5			30.5	694.1
236.9	66.3	12.5			27.4	319.9
			326.8		2.5	319.9
166.3	201.3	55.5			-10.5	477.6
	-13.8	47.5	27.1		34.1	477.6
4.5	-119.9				-49.3	-549.6
	-573.2		62.1		59.1	-549.6
6.2	31.3				15.8	252.3
	75.9				28.3	252.3
	14.3				39.0	123.1
	262.3				7.7	123.1
	70.2	140.2		89.0		757.3
	56.5	-3.4		94.0	-30.1	757.3
932.4	773.5	185.8	416.2	183.0	737.2	5,329.7
932.4	773.5	185.8	416.2	183.0	737.2	5,329.7

on Research in Income and Wealth, *The Flow-of-funds Approach to Social Accounting: Appraisal*, University Press for the National Bureau of Economic Research, 1962), pp. 111–114 (with cor-

criteria have produced some detail by liquidity (such as bonds, long- and short-term; and loans, n.e.c., long- and short-term), separation of corporation stock into that quoted on stock exchanges and that not, and separation of currency and deposits into foreign currency and national currency. Several of these breakouts were among those recommended for improving the United States FOF accounts. On the other hand, the present FOF accounts show greater detail in breaking out mortgages (subdivided into mortgages for one- to four-family houses and other mortgages), consumer credit, other loans (subdivided into open-market paper and federal loans), and security credit (subdivided into credit to brokers and dealers and credit to others). Thus in some cases the FOF accounts provide more information on the specific type of instrument, perhaps reflecting the greater degrees of specialization of United States financial institutions in these cases and the special interest of the Federal Reserve Board in financial detail.

The sectoring also provides some interesting contrasts to the FOF accounts. In the SNA, households are subdivided by socioeconomic character into proprietors, employees, and others; there is no subdivision in the FOF accounts. Further, the SNA separates private nonprofit institutions serving households, which in the FOF accounts are included in the household sector. In the SNA, both financial institutions (and subdivisions thereof) and nonfinancial enterprises are provided with "publicly owned and/or controlled" versus "privately owned and/or controlled" breakdowns, reflecting the need to provide classifications relevant to various economic systems when drawing up standard systems for international use.

REVIEW QUESTIONS

1 The FOF accounts can be viewed as a direct extension of the income and product structure into the financial markets. Explain what is meant by this statement.
2 Sketch out the structure of the FOF summary sector-by-transaction matrix. How does the matrix enforce consistency of analysis?
3 What are the major differences remaining between the OBE income and product accounts and the FOF accounts?
4 Explain the problem of float in the FOF accounts.
5 Outline the major features of financing accounts in either the Canadian National Transactions Accounts or the SNA. Stress the interrelations of the financing accounts with the other accounts, showing the structure of these integrated systems.

SELECTED REFERENCES

BOARD OF GOVERNORS OF THE FEDERAL RESERVE SYSTEM: *Flow of Funds Accounts, 1945–1968* (1970).
   An explanation of the accounts at their present stage, with historical data.
CONFERENCE ON RESEARCH IN INCOME AND WEALTH: *The Flow-of-funds Approach to Social Accounting: Appraisal, Analysis, and Applications,* Studies in Income and Wealth, vol. XXVI (Princeton, N.J.: Princeton University Press for the National Bureau of Economic Research, 1962).
   Thirteen papers presented in 1959, an introduction, and comments.
UNITED NATIONS, DEPARTMENT OF ECONOMIC AND SOCIAL AFFAIRS, STATISTICAL OFFICE: *A System of National Accounts,* Studies in Methods, ser. F, no. 2, rev. 3 (New York: 1968).
DOMINION BUREAU OF STATISTICS: *Financial Flow Accounts, 1962–1967* (Ottawa: 1969).

Balance Sheets and Wealth Statements

10

By analogy with business accounting, the chief branch of economic accounts remaining to be discussed is the balance sheet. In contrast to the accounts discussed thus far—production, income and outlay, and capital accounts—all of which relate to *flows* of output, income, and finance *during* successive periods, balance sheets relate to *stocks* or levels of assets, liabilities, and net worth at the *ends* of successive periods. Balance sheets show the condition of individual sectors, or the economy as a whole, at a point in time, and changing conditions over time.

The economic condition of the sector or the economy, reflected in balance sheet items, changes as a result of saving and investing, borrowing and lending. Balance sheets are thus directly related to capital accounts and indirectly to production and appropriation accounts. That is, that portion of net output which is not consumed is added to stock (invested), and it is financed by the saving of all sectors (income less current outlays for consumption, transfers, and taxes). But since the saving and tangible investment of each economic unit, and each sector, do not necessarily match, surplus units and sectors lend to others either directly or through financial intermediaries, giving rise to changes in financial claims. Thus, the real and financial investments of the capital accounts result in changes in assets on the balance sheet, and borrowing and saving result in changes in liabilities and net worth. For the economy as a whole, since changes in financial assets and liabilities are offsetting, the change in net worth results from saving and is equal to the change in domestic tangible assets plus net foreign assets resulting from investment. We shall discuss these relationships, and the valuation assumptions involved, in greater detail below.

Although statistically less developed, balance sheet estimates are an important adjunct to the flow estimates for the purposes of economic analysis. Indeed, some economists would claim coordinate importance for the stock estimates. In the first place, sector decision making is influenced by balance sheet structure and by the proportion between the various magnitudes of balance sheet items and coordinate flows in relation to desired stock-flow relationships.[1] For example, consumer spending is influenced by asset holdings, both liquid and total. Business orders are affected by the sales-inventory ratio (actual in relation to "normal"); and a firm's capital outlays are affected by the relation of production to the output capacity of the fixed assets, as well as by its financial condition. For these, and other types of demand analysis, balance sheet data consistent with the related flow data are finding an increasing clientele of economists.

Also for supply, or production, analysis, it is obvious that estimates of real tangible assets or "capital" are necessary, along with estimates of labor used in the production process. This is true whether the factor stocks and/or inputs are used as variables in statistical "production function" analysis or as components of the productivity ratios discussed in Chapter 6.

Indeed, if the concept of capital or "wealth" is broadened to include not only tangible nonhuman assets (land, structures, equipment, and inventories) but also human capital, including the real investments designed to enhance the quality or "efficiency" of the factors, then economic growth can be largely explained by the trends in "total capital." But in this chapter, we hew to the more conventional definition of capital and real wealth as relating to tangible nonhuman instruments of production, although the asset side of the balance sheet (and thus net worth) could be expanded to include human capital and the intangible capital embodied in both human and nonhuman agents of production.

Despite the importance of balance sheets and wealth estimates for economic analysis, the development of this aspect of the economic accounts has lagged badly. Indeed, since the beginning of the era of official national income estimation on a regular basis in 1925, no country has prepared balance sheets as a routine part of its national economic accounts. Progress in this field has largely been due to the work of individual investigators, such as Raymond Goldsmith in the United States.

Since the beginning of work on national income in the seventeenth century, many individual economic statisticians have been as interested in wealth as in income. Indeed, the mercantilists and many of the early economists from Smith to Mill (and Marx) defined income and product in terms of *material* (commodity) output, since this was the only type of production, as they saw it, which could add to wealth; all services were presumably consumed in the instant of production. Just as the early economists failed to recognize that all utility-producing activity should be included in national income, they also failed to recognized that certain intangible investment

[1] One of the early systematic expressions of the importance of balance sheet items in economic behavior was Lawrence R. Klein, "Assets, Debt, and Economic Behavior," Studies in Income and Wealth, vol. XIV (New York: National Bureau of Economic Research, 1951).

may also increase wealth, defined as income-producing capacity. But they did recognize the key role of wealth in economic growth.

Neglect of balance sheets and wealth statements by government statistical offices may be attributable in part to the feeling that they are more difficult to estimate within reasonable margins of error than are the flow estimates. It is true that there are problems peculiar to the stock estimates, particularly as regards market valuations of fixed assets, which will be further discussed below. But it is not clear that they are more difficult, on balance, than the problems associated with the income, appropriation, and capital accounts—especially when it is remembered that estimation of capital consumption allowances as a flow variable involves the same problems that attach to estimating stocks of fixed capital.

It has also been suggested that the strong influence of J. M. Keynes on the theoretical formulations of national income accounts during the first generation of burgeoning official estimates promoted the development of flow estimates with little stress on stocks as an influence on demand. But after World War II, as noted above, increasing importance was placed on asset holdings as a demand variable, and there was renewed interest in production function analysis. Indeed, with the notable success of high-employment policies in advanced countries, theoretical attention shifted relative emphasis to growth and development analysis, in which the secular increase of capital stock is a centerpiece.

With this shift of emphasis, there have been signs of progress in the direction of expanding economic accounts to include balance sheets. The revised *SNA* was designed with national and sector balance sheets as an integral part of that accounting system. Their relationship to the flow accounts and their structure and concept were described in the 1968 UN report (see Chapter 14). However, the report does not provide full definitions and classifications or standard accounts and tables; it notes that further discussion of these matters is expected in the next year or two. In various countries continued efforts are being made by individual scholars to refine concepts and accounting structure, assemble data, and prepare occasional estimates.

In the U.S.S.R., a comprehensive inventory of fixed assets was compiled, beginning in 1959. Japan conducted a sample survey of wealth in 1955. As noted in the previous chapter, the Federal Reserve Board prepares partial sector and national balance sheets, confined to levels of financial assets and liabilities. The OBE has prepared fixed capital stock estimates for the business and household sectors. With expansion of the work to include government and natural resources (OBE already has estimates of net foreign assets and unpublished business inventory stock estimates), complete balance sheets will be possible on a regular basis, joining the work of the FRB and OBE. Indeed, the present writer has prepared such balance sheets for selected years, and these estimates together with Goldsmith's will be drawn on below to illustrate the principles of balance sheet construction. But it must not be forgotten that in order to increase the reliability of the estimates, we must expand the bench-mark wealth data considerably. This should be done along the lines set forth in the report of the United States Wealth Inventory Planning Study, *Measuring the Nation's Wealth*, summarized at the end of this chapter.[2] Parallel efforts in other

---

[2] *Measuring the Nation's Wealth*, by the Wealth Inventory Planning Study, Joint Committee Print (1964). Hereinafter called the Wealth Study.

countries will be necessary as a basis for comparative studies of the structure and growth of assets among nations and their relation to income composition and growth.

THE STRUCTURE OF SECTOR AND NATIONAL BALANCE SHEETS

The basic structure of sector and combined national balance sheets can be illustrated by reference to Table 10-1, which reproduces Raymond Goldsmith's estimates for the United States at the end of 1958.

Sectors

With regard to sectoring, Goldsmith's work is similar to that of the FRB. It differs from OBE work in that a separate financial sector is distinguished. This is essential if financial flows and sector holdings of assets and liabilities are to be shown. When an integrated, comprehensive economic accounting system is developed for the United States, it is obvious that OBE will have to make provision for a finance sector and that a consistent sectoring will have to be adopted for all accounts, including balance sheets.

Goldsmith limits his household sector to nonfarm units and private nonprofit institutions; farm households are shown in combination with farm business in a separate agriculture sector. While this procedure is easier in consideration of statistical availabilities, it would be preferable to include farm households as a subsector in a combined household sector such as that presented by OBE and FRB. The Wealth Study also recommended that nonprofit institutions and personal trusts be segregated, the former as a separate sector and the latter as a financial subsector. Periodic sectoring by income or asset size class would also be informative.

Goldsmith splits the nonfinancial business sector into corporate and noncorporate (nonfarm) sectors, whereas the FRB presents in its published tables a unified business sector. Probably the split by legal form of organization, while statistically expedient, is less significant than a subsectoring by broad industry groups, which was recommended by the Wealth Study, as noted in Chapter 2. The industries would comprise companies, and thus could be grouped according to the recently developed Standard Enterprise Classification. Examination of the balance sheet patterns of the various industries would probably suggest certain consolidations to avoid excessive detail. Periodic subsectoring by company asset size class was also recommended by the Wealth Study in order to throw light on financial problems of small business and to indicate differing patterns of concentration by industry.

As shown in Table 9-1, the FRB breaks the financial sector into monetary authorities, commercial banks, and nonbank finance. In its more detailed tables, the FRB breaks nonbank finance into further divisions: savings institutions, consisting of mutual savings banks, savings and loan associations, and credit unions; insurance, consisting of life insurance companies, noninsured pension plans, and other insurance companies; and finance, n.e.c., consisting of finance companies, security brokers and dealers, open-end investment companies, agencies of foreign banks, banks in United States possessions, and other. The Wealth Study recommended that for the FRB and others specializing in financial analysis, somewhat finer industrial detail could be useful. For example, finance companies could be subdivided into consumer finance, sales finance, mortgage companies, commercial finance, and miscellaneous. As is done by Goldsmith, "other investment companies" could be shown in addition to the open-end variety. Goldsmith also included government pension and insurance funds in the finance sector; FRB keeps these in the government sector, a procedure preferred by the Wealth Study group.

The treatment of governments is fairly clear-cut. Eventually, data will permit the breakdown of the state and local governments sector into its two major components. The separate treatment of monetary authorities by the FRB permits their recombination with federal government if desired. And a subsector for other government financial operations would permit their treatment in conjunction with the finance sector, if desired by analysts.

The Wealth Study advocated that government enterprise subsectors be set up, but that statistical agencies first should reconsider and sharpen the boundaries between general government and government enterprises, with particular respect to different decision-making criteria. It would also be possible to allocate government enterprises to the appropriate industry groupings of the business sector (which could be renamed "enterprises sector"); but Goldsmith has pointed out that this treatment "would run counter to the principle that assets and liabilities under the control of one decision-making unit should be kept together."[3]

Item Classifications

Another glance at Table 10-1 indicates the four main classes of balance sheet items. In sections I and II, assets are divided into the two major classes, tangible and intangible. We prefer to call the latter group "financial assets," reserving the term "intangible" for the income-producing capacity created by intangible investments, such as education and training, research and development, health, and mobility outlays. Indeed, under broader concepts, as implied earlier, the intangible capital created by these investments could be included on the asset side of the balance sheet, with a corresponding increase in net worth—since the minor amount of borrowing to finance intangible investment is already included under liabilities.

In sections III and IV of the balance sheet are the liabilities and the equities, or the ownership category. The liabilities are, of course, financial items corresponding to financial assets other than corporate stock and other shares in equity. Although Goldsmith does not do so, one could show the stock and other shares in domestic firms under equities, together with a final net worth category. Net worth equals total assets less liabilities and shares.

The amount of detail shown under the major categories can be either collapsed or expanded further. Under tangible assets, there are basically four major types: land and other natural resources, structures, durable equipment, and inventories. The depreciable categories of structures and equipment could be broken down into the approximately thirty types of structures, twenty-two types of producers durable equipment, and twelve types of consumer durable goods shown by OBE.[4] We know that inventories can be broken down by stage—materials, in-process, and finished—as well as by sector and industry. Land can be divided according to use—agricultural, forest, grazing, site, mineral, vacant, and so on.

[3] Raymond W. Goldsmith and Robert E. Lipsey, *Studies in the National Balance Sheet of the United States* (Princeton, N.J.: Princeton University Press for the National Bureau of Economic Research, 1963), vol. I, p. 33.

[4] See tables 5.2, 5.4, and 2.6 in *Survey of Current Business,* vol. 49, pp. 37, 38, 29, July, 1969.

TABLE 10-1
National Balance Sheet, 1958
(Billions of Dollars)

172

	Nonfarm House-holds	Nonfarm Unincor-porated Business	Agri-culture	Non-financial Corpora-tions	Finance	State and Local Govern-ments	Federal Govern-ment	Total
I. Tangible assets:								
1. Residential structures	346.81	16.26	19.28	21.31	0.64	6.03	1.01	411.34
2. Nonresidential structures	26.26	25.56	16.75	180.83	4.78	133.20	35.00	422.38
3. Land	92.16	22.74	87.58	63.46	4.04	28.00	12.80	310.78
4. Producer durables	2.07	26.94	18.59	145.53	0.85	5.25	0.61	199.84
5. Consumer durables	164.73	----	14.02	----	----	----	----	178.75
6. Inventories	----	16.81	26.15	78.81	0.03	0.20	7.89	129.89
7. Total	632.03	108.31	182.37	489.94	10.34	172.68	57.31	1,652,98
II. Intangible assets:								
1. Currency and demand deposits	61.36	13.46	6.20	33.34	92.59	10.78	41.9	221.92
(a) Monetary metals	1.62	0.27	.25	0.21	23.06	----	----	25.41
(b) Other	59.74	13.19	5.95	33.13	69.53	10.78	4.19	196.51
2. Other bank deposits and shares	140.56	----	3.07	1.60	1.08	3.58	0.33	150.22
3. Life insurance reserves, private	99.70	----	6.71	----	----	----	----	106.41
4. Pension and retirement funds, private	27.80	----	----	----	----	----	----	27.80
5. Pension and insurance funds, government	65.67	----	.43	----	----	----	----	66.10
6. Consumer credit	----	4.70	----	8.21	33.19	----	----	46.10
7. Trade credit	----	11.64	----	83.37	3.64	1.70	----	100.35
8. Loans on securities	----	----	----	----	9.23	----	----	9.23
9. Bank loans, n.e.c.	----	----	----	----	53.80	----	----	53.80
10. Other loans	3.10	----	----	----	9.42	----	19.05	31.57
11. Mortgages, nonfarm	22.72	----	----	131.22	----	1.61	5.10	160.65
(a) Residential	12.79	----	----	113.52	----	1.61	5.10	133.02
(b) Nonresidential	9.93	----	----	17.70	----	----	----	27.63
12. Mortgages, farm	4.54	----	----	----	4.26	----	2.46	11.26

	(1)	(2)	(3)	(4)	(5)	(6)	(7)	
13. Securities, U.S. government	58.57	—	5.21	17.62	176.01	11.08	5.82	274.31
(a) Short term	3.16	—	—	15.20	41.63	6.00	—	65.99
(b) Savings bonds	43.02	—	5.21	1.22	2.43	—	—	51.88
(c) Other long term	12.39	—	—	1.20	131.95	5.08	5.82	156.44
14. Securities, state and local	24.79	—	—	1.63	31.23	2.44	0.97	61.06
15. Securities, other bonds and notes	11.12	—	—	2.68	74.30	0.67	—	88.77
16. Securities, preferred stock	10.37	—	—	3.55	4.36	—	—	18.28
17. Securities, common stock	332.62	—	—	75.45	39.10	—	—	447.17
18. Equity in mutual financial organizations	8.04	—	—	—	—	—	—	8.04
19. Equity in other business	98.24	—	—	—	—	—	0.42	98.66
20. Other intangible assets	0.62	—	3.81	48.14	29.78	—	18.28	100.63
21. Total	969.82	29.80	25.43	275.59	693.21	30.16	58.32	2,082.33
III. Liabilities:								
1. Currency and demand deposits	—	—	—	—	223.18	—	2.60	225.78
2. Other bank deposits and shares	—	—	—	—	151.62	—	1.22	152.84
3. Life insurance reserves, private	—	—	—	—	108.51	—	—	108.51
4. Pension and retirement funds, private	—	—	—	—	27.80	—	—	27.80
5. Pension and insurance funds, government	—	—	—	—	66.10	—	—	66.10
6. Consumer debt	44.77	—	1.33	—	—	—	—	46.10
7. Trade debt	1.83	9.00	2.30	68.78	0.21	2.00	2.83	86.95
8. Loans on securities	6.20	—	—	—	3.42	—	—	9.62
9. Bank loans, n.e.c.	2.12	12.45	4.16	25.94	5.69	—	0.81	51.17
10. Other loans	4.37	5.42	1.87	2.18	5.55	—	—	19.39
11. Mortgages	117.05	13.94	11.25	29.67	—	—	—	171.91
12. Bonds and notes	—	—	—	69.68	9.09	61.16	288.49	428.42
13. Other liabilities	—	—	—	60.84	31.20	—	1.80	93.84
14. Total	176.34	40.81	20.91	257.09	632.37	63.16	297.75	1,488.43
IV. Equities	1,425.51	97.30	186.89	508.44	71.18	139.68	182.12	2,246.88
V. Total assets or liabilities and equities	1,601.85	138.11	207.80	765.53	703.55	202.84	115.63	3,735.31

SOURCE: Raymond W. Goldsmith, Robert E. Lipsey, and Morris Mendelson, *Studies in the National Balance Sheet of the United States* (Princeton, N.J.: Princeton University Press for the National Bureau of Economic Research, 1963), vol. II, pp. 68–69, table 1.

TABLE 10-2

Financial Interrelations Ratios, United Kingdom and United States,
Selected Years, 1900–1958

United Kingdom		United States	
Year	Ratio	Year	Ratio
1900	1.90	1900	0.77
1910	2.17	1912	0.86
1920	1.07	1922	1.00
1927	2.20	1929	1.30
1937	2.58	1939	1.30
1948	1.98	1948	1.21
1958	1.64	1958	1.26

SOURCES: United Kingdom: Jack Revell, *The Wealth of the Nation: The National Balance Sheet of the United Kingdom,* 1957-1961 (New York: Cambridge University Press, 1967), pp. 72, 81, table 3.11. United States: Raymond W. Goldsmith and Robert E. Lipsey, *Studies in the National Balance Sheet of the United States* (Princeton, N.J.: Princeton University Press for the National Bureau of Economic Research, 1963), vol. I, p. 80, table 16.

The financial assets consist basically of money, time and savings accounts, insurance and pension fund reserves, credit market instruments, security and trade credit, accruals, and others. These groupings are broken down further in the tables of Goldsmith and the FRB (see Tables 9-1 and 10-1). The Wealth Study recommends additional detail with regard to length of maturities, types of accruals, sources of credit (to the extent not revealed by the sectoring), and so on; the full range of suggested items is listed in dummy stubs prepared for the Wealth Study.[5]

Liabilities follow the same classifications as the financial assets, since they are opposite sides of the same coins—with the exception of corporate stock and other shares, which are placed under equities. Net worth, as a residual item, is not broken down further.

How much detail should be shown in summary tables remains a moot question. The most significant classifications must be presented if the tables are to have useful texture. But frequently, additional detail with respect to both subsectors and item subclasses can be shown in supporting tables and related to the summary interlocking accounts, which reveal the interrelationships of the myriad details when consolidated into a manageable number of categories.

[5] See Wealth Study, *op. cit.,* appendix II-O, exhibits A-G, pp. 817-825.

TABLE 10-3
The Composition of National Wealth, by Type
(Percentages of Total)

	1929	1948	1958	1966p
Structures	43.2	48.4	49.0	49.6
Residential	21.8	25.2	24.2	24.5
Business	14.8	12.4	13.4	12.9
Public and other	6.6	10.7	11.4	12.2
Other reproducibles	28.1	30.9	31.4	31.5
Producer durables	8.7	9.4	11.7	11.6
Consumer durables	9.6	9.2	10.5	11.8
Business inventories	8.7	9.3	7.6	7.4
Monetary metals	1.1	3.0	1.5	0.7
Nonreproducible assets	25.8	19.3	18.3	16.8
Agricultural land	8.7	6.4	5.9	5.9
Business land	5.2	4.2	4.0	3.9
Residential land	8.2	5.0	5.5	4.6
Public land & other	3.8	3.7	2.8	2.4
Net foreign assets	2,8	1.4	1.4	2.0
Total wealth	100.0	100.0	100.0	100.0

p:preliminary. Reproduced from *Finance Magazine,* January, 1967, p. 13.

Structural Relationships

It will be helpful in understanding sector and national balance sheets to look at some of the structural relationships. On the asset side, Goldsmith lays stress on the "financial interrelations ratio," which is the ratio of financial assets to tangible assets. It indicates the magnitude of, and trends in, the financial superstructure of the economy in relation to its real wealth. Table 10-2 shows the financial interrelations ratio for selected points of time in the United States, as estimated by Goldsmith, compared with the like ratio for the United Kingdom, prepared by Jack Revell.

Within the two major classes of tangible and financial assets, it is of interest to examine the structural changes. Table 10-3 shows percentage distributions for selected years. Within the tangibles, the decline in the relative importance of land has been offset by a rising relative proportion of structures, so that real estate values have held their own in the total. Both producer and consumer durables have grown relatively, while inventories have fallen.

The relative trends in financial assets can be read from the table. The historical estimates provide a necessary basis for projections into the future, which are of value in forecasting levels of activity in certain sectors of the economy—particularly in the finance, insurance, and real estate industries.

On the credit side of the balance sheet, the levels and changes in proportions of the total represented by liabilities and by equities would be of interest. Changes in the relative importance of debt and ownership could foreshadow unfavorable developments in the short run.

TABLE 10-4
Real Wealth and Equities by Major Economic Sectors
(Percent of Tangible)

	Percent of Tangible Assets			Percent of Equity		
	1945	1958	1966	1945	1958	1966
Government	15	13	14	−22	−2	2
Federal	10	10	n.a.	−28	−8	n.a.
State and local	5	3	n.a.	6	6	n.a.
Agriculture	16	11	10	13	8	6
Households (nonfarm)	36	38	39	78	63	64
Business (nonfarm)	33	38	37	30	30	28
Unincorporated	7	7	n.a.	5	4	n.a.
Nonfin. corporations	26	30	n.a.	22	23	n.a.
Finance	−	1	n.a.	3	3	n.a.
All sectors	100	100	100	100	100	100

n.a.: not available.
SOURCE: R. W. Goldsmith and R. E. Lipsey, *Studies in the National Balance Sheet of the United States,* vol. I, table 1, extended to 1966 by J. W. Kendrick.   Reproduced from *Finance* Magazine, January, 1967, p. 13.

Even more significant is the comparison across sides of the balance sheet between net worth and tangible assets. Just as saving and tangible investment are unequal in individual sectors of the economy, so also are tangible asset holdings and net worth. Thus, households (nonfarm) owned 63 percent of domestic wealth in terms of net worth, but held only 38 percent of the tangible assets in 1958 according to Goldsmith's estimates, reproduced in Table 10-4. In contrast, the business sector (nonfarm, plus total agriculture) held about half the productive assets, but owned only 38 percent of total national wealth. This means, of course, that the liabilities of business exceeded its financial assets; for households, financial asset holdings exceeded debt, so that positive net financial holdings augmented tangible assets as a source of wealth. Total government held about one-eighth of the tangible assets of the nation in 1958, but had a negative net worth, since the large government debt (particularly at the federal level) exceeded the total value of assets, real and financial.

The Consolidated National Balance Sheet

Just as saving equals domestic investment plus net foreign investment, so does national net worth equal tangible assets plus net foreign assets, or national wealth. This was implied in the preceding discussion in which national wealth was allocated among the sectors in terms of both proportions of net worth and proportions of tangible wealth.

The aforementioned identity emerges when the balance sheets of the various sectors are consolidated, rather than combined as in Table 10-1. When sector balance sheets are consolidated, domestic financial assets and liabilities plus equity shares

ECONOMIC ACCOUNTS AND THEIR USES

TABLE 10-5
Summary National Balance Sheet of the United States
(Millions of Dollars)

	1948	1958	1966p
Tangible assets†	887	1,654	2,390
Financial assets‡	729	1,306	2,220
Total assets	1,616	2,960	4,610
Liabilities*	716	1,282	2,170
Equities (net worth)	900	1,678	2,440
Total liabilities and equities	1,616	2,960	4,610
Addendum:			
Net foreign assets	13	24	50

p: preliminary.
* Includes a small statistical discrepancy.
† Exclusive of gold.
‡ Exclusive of corporate stock and other equities.
SOURCE: Tangible assets as estimated by Raymond W. Goldsmith, extended from 1958 to 1966 by John W. Kendrick. The financial assets and liabilities are based on estimates of the Federal Reserve Board. Reproduced from *Finance* Magazine, January, 1967, p. 12.

wash out, and net worth is equal to tangible domestic assets plus net foreign assets, which we may call the national wealth. In terms of Goldsmith's figures for 1958 on a combined national basis, his tangible assets of $1,654 billion, plus net foreign assets (not shown) of $24 billion, gives a national wealth of $1,678 billion. This equals his total assets of $3,735 billion less liabilities of $1,488 billion, equity shares of $572 billion, and a small statistical discrepancy. Bare bones calculations of national wealth in terms of simple combined balance sheets are shown for selected dates in Table 10-5.

This result accords with the common sense of political economy. The wealth, or net worth, of a nation does indeed consist of its tangible productive capital—to which we might well add the human capital if the art of measuring human and intangible capital stocks were as far advanced as the art of measuring the nonhuman, tangible capital stocks which have traditionally been referred to as wealth. This portion of total wealth also has the quality of fungibility; the goods are owned, and thus can be bought and sold in markets, which renders the problem of valuation easier to deal with than in the case of human beings.

To anticipate the next section on valuation, it is clear that since domestic wealth consists of tangible assets, they can be "deflated" by appropriate price indexes—or physical units can be weighted by base-period prices—to yield a series in real, constant-price terms (see Table 10-6). This is not true of financial items, which do not stand for specific physical items of various types. As with the financial flows, one might deflate the financial asset and liability totals with the overall price deflator for the underlying physical assets. But such a constant-dollar series does not have the same real significance as a base-weighted aggregate of real physical items of various types, such as those which make up the real domestic wealth.

TABLE 10-6
Wealth: Total, Per Capita, and Ratio to National Product

	1900	1929	1948	1958	1966p
Total U.S. wealth:					
In current dollars (billions)	88	439	928	1,703	2,460
In constant 1947-49					
dollars (billions)	315	778	883	1,244	1,550
Population (millions)	76.8	122.4	147.9	175.6	197.7
Per capita wealth:					
In current dollars	1,145	3,586	6,274	9,698	12,443
In constant 1947-49 dollars	4,099	6,355	5,970	7,084	7,840
Net national product, in					
current dollars (billions)	16	98	250	417	674
Ratio of total wealth to					
net national product	5.6	4.5	3.7	4.1	3.6

p: preliminary.

SOURCE: Wealth estimates are from R. W. Goldsmith, *The National Wealth of the United States in the Postwar Period.* tables A-1 and A-2, extended to 1966 by J. W. Kendrick. Net national product estimates for 1929 through 1966 are based on Department of Commerce numbers with depreciation revalued to current replacement cost by J.W. Kendrick; NNP for 1900 is based on a compilation by Simon Kuznets. Reproduced from *Finance Magazine,* January, 1967, p. 12.

THE VALUATION PROBLEM

It is generally agreed that to be most meaningful, balance sheet items should be expressed in terms of market values or approximations thereof. The market value of a capital asset represents the present (discounted) value of the future net income stream expected from the use of the asset. For new capital goods, the present values equal their prices (costs) to purchasers in equilibrium—which opens up a possible avenue for approximating market valuation when market data are not at hand. In any case, market valuation of assets is consistent with the valuation of national income and product, which is also at market.

Unfortunately, firms and other organizations which prepare balance sheets do so in terms of the original (or acquisition) cost of assets. The records of households, governments, and other organizations which do not prepare balance sheets would also reflect prices paid at time of acquisition. Thus, the value data which could be collected from respondents in the several sectors would generally reflect original costs rather than current values. Since prices of assets change over time, book values cannot be substituted for market values. And depreciated fixed capital goods values cannot be used, not only because of changing replacement prices, but also because changes and differences in depreciation accounting among firms and other organizations make the net book values noncomparable.

ECONOMIC ACCOUNTS AND THEIR USES

In some cases, owners of capital goods may be able to estimate with reasonable accuracy the current market value of their properties. This is often true of home-owners, who carefully watch changes in selling prices of comparable properties in their neighborhoods. The decennial censuses of housing obtain owner estimates of current values. In other instances, extensive secondhand markets exist, so that the estimating agency may obtain data on the numbers of items by type and by age, and apply the "blue book" prices. This is notably true of automobiles, tractors, trucks, and certain types of farm machinery.

But active markets do not exist for most types of secondhand structures and equipment, which make up the going concerns of the economy. Remember that newly produced goods constitute a very small proportion of the capital stock. The chief method for approximating the market values of fixed capital goods over their life-times is by estimation of net (depreciated) replacement cost.

There are two possible approaches to estimating depreciated replacement cost of fixed assets. First, one can obtain data on the age composition of the gross de-preciable stock (before depreciation allowances) by type. Then, for each type of fixed asset, a price index for earlier years, with the given year as 100, can be multiplied by that year's purchases which remain in stock. When this is done for purchases of all prior years, by type, one has an estimate of the gross replacement value of the stock. To obtain the net replacement value, one must estimate the average economic lifetime for each type of durable good, apply an appropriate depreciation rate to each vintage at replacement cost, and then sum the depreciated replacement values of all earlier years' purchases still in stock. This is better than deflating the net book value of fixed capital, since depreciation practices of the firms involved may differ and may have changed over the period.

A simpler, but probably less accurate approach is the so-called perpetual inventory method developed and employed by Goldsmith. In summary, (1) annual gross investment by type is deflated to constant prices, (2) estimates of average economic lifetimes are used to retire the various types of structures and equipment to obtain gross stocks, (3) gross stocks are depreciated over the lifetimes to obtain net stocks, and (4) real gross and net stock estimates are reflated, by type, to current (replace-ment) prices by the same price indexes used to deflate the gross investment estimates. An advantage of the perpetual inventory method is that the resulting stock estimates are completely consistent with the investment estimates contained in the capital account. A disadvantage is that if estimates of lifetimes are in error, cumulative biases can develop in the stock estimates. One of the objectives of the United States Wealth Study proposals was to obtain data on the age distribution of depreciable assets of various types, in the various industries, and, indirectly, to get information on the average ages and survival patterns.

Pending such an inventory survey, OBE has experimented with a considerable number of variants of the perpetual inventory.[6] Differing lengths of life have been used; mortality curves have been applied, instead of retiring all items of a given

---

[6] See Lawrence Grose, Irving Rottenberg, and Robert C. Wasson, "New Estimates of Fixed Business Capital in the United States, 1925-65," *Survey of Current Business*, vol. 46, pp. 34-40, December, 1966; and "Fixed Business Capital in the United States, 1925-66," *Survey of Current Business*, vol. 47, pp. 46-52, December, 1967.

type at the end of the average age, like the one-hoss shay; differing depreciation patterns have been applied, notably straight-line versus several types of declining-balance depreciation; and adjusted construction price deflators have been prepared to correct for the probable downward bias of the conventional construction cost deflators, many of which do not allow for productivity advance. It emerges that differences in average lifetime assumptions affect the movement of stock estimates more than differences in the other variables. This underscores the need for more data on capital goods. However, it must be recognized that in depreciating relatively new types and models of durable goods, one can only be guided by past experience with similar goods. Not only may average economic lives differ from expectations, but to the extent that actual experience deviates from producers' expectations concerning the net income to be earned from new capital goods when they were bought, the decline in their market values as they age will deviate from a stylized depreciation curve. There is thus a conventional element in ongoing capital stock and depreciation estimates which cannot be avoided by the economic accountant.

As far as nonfarm business inventories are concerned, OBE already makes fairly good estimates in constant market prices as a stage in estimating the value of the inventory change. The deflation of book values of inventories could be improved by better information on the relative importance of the chief business inventory accounting methods, as well as by larger samples of firms supplying data. The data on farm inventories are almost ideal: Relatively good estimates of the number of units of the various types of crop and livestock inventories are made at the end of each quarter and year, by state, and the corresponding unit market-value data permit ready conversion into current- or constant-dollar stock estimates. Unfortunately, data on government inventories are not good; and firm data on household inventories are almost nonexistent. Estimates can be made, but by the indirect method of assuming the number of days' supply of the various perishables that are held in stock.

With regard to land and other natural resources, market-price estimates by owners, valuations by appraisal boards for certain types of public lands, and the discounting of projected net income are methods which have been used and which need expansion to cover this important category fully.

An interesting special case of nonreproducible wealth comprises art and other unique man-made items. Markets for art, coins, stamps, and most other collector items are generally active enough to allow owners or appraisers to produce fair estimates of market value—although the sensibilities of some art lovers might be hurt in the process! This category is of considerably less importance than many others, however, and will command relatively low priority in a wealth inventory.

DATA PROBLEMS

Basic data problems may seem tedious to the student who is eager to obtain the estimates of pertinent variables and proceed to analysis. But ingenuity can go only so far in substituting for underlying data. In the balance sheet area, more and better data are needed in the United States to provide reasonably accurate estimates, by sector, particularly as regards tangible wealth. In 1963 the Wealth Inventory Planning Study was set up to survey the need for additional data and lay plans whereby more information could be obtained. The study report may be consulted for details; here, a few highlights will be summarized to provide a sample of the problems.

In general, financial data are more adequate than tangible asset data. The Wealth Study recommended for the inventory years an expansion of the scope and coverage of balance sheet data collected by the Internal Revenue Service, particularly for proprietorships and nonprofit institutions. The federal government is quite well covered by the Treasury Department, but an expansion of detail obtained from state and local governments by the Census Bureau would be helpful. With regard to households, considerable financial information can be assembled by reference to estate tax data. But an expanded survey of financial characteristics of families, of the sort conducted by the Federal Reserve Board, would be necessary for bench-mark purposes.

The suggested strategy for obtaining tangible wealth estimates for industry is to introduce and/or expand asset schedules in the various economic censuses and other reporting systems (which apply chiefly to the regulated industries) that largely cover private business. Some areas, notably most private nonprofit institutions and certain other service industries, are not now covered by the federal statistical system, and some expansion of that system is needed.[7]

Although the full economic censuses—which cover most industries on a five-year cycle, and population and housing decennially—can provide control totals in terms of gross book values for a few major types of tangibles, much more detail is needed from small samples of establishments in each industry. The detail would not only be useful in its own right, but also would be necessary to revalue book data to current market (replacement) prices, and in the case of fixed assets, to depreciate on a consistent basis. Specifically, the detail should encompass the various types of structures and equipment, arrayed by year or period of acquisition. As a by-product of the detailed sample survey, data on mortality of the various types of depreciable assets could be obtained.

The tangible assets of the federal government are fairly well covered and are summarized periodically in the *Federal Real and Personal Property Inventory Report* of the House Committee on Government Operations. Even here, somewhat more detail is needed to revalue consistently in terms of market prices or reproduction costs. The problem is perhaps greatest in the case of public lands, for which the Wealth Study recommended that regional appraisal boards be set up to determine "shadow prices." In the area of state and local governments, however, virtually no tangible asset data are collected. Exploratory studies would need to be undertaken by the Governments Division of the Census Bureau to determine what records exist and thus what data could be collected. Until this is done, rough estimates based on the perpetual inventory method for reproducibles, and fragmentary data for land and inventories, will have to plug the gap.

For households, census and sample survey data exist on housing, automobiles, and major consumer durables. The Wealth Study recommended a split sample for the minor durables and for inventories. In the meanwhile, perpetual inventory estimates have been prepared by the Office of Business Economics.[8]

---

[7] At the time the Wealth Study was conducted, no census of the construction industry had been taken since 1939, but subsequently one was scheduled for 1969.

[8] Scheduled for publication in the *Survey of Current Business* in 1970.

Many technical details must be carefully planned in preparation for data collection. For example, because of the increasing relative importance of the practice of leasing equipment as well as structures, the problem of industry of use versus ownership arises. Real capital stock estimates, by industry, which are used in production functions and productivity analysis, are better made in terms of capital goods *used* by component establishments. Collecting data on rents paid and received, by category of real asset, provides a link between the ownership and use values.

On the contrary, complete balance sheets for the business sector, by broad industry groupings, which are used for financial analysis, would best relate to assets *owned* by component companies. Data have been assembled by the Census Bureau reconciling Treasury Department company data with Census Bureau establishment data. This "link project," on an occasional basis, helps provide a most important bridge between wealth estimates by industries on the alternative establishment and company bases.

These, and various other technical problems noted by the Wealth Study, can only be solved if, prior to data collection, a clear theoretical and conceptual basis is laid for the desired estimates. It has been the thesis of this chapter that balance sheet and wealth estimates are best conceived as an integral part of the national economic accounts. They will be most useful when consistent with the related flow estimates, and it is for effectuation of this purpose that data collection must be designed.

REVIEW QUESTIONS

1   What is the status of development of balance sheets and wealth statements? Are there signs of progress in this field?
2   What are the sectoring requirements for meaningful balance sheets?
3   Sector balance sheets may be combined or consolidated. Contrast the structure of the resulting national statements.
4   Describe the perpetual inventory method of estimating depreciated replacement cost of fixed assets. What are the advantages and disadvantages of this method?
5   Discuss the major data problems encountered in preparing balance sheets for the United States.

SELECTED REFERENCES

CONFERENCE ON RESEARCH IN INCOME AND WEALTH: Studies in Income and Wealth (New York: National Bureau of Economic Research, 1950 and 1951), vols. XII and XIV.

These volumes were devoted entirely to national wealth. They contain papers on techniques of measuring, problems encountered, uses, national and sectors estimates, etc.

GOLDSMITH, RAYMOND W., ROBERT E. LIPSEY (and MORRIS MENDELSON, for vol. II): *Studies in the National Balance Sheet of the United States*, 2 vols. (Princeton, N.J.: Princeton University Press for the National Bureau of Economic Research, 1963).

GOLDSMITH, RAYMOND W.: *National Wealth of the United States in the Postwar Period* (Princeton, N.J.: Princeton University Press for the National Bureau of Economic Research, 1962).

KENDRICK, JOHN W.: "Conceptual and Data Problems of Wealth Estimates in an Economic Accounting Framework," *Review of the International Statistical Institute,* vol. 34, pp. 360-368, 1966.

———: "Problems of a Census of National Wealth," *Review of Income and Wealth,* ser. XII, March, 1966, pp. 57-70.

NESTEROV, L.: "Current Position of National Wealth Estimation in the World," *Review of Income and Wealth,* ser. XV, September, 1969, pp. 271-283.
  This article reviews methods of national wealth estimation in different countries and available statistical data.

U.S. CONGRESS, JOINT ECONOMIC COMMITTEE: *Measuring the Nation's Wealth,* by the Wealth Inventory Planning Study, Joint Committee Print (1964).
  This study was also issued as vol. XXXIX of Studies in Income and Wealth.

International Comparisons
of Accounts and Aggregates

11

There is considerable analytic interest in international comparisons of economic accounts and in the combination of major aggregates into totals for multination groups.[1] For example, the study of the comparative morphology of national economic development and the association of differences in growth patterns with differences in related factors can yield important insight into historical economic dynamics. Work on this topic has also been stimulated by the practical administrative and policy needs of international organizations. During World War II a report prepared for the Combined Resources Board compared the impact of the war on civilian consumption in the United Kingdom, the United States, and Canada. The assessment of contributions of member nations to the United Nations and half a dozen other international organizations is based on national income estimates. Foreign aid is often considered in the context of national income and product, either from the point of view of percentages of

---

[1] The following paragraph is adapted from John W. Kendrick, Introduction, *Problems in the International Comparison of Economic Accounts*, Conference on Research in Income and Wealth, Studies in Income and Wealth, vol. XX (Princeton, N.J.: Princeton University Press for the National Bureau of Economic Research, 1957), pp. 5-6.

donors' national products devoted to aid or of relative incomes of recipients, as a criterion in the allocation of aid. Both the United Nations and the Organization for Economic Cooperation and Development (OECD) have framed policy goals in terms of national income and product. The United Nations adopted as a target for the development decade (1960s) a 5 percent annual rate of growth in national income in less developed countries by 1970. The OECD nations set as a target a 50 percent increase in their combined national product over the decade of the 1960s.

Two major problems are encountered in preparing international comparisons. First, the methodologies of the individual accounts must be consistent. This means that either the estimates initially must be based on standardized definitions, classifications, frameworks, etc., or the estimates must at least be subject to standardization by some international organization. Substantial progress has been made in this direction over the last twenty-five years. The League of Nations had just begun consideration of the problem when World War II intervened. In 1944 an important degree of consensus on many questions was reached by representatives of the agencies responsible for the official estimates in the United States, the United Kingdom, and Canada. Several of the participants played important roles in the subsequent efforts of international organizations to standardize the accounts. In 1953 the United Nations first published *A System of National Accounts and Supporting Tables*, which provides a framework for reporting national income and product statistics.[2] That system, known as the SNA, now has been revised to include other economic accounts. The Organization for European Economic Cooperation (OEEC) and its successor, the OECD, also were active in this field. A system of accounts, similar enough to the SNA to facilitate integration, was formulated, and within the system, in 1954, the most closely comparable set of estimates yet to appear as of that time was published, covering seventeen developed countries.[3] The latest UN compilation, the 1967 *Yearbook of National Account Statistics*, presented detailed national accounts estimates for 112 countries and territories and principal aggregates for 22 others.[4] To compile the *Yearbook*, the UN sends out an annual standardized questionnaire which requests detailed estimates for ten principal tables of the 1953 SNA. Recipient nations are also requested to indicate where the scope and coverage of their estimates differ from definitions and classifications recommended by the SNA. Data from the questionnaire are supplemented by correspondence and national source information. When published, the accounts are presented in a standard form, and differences in concept, scope, coverage, and classification are described in notes preceding and accompanying the tables. Presumably a similar procedure will be inaugurated to provide reporting within the newly revised SNA.

[2] With minor revisions, United Nations, Department of Economic and Social Affairs, Statistical Office, *A System of National Accounts and Supporting Tables*, Studies in Methods, ser. F, no. 2, rev. 2 (New York: 1964).

[3] The UN and OECD efforts are discussed further in connection with the sources and methods of income estimation in less developed countries. See Chap. 13.

[4] United Nations, Department of Economic and Social Affairs, Statistical Office, *Yearbook of National Account Statistics, 1967* (New York: 1968).

COMPARABLE VALUATION: THE PROBLEM OF
EXCHANGE RATE CONVERSION

Less progress has been achieved in finding a way to convert valuation in national currencies to a common unit, which is the second major problem. Comparisons of proportions, such as industrial or expenditure shares in the total, of rates of change, or of productivity can be conducted in national currencies, so that a common unit is not necessary. However, for comparisons or combinations of absolute levels of aggregates, some common unit must be found.

An answer that perhaps comes immediately to mind is the use of exchange rates: Simple multiplication of values in the national currency by appropriate exchange rates. The United Nations has been the foremost user of this method. A 1950 paper presenting estimates of national and per capita incomes of seventy countries converted to United States dollars was used in assessing member contributions. The *Yearbook of National Account Statistics* uses exchange rates to compile estimates of total and per capita gross domestic product, gross national product, and national income in United States dollars for 150 countries and territories.[5] Three different types of exchange rate systems were treated in the recent edition: Par values of currencies were used for countries pledged to convertibility; an average of export and import rates was used for countries with a single but fluctuating rate; an average of implied rates obtained by comparing values of exports and imports in dollars and in national currency was used for countries with a multiple exchange rate system.

Unfortunately, official exchange rates, or even prevailing market rates, may produce grossly arbitrary results. (The UN does raise a warning flag in the notes to its tables.) To obtain even approximately correct results, one would have to be sure that the average relationship of internal purchasing power of currencies was the same as the exchange rates used to make the conversion. This may not be true for a number of reasons. First, the necessary long-term equilibrium in exchange rates seldom exists. Second, for goods traded internationally, the equivalence between the relationship of internal prices and exchange rates is prevented by tariffs and other barriers to trade. Third, even if there were equivalence between prices of traded goods and exchange rates, final prices to domestic buyers would differ, owing to the differing margins for indirect taxes, domestic transportation, additional processing, etc. Finally, the bulk of the goods included in GNP is not traded internationally, so the exchange rate is directly relevant only to a small proportion of economic production.[6]

Alternatives to Exchange Rate Conversion

Milton Gilbert and Irving B. Kravis, in a study for the OEEC, developed the "binary comparison" method to avoid some of the pitfalls of using exchange rate conversion to make international comparisons of national product levels.[7] The method is

---

[5] *Ibid.*, table 7, pp. 825–836.

[6] Milton Gilbert and Irving B. Kravis, *An International Comparison of National Products and the Purchasing Power of Currencies* (Paris: Organization for European Economic Cooperation, 1954), pp. 15–16.

[7] *Ibid.* This study was extended in Milton Gilbert and Associates, *Comparative National Products and Price Levels* (Paris: Organization for European Economic Cooperation, 1958).

TABLE 11-1

Indexes and Ranks of per Capita Gross National Product,
United States and Western European Countries, 1955

	U.S. Price Weights		European Price Weights[a]		Exchange Rates	
	Index U.S. = 100	Rank	Index U.S. = 100	Rank	Index U.S. = 100	Rank
United States	100	1	100	1	100	1
Denmark	56	6–7	46	5	37	6
United Kingdom	64	2	51	2	42	4
Norway	61	3	50	3	41	5
Belgium	58	4–5	49	4	44	3
France	56	6–7	43	7	47	2
Netherlands	53	8	42	8	31	8
Germany	58	4–5	44	6	35	7
Italy	35	9	24	9	19	9

[a]Utilizing average European relative prices.
SOURCE: Adapted from Milton Gilbert and Associates, *Comparative National Products and Price Levels* (Paris: Organization for European Economic Cooperation, 1958), p. 28, table 4.

essentially the same as that used to compare change over time in the output levels of a given country; i.e., quantity data by detailed expenditure category are weighted with the prices of some relevant base period. In international comparisons, quantity data are obtained for each country to be compared, and then weighted not only with the prices of one country but also with those of each country with which the given country is to be compared.

This method requires reasonably detailed national product statistics and assumes a broad similarity of wants and of productive resources. The OEEC authors applied the method to comparisons of the United States and eight nations of Western Europe. Table 11-1 presents some of the results. Exchange rates are shown to exaggerate the gap in per capita GNP between the United States and Europe and to give distorted relationships among the European nations. Even the ranking of countries differs, particularly between the exchange rate conversion and the price weight conversion, but also between the two sets of price weights. The fundamental index number problem, that is, the problem of the choice of weights, appears as the difference between the results of the two sets of price weights. The phenomenon is due basically to the negative correlation between relative prices and quantities purchased,

TABLE 11-2
Hypothetical Quantity Consumed, Prices, and Expenditures for
Europe and the United States

	Quantity Consumed		Prices		Expenditure			
	Europe	U.S.	European (£ per Unit)	U.S. ($ per Unit)	European Price Weights		U.S. Price Weights	
					Europe £	U.S. £	Europe $	U.S. $
Food	6	10	4	5	24	40	30	50
Cars	3	12	10	8	30	120	24	96
Total					54	160	54	146

as discussed in Chapter 6. When United States prices are used as weights for the quantities, a greater weight, i.e., a higher unit value, is given to goods and services which are relatively cheaper and thus more heavily purchased in Europe, and a lower weight given to those goods and services which are relatively more heavily purchased in the United States. Thus, United States price weights bring European national products closer to the United States national product. This is illustrated hypothetically in Table 11-2, which shows that the consumption of food in Europe and in the United States is closer than is the consumption of cars. Since food is cheaper relative to cars in Europe than it is in the United States, total expenditure on the two commodities will be closer together when weighted with United States prices than when weighted with European prices.

Binary Comparison of Output by Industry of Origin

A subsequent study published by the OEEC further explored the binary comparison method, but compared national products by industry of origin rather than by final expenditure.[8] Value added for each industry was weighted with the prices of one and then the other country to be compared. Contributions of the various industries could then be aggregated to national product. Part of the reason for the industry-of-origin study was to compare the results with the expenditure approach: The authors concluded that the two studies were reasonably consistent, considering the broad character of the estimates.

In addition to the information on total product, the later study yielded important new information on the relative position of individual sectors and industries. Table 11-3 exhibits some of the results compiled for the United States and the United Kingdom, the two countries chosen for study because the basic data were most readily at hand. Once again the negative correlation between relative prices and quantity purchased is the source of striking differences when output is measured in real terms, that is, using a common set of prices. For example, agriculture and fuel

[8] Deborah Paige and Gottfried Bombach, *A Comparison of National Output and Productivity of the United Kingdom and the United States* (Paris: Organization for European Economic Cooperation, 1959).

ECONOMIC ACCOUNTS AND THEIR USES

TABLE 11-3

Index of Real Product per Capita and Percentage Distribution of
Real Product, United States and United Kingdom, 1950

| | Real Product per Capita, U.S. = 100 | | Distribution of Real Product | | | |
| | | | U.K. Prices | | U.S. Prices | |
	U.S. Prices	U.K. Prices	U.S.	U.K.	U.S.	U.K.
Agriculture	25	29	12.4	5.7	8.4	3.7
Fuels	32	40	9.7	5.6	4.3	2.6
Manufacturing	54	62	34.8	33.6	30.3	27.8
Construction	61		4.4	4.8	5.8	5.2
Transport & communications	36	60	15.1	9.9	8.6	7.6
Distribution	48	56	13.0	11.1	15.4	12.8
Ownership of dwellings	85		2.1	3.2	4.2	5.4
Services (incl. health & education)	68	71	13.8	16.7	17.2	18.2
Government	147	149	2.5	6.5	5.3	11.5
Gross Domestic Product	55	67	99.3	97.1	99.5	98.4
Net factor income from abroad	233		0.7	2.9	0.5	1.6
GNP (based on output of domestic establishments)	56	68	100.0	100.0	100.0	100.0
GNP (= Gross National Expenditure)	56[a]	67[a]				

[a]The expenditure method of binary comparison yielded index numbers of 49 and 63 at United Kingdom and United States prices, respectively.

SOURCE: Adapted from Deborah Paige and Gottfried Bombach, *A Comparison of National Output and Productivity of the United Kingdom and the United States* (Paris: Organization for European Economic Cooperation, 1959), pp. 20, 21, tables 4, 5.

production account for fairly similar percentages of production in the United States and the United Kingdom when production is measured in national currencies for each: 13 percent of United States product and 11 percent of United Kingdom product. In real terms, however, the contribution of these extractive industries in the United States is about twice that in the United Kingdom: 22 percent compared with 11 percent in United Kingdom prices and 13 percent compared with 6 percent in United States prices. The result in real terms is thus much more in line with the expected relative contribution of natural resource industries in the two countries.

The authors of the OEEC study indicated that the industry-of-origin method is not, in its present state of development, as widely applicable as the expenditure method. Among developed countries, production is more specialized than consumption; thus, unique commodities pose a problem for comparisons between countries with dissimilar economic structures. While the industry-of-origin method is clearly unsuitable for comparing a developed and a less developed country, the ease with which primary industries can be compared and the fact that production statistics are often more readily available than consumption statistics suggest that the method might have an advantage in comparing real products of less developed countries.

Irving B. Kravis, in cooperation with the United Nations, is currently engaged in further development of techniques based on binary comparisons.[9] The ultimate goal is to construct an intercountry matrix of real product and purchasing-power comparisons. Although the potential importance of the industry-of-origin, or production, approach is recognized, for the time being the study is concentrating on the expenditure approach. Shortcut methods of making per capita real product estimates are to be experimented with, since one of the drawbacks of the binary comparison method is the work load of a large number of comparisons. If comparison between all members of a group of n countries is desired, the necessary number of comparisons would be $n(n-1)$. Hitherto the method has been applied to relatively homogeneous groupings, such as within the countries of the OECD, the Economic Commission for Latin America, and the Council for Mutual Economic Assistance. The UN study will explore the possibilities of extending the method to countries heterogeneous in terms of stage of development, economic system (market-oriented or centrally planned), region, and importance of the nonmarket sectors.

Nonmonetary Indicators

The "modified nonmonetary indicator" method was derived to take advantage of the easy availability of certain statistics in many countries in the face of the scarcity of national account statistics. Beckerman described the method as follows:

> . . . the essence of the Modified Non-Monetary Indicator Method is to find the "best" statistical relationship, on the basis of inter-country comparisons for such countries for which independent estimates of relative real income or consumption levels exist, between relative real income or consumption and selected non-monetary indicators for which data are readily available in most countries, and then to use these statistical relationships to predict, from data on the non-monetary indicators, the relative real income levels of all countries for which such data exist.[10]

The nonmonetary indicators selected from among many tested as "explanatory" variables were steel consumption, cement production, number of domestic letters sent, stock of radio receivers, stock of telephones, stock of road vehicles, and meat consumption. The relative real income or consumption levels used in developing the relationships were mainly the Gilbert and Associates estimates discussed above. Because the relationships were worked out on the basis of these estimates, which are largely for high-income countries, rather dubious predictions for some low-income countries resulted. Beckerman's predictions of private consumption are contrasted with exchange rate conversion in Table 11-4. Beckerman noted that it is obviously possible to work with total income, rather than consumption. He concluded that this method appears satisfactory for the majority of countries, although there is danger of large errors in "special-case" countries, such as Argentina, where the exceptionally high meat consumption disturbs the predicted relationships.

---

[9] "Plans for International Product and Purchasing Power Comparisons" (August, 1968). (Typescript.)
[10] Wilfred Beckerman, *International Comparisons of Real Incomes* (Paris: Development Center of the Organization for Economic Cooperation and Development, 1966), p. 27.

TABLE 11-4
Private Consumption per Capita Calculated by Modified
Nonmonetary Indicator Method and Exchange Rates, Selected Countries, 1960

	Modified Non-monetary Indicator		Official Exchange Rate,[b] Index, U.S. = 100		Modified Non-monetary Indicator		Official Exchange Rate,[b] Index, U.S. = 100
	Index, U.S. = 100	Rank			Index, U.S. = 100	Rank	
United States of America	100.0	1	100.0	Algeria	13.8	30	..
Sweden	77.4	2	54.5	Yugoslavia	13.5	31	6.1
Canada	77.0	3	73.9	Mexico	13.4	32	16.2
Australia	65.4	4	57.2	Greece	12.7	33	16.4
UK[a]	61.7	5	49.9	Malaya	12.6	34	..
Denmark[a]	59.2	6	46.6	Cuba	12.2	35	..
Switzerland	59.1	7	55.6	Brazil	12.1	36	6.4
New Zealand	58.6	8	56.0	Colombia	11.4	37	10.9
Norway[a]	57.4	9	34.9	Federation of Rhodesia	11.2	38	5.4
Germany[a]	56.1	10	41.2	Turkey	9.8	39	27.2
France[a]	54.3	11	47.4	China (Mainland)	9.4	40	..
Belgium[a]	53.6	12	48.3	Iraq	9.0	41	..
Netherlands[a]	45.0	13	31.3	Syria	8.6	42	..
Finland	41.3	14	32.5	Peru	8.1	43	..
Austria	40.8	15	29.2	Morocco	8.1	44	6.7
Italy	30.8	16	22.3	Tunisia	7.9	45	..
Japan	28.7	17	12.6	Taiwan	7.4	46	5.4
Israel	27.8	18	45.8	Iran	7.3	47	..
South Africa	26.0	19	35.8	Egypt	6.4	48	..
Rumania	25.2	20	..	Ceylon	5.3	49	5.8
Argentina	23.8	21	18.5	Ghana	4.8	50	7.9
Lebanon	22.8	22	..	Saudi Arabia	4.0	51	..
Ireland	22.0	23	27.5	Thailand	3.7	52	4.0
Hong Kong	19.6	24	..	Congo (Leopoldville)	3.2	53	..
Spain	19.5	25	13.6	India	3.1	54	..
Venezuela	18.9	26	31.8	Nigeria	2.6	55	..
Portugal	17.0	27	11.6	Indonesia	2.4	56	..
Chile	16.9	28	20.9	Pakistan	2.3	57	..
Uruguay	16.2	29	..				

[a] Indicates countries for which the modified nonmonetary indicator method was not used to predict private consumption.
[b] Estimates of private per capita consumption in national currencies, as they appear in the UN *Yearbook of National Account Statistics,* converted by exchange rates.
SOURCE: Wilfred Beckerman, *International Comparisons of Real Incomes* (Paris: Development Center of the Organization for Economic Cooperation and Development, 1966), pp. 36–37, table 5.

AN ESTIMATE OF GROSS WORLD PRODUCT

Table 11-5 presents an estimate of "gross world product" prepared by the U.S. Department of State. An attempt was made to express the GNPs in purchasing-power equivalents (see the note to the table). The GNPs of the Communist countries are based on Western concepts, rather than on the material product system which those countries employ in their own estimates. This table and a table presenting time series of the GNPs for selected areas are the bases for a periodic review for the Department of State of the structure and progress of world output. The table facilitates a number of interesting comparisons. The United States is shown to dominate world production, accounting for 30 percent of the world total. Since the United States has only 6 percent of the world population, the high productivity and high standard of living of the United States economy are indicated. At the other extreme, all less developed countries (here defined as countries with less than $1,000 per capita annual income) account for about three-quarters of the world population, but only about one-fifth of total production.

Communist countries produce 23 percent of the world's goods and services, compared with 77 percent for non-Communist countries. In the latter, production (and population) is spread over a greater number of political units, whereas of the Communist countries, two of them, the U.S.S.R. and China, account for three-quarters of Communist production and slightly more of the Communist population.

The GNP of the U.S.S.R. is about 45 percent of that of the United States, a relative position that has been maintained for about a decade. During this period, the two nations have grown at roughly the same rate—5 percent or slightly less. The U.S.S.R., however, has devoted almost 30 percent of its GNP to investment in fixed assets, while the United States has devoted only 18 percent. The labor force of the U.S.S.R. is more than 50 percent greater than that of the United States, but it produced less than one-half as much. Within the indicated productivity disparity, there are differences, of course, from industry to industry, as Soviet agriculture is below average and armament production and supporting services are above average.[11]

Per capita GNP is shown for the major areas. These figures reflect both productivity gain and net population growth. In the developed countries (Communist as well as non-Communist) population growth has declined to about 1 percent a year, while in the 1960s GNP grew 5 percent, meaning that the per capita increase is about 4 percent. In non-Communist less developed countries, the 5.2 percent increase in GNP was reduced by a population increase of 2.5 percent to a per capita increase of 2.7 percent a year.[12]

The note to Table 11-5 that states that the figures should not be regarded as precise, in effect, serves to summarize this chapter on international comparisons. International comparisons are useful analytical, policy, and administrative tools. However, the comparisons are seldom wholly unambiguous. The concepts and methodologies employed by the various nations are not fully tractable to reconciliation, since they are the products of differences in natural resources, institutions, stage of economic development, and other basic factors. Further, there is no unique answer to the problem of converting values to a common currency unit. International com-

[11] U.S. Department of State, Research Memorandum, Oct. 7, 1969, pp. 11–12, table 2.
[12] Ibid., p. 9.

TABLE 11-5

World Population and Gross World Product, 1968[a]

	Population		GNP[b]		
	Millions	*Percent of Total*	*Billion 1968 Dollars*	*Percent of Total*	*Per Capita, Dollars*
Advanced countries					
U.S. (including Puerto Rico & overseas possessions)	204	6	865	30	4,238
Communist countries	312	9	509	18	1,632
U.S.S.R.	238		396		
Advanced Eastern Europe[c]	74		113		
Other Countries	420	12	888	31	2,115
Canada	21		67		
Advanced Western Europe[d]	280		616		
Japan	101		169		
Others[e]	18		38		
Less developed countries					
Communist countries	864	25	142	5	164
China (Mainland)	772		85		
Less developed Eastern Europe[f]	50		47		
Others[g]	42		10		
Noncommunist countries	1,685	48	443	16	263
World	3,485	100	2,847	100	808

[a]The figures should not be regarded as precise measurements. Demographic statistics of even the most advanced nations contain a considerable margin of error; GNP estimates are still less reliable.
[b]Western concepts of GNP are used for all countries. Figures for the United States, Canada, Japan, Western and Eastern Europe, the U.S.S.R., and Communist China are expressed in purchasing-power equivalents. The GNP for all noncommunist less developed countries are calculated as follows: The GNP total of all less developed noncommunist countries converted into dollars at the official or—where applicable—effective exchange rate amounted to $336 billion in 1967. For advanced noncommunist countries conversion at purchasing power equivalents instead of exchange rates yields a 12 percent higher GNP in dollars. The gap is probably larger for less developed nations; therefore the $336 billion is increased by an arbitrary 20 percent to $404 billion. Adding 5.8 percent for real growth and 3.8 percent for conversion to 1968 dollars yields $443 billion in 1968. Other countries are estimated separately.
[c]Czechoslovakia, East Germany, Hungary, and Poland.
[d]Excludes Turkey, Greece, Portugal, Spain, and communist countries of Europe.
[e]Australia, New Zealand, Israel, Bahamas, and Bermuda.
[f]Albania, Bulgaria, Romania, and Yugoslavia.
[g]North Korea, North Vietnam, Outer Mongolia, and Cuba.

SOURCE: U.S. Department of State, Research Memorandum, Oct. 7, 1969, pp. 14—15, table 2.

parisons must be viewed with an understanding of the statistical manipulations behind them, and hence with an element of caution.

REVIEW QUESTIONS

1 What steps have been taken over the last twenty-five years to achieve standardized definitions, classifications, and frameworks for economic accounts to facilitate international comparisons?

2 Why are exchange rates not appropriate for the conversion of estimates in national currencies to a common currency unit?

3 What are the alternatives to exchange rate conversion? What are some of the advantages and disadvantages of each alternative?

SELECTED REFERENCES

BECKERMAN, WILFRED: *International Comparisons of Real Incomes* (Paris: Development Center of the Organization for Economic Cooperation and Development, 1966).

CONFERENCE ON RESEARCH IN INCOME AND WEALTH: *Problems in the International Comparison of Economic Accounts*, Studies in Income and Wealth, vol. XX (Princeton, N.J.: Princeton University Press for the National Bureau of Economic Research, 1957).
An introduction and five papers, dealing with the then new UN account system and with conceptual problems of delimitation of economic activity.

GILBERT, MILTON, and IRVING B. KRAVIS: *An International Comparison of National Products and the Purchasing Power of Currencies* (Paris: Organization for European Economic Cooperation, 1954).
The basic work on binary comparisons of national product.

Regional Economic Accounts

12

Since World War II there has been a tremendous growth of interest in regional economics. This interest has stimulated demand for regional, or subnational, economic accounts. For example, private business often calls for regional data for market and location research. Reconstruction and economic development programs often have a regional emphasis, and therefore require data on a regional basis. In the United States, the Public Works and Development Act of 1965 provided for designation of economic development centers that have sufficient potential to foster economic growth in the surrounding area. The necessary analysis would be based on a selection of regional economic indicators.

PROBLEMS OF REGIONAL ACCOUNTS

Some of the problems of preparing, comparing, and combining economic accounts for regions are similar to those encountered in international comparisons. It is obvious, for example, that consistency of concepts and methods is necessary. Also, relative prices and price changes may differ from region to region, complicating real comparisons.

Certain problems, however, are unique to regional accounts. A primary problem is the definition of the region for which the accounts are to be prepared.

At least three criteria have been used to define a region: (1) homogeneity with respect to physical, economic, social, or other characteristics; (2) nodality, usually around some central urban place; and (3) policy orientation, related to administrative institutions.[1] The definition of the region by one or another of these criteria will depend on the objectives of the user. For example, New England, as a grouping of states, has been the subject of studies concerned with the relative economic decline of those states as industries common to all of them migrated elsewhere. The standard metropolitan statistical areas (SMSAs), which fall within the second category, are integrated economic and social units with a large volume of daily travel between a central city and the outlying parts of the area. The SMSAs are thus relevant to studies of certain kinds of transportation and urban planning. The states are obvious examples of regions with a policy orientation related to administrative institutions. The regional structure of the Federal Reserve System has been a stimulus to studies treating aspects of the somewhat artificial Federal Reserve districts. From the point of view of data requirements, the ideal compromise would be to compile the data by small administrative units, such as counties, which could then be the building blocks for larger regions tailored to fit the needs of various investigators.

A second major problem is the openness of a regional economy as compared with a national economy. This problem is directly related to the size of the region defined; the smaller the region, the more open it is likely to be. This openness makes it difficult to measure imports and exports of goods and services which, in comparison with the national economy, are important components to be accounted for. A particularly difficult problem is posed by the multiregion corporation, which has plants in several regions, but has no reason to keep accounts that will distinguish the production and income earned by region. Although several methods of allocating net income of these corporations among regions have been used by private researchers, for example, allocating the net income on the basis of the residence of the stockholders or assigning it all to the region of the corporate home office, as yet no fully satisfactory method has been found.[2] Another aspect of this problem is the individual who may be a producer in one region and consumer in another, i.e., the commuter. The distinction between income earned and income received or spent becomes critical.

Data problems are significant. Avoiding disclosure of confidential data based on censuses or administrative statistics becomes more difficult as the area becomes smaller. For example, OBE prepares income by industry and type for counties. In general, these data are available to the public, except where a check shows that operations of individual enterprises would be revealed. Interpolation between bench marks becomes riskier for small regions, since the assumption of stability is less likely to be valid. In constructing accounts for units such as nations, one can often obtain data from either buyer or seller or, as a check, from both. This flexibility does not exist in the construction of regional accounts unless accounts for all regions are constructed because, as mentioned, the buyer and seller may reside in different

[1] John R. Meyer, "Regional Economics: A Survey," in *Surveys of Economic Theory*, vol. II, *Growth and Development* (New York: St. Martin's Press of Macmillan for the American Economic Association and the Royal Economic Society, 1967), p. 243.

[2] These methods and others are described by Kalman Goldberg, "The Measurement and Allocation of Corporate Profits in Regional Sector Accounts," *Journal of Regional Science*, vol. 8, pp. 159–163, Winter, 1968.

regions, and thus the two sides of a transaction would appear in the accounts of different regions.[3]

REGIONAL INCOME AND PRODUCT

Over the years, estimates of state income, variously defined, have been available shortly after the national total. The National Bureau of Economic Research presented estimates by state in 1922, following the publication of national aggregates in 1921. The federal government first published estimates by state in 1939, five years after the first official national income estimates. In 1956 OBE revised its state income series to be consistent with the national personal income (PI) series. Personal income remains the only major series available by region. OBE now prepares these estimates, by type and industrial source, for broad geographic regions and states (quarterly) and for SMSAs and counties outside SMSAs (annually).

OBE defines state PI as the current income received by residents of the state from all sources. It is measured before deduction of income and other direct personal taxes, but after deduction of individuals' contributions to social security.[4] So defined, PI is a comprehensive measure, and is particularly useful as a purchasing-power guide.

The general character of the state PI series can be described in terms of the estimating procedure. First, state estimates of each component—by type and industrial source—are fully adjusted to and represent allocations of an independently derived national total. This procedure is followed because most components can be estimated at least somewhat better on a national basis than on a state basis. In some important instances, however, allocation has not been necessary, because direct, comprehensive data on a state basis are available. Payroll data in occupations covered by social security, civilian payrolls of federal employees, and most government transfers are examples. The allocation procedure takes the national estimate as a datum, and the state estimates are derived by multiplying a national total by percentages computed from relevant state data. As an illustration, some federal disbursements to veterans are allocated among states on the basis of the geographic distributions of the veteran population. Second, several hundred separate series are used to develop the PI totals, for the same reasons that the work at the national level is done in considerable detail.[5] Third, state income estimates are prepared utilizing uniform sources and methods for all states.[6]

[3] These and other problems are discussed in Werner Hochwald, "Conceptual Issues of Regional Income Estimation," *Regional Income*, Conference on Research in Income and Wealth, Studies in Income and Wealth, vol. XXI (Princeton, N.J.: Princeton University Press for the National Bureau of Economic Research, 1957), pp. 9-26.

[4] The relation of personal income to GNP and national income, on a national basis, is shown in Table 16-1. The state PI, in concept, parallels the national total, with the exception that income distributed by the federal government to its employees outside the continental United States is not included in the state estimates.

[5] See Chap. 13.

[6] U.S. Department of Commerce, Office of Business Economics, *Personal Income by States since 1929*, a supplement to the *Survey of Current Business* (1956), pp. 50-51. This publication remains the standard reference work on definitions, sources, and methods of estimating income by state, although concepts were modified for consistency with the 1965 revision of the national accounts.

TABLE 12-1

Total, per Capita, and Industrial Sources of Personal Income,
and Industrial Sources of Civilian Income Received by Persons
for Participation in Current Production, by State for Three Regions, 1967

State and Region	Total Personal Income	Per Capita Personal Income	Farm Income [a]	Broad Industrial Sources of Personal Income		Private Nonfarm Income [c]	Total
				Government Income [b] Disbursements			
				Federal	State and Local		
United States ————————	625,068	3,159	16,675	77,176	54,724	476,493	489,301
New England ———————	39,658	3,503	250	4,295	3,020	32,093	30,884
Maine ———————	2,585	2,657	69	405	226	1,885	1,931
New Hampshire ————	2,094	3,053	14	276	149	1,655	1,635
Vermont ———————	1,178	2,825	47	128	101	901	922
Massachusetts —————	19,197	3,541	56	2,144	1,554	15,442	14,921
Rhode Island ————	2,995	3,328	6	491	224	2,274	2,236
Connecticut —————	11,609	3,969	58	850	766	9,936	9,239
Mideast ———————	149,502	3,561	1,049	16,787	13,073	118,594	116,935
New York —————	68,916	3,759	402	6,012	7,167	55,335	52,929
New Jersey —————	25,686	3,668	109	2,464	1,760	21,354	20,787
Pennsylvania —————	37,065	3,187	378	4,052	2,789	29,846	29,476
Delaware —————	1,905	3,642	41	198	139	1,526	1,397
Maryland —————	12,595	3,421	119	2,672	1,020	8,784	10,107
District of Columbia ———	3,336	4,123	——————	1,389	197	1,749	2,238
Great Lakes —————	132,806	3,395	2,721	11,648	10,311	108,127	108,195
Michigan —————	29,151	3,396	316	2,335	2,580	23,920	23,981
Ohio ———————	33,605	3,213	416	3,171	2,409	27,609	27,483
Indiana ———————	15,980	3,196	525	1,431	1,248	12,776	13,329
Illinois ———————	40,850	3,750	902	3,532	2,873	33,543	32,811
Wisconsin —————	13,220	3,156	563	1,178	1,201	10,277	10,591

[a]Consists of net income of farm proprietors, farm wages, and farm "other" labor income, less
[b]Consists of income disbursed directly to persons by the Federal and State and local governments.
income, interest and transfer payments.
[d]Consists of wage and salary disbursements, other labor income, and proprietors' income.
[f]Less than $500,000.

SOURCE: *Survey of Current Business*, vol. 48, pp. 15, 21, August, 1968.

Farms	Mining	Contract Construction	Manufacturing	Wholesale and Retail Trade	Finance, Insurance and Real Estate	Transportation, Communications, and Public Utilities	Services	Government[e]	Other
17,166	5,180	30,155	148,910	83,950	25,710	35,418	71,644	69,698	1,470
258	30	1,916	11,533	4,983	1,807	1,738	4,867	3,627	125
71	1	125	673	320	75	118	242	289	16
15	3	116	636	255	76	85	230	214	5
49	7	72	288	138	39	54	158	117	2
58	10	884	5,052	2,543	927	915	2,608	1,862	61
6	2	149	843	373	116	119	307	311	10
59	8	570	4,042	1,353	574	447	1,321	834	31
1,082	465	6,451	36,863	19,656	7,479	9,056	18,990	16,612	282
416	91	2,540	14,682	9,357	4,440	4,364	9,614	7,301	123
112	34	1,326	7,826	3,500	1,077	1,642	3,045	2,169	57
390	324	1,711	11,468	4,638	1,297	2,129	3,994	3,476	49
42	1	96	595	192	55	75	176	161	4
122	14	702	2,207	1,714	512	720	1,618	2,469	28
- - - - -	f	76	85	255	97	126	542	1,037	20
2,800	600	6,615	43,202	17,799	4,636	7,026	13,425	11,888	206
325	108	1,386	10,626	3,684	860	1,281	2,908	2,760	42
428	173	1,661	11,599	4,373	1,081	1,785	3,370	2,958	54
540	66	859	5,654	2,008	522	839	1,346	1,474	20
928	228	2,037	11,334	6,031	1,756	2,513	4,534	3,389	63
579	24	672	3,989	1,702	417	608	1,267	1,307	25

personal contributions under the OASDHI program.
  Comprises wages and salaries (net of employee contributions for social insurance), other labor
[c]Equals total personal income less farm income and government income disbursements.
[e]Does not include earnings of military personnel.

Personal income by state, with component detail, appears quarterly in the *Survey of Current Business*, along with an analysis of regional trends. A sample of these data, showing total, per capita, and industrial sources of PI, and industrial sources of income received in current production for the states of three regions, appears in Table 12-1. OBE also shows PI by source—wage and salary disbursements (with detail), other labor income, proprietors' income, property income, and transfer payments, less personal contributions for social security.

OBE recently completed the first comprehensive estimates covering all SMSAs and counties in the United States for selected years, 1929 to 1966.[7] The published data on SMSAs were compiled to highlight the classification of SMSAs by sources of income and differences among SMSAs in the relative growth of total income and per capita income.

The statistical approach for local area income estimates generally parallels the state PI series. The state total for each income component is allocated to the local areas in accordance with proportionate shares of some related series available for all the local areas. This method makes it possible to use the best allocating series for a particular state without impairment of interstate comparability.[8]

The problem of commuters who work in one area but reside in another must be faced in dealing with local areas. For labor and entrepreneurial income, it is possible to distinguish between place of work and residence. It is not possible statistically to make this distinction for the other components of the income flow, i.e., property incomes and transfer payments, so in these components, residence is the only criterion of allocation. OBE thus prepares two versions of local area PI. In the "where-earned" version, earnings are allocated on a place-of-work basis. This version facilitates analysis of the income structure in terms of industrial origin and type of income. In the "where-received" version, earnings are allocated according to place of residence. Allocated in this way, income can be used in the analysis of consumer markets and, on a per capita basis, as an indicator of standards of living. The per capita series shown in the *Survey of Current Business* are compiled in this way.[9]

Gross State Product

In the absence of OBE estimates of regional gross product, a method of obtaining gross state product (GSP) has been developed by the author and C. Milton Jaycox.[10] This method relies principally upon the OBE estimates of GNP by industry, in conjunction with relevant components of state PI and some readily available collateral data. The troublesome sector is the private nonfarm industries, since state farm and government product can be estimated directly from available data. In the private nonfarm sector, for each industry, gross state product originating (seen as the sum of income originating plus capital consumption allowances plus indirect business taxes) is estimated from state personal income originating in

[7] Robert E. Graham, Jr., and Edwin J. Coleman, "Metropolitan Area Incomes, 1929-66," *Survey of Current Business*, vol. 48, pp. 25-48, August, 1968.

[8] U.S. Department of Commerce, Office of Business Economics, Regional Economics Division, "Sources and Methods Used in Estimating Local Area Income" (n.d.), pp. 7-8. (Duplicated.)

[9] *Ibid.*, pp. 4-5.

[10] John W. Kendrick and C. Milton Jaycox, "The Concept and Estimation of Gross State Product," *Southern Economic Journal*, vol. 32, pp. 153-168, October, 1965.

current production, blown up by national ratios of national gross product to the components.

The authors of this method illustrated it by using estimates for the state of Maryland, 1957 to 1959. The indirectly estimated items of GSP made up almost one-third of the total. No direct check of accuracy was possible, although reference to related measures suggested the plausibility of the estimates. The authors also worked out constant-dollar estimates of GSP, using the preferred double-deflation method for farm product, deflation by average compensation per general government employee for government product, and the national implicit industry gross product price deflators for the private nonfarm product.

The main defects of the estimates obtained in this way are (1) the national blowup ratios for certain industry groups may be wide of the mark for certain states, and (2) in some states average prices, especially in the short run and for local products, may vary from the national average used in deflation.

OBE's program in regional statistics calls for the development of a set of regional accounts that will be analytically useful and capable of being implemented statistically. Estimates of gross product would appear to be the cornerstone of such accounts. The expenditure approach would, to be sure, yield valuable information — consumer expenditures, to gain insight into welfare levels and market potential; government expenditures, to evaluate the impact of such spending on regions; capital expenditures, to study growth and changes in productivity; and regional exports and imports, to illuminate trade relationships with the rest of the nation. However, consumption expenditures pose a knotty problem, since they are now estimated on a national basis by the commodity-flow method, which does not yield regional data. Data on regional exports and imports are nonexistent.[11] Particularly because of the last problem, and because building up gross product by industry makes possible a rich study of comparative production and productivity trends, the industry buildup of gross product may have to serve as the controlling total of final expenditures, with net exports obtained as a residual.[12]

OTHER ECONOMIC ACCOUNTS

The greatest elaboration of regional accounts has been on input-output (I-O) tables. A distinction may be drawn between interregional (or multiregional) I-O models and regional models.[13] Interregional models identify inputs and outputs by region as well as by industry. Interregional tables exhibit two kinds of interdependence — interindustrial and interregional — which substantially increases their complexity and the data requirements. A regional I-O model is similar to a national model, but is confined to a smaller area. Studies have been done for Federal Reserve districts, states, and groups of counties, and at least one study has been done for a small community. The regional models may or may not disaggregate imports and

---

[11] Richard Ruggles and Nancy D. Ruggles, "Regional Breakdowns of National Economic Accounts," in Werner Hochwald, ed., *Design of Regional Accounts* (Baltimore: The Johns Hopkins Press for Resources for the Future, Inc., 1961), pp. 132–135.

[12] Kendrick and Jaycox, *op. cit.*, pp. 162–163.

[13] These are surveyed by William H. Miernyk, *The Elements of Input-Output Analysis* (New York: Random House, Inc., 1965), chap. 4.

exports by region and sector. Regional I-O tables may be constructed either by adjusting coefficients found in national tables or by making surveys to determine the regional coefficients. The latter method is expensive and time-consuming, but is more reliable. Particularly if projections of economic structure are to be made on the basis of the tables constructed, the more reliable method may be worth the extra cost.[14] Because of the complexity of the work in preparing I-O tables, even tables with relatively few sectors and with adjusted national coefficients, it will probably not be economical to obtain comprehensive coverage of the nation by regional tables.

Flow-of-funds accounts, balance-of-payments accounts, and balance sheets, by region, are much less developed.[15] Balance-of-payments accounts would require a completely new set of data. Flow-of-funds accounts, by region, may take on a distorted appearance, because those accounts are sectored by legal institution. For example, the flows in and out of the region of an insurance company's home office may not reflect real transfers between that region and others. Regional wealth statements and balance sheets, like their national counterparts, have yet to be compiled on a firm statistical basis and in a framework consistent with other economic accounts. The Wealth Inventory Planning Study recommended, with regard to regional statistics, that tangible wealth data be prepared on state and major SMSAs, since the establishment basis of much industry data is well suited to regional deconsolidation. The multiregion corporation arises again as a problem in the preparation of estimates of financial assets by region, and such estimates will present major difficulties.[16]

In summary, regional economic accounting is comparatively underdeveloped. Indeed, the UN puts regional accounting into the category of topics which are not yet beyond the stages of preliminary discussion. The revision of the SNA does not include provision for a regional dimension. This state of underdevelopment appears to be due in part to the fact that interest in and effort to create a theoretical framework for regional data have emerged only recently. In part it may be attributed to the need for improvements in underlying data. Despite this handicap, it is desirable that, in the United States, an agency such as OBE assume continuing responsibility for expanding regional accounts in order to ensure consistency of concept and method among state estimates and between state and national estimates, and to facilitate full exploitation of available data.

REVIEW QUESTIONS

1 What are the main problems unique to the preparation of regional as distinct from national economic accounts?

2 Describe the main features of OBE's procedure in estimating state personal income.

3 What is the status of work on regional input-output tables, flow-of-funds accounts, balance-of-payments accounts, and wealth estimates?

[14] William H. Miernyk, "Long-range Forecasting with a Regional Input-Output Model," *Western Economic Journal*, vol. 6, pp. 165–176, June, 1968.

[15] Ruggles and Ruggles, *op. cit.*, pp. 138–140.

[16] John W. Kendrick, David J. Hyams, and Joel Popkin, "The Staff Report," in *Measuring the Nation's Wealth*, by the Wealth Inventory Planning Study, Joint Economic Committee Print (1964), pp. 50 and 153.

SELECTED REFERENCES

CONFERENCE ON RESEARCH IN INCOME AND WEALTH: *Regional Income.* Studies in Income and Wealth, vol. XXI (Princeton, N.J.: Princeton University Press for the National Bureau of Economic Research, 1957).
An introduction and ten papers. Considers value and problems of regional estimates.

GRAHAM, ROBERT E., JR., and EDWIN J. COLEMAN: "Metropolitan Area Incomes, 1929-66," *Survey of Current Business*, vol. 48, pp. 25-48, August, 1968.

HOCHWALD, WERNER, ed.: *Design of Regional Accounts* (Baltimore: The Johns Hopkins Press for Resources for the Future, Inc., 1961).
See especially the introduction by Hochwald and papers by Hirsch, Perloff, and Ruggles and Ruggles.

ISARD, WALTER: *Methods of Regional Analysis: An Introduction to Regional Science* (New York: Technology Press of Massachusetts Institute of Technology and John Wiley & Sons, Inc., 1960).
See especially chaps. 4, 5, and 8.

KENDRICK, JOHN W., and C. MILTON JAYCOX: "The Concept and Estimation of Gross State Product," *Southern Economic Journal*, vol. 32, pp. 153-168, October, 1965.

MIERNYK, WILLIAM H.: *The Elements of Input-Output Analysis* (New York: Random House, Inc., 1965).
See chap. 4, "Regional and Interregional Input-Output Analysis."

Sources and Methods
of Estimating the National
Income and Product Accounts

13

This chapter contrasts to some extent with the preceding chapters, which dealt in large part with conceptual issues—the conceptual formulation of significant aggregates, the relations of aggregates within accounts, the structure of an integrated system of economic accounts, and so on. This is more a how-to chapter. Its purpose is to impart a sense of reality, or concreteness, to the estimates that emerge from the statistical agencies and, more important, to provide a means of gauging the reliability of the estimates and their appropriateness for different uses.

The chapter first treats, in a general way, sources and methods of estimation of the United States national income and product accounts. Next, it describes, component by component, the sources and methods used in preparing the National Income and Product Account basic summary table. Although tedious, this provides the basis upon which to discuss the reliability of the estimates. Finally, to stress issues of reliability and to show the interesting contrasts with national income estimation in developed countries, such as the United States, the last section of the chapter describes sources and methods of national income estimation in less developed countries.

SOURCES

The notable characteristic of the United States sources is diversity—in terms of collecting agency, purpose of data collection, periodicity, reliability, and other factors. With few exceptions, the data used are not collected for the purpose of being transformed into income and product estimates. Data collected by federal government agencies for other purposes provide the backbone of the estimates.[1] These data may be classified as nonadministrative and administrative. Nonadministrative statistics include the periodic economic and population censuses which are processed and used in a variety of ways. Also, there are a number of sample surveys, including those which obtain data on manufacturing operations, corporation finance, and households. Administrative statistics are by-products of government administrative functions, such as welfare and social security programs, tax collection, and regulatory activities. The items for which OBE does collect its own data are travel expenditures abroad and plant and equipment expenditures. Government statistics are supplemented from private trade associations, labor organizations, research organizations, and welfare, educational, and religious groups.

Sources are also diverse as to underlying statistical technique and periodicity of collection. For bench marks, i.e., actual measurements that serve as statistical bases, use is made of the decennial Census of Population, extensive business data collected by the Bureau of the Census, usually every five years, and wage and salary data compiled annually by the Bureau of Employment Security. Income and financial data are compiled annually by the Internal Revenue Service, but are available in complete form only after several years' lag. Annual data sources are often based on samples, such as the annual Survey of Manufactures. Quarterly and monthly data sources usually are based on samples. These include the *Quarterly Financial Report for Manufacturing Corporations* prepared by the Securities and Exchange Commission and the Federal Trade Commission, the monthly surveys of wages and employment by the Bureau of Labor Statistics, and the monthly surveys of retail and wholesale trade by the Census Bureau based on probability samples.

METHODS

The data pulled together from these diverse sources undergo considerable processing. In part, this involves adjustment of the data to the stipulated definitions of the economic aggregates. An example is the adjustment of corporate profits tax receipts from a cash basis to an accrual basis. Gaps in information may have to be filled by referring to sources that are themselves incomplete. Conflicting evidence may be received from different sources or for slightly differing periods. The director of OBE, George Jaszi, stresses the amount of judgment required in the preparation of the estimates: "The estimating is not a mechanical job. It is not a question of adding up a lot of reported figures. Judgment necessarily enters at every step of the estimating procedure."[2]

[1] A useful introduction to federal government data sources, discussing general procedures and detailing specific programs and publications, is contained in U.S. Bureau of the Budget, Executive Office of the President, *Statistical Services of the United States Government*, rev. ed. (1968).

[2] George Jaszi, "The Statistical Foundations of the Gross National Product," *Review of Economics and Statistics*, vol. 38, p. 208, May, 1956.

Among the estimating procedures are extrapolation and interpolation, which make it possible to produce income and product figures for a series of years from one or more pivotal years for which data are more reliable or more abundant. Extrapolation projects figures from one year, either forward or backward in time, to other years. Interpolation fills in the figures between two years for which information is available. Because interpolation deals with two base periods, the extent of uncertainty is somewhat less than in extrapolation. The results of both methods become less reliable the longer the period covered by the calculated estimates.

The basic commodity-flow procedure was developed by Simon Kuznets in the 1930s and has since been adopted by OBE. The method is a complex one of obtaining the retail value of consumer purchases of commodities or the value of producers' purchases of durable equipment by starting from the value at manufacturers' prices of manufacturing production. For consumer purchases, this method is preferable to the alternative of utilizing retail sales data, which are detailed by type of store, or by type of department in department stores, and thus does not provide information by commodity group. The commodity-flow procedure followed by OBE in the case of consumer purchases has several steps.

1 From among the detailed list of products enumerated in the Census of Manufactures, those which are destined for consumer use without further processing in manufacturing are segregated. This involves, in addition to the straight selection of products that are destined solely for consumers, an allocation of products whose use is mixed, e.g., an estimate of how much flour is used by housewives direct and how much is raw material used by bakeries.

2 Where necessary, manufacturers' production of finished consumer commodities is converted into manufacturing shipments by allowing for change in manufacturing finished inventories.

3 Sales by nonmanufacturing producers of commodities destined for consumer use are then taken into account. This includes products of agriculture and commericial fisheries.

4 Transportation charges to the first buyer are added.

5 The total of producers' sales are classified according to broad sales outlets: exports, consumers, wholesalers, and retailers.

   a Producers' exports are eliminated.

   b Producers' sales to consumers need no further processing.

   c Imports are added to domestic sales to wholesalers, and wholesalers' inventory change and markups are taken into account to derive wholesalers' sales. These, in turn, are classified into sales to retailers and to consumers.

   d Wholesalers' sales to retailers are combined with producers' sales to retailers, and the change in retailers' inventories, and markups, including retail sales taxes, are added to derive retail sales to consumers.

6 The consumer purchases total represents the sum of producers', wholesalers', and retailers' sales to consumers.[3]

This method has been described in some detail to give the reader an appreciation of the complexity of the estimating procedure. Most recently, since the national

---

[3] *Ibid.*, pp. 208-209.

income and product estimates and the input-output tables have been integrated, the procedure has been modified to allocate service charges, as in the case of transportation and trade, to fill in a matrix of values.

SPECIFIC SOURCES AND METHODS FOR GROSS NATIONAL PRODUCT AND CHARGES AGAINST GROSS NATIONAL PRODUCT

Specific sources and methods are briefly outlined below for the components of the two sides of the National Income and Product Account, that is, for the components of GNP and charges against GNP (see Appendix A, Table A-1). The basic references for such a description are still the 1954 and the 1958 supplements to the *Survey of Current Business*.[4] The description applies to the annual current-dollar estimates. The quarterly or, in some cases, monthly estimates are generally based on more limited information, and their preparation may utilize different, or additional, substitute sources and methods. A description of how quarterly estimates are made is contained in *U.S. Income and Output,* where the system of quarterly reporting was expanded. The methodology and the kinds of price information needed for deflating the current-dollar series to constant dollars were treated in Chapter 6. The methodology described here does not apply to the third method of arriving at the national output total, the estimation of industry gross product.[5] Further, other compilations of national income data, such as size distribution of income or income by states, have specialized methodologies.

Gross National Product

Personal consumption expenditures Over 80 percent of personal consumption expenditures for commodities is estimated by commodity-flow methods. This means that the basic source of information is the commodity detail on value of shipments provided by the Census of Manufactures, supplemented for nonmanufactured items by information from the Department of Agriculture, Bureau of Mines, and Fish and Wildlife Service. Transportation charges are computed from data compiled by the Interstate Commerce Commission and other sources. Trade markups are derived from the Census of Business and Internal Revenue Service data. Between commodity-flow bench-mark years, the estimates are interpolated by the Retail Trade Report, the annual Survey of Manufactures, and other sources. Of the commodities not

[4] U.S. Department of Commerce, Office of Business Economics, *National Income,* a supplement to the *Survey of Current Business* (1954); U.S. Department of Commerce, Office of Business Economics, *U.S. Income and Output,* a supplement to the *Survey of Current Business* (1958). A few recent changes are mentioned in "The National Income and Product Accounts of the United States: Revised Estimates, 1929-65," *Survey of Current Business,* vol. 45, pp. 6-22, August, 1965. Relevant sections of these publications have been reprinted in George Jaszi et al., *Readings in Concepts and Methods of National Income Statistics* (Washington, D.C.: National Technical Information Service, 1970). A useful summary of the GNP components is in "Explanatory Notes to the Statistical Series," in U.S. Department of Commerce, Office of Business Economics, *Business Statistics, 1967,* a supplement to the *Survey of Current Business* (1967).

[5] The specific methodology is detailed in U.S. Department of Commerce, Office of Business Economics, "GNP by Major Industries: Concepts and Methods" (April, 1966). (Mimeographed.)

estimated by commodity-flow methods, passenger cars, gasoline and oil, and tobacco products make up the largest part. Available quantity and price information on these products permits their estimation by retail valuation (quantity purchased multiplied by average retail price).

Preparation of the services component of personal consumption expenditures draws upon several hundred different series. Periodic censuses provide bench marks for the rental value of housing (Censuses of Population, Housing, and Agriculture); auto repairs, barbershops, laundries, movie theaters, and similar repair and personal service establishments (Census of Business); and other components that together constitute half of the dollar value of consumer services. In the case of service establishments, information for years between censuses is available from the Census Bureau surveys reported in *Monthly Selected Service Receipts*. Annual reports of government administrative agencies are available for telephone, transportation, and educational outlays. Private organizations provide data on insurance, hospitals, electricity, gas, local transport, and religion and welfare. Information on physicians, lawyers, and other professional services is obtained from the Internal Revenue Service.

Gross private domestic investment   An improvement in the sources for the construction component of investment was incorporated in the 1965 revision. The new construction series is now provided by the Census Bureau. The Bureau utilizes two new and continuing sample surveys. One provides information on the value of construction put in place for private nonfarm nonresidential buildings, adjusted with data on value of contract awards from the F. W. Dodge Division of McGraw-Hill, Inc. The other is a quarterly survey of local government construction. For other types of construction, several methods are used, depending on the type of information available. For housing, building-permit and average-cost data derived from monthly sample surveys are the basic series. The responsible federal agencies provide information on federally owned construction. For privately owned utilities, telephone, and telegraph, companies or trade associations and federal regulatory agencies provide data. Farm construction expenditures are prepared by the Department of Agriculture on the basis of a 1955 bench-mark survey which is extrapolated by changes in farm income and other relevant data.

Producers' durable equipment is estimated chiefly by the commodity-flow method; in 1947 almost 90 percent of this component was so estimated. Thus, for bench-mark years, the major sources are the manufactures and trade censuses. For selected intermediate years, "secondary" bench marks are developed from data collected by the Census Bureau in the annual sample Survey of Manufactures. An alternative estimate is derived by adjusting OBE's plant and equipment survey to remove construction and add areas not covered by the survey. The movement in postbench-mark periods is the average of the movement of the commodity-flow and the plant and equipment series.

Business inventory change is defined as the change in physical volume of inventories valued at average prices of the period. In nonfarm inventories, the basic data available are book value data. The book value of manufacturing and trade inventories, which make up over 90 percent of the nonfarm total, is derived from Census Bureau sample surveys of wholesalers, retailers, and manufacturers. Annual inventories of all other nonfarm industries are obtained from Internal Revenue Service data. Because different accounting methods underlie the firms' reports, and these methods vary widely with respect to both scope of the cost elements and costing procedures, complex adjustment, including the removal of price change, is called for to arrive at estimates consonant with the inventory definition. The change in farm inventories is estimated separately by the Department of Agriculture from physical quantity data and current prices.

Net exports of goods and services   The largest components of net exports are merchandise imports and exports, data for which are obtained from import entry forms and shippers' export declarations filed with the Customs Bureau, compiled by the Census Bureau, and adjusted for coverage, timing, and valuation. Other sources include reports from the following: United States companies on branches and subsidiaries abroad, and foreign companies on branches and subsidiaries in the United States; government agencies on their loans, purchases, and sales abroad; firms and federal administrative agencies on transportation; travelers on their expenditures abroad, or in the case of foreign travelers on their expenditures in the United States; and agencies or companies handling payments for other services such as income on investments, insurance, royalties, and fees.

Government purchase of goods and services   The essential source for federal expenditures on goods and services is the *Monthly Statement of Receipts and Expenditures of the United States Government* issued by the Treasury Department. From these data, certain deductions are made (public debt interest, grants-in-aid to state and local governments, transfer payments, subsidies, capital transactions, net expenditures of government enterprises); and to these data certain additions are made (capital formation of government enterprises). The residual, after timing adjustments, represents purchases of goods and services.

State and local government purchases of goods and services are derived from fiscal-year reports made by these government to the Census Bureau in a manner analogous to that used in deriving federal purchases. Since the data are on a fiscal-year rather than a calendar-year basis, major components are converted to a calendar-year basis by reference to the movements of relevant monthly data on payrolls, construction, and others.

Charges against Gross National Product

Compensation of employees   Over half of the total charges against gross national product is wages and salaries. The estimates of wages and salaries are considered extremely reliable, since a very large proportion of the information comes from payroll statistics, either from reports related to unemployment insurance and social security programs or reports of federal, state, and local government. In only a few instances, such as the estimates of tips as percentages of revenues in applicable industries, are indirect methods employed. Information on the supplements to wages and salaries comes from labor-management agreements, insurance company data, and studies compiled by the Securities and Exchange Commission, the Internal Revenue Service, the Department of Labor, and the Social Security Administration.

Proprietors' income Business and professional proprietors' income is estimated from income tax returns to the Internal Revenue Service. This information must be adjusted for incompleteness of the Internal Revenue Service universe and for under-statement of net income on tax returns. Proprietors' income from farming is developed by the Department of Agriculture on the basis of an extensive reporting system. Basically, the procedure is to obtain an estimate of realized gross earnings (cash receipts from marketings, government payments, and nonmoney income) from which production expenses are subtracted to obtain net income.

Rental income of persons Rental income of persons is estimated as the sum of three components. The return from rented nonfarm property is in large measure based on totals of net rents and royalties reported for income tax purposes. Imputed income derived from owner-occupied dwellings is found by estimating the number of dwellings, obtained from the Census of Housing and sample surveys, and multiplying this by an annual rent similarly obtained. For intercensal years the number of dwelling units is interpolated or extrapolated, using estimates of new construction and demolition; annual rent is determined by reference to the rent component of the Consumer Price Index and information on the number of rooms in new dwellings added to the stock. From this gross estimate, estimates of average expenses, maintenance costs, and depreciation are subtracted to obtain net imputed rent. The third component is rent from farm realty, which is prepared in conjunction with the estimates of farm income.

Corporate profits and inventory valuation adjustment Corporate profits, except for the most recent year, are based on tabulations of unaudited corporate income tax returns published by the Internal Revenue Service in *Statistics of Income*. These data are adjusted statistically and conceptually; the latter adjustment involves the inclusion in profits of domestic depletion allowances, defaulters' gains, and excess of additions to bad debt reserves over losses actually incurred, exclusion of capital gains and losses, shifts in the timing of foreign income, and other items.[6] For the most recent years, extrapolations are based on the *Quarterly Financial Report for Manufacturing Corporations* of the Federal Trade Commission and Securities and Exchange Commission, reports of federal regulatory agencies, and compilations of publicly reported company profits.

Inventory valuation adjustment is the excess of the physical volume of the change in inventories valued at average prices of the period over the book values of the change in inventories reported to the Internal Revenue Service. It is included as an element of earnings from current production, consistent with the treatment of inventories in the GNP. (A parallel adjustment is made for noncorporate enterprises, but it is not shown separately.)

Net interest Net interest is the excess of interest payments of domestic business over its interest receipts (excluding interest paid by consumers and by government),

---

[6] See table 7.5, "Relation of Corporate Profits, Taxes, and Dividends in the National Income and Product Accounts to Corresponding Totals as Tabulated by the Internal Revenue Service," *Survey of Current Business*, vol. 49, p. 46, July, 1969.

plus net interest received from abroad. Monetary components of the interest paid and received by domestic businesses are obtained from the Internal Revenue Service and by applying interest rate data to mortgage figures obtained from the Federal Home Loan Bank Board. A portion of imputed interest is equal to the value of financial services received by persons from financial intermediaries without explicit payment. Calculated as the monetary return on investment of deposits less monetary interest paid on deposits in the case of commercial banks, and the same less profits in the case of mutual depositories, the required data are available in the annual reports of the Federal Deposit Insurance Corporation and the Board of Governors of the Federal Reserve System. The remaining portion of imputed interest represents property income received by life insurance companies and noninsured pension funds less profits of life insurance companies, for which data are obtained mainly from the Internal Revenue Service. Net interest received from abroad is estimated as part of the balance of payments.

Business transfer payments   The component estimates—of corporate gifts to non-profit institutions, consumer bad debts, and a few other minor items—are based in large part on data contained in tax returns.

Subsidies less current surplus of government enterprises   Subsidies paid by the federal government are compiled from Treasury reports. The current surplus of government enterprises applies to both state and federal governments. For federal enterprises, the necessary data, after certain adjustments, are found either in the profit and loss statements of those enterprises organized as corporations or in the financial statements reconstructed from available budgetary data for the others. Information on state enterprises is calculated from summary operating statements compiled by the Census Bureau for certain years, and interpolated and extrapolated for other years on the basis of whatever data may be available.

Capital consumption allowances   The depreciation component of capital consumption allowances, for unincorporated enterprises and corporations, is obtained from tax return data. The valuation of these charges reflects the accounting practices pursued under Internal Revenue Service regulations, except in the case of farm depreciation. For the farm sector, the Department of Agriculture prepares estimates on the basis of replacement cost rather than original cost. Estimates of the other component, accidental damage to fixed capital, are based on losses reported to insurance companies, to police, and to government agencies in cases of weather damage and damage to transport facilities.

Reliability and Revisions

The United States national income and product accounts probably surpass those of any other country with respect to the accuracy of the aggregates and much of the detail shown.[7] One important factor is that, comparatively, the statistical

[7] National Economic Accounts Review Committee, *The National Economic Accounts of the United States: Review, Appraisal, and Recommendations, Hearings before the Subcommittee on Economic Statistics of the Joint Economic Committee,* 85th Cong., 1st Sess., 1957, p. 217.

information available for estimating the accounts is abundant and generally reliable. Further, certain characteristics of the estimates and the methods used to produce them contribute to overall reliability. First, OBE points to a tradition of detailed estimating that utilizes all available source material. The published detail has behind it much greater worksheet detail, so the published items are not only the sums of components that are estimated independently, but each component is likely to represent the product of several estimating steps.

Second, the procedure of estimating in detail brings into play what has been called the "guardian angel" of national product estimation, the phenomenon of offsetting errors. It has been found that errors made in detailed components tend to offset each other when the various series are aggregated, so that errors in broad totals of income and product are substantially smaller than those in the components.

Third, estimation in an accounting framework provides powerful checks on the estimates. The most obvious check is that the gross national product as the sum of product flows must, in principle, equal the sum of income and other charges against gross national product and the sum of gross product originating in the various sectors and industries. If the statistical discrepancies produced by a preliminary set of estimates are beyond reason, this is a signal to look for errors in the component estimates, which, as was noted above, are derived largely from independent sources.

Fourth, there is a check on the reliability in terms of past trends and relationships. A preliminary set of estimates that produced individual components that were out of line either with a component's past history or with the functional relations with other components would lead to an investigation. For example, if a fairly steady series, such as consumer purchases of services, were to show an erratic change from one year to the next or if personal consumption expenditures were to show a marked change in relation to disposable personal income, this would be a signal to the estimators to check these components.

Even though the comparative reliability of the United States accounts may be admitted and the various checks on reasonableness and reliability recognized, we still do not know just how reliable the estimates are. There have been requests that the OBE estimators provide mathematical measures of error based on sampling probabilities, or a letter grading system for the various components, or plus or minus ranges to the numerical estimates. OBE has declined to provide such indicators, and in general is supported in this judgment by the National Accounts Review Committee. Sampling errors are not considered the major errors in the accounts. More important are errors in estimating procedures and errors in the basic sources—undercoverage or faulty reporting or recording, for example. These nonsampling errors, however, are not susceptible to quantification. It is suggested than even indicators of relative accuracy would give an erroneous impression of mathematical precision, especially since the margin of error does not remain the same at all times, for example, as between bench-mark and other years, and since a great number of data sources of varying quality are used in preparing the individual components.[8]

OBE estimators suggest that the user must study the sources and methods used in preparing the accounts, and combine this analysis with continued use of the

[8] John Gorman of OBE made the point, in his review of this chapter, that given data sources also deteriorate or improve.

212   ECONOMIC ACCOUNTS AND THEIR USES

statistics, in order to form a judgment of their reliability vis-à-vis his own needs and purposes. It is in this light that even the brief description of sources and methods provided above takes on importance. In *National Income*, OBE suggested four factors pertaining to the sources and methods that affect reliability:

1   Complexity of the reported item. One must consider whether the economic unit is reporting on an item which is a straightforward transaction of simple definition—often associated with a monetary transaction—or an item that requires complex calculations or is vague in definition.

2   Quality of records kept. One must consider whether the records of the reporting unit are adequate to provide reliable data or even any data at all. The inadequacy of records of small proprietorships and consumer units, for example, is a major problem of national income accounting.

3   Design of the reporting system. Other things equal, complete enumerations (censuses) are more reliable than samples, and large samples more reliable than small samples. Possible gaps in information must also be considered.

4   Estimating procedure employed. If the data come in nearly the same form as that in which they enter the final estimates, potential error in procedure may be reduced. However, this does not mean that the simpler the procedure the more reliable the estimate; absence of a complex procedure may merely indicate use of one broad guess in the absence of information.[9]

A few illustrations of the application of these factors will give an indication of what is required. There is little doubt that on the income side the wages and salaries component ranks highest in reliability. It is based on a relatively simple concept; the quality of the record-keeping system is high, as is the quality of the reporting system, both of which are by-products of the comprehensive social security system; the adjustments of reported totals are small and statistically well founded. On the other hand, estimates of change in business inventories present a reliability problem. The item is a complex one, requiring decisions of cost allocations and valuation by the reporting unit. Particularly for the noncorporate sector, records are inadequate, and the reporting system is not entirely satisfactory. The item of change in inventories is estimated as a residual between large and volatile totals, and is thus subject to significant percentage errors. The estimating procedure involves complex adjustment, often on the basis of less than secure statistical assumptions.

Revisions

Closely related to the subject of reliability in general is the subject of revisions in the estimates. In effect, a discussion of the size and character of subsequent revisions is a discussion of the reliability of the initial estimates.

The impetus behind successive revisions is the availability of additional and more reliable sources of data. Preliminary estimates of the series included in the national income and product accounts are published in the *Survey of Current Business* in the first month after the close of the quarter; revised figures for each quarter are shown in a subsequent issue. In the July issues, estimates of the three most recent years are revised. The July, 1969, issue, for example, updated previous estimates for 1966 to 1968. The new data incorporated into the estimates at that time

---

[9] U.S. Department of Commerce, Office of Business Economics, *National Income*, 1954, *op. cit.*, p. 62.

included Internal Revenue Service statistics, which provided the basis for estimating profits for 1966 and 1967; state unemployment insurance payroll statistics, which provided new information for wage and salary estimates for 1968; the 1967 preliminary data from the annual Survey of Manufactures; new Census Bureau data on business inventories, which provided the principal sources of information for nonfarm inventory change for 1966 to 1968; the fiscal 1970 Budget and other federal government reports; and Census Bureau reports of finances of state governments for fiscal year 1968 and local governments for fiscal years 1967 and 1968. Periodically—as in 1954, 1958, and 1965—comprehensive revisions are made to incorporate major additions to the statistical source data and, in the years cited, some definitional change in the income and products totals and their components. In the 1965 revisions, for example, the results of the 1958 Censuses of Manufactures, Business, and Mineral Industries and the 1960 Censuses of Population and Housing were incorporated.

Several studies have attempted to assess the nature and size of the revisions as a key to the reliability of the initial quarterly estimates. Of course, this only gets at one possible source of error, that of using less than complete information for the initial estimates. In other words, the revised estimates, however good or bad, become the standard of comparison. A study by the Office of Statistical Standards of the Bureau of the Budget sought to evaluate the bias upward or downward, dispersion, and missed direction of first estimates of quarter-to-quarter movements in selected series.[10] An evaluation was done by Rosanne Cole of the National Bureau of Economic Research as part of a larger study of short-term forecasting accuracy.[11] Because of the lags in the availability of primary data, the provisional estimates can be viewed as extrapolations, and the revisions are largest for the series which show considerable variability and weak serial correlation with the related series. Of the six revisions through which the GNP estimates pass, successive revisions, as a rule, make each set a more accurate prediction of the final set. Least accurate are the revisions one month after the advance estimates; only about 50 percent of these early revisions reduce error. Several kinds of bias have been isolated. The initial quarterly estimates tend to understate increases and overstate decreases in aggregate economic activity. The errors are primarily the result of overestimating changes in inventory investment and understating changes in personal consumption expenditure. During contractions, the two kinds of error reinforce each other, but during expansions, they tend to offset each other. Over the longer term, the initial figures tend to understate the growth trend throughout the period 1947 to 1963. With regard to components, early income-side estimates are only slightly more accurate than corresponding expenditure-side estimates. The differences in the primary data which tend to favor the early income estimates, such as the large percentage of income which can be based on fairly satisfactory payroll data, are apparently offset by the lack of early profits data.[12]

[10] The method is explained and carried forward to 1961 by George Jaszi, "The Quarterly National Income and Product Accounts of the United States, 1942-62," in Simon Goldberg and Phyllis Deane, eds., *Studies in Short-term National Accounts and Long-term Economic Growth, Income and Wealth*, ser. XI (London: Bowes & Bowes, Publishers, Ltd., 1966), pp. 117-139.

[11] Rosanne Cole, *Errors in Provisional Estimates of Gross National Product* (New York: National Bureau of Economic Research, 1969).

[12] *Ibid.*, pp. 91-96.

SOURCES AND METHODS OF NATIONAL INCOME ESTIMATION
IN LESS DEVELOPED COUNTRIES

The importance of a knowledge of the sources and methods used in preparing the United States national income statistics has been stressed as a means of gauging the reliability of the estimates and recognizing their limits. A similar knowledge is equally important when working with national income statistics of other nations, particularly the less developed countries, for one cannot assume that the structure of their economies will permit the collection of parallel data or the use of similar sources.

Indeed, less developed countries present special problems to national income estimators. First of all, these countries may exhibit "dualism," i.e., the simultaneous existence of traditional and modern modes of production and living. As a result, sources and methods that give tolerably reliable results in one part of the economy might be totally inapplicable in the other. Subsistence production is often important in less developed countries. This implies that neither quantity information, such as on the physical quantity of labor input or product output, nor value information is readily available. Small production units are prevalent, making sample and census work extremely difficult. Variation in quality, size, and design of a particular commodity, or even absence of uniform units of measurement, complicate classification and enumeration.

The above characteristics suggest, *ceteris paribus*, a paucity of statistical information upon which to base national income and product estimates. Furthermore, only in recent years, owing in large measure to the emphasis on planned economic development, has provision of useful and up-to-date statistics been considered important. With regard to methods, the fact that developing countries by definition are changing countries means that extrapolating from bench-mark data on the basis of estimating assumptions embodied in fixed coefficients becomes very hazardous.

As a result of the paucity of data and the inapplicability of commonly employed methods, there is wide shading in the quality of national income and product estimates throughout the world, with the less developed nations generally on the lower end of the quality scale. Table 13-1 shows an evaluation of national account statistics for sixty-four countries, by continent, as of 1956. The ratings take into consideration the extent and quality of the source data available and the methods employed. A concentration of lower-quality ratings of countries in Asia, Africa, and Latin America is apparent.

Efforts to Improve Economic Accounts

Substantial effort is being devoted to improving the economic accounts of the less developed countries, both by the countries themselves and by international organizations. The UN has maintained a long-standing interest in this effort. After the *SNA* was published in 1953, the handbook, *Methods of National Income Estimation*, was prepared as an aid to preparing national income statistics, with the needs of the less developed countries given particular attention.[13] Subsequently, the UN

---

[13] United Nations, Department of Economic and Social Affairs, Statistical Office, *Methods of National Income Estimation*, Provisional Issue, Studies in Methods, ser. F, no. 8 (New York: January, 1955).

TABLE 13-1
Quality Rating of National Accounts Statistics, 1956

	All	Very Good	Good	Fair	Weak
Africa	9	..	1	2	6
America, North	11	2	1	5	3
America, South	8	..	2	4	2
Asia	15	..	2	5	8
Europe and Oceania	21	15	3	2	1
Total	64	17	9	18	20

SOURCE: U.S. Congress, Joint Economic Committee, *International Economic Statistics*, A memorandum prepared for the Subcommittee on Economic Statistics of the Joint Economic Committee by the Office of Statistical Standards of the Bureau of the Budget, Joint Committee Print (1958), p. 42.

not only has published a *Yearbook of National Account Statistics,* but has also provided a survey of national accounting practices, with a view to their ultimate improvement through analysis and comparison.[14]

The document describing the revision of the SNA devotes a chapter to the need to adapt the full system of accounts to developing nations.[15] Schemes of classification are suggested to supplement the classification of industries according to kind of activity: (1) classification into modern and traditional modes of production, based on such criteria as the resources and technology used, the manner of organization and management, and the scale of operation; and (2) classification into privately and publicly owned or controlled establishments. Three areas are suggested for which it may be useful to compile special series of data: geographic and/or economic areas, as for rural and urban portions of the nation; leading sectors in economic growth, such as export industries, industries supplying import substitutes, or industries supplying goods to a national market; and the public sector, in view of the usually important role in economic development that it plays. An order of priority in compilation for the standard accounts and tables is presented, based on a weighing of the difficulty of collecting basic data against the urgency of need. The highest priority is given to the consolidated accounts and many of the flows of the deconsolidated production accounts (and associated current-price tables), external transactions, government activities, and financial transactions of monetary authorities.

The Organization for Economic Cooperation and Development has also encouraged standardization and improvement of national accounts, not only for its

[14] United Nations, Department of Economic and Social Affairs, Statistical Office, *National Accounting Practices in Sixty Countries,* a supplement to the *Yearbook of National Accounts Statistics,* Provisional Issue, Studies in Methods, ser. F, no. 11 (New York: 1964).
[15] UN, *SNA,* 1968, chap. IX, pp. 207-229.

ECONOMIC ACCOUNTS AND THEIR USES

economically developed member nations, but also for less developed countries. The Development Center of the OECD publishes a series of documents containing national accounts data and detailed bibliographies for selected developing nations. The dual aim of this program is to provide a readily accessible collection of data and a critique of the figures, which will assist in interpretation and, perhaps, encourage improvement, resulting in greater reliability and comparability.[16]

Estimating Methods

Of the three methods by which national income may be estimated—the sum of value added or income originating by industry, the sum of factor shares, and the sum of final expenditures—the basic approach in less developed nations is to build up value added by industry. Although there are differences from nation to nation, it is possible to generalize on the sources and methods used in preparation of value-added estimates for the major industries.[17]

The estimates for the agricultural sector are particularly important because of the predominance of agriculture in the economies of the countries. The value added for agriculture is commonly obtained by estimating the value of gross output and deducting the expenses of production. Total physical output for the major crops is derived by multiplying acreage by average yield. Annual surveys of crop cuttings and acreage are seldom available, so that intercensal estimates are often based on presumed changes in crop acreage and average yield. Price statistics may be deficient in that they represent town prices, which overstate the production value of output; offsetting this tendency is the fact that often the price statistics are based on harvest prices, which are usually the annual low. Prices may also vary substantially from one part of a country to another. Both output and price data are shakier for minor crops, especially animal production, than for major crops. Appropriate statistics on expenses of production are even harder to obtain, except those for a few commercial crops. Frequently, resort is made to deduction of round percentages from the gross value to obtain the net value added based on fragmentary information.

Manufacturing value added may be derived from physical production data. The annual estimates of gross output are often obtained by extrapolating bench-mark census or survey data on the basis of current indexes. The bench-mark data may be plagued with undercoverage. It is also common for the manufacturing indexes to be constructed from returns sent in by a fixed sample of establishments selected in a remote base year, thus omitting the increase in production due to the addition of new firms. Alternative to the use of physical production data, value added may be obtained from income data. Total wages and salaries paid may be estimated and a percentage addition made for profits, usually based on tax sources, and other factor

---

[16] See, for example, *National Accounts of Less Developed Nations* (Paris: Organization for Economic Cooperation and Development, 1967).

[17] Basic material appears in the two UN documents mentioned above: *Methods of National Income Estimation* and *National Accounting Practices in Sixty Countries.* Useful commentary and summarization are available in Harry T. Oshima, "National Income Statistics of Underdeveloped Countries," *Journal of the American Statistical Association,* vol. 52, pp. 162–174, June, 1957; and Emanuel Levy, "National Income Accounting in Developing Countries," *Finance and Development,* vol. 5, pp. 26–30, June, 1968.

income. The wages and salaries paid are often based on number employed times an average wage. The demarcation of those who are employed is more difficult in less developed countries than in developed countries, because housewives and students do a significant amount of work that may be difficult to distinguish from that done by persons more easily classified as economically active. The income data, by which the number of employed is multiplied, may come from several sources, including social security data, industrial censuses, income censuses, tax statistics, or sample surveys. The quality of the data may be impaired by the limited coverage or the seasonality of earnings.

Construction industry value added is usually based on physical estimates of construction, although the data available are crude. Direct information may be available for government construction only. Systems of building permits, which could provide the backbone of the estimates, are effective only in the larger towns. Trade and service estimates are even cruder. They may not be obtained by direct measurement at all, but by making their level and movement a function of the level and movement of output in other areas of the economy. As an example, for trade, the gross output of commodity-producing sectors, after adjustment for exports and imports and output supplied directly to consumers, may be used to estimate the value of goods entering trade. Customary markups may then be added to obtain gross profit, and expenses deducted to reach net value of services of trade. When direct estimates are obtained, the income method is commonly utilized.

The difficulty of obtaining data on factor incomes or expenditures on final products dictates that the value-added approach should be the basic one. Some countries are able to utilize the other approaches, as well, and still others prepare estimates of only certain components, such as the investment component of the expenditure approach. The essential problem with the expenditure approach is that personal consumption expenditure in many, if not most, countries is obtained as a residual after deducting the estimatable components of government consumption plus investment from domestic product plus net imports. An important item on the agenda for less developed countries is to prepare surveys of household expenditure; these could be an economical means of rounding out the expenditure approach as a much-needed check on the aggregate value-added estimate.

REVIEW QUESTIONS

1 Explain why diversity is the notable characteristic of the primary sources of data for the income and product accounts.
2 What is the commodity-flow procedure? What are the steps in applying the procedure to the estimation of consumer purchases?
3 What are the sources of primary data and methods used in preparing estimates of the major components of GNP by type of expenditure?
4 What are the sources of primary data and methods used in preparing estimates of the major components of charges against GNP, i.e., the income side of the summary account?
5 How can the reliability of the GNP estimates be judged?
6 What are major sources and estimating methods used in less developed countries to prepare national income estimates?

SUGGESTED REFERENCES

JASZI, GEORGE: "The Statistical Foundations of the Gross National Product." *Review of Economics and Statistics,* vol. 38, pp. 205-214, May, 1956.

——: "The Quarterly Income and Product Accounts of the United States, 1942-62," in Simon Goldberg and Phyllis Deane, eds., *Studies in Short-term National Accounts and Long-term Economic Growth, Income and Wealth,* ser. XI (London: Bowes & Bowes, Publishers, Ltd., 1966).

UNITED NATIONS, DEPARTMENT OF ECONOMIC AND SOCIAL AFFAIRS, STATISTICAL OFFICE: *National Accounting Practice in Sixty Countries,* a supplement to the *Yearbook of National Accounts Statistics,* Provisional Issue, Studies in Methods, ser. F, no. 11 (New York: 1964).

U.S. DEPARTMENT OF COMMERCE, OFFICE OF BUSINESS ECONOMICS: *National Income,* a supplement to the *Survey of Current Business* (1954).

——: *U.S. Income and Output,* a supplement to the *Survey of Current Business* (1958).

The two publications from OBE remain the basic references on sources and methods of preparing the income and product estimates in the United States.

An Integrated System of Economic Accounts: Recapitulation

14

In the opening chapter, we presented a "vision" of an integrated set of economic accounts to provide a framework for the subsequent chapters devoted to discussion of the various component accounts and other aspects of the system. In that discussion, we tried to indicate the relation of each account to the ones which preceded and/or followed it. But now, before going on to a discussion of the uses, we shall provide a general summary of the economic accounts viewed as an integrated whole, with particular emphasis on their overall structure, or design.

The summary is general, because we are not describing a specific set of economic accounts. We shall refer to the United States and the UN accounts, indicating various criticisms of their design and suggestions for improvement. This summary really relates to our own "ideal" set of accounts, which we sketch in general outline but not in specific detail (except for the current and capital accounts presented in Chapter 8). In many respects, the system we describe is quite similar to that recently developed independently by Richard and Nancy Ruggles.[1] We could have worked out a very specific and detailed structure and set of definitions, but that is unnecessary. For the student, the important thing

[1] Nancy Ruggles and Richard Ruggles, *The Design of Economic Accounts* (New York: National Bureau of Economic Research, 1970).

is to see the general system, to understand the major variables and the structure, but not to become enmeshed in the details, particularly those of a proposed system which will never be effectuated in entirety. As we have stressed from the beginning, the accounts should be considered fluid. Further improvements will be made, even on our ideal system, and it would be a mistake to try to crystallize it. Also, this summary is general, because the preceding chapters discuss basic concepts and the component accounts rather thoroughly.

The Production Account

In summary, the production account comprises the basic income and product estimates, which were not only the focus of historical development but have become the cornerstone of modern economic accounting systems. The production account is the cornerstone because, on one hand, it may be deconsolidated into value added by industry (of establishments) and the industry production estimates further disaggregated in terms of input-output tables, while on the other hand, it may be linked by institutional sector to income and outlay accounts, sector capital accounts, and balance sheets. Consolidated balance sheets yield aggregate wealth estimates, which represent the cumulation of net tangible investment either by sector or by industry — thus linking the two types of classification underlying the accounts.

In view of their central importance, the concepts of income and product and their components have received much attention in the literature, and we have reviewed most of the chief issues. In many cases, alternative concepts are useful for different purposes. Thus, *domestic* product, the aggregate used in the UN accounts, is preferable for production analysis, while *national* income and product, featured in the United States accounts, is preferable for analysis of sources and disposition of income. *Net* income and product is clearly better than *gross* from a welfare viewpoint, while gross investment and product may be more useful for analysis of demand and short-run supply capabilities. Confining the scope of the economy largely to market activity is statistically more practicable and does not prejudice analysis of business conditions and fluctuations; on the other hand, expanded imputations for nonmarket activity would improve the accuracy of intertemporal and interspatial comparisons.

It will be recalled that it is in the last area that we made a series of recommendations for improvement of the production and related accounts. We urged that the scope of national income and product be expanded by including imputations for the rental values of nonbusiness durable goods (in addition to owner-occupied residences) and imputations for the value of nonmarket labor activities, particularly productive household work, volunteer labor outside the home, and the opportunity cost of school work. Not only would such imputations improve trend analysis and international comparisons, but also they would provide a more accurate picture of the relative importance of nonbusiness sectors and of types of factor compensation. Even if expanded imputations were not integrated as a regular feature of the accounts, periodic estimates of nonmarket activity would still be very useful for analytical purposes.

The income, or debit, side of the production account is generally broken down according to legal forms. We have pointed out that, for practical statistical analysis of income distribution, the net income of proprietors must be divided between its labor and property components. Richard and Nancy Ruggles have further recommended that "profits" as measured should be divided between an imputed interest on equity capital and "pure" profits.[2] While analytically of considerable interest, this proposal poses many conceptual and statistical problems, especially if it were to be implemented for many industries, since estimates of net worth, possibly revalued on a current basis, and appropriate interest rate(s), would have to be provided for each. Here, again, such estimates might best be prepared on an occasional basis rather than become an integral part of the production account, at least until after the experimental phase of the work were over.

One final broad comment on the income side of the production account: It seems clear that depreciation should be revalued from book values (original cost) to current replacement cost, if net product is to represent market prices or approximations thereof. This means that profits would be subject to a "depreciation valuation adjustment," which would make the estimates economically more meaningful.

On the credit side of the production account, the practice of classifying final demand by major sectors is well established as an aid to analysis of the decision-making processes by tying in with the sector income-outlay and capital accounts, which we turn to later. Further, a detailed breakdown by commodity type of consumption and investment, private and public, and exports and imports, is essential not only to demand analysis, but also to analysis of the structure of production, by industry, which we consider below.

Commodity detail is likewise essential for deflation of gross product by appropriate price indexes. Factor costs may likewise be deflated by factor-price indexes or used to weight together input measures, such as man-hours or real capital stock utilized in production. The relationships of real product to real factor cost, either as ratios or as the "scalar" in statistical production functions, provide a basis for estimating rates of change in total factor productivity.

INDUSTRY DISAGGREGATION OF THE PRODUCTION ACCOUNT

For purposes of production and productivity analysis, the production account may be disaggregated by industries composed of establishments, in contrast to the institutional sectoring used in tracing income and financial flows. The commodity detail of the GNP permits the final goods and services to be traced back to industries of origin. The final sales together with sales of intermediate products constitute the total production of the various industries. The total value of output less the cost of purchased intermediate goods equals value added. The sum of value added (net output) for all industries—and in production analysis, the productive activities of nonenterprise sectors are classed as "industries"—equals the gross national income and product.

These relationships are shown in Diagram 14-1. The revised UN system of national accounts provides for estimates of income and product originating by industry, or "activity," both as the sum of factor costs and other charges and as the difference between the total value of production and intermediate product costs. The latter approach is currently used by the U.S. Department of Commerce for about

[2] *Ibid.*, pp. 54–58.

ECONOMIC ACCOUNTS AND THEIR USES

DIAGRAM 14-1

Deconsolidation of the aggregate production account, with investment account and wealth statement, by industry.

Sales → Industry	Intermediate A	B · · · N	Total intermediate sales	Final demand	Total value of production
Purchases ↓ A					
B .					
: N					
Total intermediate purchases					
Factor purchases					
Other charges					
Total costs of production					

(a) Production account

		Industry				(Derivation)
		A	B	N	Total	
1.	Gross investment					(2+3+4)
2.	Structures					
3.	Equipment					
4.	Inventories					
5.	Capital consumption					
6.	Net investment					(1−5)
7.	Revaluations					
8.	Change in wealth					(6+7)
	Wealth:					
9.	First of period					
10.	End of period					(9+8)

(b) Investment account with revaluation

half the private industries for which real product estimates are prepared. The approach based on dual streams of commodity flows is essential to the double-deflation method of estimating real product by industry. That is, the value of gross production, by categories of goods and/or services, is deflated by appropriate indexes of prices received by the establishments of the industry; purchased intermediate products are likewise deflated by category; and real product emerges as the difference between the two real flows. The real industry product may then be related to real factor cost of the industry, estimated as described at the national level, in order to obtain index numbers of total factor productivity, by industry, essential for analysis of changing industrial structure.

When data are collected on the industry origins and/or destinations of intermediate product, it becomes possible to show interindustry sales and purchase relationships in terms of a rectangular "input-output" matrix, as also depicted in Diagram 14-1. In Chapter 5, we saw how useful this information can be, providing a basis for estimating the direct and indirect requirements for the production of each industry with a given change in final demand.

Many countries have produced input-output matrices, at least for one year. In the United States input-output matrices were recently integrated with the national income and product accounts. The new UN system is set up to show these interrelationships among industries, and commodity groupings as well. Commodity groupings have the advantage of being "pure," whereas industries produce not only the primary commodities in terms of which they are defined, but frequently some fraction of secondary products. The advantage of industry classifications is that production can be related directly to the inputs, factor and intermediate, used by the producing units. If pure commodity groupings are used in interindustry studies, inputs and costs must be reallocated among commodity groupings according to some arbitrary prorating device.

In an estimation of stocks of capital resources utilized by industry, it is desirable for production analysis to record gross investment by industry (of establishments). This makes possible the estimation of gross and net stocks of capital at the beginning and end of each period by means of the perpetual inventory method, given appropriate information concerning mortality experience of major types of depreciable capital goods in the various industries, and depreciation curves. The estimates may be expressed in terms of current prices if provision is made for the revaluation of assets held at the beginning and end of the period to reflect price changes. The price indexes can, of course, be used to deflate the wealth estimates. The real wealth estimates can then be used in conjunction with the real output estimates to obtain capital coefficients, by industry. Or, since consistent industry employment and man-hour estimates ideally would be contained in supporting tables, statistical production functions may be fitted to the industry output and input estimates, or estimates of total factor productivity can be prepared by industry along lines suggested above.

SECTOR INCOME, INVESTMENT, AND FINANCING ACCOUNTS

The income-outlay, saving-investment, and financing accounts are based on an institutional sectoring. That is, organizations are grouped in terms of decision-making similarity as regards disposition of income and the investment of savings or the financing of borrowing.

It is generally argued that at least three chief sectors must be distinguished:

households, business (or enterprises), and governments. The rest of the world is often called a sector, but actually it represents a separate account into which are placed the foreign transactions of the various domestic sectors. Private nonprofit institutions are a problem, since they do not fit into the triad of major sectors. The Commerce Department combines them with households, while the SNA would make a separate sector of those which service households. In view of the small size of private nonprofit institutions in aggregate value of income and product, and certain analogies with enterprises, Richard and Nancy Ruggles would combine them with the business sector. As in all classifications, reality is not always tidy!

The several sectors may, of course, be broken down still further. For example, the general governments sector may be divided among central, state, and local governments. It is essential, if financing accounts are to be shown, that the business sector be broken between financial and nonfinancial subsectors. The major types of financial institutions may be distinguished, and the nonfinancial organizations may be divided into many industrial groupings if desired and if data permit. Here, as elsewhere, in macroeconomic accounting, a balance must be struck between the utility of additional information and the loss of comprehensibility. But the recognition of major industry groups in which decision-making criteria and financial structures differ markedly would seem to be warranted. The industry grouping should comprise companies rather than establishments, of course, since the managements of companies or other enterprises as a whole make the ultimate decisions with respect to saving, productive investments, and financing.

The structure of the official United States economic accounts, as depicted by Richard and Nancy Ruggles, is reproduced in Diagram 14-2. The inadequacies are apparent from the viewpoint of an integrated system. No business sector account is distinguished, since business net income and corporate saving emerge in the production account, and business investment largely constitutes total investment, by OBE definitions. It follows, of course, that financial and nonfinancial businesses are not distinguished, so that meaningful financing accounts cannot be elaborated on the basis of the present OBE system.

The OBE system distinguishes only a national saving-investment account. The savings of the several sectors are credited to this account, to which all domestic and net foreign investments are debited. This treatment partially hinges on OBE's narrow definition of investment. By that definition, domestic investment is confined to business investment, although the latter is stretched to include investments in owner-occupied residences, but not other consumer durables or government durables. We recommend strongly (Chapter 8), as do Richard and Nancy Ruggles, that investment be defined broadly to include durable goods purchases by all sectors, inventory accumulation, outlays for development of natural resources, and also expenditures for intangibles which enhance future income- and output-producing capacity.

When future-oriented outlays by all sectors are classed as investment, the desirability of showing saving-investment accounts for all sectors—i.e., disaggregating the OBE national saving-investment account—becomes clear. Each sector is then seen to save, or dissave, depending on whether its income exceeds its current (noninvestment) outlays. This saving, plus or minus, can then be carried down as a credit to the sector's saving-investment account, to which its total investments are debited. To the extent that its saving exceeds (or falls short of) its investments, the sector is a net lender to (or borrower from) other sectors, directly or through financial intermediaries.

Thus far, the development of sector capital accounts was provided for in the old, as well as the new, UN standard system of national accounts. The SNA is more informative than the OBE system, in that saving, investment, and net lending or borrowing are shown for all sectors, except business, which in the old SNA was merged with the national accounts. For the entire nation, as shown by the OBE and UN accounts, following Keynes's ex post definitions, saving and investment are

DIAGRAM 14-2
The structure of the United States national income accounts. Source: Nancy Ruggles and Richard Ruggles, *The Design of Economic Accounts* (New York: National Bureau of Economic Research, 1970), p. 29.

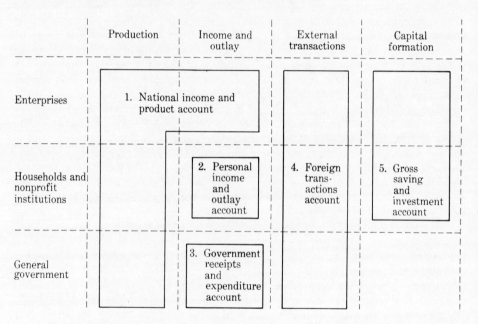

equal. For each sector, however, saving may exceed or fall short of investment, giving rise to "net financial investment" plus or minus (i.e., net lending or borrowing). Equality is established on a sector basis only if net changes in financial investments are shown in addition to real investments and if the net increases in liabilities are shown in addition to saving as sources of funds.

This further elaboration of capital accounts is contained in financing, or flow-of-funds, accounts. We reviewed the system of the Federal Reserve Board, which adapted the OBE sector accounts to accommodate capital financing. The advantage of the financing accounts is that they detail the various types of instruments in

ECONOMIC ACCOUNTS AND THEIR USES

DIAGRAM 14-3

The structure of the revised United Nations system of national accounts. Source: Nancy Ruggles and Richard Ruggles, *The Design of Economic Accounts* (New York: National Bureau of Economic Research, 1970), p. 17.

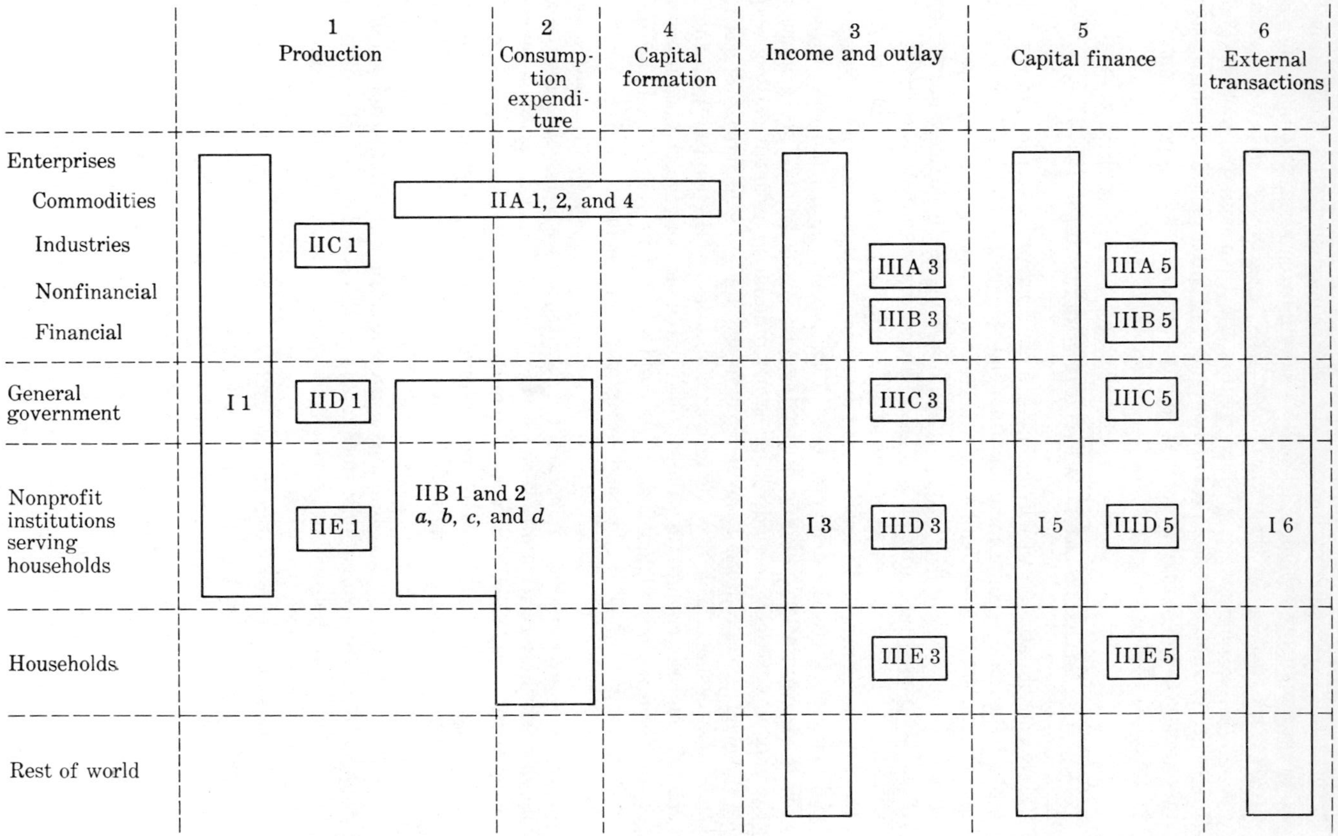

227

terms of which lending and borrowing are accomplished, thus facilitating financial analysis. Financing accounts, as well as saving-investment accounts, for all sectors, are likewise provided by the revised SNA. The new UN system is depicted in Appendix B and in Diagram 14-3, which follows the treatment by Richard and Nancy Ruggles. As in the FRB system, nonfinancial and financial business sectors are distinguished. These may be further subdivided, and major types of financial assets and liabilities shown at various levels of detail.

BALANCE SHEETS AND WEALTH ESTIMATES

Deconsolidation of the saving-investment account by sector, and its elaboration into a full capital account including financial transactions, opens the way to development of balance sheets and wealth statements depicting an important aspect of economic conditions of the nation, by major sector, at the ends of successive periods. If the balance sheet carries assets and liabilities at original cost, the tie-in is very simple. At any point in time, assets and financial liabilities are shown in the balance sheet for the same classifications used in the capital account. Total assets less financial liabilities gives the residual, "net worth," on the right-hand side of the balance sheet. The capital account shows the *changes* in the balance sheet items between the ends of successive periods. That is, net tangible investment and net acquisition of financial assets represent the changes in the items on the left-hand, asset, side of the balance sheet. The net changes in liabilities of the capital-financing account should equal the changes in balance sheet liabilities between the beginning and end of the given period, while net saving should equal the change in net worth, the balancing category on the right-hand side of the balance sheet.

Actually, the balance sheet is more useful if it is expressed in terms of market prices, or approximations to market, for consistency with the valuations used in the income and product accounts. When it is expressed in market prices, changes in the balance sheet reflect not only net saving and investment and net changes in the financial assets and liabilities from the capital account, but also changes in the market value of existing assets and liabilities between the beginning and end of the period (and of new investments or issues of assets and liabilities between the average price during the period and that obtaining at the end of the period). Currency and deposits are not subject to revaluations, since money is the standard of value. The change in net worth reflects not only net saving, but also the excess of asset revaluations over revaluations of liabilities.

These principles are illustrated in Table 14-1, taken from the UN report; it shows simplified hypothetical opening and closing balance sheets for a nation. Although the new SNA does not include balance sheets, the system is set up in such a way that they can be added when the system is elaborated in this direction at a later time. The report discusses the relationship of balance sheets to the flow accounts in general terms, and the matrix presentation of the new system provides rows and columns for opening assets, revaluations, and closing assets, in addition to the flow accounts, as shown in Table 14-2, also taken from the UN report. The heavy lines within the matrix delineate the flow accounts which compose the present system. The balance sheet items have been pulled out of the matrix, and opening and closing statements are shown in Table 14-3.

TABLE 14-1
Opening and Closing Balance Sheets, All Institutional Sectors

	Assets					Liabilities and Net Worth			
	Opening Assets	*Acquisition of Assets*	*Revaluation of Assets*	*Closing Assets*		*Opening Liabilities*	*Issue of Liabilities*	*Revaluation of Liabilities*	*Closing Liabilities*
Currency and deposits	275	12		287	Currency and deposits	296	14		310
Securities	457	3	−25	435	Securities	442	8	−26	424
Other financial assets	517	43	4	564	Other financial liabilities	479	37	3	519
Net tangible assets	661	28	42	731	Net worth	693	27	44	764
Total	1,910	86	21	2,017	Total	1,910	86	21	2,017

SOURCE: United Nations, *A System of National Accounts* (1968), p. 32, table 2.16.

Having national balance sheets, by major components, one can readily derive wealth statements. It will be recalled from Chapter 10 that, when sector balance sheets are consolidated (rather than combined, as in Table 14-1), the domestically issued and held financial claims cancel out. If domestic liabilities to foreigners are netted against domestic claims on foreigners, one is left with the identity that national net worth equals domestic tangible assets plus net foreign assets (net claims on the rest of the world). This is depicted for the beginning and end of the period in Table 14-4.

The changes in the several items may be related to the UN matrix (Table 14-2) as follows. Closing net worth is linked to opening net worth by the entries in columns 6 and 14: 764 = 693 + 27 (net saving) + 44 (net revaluation). Closing tangible assets are linked to opening tangible assets by the entries in rows 6, 7, 8, and 14: 731 = 661 − 19 (capital consumption) + 6 (inventory accumulation) + 41 (gross fixed investment) + 42 (revaluation). Closing net foreign assets (33) are linked to the opening value (32) by the entry in row 12, column 11, net foreign investment (1).

In principle, the domestic net tangible assets shown in the national balance sheet should equal the sum of the net tangible assets commanded by each producing industry of the economy (see above, Diagram 14-1). We have now come full circle: The sector and industry approaches to domestic wealth converge. Note, however, that by the sector balance sheet approach, the sum of net tangible assets can also be viewed as the sum of net worth for the domestic sectors. And for each sector, the two would generally not be equal, since the financial assets of each sector would

TABLE 14-2
A Primary Disaggregation of the National Accounts, Including Balance Sheets

			1	2	3	4	5	6	7	8	9	10	11	12	13	14	15	16
Opening assets	1	Financial claims										1,249		165				
	2	Net tangible assets										661						
Production	3	Commodities				245	166		6	41			50					
	4	Activities			443		44											
Consumption	5	Consumer goods/purposes						210					2					
	6	Income and outlay			14	241						-19	13					
Accumulation	7	Increase in stocks										6						
	8	Fixed capital formation										41						
	9	Financial claims										58		18				
	10	Capital finance	1,217	693				27			59				-23	44	1,253	764
The rest of the world	11	Current transactions			51	1	2	12										
	12	Capital transactions	197	-32							17		1		0	-2	214	-33
Revaluations	13	Financial claims										-21		-2				
	14	Net tangible assets										42						
Closing assets	15	Financial claims										1,286		181				
	16	Net tangible assets										731						

NOTE: In the columns: opening and closing assets are balanced by opening and closing liabilities; and net tangible assets are balanced by net worth. The left side of the accounts (termed outgoings by the UN report) is shown across the rows; the right side (incomings) is shown down the rows.

SOURCE: United Nations, *A System of National Accounts (1968)* p. 9, table 1.6.

230

TABLE 14-3

National Balance Sheets

OPENING OF PERIOD

Assets		Liabilities and Net Worth	
Financial (1, 10)	1,249	Liabilities (10,1)	1,217
Domestic	1,052	Domestic	1,052
Foreign (12,1)	197	Foreign (1, 12)	165
Tangible, net (2, 10)	661	Net Worth (10, 2)	693
Total	1,910	Total	1,910

CLOSING OF PERIOD

Assets		Liabilities and Net Worth	
Financial (15, 10)	1,286	Liabilities (10,15)	1,253
Domestic	1,072	Domestic	1,072
Foreign (12, 15)	214	Foreign (15, 12)	181
Tangible, net (16, 10)	731	Net Worth (10, 16)	764
Total	2,017	Total	2,017

NOTE: The numbers in parenthesis relate to the row and column, respectively, of Table 14.2. Domestic financial assets were derived as a residual.
SOURCE: Derived from Table 14-2.

generally be larger or smaller than its liabilities. This underscores the significance of the two meanings that may be attached to the concept of wealth in a closed economy: It may be viewed either as net worth or as the underlying net tangible assets. In an open national economy, however, net foreign claims must be added to the domestic net tangible assets to equal the national net worth. In a regional economy, as discussed in Chapter 12, net claims on the rest of the nation would also be included in regional net worth.

THE ROAD AHEAD

No nation has as yet produced the kind of comprehensive integrated economic accounts envisaged in this volume and by the revised United Nations system of national accounts. In the United States, we have a considerable distance to go before even a first approximation to an integrated system will be realized. In particular, the official Commerce Department income and product accounts must be restructured to

TABLE 14-4
National Wealth

OPENING OF PERIOD			
Assets		*Net Worth*	
Net tangible assets	661		
Net foreign claims	32		
Total	693	Total	693

CLOSING OF PERIOD			
Assets		*Net Worth*	
Net tangible assets	731		
Net foreign claims	33		
Total	764	Total	764

SOURCE: Derived from Table 14-3.

permit elaboration in the direction of both national and sector capital-financing accounts and balance sheets, permitting coordination with the Federal Reserve Board flow-of-funds accounts. Then, OBE estimates of tangible asset stocks must be extended to cover all types and sectors, so that in conjunction with the FRB estimates of financial assets and liabilities, complete balance sheets and wealth statements for the nation and its major sectors can be provided. Finally, price indexes for all types of tangible assets and financial claims must be developed in order to fill out a revaluation account to provide the missing link between capital accounts and balance sheets based on market valuations.

As integrated systems of economic accounts are gradually developed in the United States and other countries, the design of the systems will undoubtedly be improved. Despite the many advantages of the revised SNA over the 1953 SNA system—above all, structuring the accounts as an integrated whole—further revisions will undoubtedly be made in the SNA both as a guide to country statistical developments and as the basis for standardized international reporting to facilitate comparisons. As noted earlier, the revised SNA does not delineate the structure of balance sheets in the standard accounts or in the supporting tables. This task is deferred to a later report. Even the UN standard flow accounts have been criticized justly as follows: "The new UN system in its consolidated form thus provides too little information about the economic activities and the interrelationships of sectors, but in even the initial deconsolidation it provides such a complex and detailed network of flows that the relationships are obscured."[3]

[3] *Ibid.*, p. 37.

We have purposely kept the discussion of an integrated system of economic accounts in this volume on a fairly general level, recognizing that substantial revisions in the various national systems and in the UN system are inevitable and desirable as concepts and statistics improve. We believe that our major proposals— for expanding the imputations for nonmarket activity and for broadening the concept of investment to include intangible as well as tangible capital goods—are constructive; but even in these areas considerable experience in preparing estimates, and using them for analysis, will be needed before the necessary alterations of economic accounts to accommodate these variables should be crystallized.

Finally, we would be remiss not to say a few words about the movement in a number of countries to develop *social* accounts, in the true meaning of the word. Impressed by the success of economists in developing economic accounts as means of ordering vast amounts of information into a systematic framework useful for analysis, appraisal, forecasting, and/or goal setting, social scientists from a number of disciplines have been working toward the development of a similar body of social statistics.[4] It is hoped that eventually the United States may have an annual "social report" as a basis for evaluating past progress and charting future measures, and possibly a "Council of Social Advisers," which would have functions in the broader social realm comparable to those exercised by the present Council of Economic Advisers.[5] But it is generally believed that much more conceptual and statistical developmental work will be necessary before a full system of social accounts can be constructed.

To some extent, the economic accounts can present additional detail, which may be of broad social significance, by the use of techniques of deconsolidation and disaggregation. For example, the household account can be disaggregated to show income and outlay for various socioeconomic groupings. As Richard and Nancy Ruggles have written: "Samples of households providing information on such things as wages, other income, financial transactions, and assets and liabilities need to be linked with social and demographic information relating to age, education, work status, family composition, place of residence, occupation, etc."[6] Micro-data sets can also be developed from government and business records. An important prerequisite for assembling detailed data is adequate provision for preserving the confidentiality of individual records.

In some areas, social data can be organized according to principles used in economic accounts. This would apply in the area of human stocks and flows, for example, with regard to which the recent UN report on the revised SNA speculates about possibilities of formulating what may be called a population matrix:

> Such a matrix makes it possible to bring together in a coherent form demographic, educational, manpower, and other social statistics which have a bearing on the economic and social characteristics of a population so that the changing structure of that population in terms of these characteristics can be measured. Just as the row and column pairs in the economic matrices set out in this report represent accounts

---

[4] See, for example, Raymond A. Bauer, ed., *Social Indicators* (Cambridge, Mass.: The M.I.T. Press, 1966).

[5] See U.S. Department of Health, Education, and Welfare, *Toward a Social Report* (1969).

[6] Ruggles and Ruggles, *op. cit.*, p. 135.

which balance, so the same is true in population matrices because all who flow into a period, whether through survival from the preceding period or through birth or immigration in the period itself, must necessarily flow out of the period, either through death or emigration in the period itself or through survival into the following period. The economic and population matrices (or accounts) would have many areas in common, such as the distribution of labour force activities and the distribution of the population over different types of household and institution. Eventually it would be desirable to link the two systems, much as it was proposed above to link statistics of the distribution of income, consumption and wealth to the SNA.[7]

But there are also many areas of social statistics, such as those relating to crime, health, attitudes, environmental factors, and so on, which could not be fitted into accounts in the sense that the term is used in business and economic accounting. It would be preferable to present statistics in these areas in supplemental tables and to call them "indicators."[8]

Since this book is about economic accounts, we shall not pursue the subject of social accounts and indicators in greater depth. The social statisticians are at a considerably earlier stage of development than we, and it could well be that their progress will be more rapid than ours, as we seek to refine what is becoming a well-charted field. But there is enough left to do in our field, as well as in theirs, for many years to come.

REVIEW QUESTIONS

1 What six major types of economic accounts make up the integrated system?
2 What are the main deficiencies of the present official United States national income accounts from the viewpoint of elaboration into a complete, consistent system?
3 Why are different types of sectoring required for disaggregation of the production account to show interindustry relationships and industry product, and to show sector income, capital finance, and balance sheets?
4 Why are revaluation accounts necessary to link capital accounts with balance sheets when market valuations are used?
5 In what two ways may national wealth, by sector, be interpreted?
6 Are social accounts feasible in the same sense as are economic accounts?

SELECTED REFERENCES

KENDRICK, JOHN W.: "National Income and Product Accounts," *International Encyclopedia of the Social Sciences*, vol. XI (New York: The Macmillan Company and The Free Press, 1968).

NATIONAL ACCOUNTS REVIEW COMMITTEE: *The National Economic Accounts of the United States: Review, Appraisal, and Recommendations, Hearings before the Subcommittee on Economic Statistics of the Joint Economic Committee*, 85th Cong., 1st Sess., 1957.

RUGGLES, NANCY, and RICHARD RUGGLES: *The Design of Economic Accounts* (New York: National Bureau of Economic Research, 1970).

UNITED NATIONS, DEPARTMENT OF ECONOMIC AND SOCIAL AFFAIRS, STATISTICAL OFFICE: *A System of National Accounts*, ser. F, no. 2, rev. 3 (New York: 1968).
See especially chaps. II and VIII.

[7] UN, *SNA*, 1968, p. 15.
[8] The Department of Health, Education, and Welfare currently prepares a monthly publication called *Social Indicators*.

ECONOMIC ACCOUNTS AND THEIR USES

Uses of Economic Accounts: General Survey

15

Economic accounts are tools as well as pedagogic devices. The test of tools is their usefulness. In this chapter we are concerned with the practical usefulness of the five different kinds of economic accounts. The economic accounts of the United States, and those conforming to the OECD and UN systems, are general-purpose tools in that they are designed to be useful to different types of users and for different purposes. Uses of the accounts may be classified in several ways.

I   Method of use
    A.   Instrumental, for example
        1.   Check of coverage and consistency of statistics
        2.   Indicator, e.g., use of an aggregate to determine contributions to or from political bodies
    B.   Substantive, for example
        1.   Operations with broad aggregates and their components, e.g., economic barometers or structural analyses
        2.   Operations with relationships among components, e.g., functional relationships
II Type of user
    A.   International organizations

B. Governments: federal, state, and local
C. Private groups: business, labor organizations, nonprofit institutions, households
III Purpose of use
A. Analysis
B. Projections and forecasts
C. Policy formulation

The matrix shown in Table 15-1 is built around the classification by purpose of use. *Analysis* of past behavior and relationships as recorded in statistics is often a first step in an investigation. The analysis is often guided by theory. Theory must pick out key variables and relationships. The accounts, and the data series within their frameworks, must combine detail into manageable and useful categories. Thus there is an interaction of theory, which suggests significant variables, and the accounts, which provide the data with which to test and refine theory, which may in turn suggest further refinements of the accounts. *Projections and forecasts* extend estimates of variables and relationships into the future. Projections are conditional upon assumptions; alternative assumptions may be provided to demonstrate a range of values. Forecasts are attempts to predict the most likely course of future events. Projections and forecasts may be for the purpose of estimating future values of accounting aggregates, such as GNP or total wealth. Or the projections and forecasts of accounting aggregates may be part of the background for other types of projections. *Policy formulation,* or decision making as it may be called in the private sector, is often the final step in the process that begins with analysis; it includes implicit or explicit projections and forecasts. Establishing quantitative targets in terms of the accounting variables may be part of the process. Policy formulation may be adaptive, in the sense that measures are taken to bring a unit into conformity with the projections of the whole, or, as is often the case with government policy formulation, the purpose may be to alter the forecast course of events. Particularly with regard to government policy, the formulation of recommended policy and efforts to influence the actual decision makers by academic experts and non-profit organizations, among others, should be included.

For each of the five kinds of accounts, illustrative uses in analysis, projections and forecasts, and policy formulation are entered in the cells of the matrix. It should be stressed that these entries and the discussion below relating to them are indeed illustrative, and by no means exhaustive. In some cases a particular work has been cited to help identify that use. The uses represent a spectrum of complexity and sophistication, from selection of one or more aggregates as a barometer of economic activity to complex models using several accounts. Even in a country where the extent of development of the accounts will support sophisticated use, such use may not be necessary for all users and purposes. In some of these illustrative uses there is a clear continuum between analysis, projection and forecasts, and policy formulation. This continuum has been emphasized by connecting lines across the page. More difficult to exhibit is the use of several types of account for the same project. For example, in *Projections, 1970,* by the Bureau of Labor Statistics, this is done within the frames of both the income and product accounts and input-output analysis. It has been classified with input-output uses because that characteristic distinguishes it from other undertakings similar in purpose.

ECONOMIC ACCOUNTS AND THEIR USES

A precautionary word: The accounts are not fully comprehensive. Some economic variables—not to mention many social, political, and other noneconomic variables—lie outside the accounts. The demographic variables, such as population, labor force, households, etc., are ready examples. Users must often bring in these other variables. Common to the illustrative uses is the fact that the economic accounts provide their focal points and integrating frameworks.

CHECKS OF COVERAGE AND CONSISTENCY OF STATISTICAL DATA

Before launching into substantive uses, let us note that the economic accounts are important tools in the development of a complete and reliable statistical system. An advantage of the accounting approach, which was recognized in the 1940s in relation to the income and product accounts, is that it is a great aid in defining the tasks of statistical collection. Once a particular framework providing a useful picture of the economic structure is sketched out, a list of required statistics emerges. Furthermore, collection of nonaccount statistics, e.g., on prices and employment, can be tailored to be consistent with the accounts. This is an important use, particularly for the developing nations, which are in the process of setting up statistical programs.

Within an account, the equalities—such as the triple equality of income, expenditures, and output by industrial source in the national income accounts, or the equality of saving and investment in the flow-of-funds accounts—provide statistical checks when the estimates are separately derived. When the different sets of accounts are integrated, there are possibilities of additional checks. For example, the preparation of the 1958 input-output table required a complete accounting of all product flows, not only those to final consumers. This provided a new and powerful check, which improved the accuracy of the estimates of the level of GNP. Also, it should be possible to check certain items calculated as residuals, such as saving in the income and product accounts, against direct estimates, such as changes in assets and liabilities in the financial accounts.

THE NATIONAL INCOME AND PRODUCT ACCOUNTS

This section elaborates upon some of the uses of the national income and product accounts that are entered in the matrix. Similar sections follow for the other types of economic accounts.

Analysis

The most elementary use of national income estimates is to trace the fluctuations and growth in total economic activity. For this purpose one or more of the major aggregates, e.g., national income or personal income, are prepared at least on an annual basis and possibly quarterly or monthly. Much of the work in the United States in the 1920s and in some of the developing countries today is of this nature. When carefully constructed estimates are not available, the estimates of a benchmark year may be extrapolated forward on the basis of some available, and perhaps indicative, series. Railroad gross receipts, for example, were used for this purpose in the United States before regular annual estimates became available.

TABLE 15-1
A Summary Matrix of Uses of Economic Accounts

INCOME AND PRODUCT ACCOUNTS		
Analysis	*Projections and Forecasts*	*Policy Formulation*

Production Accounts
Aggregates & structure:
1. Aggregates: income, product, & major components–fluctuations & growth
2. Structure: comparison over time & space
  a. Type of expenditure, e.g., consumption versus investment, public versus private, domestic use versus exports
  b. Income shares, e.g., wages, profit, etc.
  c. Industrial source
 	
Interrelations:
1. Cost-profit patterns: change over time & comparison by industry[1]
2. Production analysis
  a. Decomposition of growth into input, productivity, & related variables[2]
  b. Statistical production functions[3]
	Demand projections:
	1. Government: forecasts underlie the *Budget* and *Economic Report*[7]
	2. Business: forecasts of general business conditions & as step in "top-down" industry or product forecasts; used as background for sales forecasts, short-run budgeting, financial planning, etc.[8]
	
	Supply projections
	1. Government: Joint Economic Committee staff, *U.S. Economic Growth to 1975*[9]
	2. Business: background for planning capital expenditures, R&D, diversification, etc.[8]
		Instrumental Decisions
		1. International: contributions to organizations, e.g., UN, based on national incomes of members
		2. Grants-in-aid to local government: federal share varies with state incomes
		
		Substantive Policy Formulation
		Government
		1. Agency planning, e.g., demand for postal service related to personal income
		2. Policy of maximum growth, employment, & purchasing power (fiscal policy, monetary policy, etc.)
		
		Business background for executive decisions[11]
		
		International: development goals, e.g., UN & OECD growth targets for 1960s

Development planning: formulation and implementation[1][2]

International comparisons:
1. Growth analysis
   a. Comparative analysis of industrial structure, income distribution, product use, etc.[4]
   b. Comparative analysis of changes in inputs and output per unit of input[5]
2. Current appraisal: *OECD Economic Outlook*–demand, output, costs & prices by country & OECD area[6]

Multination forecasts: *OECD Economic Outlook*[6]

Sector Income & Outlay Accounts
Personal income size distribution
Sector demand analysis: consumption functions, government expenditure analysis, investment demand

Sector saving

Projections of the "Nation's Economic Budget," built upon sector income & outlay accounts[10]

INPUT-OUTPUT TABLES[1]

Government policy
1. National security: mobilization & postattack survival
2. Expenditure: changes in spending for defense, public works, foreign aid, etc.
3. Trade policy
4. Manpower development policy

Resource planning: water supply, land reclamation, energy supply

Structural analysis, e.g., rankings by percent of output sold to final demand, degree of industry dependence for inputs on other industries[2]

Output & employment analysis: repercussions of changes in total, &/or components of, output
1. Emphasis on total economy[3]
2. Emphasis on specific locality[3]
3. Emphasis on specific sectors or industries, e.g., imports, construction[4]

BLS, *Projections,1970*–industrial distribution of employment (using interindustry employment table)[7]

Projection of regional & industry impact of hypothetical cut in military spending[8]

239

TABLE 15-1 (Continued)

Analysis	Projections and Forecasts	Policy Formulation
Market analysis, e.g., comparison of firm's sales distribution with industry's to suggest potential markets	Industry projections[9]	Business: marketing, investment programming, raw materials supply planning, etc.
Price and/or wage analysis: impact of change on other industries		Wage-price policy, involving labor, business, & possibly government
Growth analysis 1. Changes in interindustry structure over time, indicating technological change[5] 2. Interregional & international comparison of interindustry structure, e.g., using triangulated & skyline tables[6]		Development planning, especially for structural change aspects[10]
FLOW-OF-FUNDS ACCOUNTS[1]		
Relation of financial to real variables, e.g., cyclical variation in direction & volume of financial transactions[2]	Projection of short-term financial market flows[4]	Government: monetary & debt management policy
Financial behavior analysis 1. Sector expenditure and financial activity as related to adjustment toward desired net worth, form of asset held, volume & type of liability incurred	Projection of "residual sources," i.e., acquisition of certain sectors of certain instruments, as guide to future interest rates[5]	Business: management of financial institutions and corporate financial planning

240

2. Market analysis, e.g., capital market (variously defined)[3]

Sensitivity of financial flows to legal & institutional factors

Development planning, financial aspects[6]

BALANCE-OF-PAYMENTS ACCOUNTS

Government actions occasioned by postwar payments developments[4]

1. Foreign aid: initial response to dollar shortage; later payments impact minimized
2. Tax: interest equalization tax
3. Military: initial off-shore procurement; later sales to allies
4. Monetary: discount rate changes; foreign-exchange operations
5. Investment: limitations on direct investment abroad & bank loans to foreigners

Commercial policy, including aids to exporters

Business

1 Export expansion
2. Overseas investment decisions

International policy

1. Trade: tariff negotiations, commodity agreements, etc.
2. Monetary & liquidity
3. Development aid

Short-term projections: Forecasting, by component[1]

Long-term projections: Projections of "basic balance" given price, cost, output, output per manhour assumptions for U.S. and Western Europe[2]

Foreign Trade component: Dept. of Commerce, *U.S. Foreign Trade: A Five-year Outlook*[3]

Export market surveys

National economy within international economy, e.g., export competitiveness, monetary ease or tightness affecting capital flows

Aggregates & structure: changes over time, in relation to economic & noneconomic factors

1. Current account
2. Capital account
3. "Deficit"

Interrelations of components, e.g., exports to imports, direct investment, bank loans, etc.

Demand analysis: export or import demand, in aggregate or by product or industry

Returns on foreign investment, comparison over time & between areas and industries

241

TABLE 15-1 (Continued)

BALANCE SHEETS[1]

Analysis	Projections and Forecasts	Policy Formulation
Wealth aggregates & structure: comparison over time & space	Projection of average annual rate of growth of wealth, given output growth & saving-investment ratio[5]	Sector budgeting, e.g., government capital budgeting
1. Type of asset, e.g., natural resources, structures, equipment, inventory		
2. Sector of ownership & use	Projections of certain tax yields, e.g., estate, capital gains, property	Tax policy
3. Asset-size class		Welfare policy (adjunct to income-size class)
4. Age composition	Background for general economic projections, especially of potential output	
Financial aggregates & structure	Projections of volume & structure of demand & supply in financial markets	Financial policy
1. Composition of assets, e.g., by type & maturity class		1. Government: monetary & debt-management policy
2. Structure of debt		2. Business: management of financial institutions, corporate financial planning, etc.
3. Asset-debt ratios		
4. Financial interrelationships ratio (tangible assets-financial assets)		
Capital stock-output relationships	Projected capital and capital-financing requirements, used in general economic projections, company capital budgeting, capital-goods market projections	Growth & development policy, based on share of investment, adequacy of saving, external financing, etc.[6]
1. Capital-output ratios, e.g., levels & trends, total & by industry or sector[2]		
2. Capital productivity		Business: management-control tool
a. Total economy		
b. Companies & agencies[3]		
Sector behavior analysis	Background for projected productivity advance & its effects via interrelations with cost, output, etc.	Policies, e.g., manpower & relocation, to facilitate adjustment to technological change
1. Expenditure decision analysis, e.g., including liquid assets or stocks		

Policies to influence the rate of expenditure, e.g., income tax, depreciation policy on productive assets

Wage-price policy

Public utility regulation

Business investment decisions

Demand projections, e.g., consumer goods, especially durables, housing, business investment

of durables in consumption functions; productive stock, by age distribution, as influencing investment

2. Imputed interest on stocks, e.g. on household durables to yield consumption flows in use values

Rate of return analysis

Velocity of turnover analysis

Capital density analysis: capital per capita or per worker

International comparison, e.g., of wealth structure & capital-output ratios[4]

INCOME AND PRODUCT ACCOUNTS:

[1] Martin L. Marimont, "GNP by Major Industries," *Survey of Current Business* vol. 42., pp. 10-13, October, 1962.
[2] Edward F. Denison, *The Sources of Economic Growth in the United States and the Alternatives before Us*, Supplementary Paper no. 13 (New York: Committee for Economic Development, 1962), and John W. Kendrick, "Introduction: Productivity and National Income Accounting," in Conference on Research in Income and Wealth, *Output, Input, and Productivity Measurement*, Studies in Income and Wealth, vol. XXV (Princeton, N. J.: Princeton University Press for the National Bureau of Economic Research, 1961), pp. 3-20.
[3] Robert M. Solow, "Technical Change and the Aggregate Production Function," *Review of Economics and Statistics*, vol. 39, pp. 312-320, August, 1957.
[4] Simon Kuznets, *Modern Economic Growth: Rate, Structure, and Spread* (New Haven, Conn.: Yale University Press, 1966).
[5] Edward F. Denison, *Why Growth Rates Differ* (Washington, D.C.: The Brookings Institution, 1967).
[6] *OECD Economic Outlook*, no. 4, December, 1969.
[7] *Techniques of Economic Forecasting*, with an Introduction by C. W. McMahon (Paris: Organization for Economic Cooperation and Development, 1965).
[8] William F. Butler and Robert A. Kavesh, eds., *How Business Economists Forecast* (Englewood Cliffs, N.J.: Prentice-Hall, Inc., 1966).
[9] U.S. Congress, Joint Economic Committee, *U.S. Economic Growth to 1975: Potentials and Problems*, Study prepared for the Subcommittee on Economic Progress, Joint Economic Committee, Joint Committee Print, 89th Cong., 2d Sess. (1966).
[10] Grover Wm. Ensley, "A Budget for the Nation," *Social Research*, vol. 10, pp. 280-300, September, 1943.

TABLE 15-1 (Continued)

[11] Paul Kircher, "A Survey of Business Uses of the Data," in Conference on Research in Income and Wealth, *A Critique of the United States Income and Product Accounts*, Studies in Income and Wealth, vol. XXII (Princeton, N. J.: Princeton University Press for the National Bureau of Economic Research, 1958), pp. 394-402.
[12] United Nations, Economic and Social Council, Economic Commission for Latin America, *The Use of National Accounts for Economic Analysis and Development Planning*, 10th Sess. (E/CN.12/671), Apr. 16, 1963.

INPUT-OUTPUT TABLES:

[1] Surveys of uses, oriented to the United States, are found in Morris R. Goldman, Martin L. Marimont, and Beatrice N. Vaccara, "The Interindustry Structure of the United States: A Report on the 1958 Input-Output Study," *Survey of Current Business*, vol. 44, pp. 11-13, November, 1964, and National Accounts Review Committee, "The Economic Accounts of the United States: Review, Appraisal, and Recommendations," in U.S. Congress, Joint Economic Committee, *The National Economic Accounts of the United States, Hearings* before the Subcommittee on Economic Statistics of the Joint Economic Committee, 85th Cong. 1st Sess., 1957, pp. 244-246. A survey including uses in centrally planned economies is in "Input-Output: National Tables and International Recommendations for Development and Standardization," *Economic Bulletin for Europe*, vol. 16, pp. 5-12, November, 1964.
[2] Goldman, Marimont, and Vaccara, "The Interindustry Structure of the United States: A Report on the 1958 Input-Output Study," pp. 13-16.
[3] National Planning Association, *Local Impact of Foreign Trade* (Washington, D.C.: 1960).
[4] Claiborne M. Ball, "Employment Effects of Construction Expenditures," *Monthly Labor Review*, vol. 88, pp. 154-158, February, 1965.
[5] Anne P. Carter, "Changes in the Structure of the American Economy, 1947 to 1958 to 1962," *Review of Economics and Statistics*, vol. 49, pp. 209-224, May, 1967.
[6] Wassily Leontief, "The Structure of Development," in *Input-Output Economics* (New York: Oxford University Press, 1966), pp. 41-67.
[7] U.S. Department of Labor, Bureau of Labor Statistics, *Projections, 1970: Interindustry Relations, Potential Demand, Employment*, Bulletin no. 1536 (1966).
[8] Wassily Leontief et al., "The Economic Impact--Industrial and Regional--of an Arms Cut," in *Input-Output Economics* (New York: Oxford University Press, 1966), pp. 184-222.
[9] "Planners Put Big Picture on a Grid," *Business Week*, Sept. 23, 1967, pp. 62-67, and "They Call It Instant Research," *Business Week*, Jan. 25, 1969, pp. 62-66.
[10] Michael Bruno, "The Use of National Accounting Frameworks for Economic Policy and Development: A Survey of Israel's Experience, 1958-61," in Colin Clark and Geer Stuvel, eds., *Income Redistribution and the Statistical Foundations of Economic Policy*, International Association for Research in Income and Wealth, Income and Wealth, ser. X (London: Bowes & Bowes, Publishers, Ltd., 1964), pp. 1-22.

FLOW-OF-FUNDS ACCOUNTS:

[1] Sketches of several uses are found in Morris A. Copeland, "Some Illustrative Analytical Uses of Flow-of-funds Data," in Conference on Research in Income and Wealth, *The Flow-of-funds Approach to Social Accounting*, Studies in Income and Wealth, vol. XXVI (Princeton, N.J.: Princeton University Press for the National Bureau of Economic Research, 1962), pp. 195-221.
[2] Sue N. Atkinson, "Financial Flows in Recent Business Cycles," *Journal of Finance*, vol. 20, pp. 14-35, March, 1965.
[3] James J. O'Leary, "Application of Flow-of-funds Data to Capital Market Analysis," in Conference on Research in Income and Wealth, *The Flow-of-funds Approach to Social Accounting*, Studies in Income and Wealth, vol. XXVI (Princeton, N.J.: Princeton University Press for the National Bureau of Economic Research, 1962), pp. 263-285.
[4] Stephan Taylor, "Uses of Flow of Funds Accounts in the Federal Reserve System," *Journal of Finance*, vol. 18, pp. 249-258, May, 1963.

244

[5]William C. Freund and Edward D. Zinbarg, "Application of Flow of Funds to Interest-rate Forecasting," *Journal of Finance*, vol. 18, pp. 231-248, May, 1963.

[6]John G. Gurley and E. S. Shaw, "Financial Aspects of Economic Development," *American Economic Review*, vol. 45, pp. 515-538, September, 1955.

BALANCE-OF-PAYMENTS ACCOUNTS:

[1]Lawrence A. Mayer, "Forecasting Foreign Trade and the Balance of Payments," in William F. Butler and Robert A. Kavesh, eds.. *How Business Economists Forecast* (Englewood Cliffs, N.J.: Prentice-Hall, 1966), pp. 244-288.

[2]Walter S. Salant et al., *The United States Balance of Payments in 1968* (Washington, D.C.: The Brookings Institution, 1963).

[3]U.S. Department of Commerce, Bureau of International Commerce, *U.S. Foreign Trade: A Five-Year Outlook* (1969).

[4]Review Committee for Balance of Payments Statistics, *The Balance of Payments Statistics of the United States: A Review and Appraisal* (Washington, D.C.: Government Printing Office, 1965), p. 14.

BALANCE SHEETS:

[1]Raymond W. Goldsmith, "Measuring National Wealth in a System of Social Accounting," in Conference on Research in Income and Wealth, *Studies in Income and Wealth*, vol. XII (New York: National Bureau of Economic Research, 1950), pp. 73-79, and "The Staff Report" and appendix I-A: "Uses of Wealth Estimates" of the Wealth Inventory Planning Study, *Measuring the Nation's Wealth*, Joint Committee Print (1964).

[2]Simon Kuznets, *Capital in the American Economy: Its Formation and Financing* (Princeton, N.J.: Princeton University Press for the National Bureau of Economic Research, 1961).

[3]John W. Kendrick and Daniel Creamer, *Measuring Company Productivity*, Studies in Business Economics, no. 89 (New York: National Industrial Conference Board, 1965), and Executive Office of the President, Bureau of the Budget, *Measuring Productivity of Federal Government Organizations* (1964).

[4]Raymond Goldsmith, Christopher Saunders, and T. van der Weide, "A Summary Survey of National Wealth Estimates," in *The Measurement of National Wealth*, Raymond Goldsmith and Christopher Saunders, eds.. International Association for Research in Income and Wealth, Income and Wealth, ser. VIII (London: Bowes & Bowes, Publishers, Ltd., 1959), pp. 1-34.

[5]John W. Kendrick, "The Wealth of the United States," *Finance*, vol. 85, p. 34, January, 1967.

[6]V. V. Bhatt, "Some Further Notes on Aggregate Capital-Output Ratio," *Indian Economic Journal*, vol. 11, pp. 383-399, April-June, 1964.

Structure   Analysis of the industrial source of United States income was done by George Tucker as early as 1843. Although national income by industry has been available for some time, it was not until 1962 that GNP by industry was published by OBE. Analyses done with a view toward issues of equity—the labor share vis-à-vis the profit share, and the size distribution—received attention at the turn of the century and have been carried forward with refinements and improvements. The major impetus to statistical analysis, and the specification of variables on the sources side of the accounts, came with Keynesian theory. To enumerate the specific analytical uses to which the accounts were applied in the subsequent development of income and employment theory would be to review the development of that theory over more than thirty years, a task which is beyond the scope of this book.

One instance is of particular historical significance. At the beginning of World War II, national income, as the net value of current output seen as the sum of net income of the factors of production, was the most familiar comprehensive measure of output. When the war program for fiscal year 1943 was projected to require $56 billion, this $56 billion was subtracted from the national income to indicate output available for civilian consumption. This did not produce meaningful results. It was only when estimates of GNP by expenditure category at market prices were developed that it was possible to show the disposition of economic resources required for the war program, the necessary change in the structure of production, and the magnitude of the fiscal problem involved.[1] That these aggregative statistics were adopted as the operative framework of wartime anti-inflationary policy and overall resource programming is said to have been one of our important technical advantages that helped to win the war.[2]

Interrelations   With estimates of gross product by industry in current and constant prices, it is possible to examine cost-profit patterns. The implicit deflators by industry are obtained by dividing current-dollar gross product by real gross product. The number of points in the implicit price index associated with the major income and cost components (employee compensation, net interest, capital consumption allowances, indirect business taxes, and profit-type incomes) of current-dollar GNP may be obtained by dividing that component by real gross product. If the points calculated for a given component increase over time by a larger percentage than those calculated for other shares, this indicates that the particular unit cost has increased disproportionately. This technique revealed, for example, that, in the postwar period, in most major industries (private business group) payroll costs and capital consumption allowances per unit of output increased more rapidly than prices, and profit margins remained stable.[3]

---

[1] Milton Gilbert, "War Expenditures and National Production," *Survey of Current Business*, vol. 22, pp. 9-16, March, 1942; Milton Gilbert and R. B. Bangs, "Preliminary Estimates of Gross National Product, 1929-1941," *Survey of Current Business*, vol. 22, pp. 9-13, May, 1942.

[2] John P. Lewis and Robert C. Turner, *Business Conditions Analysis*, 2d ed. (New York: McGraw-Hill Book Company, 1967), p. 13.

[3] Martin L. Marimont, "GNP by Major Industries," *Survey of Current Business*, vol. 42, pp. 10-13, October, 1962.

Production analysis   Some of the uses of the income and product accounts in production analysis, utilizing the deflated estimates, were mentioned in Chapter 6. In particular, factoring growth into its input and productivity components is a useful start for further investigations.

International comparisons   The OECD has initiated publication of up-to-date analysis of current and prospective demand and output, costs and prices, trade, employment, and other major economic variables for member countries at half-yearly intervals.[4] The assessment is done by the Secretariat of the Organization in the Department of Economics and Statistics, and does not necessarily agree with the national authorities of thé countries concerned. This project is significant in two respects. First, the emphasis is on international repercussions of domestic developments, and the assessment is built up from internally consistent forecasts for national aggregates. This internal consistency is achieved in part by utilizing a foreign trade matrix which reflects the interdependence of the OECD area, and is a considerable step beyond simple aggregation of national forecasts. Second, the analysis is prepared within the frames of the OECD standardized system of national income and product accounts and the OECD-IMF (International Monetary Fund) balance-of-payments accounts.

Projections and Forecasts

The methods of preparing short- and long-range projections are discussed in Chapters 16 and 17. The point to be made here is that the income and product accounts are, at the present time, the most frequently used frame for projections of economic activity. The staff of the Joint Economic Committee prefaced their recent study of long-term growth with this statement about their use of the national income and product accounts: "While other conventions or premises might be used to view and measure the economy's performance, these particular accounts are the most thoroughly developed, accurate, and generally understood set of numbers."[5]

The nation's economic budget   Projections of income and outlay, by sector, are the distinguishing feature of the nation's economic budget as a projection tool. The framework is essentially a rearrangement of the aggregates of the appropriation accounts of the sectors, including the business sector, implicit in the United States official accounts. Table 15-2 shows this framework under the title Gross National Product: Receipts and Expenditures by Major Economic Groups.[6] For each sector, receipts, expenditures, and excess of receipts or expenditures are shown. Sector receipts and expenditures both sum to GNP (including a statistical discrepancy), and the excess of receipts or expenditures must cancel out, demonstrating the transfers of pur-

---

[4] *OECD Economic Outlook.* Published in July and December, beginning in 1967. See especially the Technical Notes.

[5] *U.S. Economic Growth to 1975: Potentials and Problems,* a staff study prepared for the Subcommittee on Economic Progress, Joint Economic Committee Print, 89th Cong., 2d Sess. (1966), p. 2.

[6] The conceptual tool was worked out in the Budget Bureau during the early 1940s. Its official debut was in the Budget of January, 1945, with the title "The Nation's Budget." The *Economic Reports of the President* from 1947 to 1953 incorporated its analytical framework. Since that time it has appeared in statistical compilations under various titles.

TABLE 15-2
Gross National Product: Receipts and Expenditures by Major Economic Groups, 1965–1968
(Billions of Dollars)

	1965			
	Receipts	*Expendi-tures*	*Excess of Receipts or Expend-itures (–)*	*Receipts*
Persons:				
Disposable personal income – – – – – –	473.2	------	------	511.9
Less: Interest paid by consumers and personal transfers to foreigners - - - - -	12.0	------	------	13.0
Disposable personal income excluding interest paid by consumers and personal transfers to foreigners – – – – – – – – – – – –	461.3	------	------	498.9
Personal consumption expenditures – – – – – –	------	432.8	------	------
Personal saving – – – – – – – – – – – – – –	------	------	28.4	------
Business:				
Gross retained earnings – – – – – – – – – – – –	84.7	------	------	91.3
Gross private domestic investment – – – – – –	------	108.1	------	------
Excess of investment (–) – – – – – – – – –	------	------	–23.4	------
Government:				
Tax and nontax receipts or accruals – – – –	189.1	------	------	213.3
Less: Transfers, etc. – – – – – – – – – – – –	49.9	------	------	55.5
Net receipts – – – – – – – – – – – – – – – –	139.2	------	------	157.9
Purchases of goods and services – – – – – – – –	------	137.0	------	------
Surplus or deficit (–), national income and product accounts – – – – – – – – – –	------	------	2.2	------
Foreign:				
Net transfers to foreigners – – – – – – – – – – –	2.8	------	------	2.8
Net exports – – – – – – – – – – – – – – – – – –	------	6.9	------	------
Net foreign investment – – – – – – – – – –	------	------	–4.1	------
Statistical discrepancy – – – – – – – – – – – – – –	–3.1	------	–3.1	–1.0
Gross national product – – – – – – – – – – – – – –	684.9	684.9	------	749.9

SOURCE: *Survey of Current Business,* vol. 49, p. 44, table 7.1, July, 1969.

1966		1967			1968		
Expenditures	*Excess of Receipts or Expenditures (−)*	*Receipts*	*Expenditures*	*Excess of Receipts or Expenditures (−)*	*Receipts*	*Expenditures*	*Excess of Receipts or Expenditures (−)*
-----	-----	546.6	-----	-----	590.0	-----	----
-----	-----	13.9	-----	-----	15.0	-----	----
-----	-----	532.6	-----	-----	575.0	-----	-----
466.3	----	-----	492.3	-----	-----	536.6	----
-----	32.5	-----	----	40.4	-----	-----	38.4
-----	-----	93.3	-----	-----	96.7	-----	-----
121.4	-----	-----	116.0	-----	----	126.3	----
-----	−30.1	-----	-----	−22.7	-----	-----	−29.6
-----	-----	228.4	-----	-----	264.2	----	----
-----	-----	62.8	-----	-----	70.6	-----	-----
-----	-----	165.6	-----	-----	193.6	-----	-----
156.8	-----	-----	180.1	-----	-----	200.3	-----
-----	1.1	-----	----	−14.5	-----	-----	−6.7
-----	-----	3.0	-----	-----	2.9	-----	----
5.3	-----	-----	5.2	-----	----	2.5	----
-----	−2.4	-----	-----	−2.2	-----	-----	0.3
-----	−1.0	−1.0	-----	−1.0	−2.5	-----	−2.5
749.9	-----	793.5	793.5	-----	865.7	865.7	----

chasing power from one sector to another. The format may be used either to record these flows ex post or to make projections. In the latter case, certain flows are stipulated exogenously, the other flows implied by behavioral relations filled in, and the results checked for consistency and reasonableness.

Policy Formulation

A use of the income and product accounts that receives nationwide publicity is the analysis, projections, and, ultimately, policy formulation called for by the Employment Act of 1946. The Employment Act makes the federal government responsible for policies to attain maximum employment, production, and purchasing power, and calls upon the government to utilize all practical means to do so, with the assistance and cooperation of the private sector and other levels of government. The act established the Council of Economic Advisers in the executive branch and the Joint Economic Committee in the legislative branch to assist in achieving these goals by providing a coordinated overview of the economic impact of the entire spectrum of government activities. Much of the work of the Council and the Joint Economic Committee has been explicitly framed within the income and product accounts. Their publications provide a record of more than twenty years' use of these accounts in policy formulation.[7]

Two devices developed in the process of carrying out this responsibility and specifically drawing upon the accounts serve as illustrations. The first of these, the gap between actual and potential GNP, was spotlighted in the 1962 *Economic Report of the President*.[8] Chart 15-1, reproduced from that report, illustrates the technique. In mid-1955, unemployment was close to 4 percent, and evidence suggests that output was close to potential. Thus GNP in mid-1955 is taken as the base for a trend line of growth of GNP. That trend line, for the post-Korean period until 1962, adjusted for changes in unemployment levels, has averaged 3-1/2 percent. Therefore, from the mid-1955 base, a trend line is shown rising at an annual average rate of 3-1/2 percent. The difference between the potential GNP, so calculated, and the lower actual GNP produced the gap. The gap implied between the next year's potential GNP and the current level of GNP represented the challenge to economic policy. Projections of attainable GNP based on alternative assumptions about unemployment were illustrated. Since 1962 the trend line of potential GNP was set at 3-3/4 percent from the fourth quarter of 1962 to the fourth quarter of 1965, and at 4 percent from the latter date through 1968. From 1965 to 1968 the actual GNP was above the potential because unemployment was below 4 percent.

The full- or high-employment surplus sought to interpret the economic significance of a given federal budget. To do this it was essential to distinguish automatic changes in federal revenues and expenditures (in terms of the national income accounts) from discretionary changes. Tax revenues and some expenditures, such as

---

[7] See the *Economic Report of the President,* issued (usually) in January since 1947, and hearings, staff materials, and reports of the Joint Economic Committee. Symposia issued at the tenth and twentieth anniversaries of the Employment Act provide useful evaluations. See Gerhard Colm, ed., *The Employment Act: Past and Future* (Washington, D.C.: National Planning Association, 1956), and *Twentieth Anniversary of the Employment Act of 1946: An Economic Symposium, Hearings before the Joint Economic Committee,* 89th Cong., 2d Sess., Feb. 23, 1966.

[8] pp. 49–53.

ECONOMIC ACCOUNTS AND THEIR USES

unemployment compensation payments and agricultural support payments, depend on the level of economic activity, defined in terms of GNP, so there is a range of possible surpluses or deficits associated with a given budget program. In Chart 15-2 this range of surpluses or deficits is shown along each of two lines representing budget programs. The discretionary element is shown by shifting the line up or down. Budget programs may be compared by calculating the surplus or deficit at some given level of economic activity. The hypothetical full-employment level, shown at the right-hand side of the chart, is a convenient point. The chart shows the 1960 program to be more expansionary than that of 1962.

CHART 15-1
Gross national product, actual and potential. Source: *Economic Report of the President, 1962* (Washington, D.C.: Government Printing Office, 1962), p. 52.

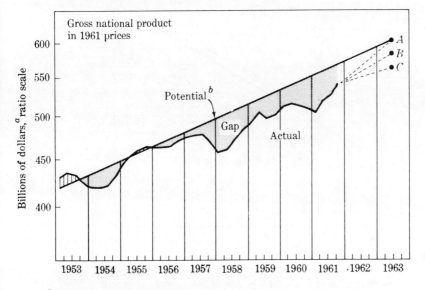

^{a} Seasonally adjusted annual rates
^{b} 3 $1/2$ % trend line through middle of 1955

Note: *A*, *B*, and *C* represent GNP in middle of 1963 assuming unemployment rate of 4%, 5%, and 6%, respectively

Business decision making   Evidence points to increasing use by business of national income estimates. Firms are recruiting their own resident economists, who by training are familiar with this tool.[9] At a recent meeting of the Federal Statistics Users' Conference, the majority of whose members are business firms, OBE economists discussed the sources and methods of preparing the quarterly estimates; this program brought one of the largest responses in the conference's history.[10] A survey

[9] "The Value of 'Practical Eggheads,'" *Business Week*, Feb. 13, 1965, p. 52.
[10] Meeting held Mar. 26, 1969, in Washington, D.C.

taken in 1955 indicates roughly how business uses the national income data.[11] The most frequent use is as background for executive decisions, presumably in areas such as production, purchasing, finance, marketing, inventories, and capital spending. The second most frequent use is in speeches of executives on business conditions.

CHART 15-2
Effect of level of economic activity on federal surplus or deficit. Source: *Economic Report of the President, 1962* (Washington, D.C.: Government Printing Office, 1962), p. 79.

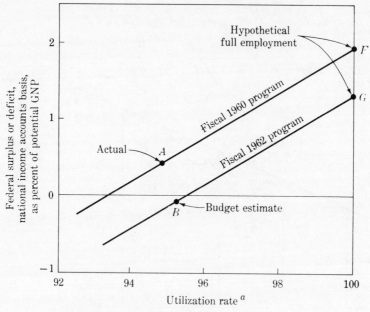

^aActual GNP as percent of potential GNP

These two uses are closely related, since most such speeches are delivered to other businessmen. Kircher shows the spectrum of other uses by firms reporting regular and occasional use of national income data.

Development planning For this illustration, we will draw upon a document prepared for the 1963 session of the Economic Commission for Latin America. *The Use of National Accounts for Economic Analysis and Development Planning* attempts to define the types of national accounts and related tables needed for planning and

[11] Paul Kircher, "A Survey of Business Uses of the Data," *A Critique of the United States Income and Product Accounts*, Conference on Research in Income and Wealth, Studies in Income and Wealth, vol. XXII (Princeton, N.J.: Princeton University Press for the National Bureau of Economic Research, 1958), pp. 394–402.

ECONOMIC ACCOUNTS AND THEIR USES

presents a list of basic series requested for elaboration and analysis of such tables.[12] The statement of purposes for which these statistics are needed, a précis of which is below, demonstrates the close connection between analysis, projection, and policy formulation.

To formulate a consistent and workable development plan, planners need a fairly detailed picture of the economic situation in the base year and of development during a reasonably long historical period. To reveal basic weak and strong points in the economic structure and to show to what extent a balanced development has so far been achieved, they need a quantitative assessment of general economic growth and of the contribution of the various industries and factors of production to this growth. To obtain an idea about the investment effort necessary for an increase in the product of a given magnitude, they must know the share of total resources which has been devoted to replacement and additions to the capital stock, and must have some idea of the magnitude of this capital stock. To achieve a reasonably detailed analysis, they need at least some information about investment and capital stock by main sectors.

For more sophisticated model building, information on the likely effect of increases in imports, exports, or the production of specific industries on the general level of economic activities or the production of individual industries would be extremely useful. Also, it would be of great usefulness to obtain as much information as possible about the pattern of private and public savings and its allocation for financing capital formation in the various industries. Although extremely difficult to obtain, distribution of total personal income by size and social strata would be of the utmost value not only because development plans are usually socially oriented but also because an assessment of the savings potential of the nation is needed. Last but not least, in countries with pronounced regional differences, at least some information on the magnitude of the main national accounts, by region, is required.

National income and national accounts estimates also furnish the raw material for the construction of balances of total demand and supply by main components, which are indispensable in revealing the existence and sources of inflationary pressures or pressures on the balance of payments. Such balances make it possible for planners to take measures which may prevent future monetary disequilibrium or a balance-of-payments crisis.

At the stage of implementation, it is necessary to make frequent checks on progress so that the direction of the effort may be changed or modified, if need be, in the light of developments during the plan period. Intermediate projections and reliable and up-to-date estimates of national accounts are required for such checks.

National budgets, or one-year economic plans, which present as complete a picture as possible of the likely developments in the year to come and are intended to form a consistent framework for short-term economic policy, have been found useful in many countries. In addition to their primary use in facilitating short-term policy decisions, the national budgets could also be very useful instruments in connection with implementation of long- or medium-term plans.

Given this statement of purposes for which the statistics are needed, the following priority was indicated according to the usefulness of the series in development planning.

[12] United Nations, Economic and Social Council, Economic Commission for Latin America, 10th Sess. (Apr. 16, 1963).

I Series without which even "rudimentary planning and economic analysis would be difficult"
   A. Gross domestic product (GDP) by industrial origin, at current and constant prices
   B. GNP by expenditure category, at current and constant prices
   C. Gross fixed capital formation
      1. By type of capital good
      2. By public and private sectors and, if possible, by industry of use, at current and constant prices
   D. General government income and current and capital expenditures, by economic and functional categories
   E. International transactions
II Minimum requirements: in addition to A through E above
   A. Private consumption by main groups, at current and constant prices
   B. Distribution of national income at current prices
   C. A system of national accounts
III Estimates to be developed over the longer term
   A. Input-output tables
   B. Inventory of existing fixed capital
   C. Flow-of-funds analysis[13]

INPUT-OUTPUT TABLES

Chenery and Clark find that the main test of the usefulness of interindustry techniques is the extent to which the structure of interindustry transactions may be an important factor.[14] It is not surprising, therefore, that many of the applications relate to mobilization and postmobilization readjustment, the industrial distribution of employment, and economic development. As mentioned in Chapter 5, early interest in the technique by BLS arose over concern with post-World War II employment readjustment. A major product of this work was the pioneering *Full Employment Patterns, 1950.*[15] The primary objective was to obtain a statistical picture of the output and employment, by industry, under full-employment conditions after readjustment. Given projections of employment, purchasing power, and final demand for products, industry output and employment patterns could be obtained by utilizing interindustry analysis and supplementary data on employment. The patterns thus obtained could be matched against full-employment potential, and alternative implications for policy drawn.

The 1947 input-output table was developed primarily for testing the economic feasibility of various mobilization plans. The so-called emergency model was the principal application of the government's research program.[16] This analysis dealt

---

[13] *Ibid.*, pp. 6-11.

[14] Hollis B. Chenery and Paul G. Clark, *Interindustry Economics* (New York: John Wiley & Sons, Inc., 1959), p. 7.

[15] Jerome Cornfield, W. Duane Evans, and Marvin Hoffenberg, *Full Employment Patterns, 1950,* U.S. Department of Labor, Bureau of Labor Statistics, serial no. R. 1868 (1947). Originally summarized in *Monthly Labor Review,* vol. 44, pp. 163-190 and 420-432, February and March, 1947.

[16] This model is discussed by Chenery and Clark, *op. cit.*, pp. 271-276, and most recently, including some now declassified material, by William R. Bailey, "An Appraisal of Input-Output Analysis Based on a Documentation of the Interindustry Relations Study for 1947," unpublished doctoral dissertation, The George Washington University, Washington, D.C., 1966, pp. 48-71.

with the rearmament program stemming from the Korean War. The emergency model was solved for total output by industry necessary to satisfy military and civilian demand for final products.

An article by Leontief carried on the interest in the implications for defense expenditures in terms of the 1958 table.[17] He worked out the effect of a hypothetical reduction in military demand accompanied by an increase in nonmilitary demand on the industrial and regional distribution of employment in the United States. The impact was measured in terms of the shifts in the labor force—the number of workers who would have to look for new jobs in a different industry in the same region and in the same or a different industry in another region.

Projections of the Industrial Distribution of Employment

The OBE 1958 input-output tables were used as the basic analytical tool for evaluating alternative economic policies and projections—a major phase of the work of the Interagency Growth Study Project. The project, started by the Department of Labor and drawing upon other government agencies and private research organizations, attempted to develop a comprehensive and integrated framework for analyzing the implications of long-term economic growth. The several stages of work in developing projections of the industrial distribution of employment were explained in *Projections, 1970*.[18] First, an estimate of potential real GNP in 1970 was made on the basis of alternative assumptions about the rate of unemployment. Real GNP was then distributed among the major components of final demand, again on the basis of alternative assumptions, and then among detailed items, consistent with the input-output tables. The 1958 input-output table was projected to the year 1970 to reflect changes in input-output relations as well as changes in unit labor requirements. From this projected table, an interindustry employment table, showing total employment attributable to a billion dollars worth of final demand, was derived. The end product is employment requirements by industry. These employment requirements are essential to the development of requirements by occupations which the Labor Department needs to implement its responsibilities in guidance and training.

Development Planning

There is a fast-growing literature on the uses of input-output techniques in development programs.[19] Most such programs aim to initiate major structural changes in the economy. Input-output tables can be used to depict where an economy stands at a moment in time and where it might be some years hence. Using input-output techniques, planners are often able to gain a grasp of the total structural changes and their implications that would be difficult to achieve by any other means.

Use of input-output methods in developing countries requires adaptation. For

---

[17] Wassily Leontief et al., "The Economic Impact—Industrial and Regional—of an Arms Cut," in *Input-Output Economics* (New York: Oxford University Press, 1966), pp. 184–222.

[18] U.S. Department of Labor, Bureau of Labor Statistics, *Projections, 1970: Interindustry Relations, Potential Demand, Employment*, bulletin no. 1536 (1966). The analysis in this report is being extended to 1975 and 1980.

[19] See, for example, the papers in Tibor Barna, ed., *Structural Interdependence and Economic Development*, International Conference on Input-Output Techniques (New York: St. Martin's Press, Inc., 1963).

example, there are extensive data problems, such as the prevalence of very small scale industry or agricultural production for own consumption. External factors may have a strong influence on input coefficients. Often special attention must be given to imports.

The case of Israel is illustrative.[20] By 1958 the major task of economic policy was to bring about a change in the composition of output. The balance-of-payments gap had to be closed, while imports went on rising in the face of projected falling prices for the major export. Potential import substitution was confined to a few branches of manufacturing. When choosing a tool for analysis, planners considered the relatively short span for which data existed, and also the limited value of time-series analysis of aggregates in a rapidly changing economy. The outcome was that for the analysis of development alternatives, 1958 to 1964, a crude 20×20 input-output model was constructed. Work advanced to the preparation and analysis with a much larger model; the largest table for which the total requirements matrix was worked out was 77×77, although basic data had been collected in a less aggregated form. Further research was expected to remedy certain deficiencies, improve data, and coordinate the analysis with policy needs.

FLOW-OF-FUNDS ACCOUNTS

The flow-of-funds accounts are often regarded as a virtually untapped statistical reservoir or as an accounting system that has not yet found its Keynes to provide a theoretical structure for the data contained in it. However, there is a growing body of literature on uses of the accounts, describing some of the aspects of business cycles, monetary policy, and debt-management policy that can be illuminated by working with the flow-of-funds accounts.

Analysis

Provision of a consistent framework for analysis of real and financial variables, especially in the short run, was one of the major uses foreseen by the originators of the flow-of-funds accounts. Progress in empirical analysis was difficult until quarterly, seasonally adjusted data became available late in 1962. Sue N. Atkinson has used the flow-of-funds tabulations to seek cyclical regularity with respect to financial assets acquired, assumption of liabilities, and net contributions to or drawings on the financial markets by major sectors.[21] The cycles of 1953 to 1957, 1957 to 1960, and 1960 to 1962, with the turning points as defined by the National Bureau of Economic Research, were used in the analysis.

The investigator concluded that the nonbank sectors showing the greatest consistent variation in lending and borrowing activities were the consumer and corporate sectors. The consumer becomes increasingly active as both borrower and lender as

[20] Michael Bruno, "The Use of National Accounting Frameworks for Economic Policy and Development: A Survey of Israel's Research Experience, 1958–61," in Colin Clark and Geer Stuvel, eds., *Income Redistribution and the Statistical Foundations of Economic Policy,* International Association for Research in Income and Wealth, *Income and Wealth,* ser. X (London: Bowes & Bowes, Publishers, Ltd., 1964), pp. 1–22.

[21] Sue N. Atkinson, "Financial Flows in Recent Business Cycles," *Journal of Finance,* vol. 20, pp. 14–33, March, 1965.

the economy moves into fast expansion. Recession reduces the accumulation of income-earning assets sharply; government bonds particularly are sold off in a move to a more liquid position. Corporate borrowing rises by relatively small amounts in early expansion but net lending increases sharply, reducing net borrowing to a low or negative level. At later stages of expansion, previously loaned corporate funds are withdrawn to cover the corporations' own needs, and bank borrowing in particular increases. The federal government and rest-of-the-world sectors have behaved erratically in recent recessions. The banking sector accumulates assets, mostly government bonds, at a maximum rate in recession. During recovery the government bonds are sold off, principally to the consumer sector, to finance an increasing volume of loans.

Projections and Forecasts

Stephan Taylor has described the use by the Federal Reserve System of the flow-of-funds accounts as the framework within which to make short-term macroeconomic projections that will depict the volume and structure of financial market flows.[22] The notable feature of the projections is that they emphasize the nature of the accounts as a closed system for the economy as a whole. The matrix framework forces consistency both between and within the financial and nonfinancial segments of the economy.

The projection procedure follows that used in national income and product projections for a considerable distance (see Chapter 16), working sector by sector. For the consumer sector, for example, the income and product projections yield personal saving and spending for durables and houses. This spending provides the main basis for estimating consumer borrowing. Thus, capital account sources—saving and borrowing—can be set against nonfinancial investment, with net financial investment as a residual. Financial investment is allocated among flow-of-funds transaction categories by the use of behavioral information—drawing upon the flow of funds as a body of historical data, income estimates of the model, and broad assumptions about monetary and debt-management policy. The result is a complete, balanced, sector statement of sources and uses of funds. Similar balanced statements are put together for the other nonfinancial sectors. As the next step, financial intermediaries' receipts are found residually as the sum of flows (mostly deposits and insurance reserves) from the asset side for nonfinancial sectors, and intermediaries' lending is found as the residual of total borrowing (in each form of financial investment) less lending in such form already projected for the nonfinancial sectors. The projection within the matrix is at least internally consistent if these intermediaries' receipts closely approximate lending.

Inspection of the matrix may indicate that the combination of projections for the nonfinancial sectors has resulted in grotesque patterns of flows for banks and intermediaries. This indicates that the model cannot be financed through reasonably normal means. Rounds of successive adjustment of the original projection are called for.

The aim of the projections is to show the volume and structure of the financial flows on the basis of assumptions for the GNP demand components, and ultimately

[22] Stephan Taylor, "Uses of Flow-of-funds Accounts in the Federal Reserve System," *Journal of Finance*, vol. 18, pp. 249-258, May, 1963.

to determine the instrumental action that appears to be consonant with the demand conditions. These projections are made, apparently, as a point of discussion and have no official status as guidelines to Federal Reserve policy formulation. Experience has shown the projections to be a useful indication of the intensity of credit demand. Further, putting the projections into the flow-of-funds structure has been especially valuable in anticipating unusual market conditions.

BALANCE-OF-PAYMENTS ACCOUNTS

The balance-of-payments accounts show the international transactions of the United States economy. The structure of those accounts is designed to facilitate analysis, projection, and policy formulation within the international sphere. For this reason, these accounts are treated separately here, rather than subsumed under the flow-of-funds accounts. Actually, the data in the statement of sources and uses of funds for the rest-of-the-world sector, found in the flow-of-funds tables, are identical to the balance-of-payments data. However, the financial items are classified to conform to the flow-of-funds categories, and so present a different picture from that brought out in the balance-of-payments structure (see Chapter 9).

Analysis

In the most general sense, the balance of payments reflects the position of the United States economy within the international economy. Major forces impinging upon that position, such as a decline in export competitiveness, would be reflected in the balance of payments.

The several accounts within the balance of payments are amenable to separate analysis. Within the current account, merchandise trade patterns may be traced, indicating shifting importance over time of trading partners or types of products. The capital account may be used to provide a history of United States net investment—first reflecting the role of foreign investment in the United States and, more recently, the United States net investment abroad. Attention often centers on the "deficit," especially because the nation's role as a reserve currency country makes analysis of the deficit an important policy variable. Where exactly the line is drawn, below which the items are included in the deficit, will vary with the purpose of the analyst.

Interrelations of components The components of the balance of payments are closely interrelated, and the interrelations defy easy analysis. The following examples are drawn from the Brookings Institution study by Walter S. Salant et al.[23] Negative feedbacks occur when the effect of changes in some transactions induces changes in the opposite direction in other transactions. There may be a negative feedback from foreign investment—particularly direct investment—to exports of goods and services, because United States firms investing abroad tend to purchase equipment, components, and services for their foreign plants from firms or individuals in the United States. Also, aid to developing countries, even if not tied to United States procurement, tends to be spent in the United States, the extent depending on many

---

[23] Walter S. Salant et al., *The United States Balance of Payments in 1968* (Washington, D.C.: The Brookings Institution, 1963), pp. 16–18.

ECONOMIC ACCOUNTS AND THEIR USES

factors, such as United States competitiveness, geographic location, political relations, etc. Changes in United States imports from some countries will change United States exports to them, because in these countries foreign expenditures are closely geared to foreign exchange receipts. Many United States exports embody imported goods, creating yet another negative feedback. As an example of positive feedbacks, United States imports and foreign travel by United States citizens may involve changes in the same direction in United States payments for freight and passenger transport. These interrelations of component items are important because it is often the net effect—as on the deficit—on which interest centers.

Projections

The Balance of Payments Division of OBE prepares projections for use within the government. In particular, use is made of these projections for "gold budget" reviews and by the Cabinet Committee on the Balance of Payments. As balance-of-payments issues became increasingly prominent in the early 1960s, government officials felt that a comprehensive and independent study of the balance-of-payments outlook was desirable. In 1962 the Council of Economic Advisers commissioned the Brookings Institution to prepare such a projection. The Council requested that the Brookings study focus on 1968, and stipulated most of the initial assumptions. This study is significant not only for the quantitative projections, which were highly speculative, since they dealt with net balances, but especially for setting out the process of obtaining the results, thus identifying the kinds and directions of the various influences.[24]

Recently the Department of Commerce developed five-year projections of the trade component of the balance of payments to assist in formulating recommended courses of action to improve export growth.[25] In the preparation of export projections, three approaches were used: (1) estimates by industry/commodity experts, (2) estimates by regional experts, and (3) estimates based on a survey of manufacturers' expectations of foreign sales. Two approaches were used to project import values: (1) commodity import estimates and (2) a major end-use categories estimate. Besides serving as a statistical check of the projections, the alternative approaches brought to the fore different sets of factors that influence the trade outlook.

Policy Formulation

Recent concern over the trend in the United States balance of payments has resulted in a number of actions in diverse policy areas. Those listed in Table 15-1 are self-explanatory. In addition, international organizations develop policies within the broader context of one nation's surplus necessitating a deficit in one or more countries. Some of the policy areas upon which these considerations impinge are trade; monetary and liquidity problems, particularly the provision of adequate facilities to settle deficits; and multilateral development aid.

---

[24] A comparison of the projections with the actual results in 1968 is of little validity, since crucial assumptions regarding output levels, price changes, military expenditures, and foreign aid have not been approximated in reality. Also, legislative and administrative regulation of capital flows has altered the institutional environment.

[25] The actual projections are of the Census Bureau trade statistics, which are the raw material for the balance-of-payments trade figures. U.S. Department of Commerce, Bureau of International Commerce, *U.S. Foreign Trade: A Five-Year Outlook* (1969).

BALANCE SHEETS

Official balance sheets or wealth statements, based on adequate data and comprehensive in nature, have not been prepared for the United States. Many of the uses suggested in the matrix are potential uses or uses that have not been fully exploited. Thus the entries lack some of the specificity found in the uses of the other accounts. However, because a discussion of potential uses is in the nature of a case for the preparation of official balance sheets, it is especially important that the connection between analysis, projection, and policy formulation be established. Therefore, the discussion below runs across the matrix for the several uses discussed.

Structural analysis of wealth estimates, utilizing the various ways that wealth may be classified, is useful and interesting in many respects. Asset size class distributions may be used as an illustration. Asset size classes of establishments and firms may be utilized in tracing industrial concentration and may be related to regulatory and antitrust policy. Similar distributions for households may be used in analysis of relations between income and property holdings. Such distributions have bearing on tax policy, especially on property, inheritance, and estate taxes, and on need criteria in welfare policy.

Capital Stock Relations

Analysis of capital-output ratios, tracing changes over time and differences between sectors, often takes its rationale from the reasoning of a Harrod-Domar type of growth model. Stated in a much simplified form, this means that, if technological and other requirements call for a given ratio of capital stock to desired output, say, 3 to 1, and if the desired rate of growth of output is x percent per year, the capital outlays must equal $3x$ percent of output. Although (marginal) capital-output ratios have varied from 2 to 5 in the postwar period for individual less developed countries, the ratios are useful for preliminary work on economic development planning. The UN Economic Commission for Latin America, in particular, has worked on this approach. Rough empirical work in the early stages of formulating a plan, comparison with similarly situated countries, and engineering data can supplement judgment in estimating the ratio.

Ratio analysis provides a broad aggregative framework for a development plan. Given the desired rate of growth, it is possible to deduce, as suggested above, the proportion of output that ought to be devoted to capital formation, and given the probable magnitude of external assistance, the required saving effort. Within the aggregative framework, analysis of output and capital by sectors, with iterative checking of requirements against feasibility, is necessary. Further, when the plan is implemented, the estimated ratio can be compared with the realized ratio for guidance in subsequent planning periods.[26]

Capital productivity (the output-capital ratio) changes over time, and there are differences between sectors, industries, and smaller units. The ratios can be combined with labor productivity ratios to yield total productivity ratios, making it possible to calculate net saving in resources per unit of output. For firms and government

---

[26] V. V. Bhatt, "Some Further Notes on Aggregate Capital-Output Ratio," *Indian Economic Journal*, vol. 40, pp. 383–399, April–June, 1964.

ECONOMIC ACCOUNTS AND THEIR USES

agencies, the productivity ratios can be used as management control tools. Changes in capital or total productivity can be related to such variables as industry structure, profit rates, and scale of output to identify causes of productivity change. This work can serve as the basis of projections of productivity change and, ultimately, for formulation of policy designed to facilitate adjustment to economic and technological change.

Sector Behavior

Increasingly, stocks, in terms of volume and structure, are being incorporated into analyses of income and production. With regard to households, liquid assets may influence spending-saving decisions, or the stock of consumer durables may be related to expenditures on them. Similar relationships may be built up for business, relating, for example, stock of inventories to rate of sales. Such relationships may be incorporated into demand projections, which provide background for policies to influence expenditures, either for growth or stability.

Financial Aggregates and Structure

The composition of assets may be related to shifts in the financial institutional structure, such as the growth of intermediaries. These shifts may affect the response of the economy to monetary policy measures. The proportion held as money, or changes in liquidity, may be related to business cycles and monetary policy. The structure of debt is critical to debt-management policy. The financial interrelationships ratio—the ratio of financial to tangible assets—gives an indication of the financial superstructure of an economy, and may indicate growing imbalances.

REVIEW QUESTIONS

1 That the uses of economic accounts may be classified in several ways emphasizes the general-purpose nature of economic accounts. What are some of the ways in which uses may be classified?
2 Explain the possibility of using the accounts to guide the development of a statistical system and to provide statistical cross-checks.
3 For each of the five kinds of accounts, cite one or more uses for each of the following categories of use: analysis, projections or forecasts, and policy formulation.
4 Characterize each of the five kinds of accounts by reference to the nature of the uses made of, or foreseen for, each of them.

SELECTED REFERENCES

See the notes to Table 15-1.

Short-term Forecasts of Aggregate Economic Activity

16

In the closing months of the year, when the "forecasting season" is in full swing, periodicals of all kinds report numerous attempts to forecast economic activity over the near year or two. Over the short term, when productive capacity is relatively fixed, interest centers on the demand for goods and services as the determinant of the level of economic activity. GNP, by type of expenditure, that is, by demand sector, thus is a logical framework for forecasting.[1]

Short-term forecasts, with varying degree of sophistication and explicitness, are used in all sectors of the economy. Businesses may make forecasts of overall economic activity as a general frame of reference or to provide a starting point for "top-down" forecasts of industry or product sales. Governments engage in forecasting as a background for their fiscal planning, since both receipts and expenditures are affected by the level of economic activity. As well, the federal government may seek to influence the level of economic activity if it foresees that either recessionary or inflationary forces are taking hold. Further, the activities of certain government agencies or departments, such as the Post Office, are closely correlated with economic activity, and forecasts help them plan. Households, too,

[1] A useful summary of representative forecasts, showing GNP and components, prices, and other selected data, is compiled by the Federal Reserve Bank of Richmond each year. See *Business Forecasts for 1969* (Richmond, Va.: Federal Reserve Bank of Richmond, February, 1969).

may consult forecasts, especially in financial investment planning or when considering major investments, such as houses.

This chapter first presents an introductory survey from a forecaster's point of view of selected studies of the behavior of the demand sectors. Background material of this kind is essential to the development and subsequent appraisal of forecasts. Also, sources of current data and other information are suggested. Thereafter, a judgmental model and an econometric model are described. The two forecasting models may be viewed as alternative methods of bringing together in a systematic manner the sector demand analyses in order to produce a consistent forecast of aggregate economic activity. In a judgmental model, the forecaster is relatively free to use his experience to change constants and add variables as he sees necessary according to the economic situation. A model elaborating the Keynesian theory of income determination is taken as representative of judgmental models. The relatively aggregative OBE model is taken as representative of the econometric approach to forecasting. A brief comparison of forecasting techniques drawing upon recent studies concludes the chapter.[2]

SURVEY OF DEMAND SECTORS

The forecaster must have a thorough knowledge of the past behavior of the individual demand sectors, of the relative reliability of the statistical series with which he will work, and of sources of up-to-date information. For practically all the major demand sectors there exist comprehensive studies of their behavior over a considerable period of time. Many of the studies concentrate on the post-World War II period, when improvement in the statistical data and development of econometric techniques made possible increasingly refined analysis.

Necessary knowledge of the statistical series encompasses not only the measures of GNP demand components (see Chapter 13), but also related series, and especially what may be called analytical series. The analytical series include diffusion indexes and the "cyclical indicators" identified by the National Bureau of Economic Research. "Leading indicators," as distinguished from the roughly coincident and lagging indicators, are those series which have been found usually to reach peaks and troughs before corresponding turns in aggregate economic activity. They are of particular interest to the forecaster. Diffusion indexes show the percentage of components of a particular aggregate rising over a given span of time. They reflect the direction of change among components, not the magnitude. They tend to lead the corresponding aggregate at cyclical turning points.

Sources of current information are too numerous for most forecasters to try to pull together themselves. Thus, secondary sources, such as newspapers, business magazines, and, for federal statistics, the major statistical publications, must often be relied upon. The monthly *Survey of Current Business*, published by OBE, presents about 2,500 statistical series. A weekly supplement provides selected weekly and monthly data subsequent to the latest monthly publication. A biennial supplement,

---

[2] The literature in the short-term forecasting field is vast. In addition to the specific references which follow, several books listed in the Selected References are helpful. They include several volumes of conference papers and general discussions of forecasting techniques.

Business Statistics, provides historical data and explanatory notes for the series regularly appearing in the *Survey of Current Business.* The *Federal Reserve Bulletin* and *Economic Indicators,* the latter prepared by the Council of Economic Advisers and published by the Joint Economic Committee, are also helpful. Of special value is *Business Conditions Digest (BCD),* formerly *Business Cycle Developments.* This is published monthly by the Census Bureau, and is intended to provide statistical information arranged to facilitate analysis of the economy. The expanded publication presents national income and product data; the cyclical indicators, mentioned above; diffusion indexes and anticipations and intentions survey series; certain key indicators in particular sectors, such as balance of payments and federal government activities, and prices; selected analytical ratios (manufacturing output to capacity, personal saving to disposable personal income, output per man-hour, etc.); and international comparisons of prices, industrial production, and stock prices.

The background discussion below relates to the major GNP demand components. For many forecasting purposes, more disaggregative analysis would be required, and the implied income components worked out. Also, the course and implications of developments in prices, employment, monetary variables, and other elements of the economic situation would be brought to bear on the forecast.

Government Purchases of Goods and Services

It has been said by an experienced practitioner, "Forecasting Federal expenditures is still a wide open field."[3] Part of the difficulty is that on both the receipt and expenditure sides there are built-in stabilizers; their effect must be brought together with likely discretionary changes in policy to gauge the future impact of federal activity. Comprehensive studies of the federal sector's impact on the course of economic events include *Federal Receipts and Expenditures during Business Cycles, 1879-1958,* by John M. Firestone and *Federal Fiscal Policy in the Postwar Recessions* by Wilfred Lewis, Jr.[4] Firestone found that in peacetime cycles, federal revenue tended to serve as a built-in stabilizer, whereas federal expenditures did not conform to cycles, but rather rose during recessions and recoveries. Lewis examined the strengths and weaknesses of fiscal policy as it operates within our economic and political institutions, and provided insights into the workings of the processes that make this sector exogenous in nearly all forecasts.

The forecaster's basic documents are *The Budget of the United States,* presented each January for the fiscal year beginning in July, and a *Midyear Budget Review,* usually available in August, which summarizes congressional action on the proposals presented earlier in the year. Emphasizing the importance of these documents is the fact that one forecasting model, specifically of short-term federal purchases of goods and services, relates current purchases to current budget recommendations and actual

[3] Samuel M. Cohn, "Problems in Estimating Federal Government Expenditures," *Journal of the American Statistical Association,* vol. 54, p. 729, December, 1959.
[4] John M. Firestone, *Federal Receipts and Expenditures during Business Cycles, 1879-1958* (Princeton, N.J.: Princeton University Press for the National Bureau of Economic Research, 1960); and Wilfred Lewis, Jr., *Federal Fiscal Policy in the Postwar Recessions* (Washington, D.C.: The Brookings Institution, 1962).

purchases lagged one year.[5] Given the latest quarterly federal purchases, the fiscal year estimates make possible a smooth quarterly projection as a first approximation. This projection may be tempered by information on special circumstances that may bunch or stretch out expenditures (or receipts), announcements of changes in administration policy, or knowledge of national needs and moods that may eventually find effect in policy changes.

A recurring problem is the need to translate estimates as they normally appear in federal budget documents to the national income and product basis to achieve consistency with the other elements of the forecast. By the mid-1960s, three separate budget concepts had come into use. Differences between the concepts in timing, netting, and treatment of certain items meant that there were differences in the totals shown.[6] Beginning in January, 1969, two of the budget concepts—the administrative and cash budgets—were replaced by a unified budget. This unified budget, first used in presenting the fiscal 1969 budget, generally moved closer to the national income accounts concept, and there are plans to bring the two concepts yet closer. However, there will continue to be differences between the two, since they have somewhat different focuses. The forecaster may refer to reconciliation methods and to presentations of the budget estimates in national income accounts terms, which appear in *Special Analyses, Budget of the United States,* and in articles, usually in February and later following the *Midyear Budget Review,* in the *Survey of Current Business,* and to the reconciliation table in the national income number (usually July) of the *Survey of Current Business.*

State and local government expenditures in the post-World War II period have shown a steady upward trend. The pace has been determined, on the one hand, by such factors as population growth, urbanization, and suburbanization, and, on the other hand, by the feasible rate of expansion of limited financial resources. A forecaster may generally extrapolate the recent trend with some certainty. As a check, a sample of budget plans of quantitatively large state and local governments may provide assurance that major alterations in underlying forces are not in prospect.

Gross Private Domestic Investment

Residential construction is a volatile component, a characteristic highlighted by the size of the sector. Interest centers, within the sector, on expenditures for new dwelling units, a term defined to include apartments and single-family houses. A common approach is to estimate nonfarm housing starts, a series maintained by the Census Bureau, and multiply that figure by an estimated average price per unit. A model designed by Sherman J. Maisel suggests the variables that the forecaster may consider in making an estimate of starts: interest rates; deviation of vacancies from a straight-line trend; the rent component of the Consumer Price Index, assumed to represent prices and expectations; the residential construction cost component of the GNP implicit deflator index; the estimate of new removals of dwelling units from

---

[5] Murray Brown and Paul Taubman, "A Forecasting Model of Federal Purchases of Goods and Services," *Journal of the American Statistical Association,* vol. 57, pp. 633–647, September, 1962.

[6] See "Three Measures of Federal Financial Transactions," *Special Analyses, Budget of the United States, 1968* (1968).

the market (based on estimates of the stock of housing and time); and net household formation (predicted from population, time, and unemployment).[7]

An approach of this kind may be supplemented with foreshadowing and anticipatory series. The F. W. Dodge Division of McGraw-Hill, Inc., prepares a series on construction contracts; building permits and applications for Federal Housing Administration and Veterans Administration loans are available monthly (all appear in the *Survey of Current Business*). There are also surveys of intentions. The Census Bureau's Survey of Consumer Buying Expectations asks respondents to indicate the probability of purchasing a house and the expected price of the house. The National Association of Home Builders periodically surveys builders' intentions. A fall issue of *Construction Review* contains a forecast of construction expenditures for the coming year prepared jointly by experts at the Departments of Commerce and Labor.

Business fixed investment   Explanatory variables in empirical studies of business fixed investment have included output, sales, profits, depreciation allowances, stock yields, interest rates, age and stock of capital, capacity, prices, value of the firm, and expectations.[8] Progress has been difficult, however, because, as Robert Eisner notes, investment more than other variables is forward looking, and it is difficult to design an investment relation from ex post variables which fit the usually expectational variables of the investment relation.[9]

Many forecasters, including some working with econometric models, place main reliance on the OBE-SEC survey of actual and planned expenditures of private business (except farming, real estate, professional, and nonprofit and other institutions) for new plant and equipment. This survey assumes that capital budgets are frequently confined to a calendar-year period, so only the March *Survey of Current Business* contains expectations for nearly a full year in advance; later surveys extend ahead only seven to four months. McGraw-Hill Publishing Company makes a survey for the full year ahead twice a year, and the results are reported in *Business Week* in about April and November. The concepts in the two surveys are comparable, so the McGraw-Hill survey may be used to supplement the OBE-SEC survey. These plant and equipment surveys have a good record in predicting direction of movement. However, in quarters of expansion, the projections tend to be low, and in periods of contraction, they tend to be high.

There are other symptomatic, as opposed to causal, series whose importance is suggested by theory and empirical testing. The National Industrial Conference Board reports quarterly capital appropriations from a survey of large manufacturing corporations. This series has been identified as a leading indicator, and it has also shown a rather clear tendency to lead the OBE-SEC expenditure expectations series. Monthly data are available on contract awards for nonresidential construction (F. W.

[7] Sherman J. Maisel, "A Theory of Fluctuation in Residential Construction Starts," *American Economic Review*, vol. 53, pp. 359–383, June, 1963.

[8] Some of the empirical studies are discussed by Robert Eisner, "Investment: The Aggregate Investment Function," *International Encyclopedia of the Social Sciences*, vol. VIII (New York: The Macmillan Company and The Free Press, 1968), pp. 185–194. See also Robert Eisner, "Investment and the Frustrations of Econometricians," *American Economic Review*, vol. 59, pp. 50–64, May, 1969.

[9] Robert Eisner, "Investment and the Frustrations of Econometricians," *ibid.*, pp. 50 and 64.

Dodge Division, McGraw-Hill, Inc.) and on new orders for machinery and equipment. The monthly series also lead capital outlays, but by shorter lead times than appropriations.

Capacity measures may be utilized to gauge the relative need to expand productive facilities. The OBE-SEC survey report is accompanied by data on manufacturers' evaluation of their capacity in light of current and prospective sales for the next twelve months. *BCD* shows the ratio, quarterly, of output to capacity in manufacturing. Profits and profit margins are also important. *BCD* presents several such series, classified as leading indicators, and a diffusion index of net profits in manufacturing and trade. Another significant leading indicator shown in *BCD* is the ratio of price to unit labor costs. Wesley Mitchell was a leader in systematically documenting the changes in this ratio over the cycle—its rise, with subsequent pressure on profits, during the upswing, as wages increase, overtime increases, and productivity drops; and its fall during downswings, reflecting the decreases in wages, reduced overtime, and productivity increases. Financial statistics may also be considered, particularly with regard to the restrictive effects on new investment that rising interest rates, coupled with credit rationing and falling equity prices, may have on expenditures on plant and equipment.

Inventory investment   Swings in inventory investment have been an outstanding feature of economic fluctuations in the United States. Measured on an annual basis, they accounted for at least 42 percent of the decline in national product in every post-World War I contraction except that of 1929 to 1932.[10] The post-World War II downturns have often been called "inventory recessions," because, on the basis of seasonally adjusted quarterly data, the declines in inventory demand have been almost as great as the declines in GNP.

Forecasting inventory investment is hazardous for several reasons. First, although inventory levels in relation to output do not deviate from a secular norm for long periods of time, there are abrupt and quantitatively large shifts over the short run. Second, it is "change in business inventories" that enters GNP, the first difference between levels. Thus, to develop a meaningful picture, economists must go behind the GNP component to study changes in the larger aggregates. Third, as it appears in the accounts, inventory investment is measured as the change in the physical volume of business inventories valued at current prices. In periods of rapidly changing prices, one must keep in mind the necessity of making the inventory valuation adjustment to the basic series. Fourth, the commonly used monthly inventory series on manufacturing and trade must be supplemented to account for inventory change in the construction and extractive industries (including agriculture).

Inventory developments, as a basic procedure, may be evaluated in light of current and prospective output changes in the final demand sectors. Series on inventory-sales ratios are valuable in appraising trends. The ratio may be taken as indicating any deviation between actual and "desired" inventory situations, and the direction

---

[10] Thomas M. Stanback, Jr., *Postwar Cycles in Manufacturers' Inventories* (New York: National Bureau of Economic Research, 1962). This paper was submitted to the Joint Economic Committee as part of the study "Inventory Fluctuations and Economic Stabilization." Other papers submitted are also of interest. They appeared as Joint Committee Prints, in four parts (1961 and 1962).

and size of the deviations related to the intensity of the adjustment effort. These trends, by industry and level of fabrication, may be used to appraise special situations, such as strikes, that may disrupt the usual inventory adjustment patterns. General price movements and price expectations may also be significant. For example, rising prices in a tight demand situation may lead to anticipatory inventory buying. Another factor to consider is interest rates. Rising interest rates and reduced credit availability may signal that inventories will be pared to cut costs.

An estimating equation for change in trade and manufacturing inventory at book values, prepared by Nestor Terleckyj, highlights three lagged variables. For forecasting inventories three and six months in advance, Terleckyj found the inventory-sales ratio at the beginning of the period, the average ratio of new orders to sales in the quarter immediately preceding, and the ratio of unfilled orders to sales at the beginning of the period to be significant variables.[11]

In this sector, too, there are anticipations surveys. OBE began reporting manufacturers' sales and inventory expectations in 1961. A survey is conducted each quarter, for the current and following quarters; it provides detail for durables and nondurables manufacturers. Reporting companies also evaluate as "high," "about right," and "low" the condition of actual inventories relative to sales and unfilled orders. This is reported in *BCD*, shown as the percentage of manufacturers who consider their inventory high less the percentage who consider their inventory low. The National Association of Purchasing Agents and *Fortune* also survey inventory intentions.

Net Exports

As the difference between two larger magnitudes, the component "net exports of goods and services," like inventory change, is difficult to forecast.

Merchandise imports may be related with a fair degree of success to domestic output. Some separation of the components that are income- and price-elastic, such as food and beverages, from components that are more closely related to production, such as raw materials, may be useful. Of the remaining components, net military outlays may be estimated after due consideration of political events, and net expenditures on services have shown a slight upward trend in recent years.

Ilse Mintz found that merchandise exports in the post-World War I period rose when business activity expanded and fell when it contracted, even duplicating to some extent the amplitude of domestic fluctuations. Much of this agreement between export value and domestic activity is explained by agreement in timing between foreign and domestic business cycles.[12] Thus, it is appropriate to examine business conditions in other countries, particularly in the major industrial countries that are customers of the United States. The international comparisons in *BCD* and *Main Economic Indicators* (prepared monthly by the Organization for Economic Cooperation and Development), both of which maintain series on industrial production, are

[11] Nestor Terleckyj, "Measures of Inventory Change," in Joint Economic Committee, *Inventory Fluctuations and Economic Instability,* Joint Committee Print (1961), part II, pp. 190–191.

[12] Ilse Mintz, *Cyclical Fluctuations in the Exports of the United States since 1879* (New York: National Bureau of Economic Research, 1967), p. 278.

convenient for this purpose. Special conditions may be noted, such as poor harvests abroad, political events, e.g., the Suez crisis in 1957, and changes in monetary reserve positions of trading partners.

Personal Consumption Expenditures

Post-World War II study indicates that consumption expenditure does not follow a simple, "passive" relation to income, as Keynes's armchair formulation suggested, although it is certainly steadier than the other GNP components. There is ample evidence of shifts in the consumption function that are independent of current-period income.[13] Liquidity, credit terms, rapidity of income change, stock of durables, and other variables in addition to disposable personal income have influenced the level of total consumption expenditures and, especially, the composition of goods and services purchased.

Of the three major components, the durables component is of the greatest concern to the forecaster because of its volatility. Consumer nondurables and services, as a percentage of disposable personal income, generally move inversely with economic activity about a slightly rising trend line. It is with respect to durables that household stocks, debt and asset variables, and rate of change in income come into play most strongly as explanatory variables.[14] It is often useful to separate automobile expenditures from other durables to take advantage of the substantial body of specialized analysis and information that is available.

Important evidence on future consumption expenditures, especially on demand for durables, can be found in consumer surveys. *Consumer Buying Indicators,* which reports the Census Bureau's quarterly Survey of Consumer Buying Expectations, provides indexes of expected car purchases (new and used) and of expected expenditures on houses and household durables. The Census Bureau initiated this survey in 1959, with a major improvement in 1966, and over that period the intention survey was found to be a helpful forecasting tool. In addition, there are privately conducted surveys. The National Industrial Conference Board publishes a monthly report on consumer attitudes and buying plans. The Survey Research Center at the University of Michigan emphasizes consumers' attitudes toward their financial position and economic well-being, and constructs an Index of Consumer Sentiment (reported in *BCD*).

A JUDGMENTAL MODEL

The model described below is a useful background for judgmental projections within the gross national product framework. The validity of the aggregate which it produces depends mainly on the validity of the projections of the autonomous sectors

---

[13] Two surveys of this field are Robert Ferber, "Research on Household Behavior," in American Economic Association and Royal Economic Society, *Surveys of Economic Theory* (New York: St. Martin's Press, Inc., 1966), vol. 3; and Daniel B. Suits, "The Determinants of Consumer Expenditure: A Review of Present Knowledge," in Daniel B. Suits et al., *Impacts of Monetary Policy* (Englewood Cliffs, N.J.: Prentice-Hall, Inc., 1963), pp. 203-223.

[14] See, for example, Arnold C. Harberger. ed., *The Demand for Durable Goods* (Chicago: The University of Chicago Press, 1960).

of government purchases, private investments, and the multiplier relations linking these variables to personal consumption. In short, the validity of the aggregate depends mainly on the judgmental elements of the model. The general approach is not unlike many small- to medium-scale forecasting operations which are limited in the resources upon which they can draw, especially computer time.[15]

The Basic Model

The first approximation represents an elaboration of the Keynesian theory of income determination. The model defines aggregate demand to conform to the OBE national income and product accounts. Thus, "leakages" from the stream of spending for consumption comprise not only personal saving, but also corporate saving, taxes (less transfers), and imports. "Offsets" to these leakages are provided not only by domestic investment, but also by exports and government purchases, treated as exogenous variables in this model.

The symbols used in the model are identified below:

Y_n: Net national product
C: Personal consumption expenditure
I: Net private domestic investment
G: Government purchases of goods and services
X: Exports of goods and services
M: Imports of goods and services
T: Net tax receipts
T_x: Tax and nontax payments
T_r: Transfer payments by government
Y_d: Disposable personal income less personal transfers
S: Corporate savings (corporate profits after tax less dividend payments)
*: Variables treated as exogenous
Δ: Change

Definitional equations There are three definitional equations. The first defines the components of net national product:

$$Y_n = C + I^* + G^* + X^* - M$$

Transfer payments by government are netted against tax and nontax payments to obtain net tax receipts:

$$T = T_x - T_r$$

Disposable personal income is defined so that consumption (and personal saving) may be related directly to this version of income:

$$Y_d = Y_n - T - S$$

Behavioral equations There are four behavioral equations. One relates consumption (and its complement, personal saving) to disposable personal income:

$$C = a + cY_d$$

---

[15] An example of a judgmental forecast is John W. Kendrick, "Disinflation without Recession in 1969," a paper presented at the Annual Agricultural Outlook Conference, Washington, D.C., Feb. 17, 1969; it appeared in the *Commercial and Financial Chronicle*, Feb. 27, 1969, pp. 1, 14-15.

The leakages due to imports, net tax receipts, and corporate saving are stated as functions of national product:

$$M = d + mY_n$$
$$T = b + tY_n$$
$$S = e + sY_n$$

In each behavioral equation there are two parameters. The parameters a (and $1-a$) and d, b, and e are the "no-income" levels of consumption (and saving), and "no-production" levels of imports, net tax receipts, and corporate saving, respectively. The parameters c, or really $1-c$, and m, t, and s determine the size of the leakage that will be induced by the associated disposable personal income and national production.

Substitutions

The final expenditure expression is obtained by making successive substitutions. The behavioral statements for net tax receipts and corporate saving are substituted in the definitional equation for disposable personal income:

$$Y_d = Y_n - b - tY_n - e - sY_n$$

This expanded statement for disposable personal income is substituted in the behavioral equation for consumption expenditure:

$$C = a + c(Y_n - b - tY_n - e - sY_n)$$
$$C = a + cY_n - cb - ctY_n - ce - csY_n$$

The relation between consumption expenditure (and saving) and national product is thus stated. The expanded equation for consumption plus the behavioral equation for imports is added to the exogenous variables in the definitional equation for national product:

$$Y_n = a + cY_n - cb - ctY_n - ce - scY_n + I^*$$
$$+ G^* + X^* - d - mY_n$$
$$Y_n + ctY_n - cY_n + scY_n + mY_n = a - cb - ce + I^* + G^* + X^* - d$$
$$Y_n(1 - c + ct + sc + m) = a - cb - ce - d + I^* + G^* + X^*$$
$$Y_n = \frac{(a - cb - ce - d) + I^* + G^* + X^*}{1 - c + ct + sc + m}$$

When one level of national product is subtracted from another, the constant in the numerator cancels out, and the equation resulting is for the change in national product:

$$\Delta Y_n = \frac{1}{1 - c + c(t + s) + m} \Delta(I^* + G^* + X^*)$$

The fraction shown is the "multiplier" applicable to the change in the exogenous variables. The size of the multiplier depends on the parameters of induced leakage to personal saving, $1-c$; of the proportion of induced net tax receipts and corporate saving that would have been spent if government and corporations had transferred their flows to consumers, $c(t + s)$; and of induced imports, m.

In the formulation of the model, investment, exports, and government purchases of goods and services are treated as exogenous. This means, essentially, that in the preparation of the forecasts for these sectors the forecaster will draw upon all information he considers relevant to the particular forecasting period, as described in the first section of this chapter. The forecast thus prepared is then inserted into the model. However, these sectors are in reality only "semiautonomous." Investment plans, for example, are made in the context of certain sales expectations. If a first approximation to the GNP projection, using expected or planned change in the exogenous variables times the multiplier, adds up to a larger (or smaller) increase in GNP than expected by business in formulating investment plans, the investment projection should be modified accordingly. The government purchase projection would be modified chiefly to the extent that the overall projection implied more (or less) inflation than was implied in the original forecast based on the President's budget plan as adjusted for anticipated congressional action. The export projection might be modified slightly to the extent that the initial GNP forecast exceeded (or fell short of) that assumed, since this would affect imports and thus (indirectly, and with a lag) exports. In the final version of the projection, the exogenous variables would be inserted in the model as adjusted for the "feedback" induced by a divergence of actual from anticipated final sales. This method of successive approximations is thus a means of taking into account the interdependence of the sectors that finally results in a level of income and final output.

Projecting Personal Consumption Expenditures and Total GNP

The first approximation to forecast change in GNP and consumption expenditures is obtained by applying the appropriate multiplier to the projected change in the aggregate semiautonomous variables. This yields a change in level of GNP, from which the change in the semiautonomous variables may be subtracted to obtain change in personal consumption expenditures.

A rough multiplier is most readily obtained by taking the average relationship between changes over recent cycles—treating expansions and contractions separately. In recent cycles, the multiplier in expansions was approximately 2, and in contractions 1. It would be valuable to determine the parameters of the several leakages separately to facilitate adjustment for a forecast period in light of expected changes in the behavioral relations. Once determined, the multiplier can be varied up or down within two standard deviations, based on interpretation of the results of consumer surveys.

The second approximation to the consumption expenditure projection is made as follows. Given the first approximation to GNP just obtained, the reconciliation items between GNP and disposable personal income (DPI) can be projected largely as by-products of, or based on relationship to, variables that have already been obtained (see section below).

Next, a second approximation to the consumption expenditure projection can be obtained, based on a regression between consumption and DPI or based on past quarterly ratios between the two variables in similar phases of the cycle. The projected values may be varied within two standard deviations of the values thus obtained, depending on results of consumer surveys. This second approximation to the consumption expenditures forecast can then be substituted to get a new GNP total, making allowance for the effect of the adjustment on DPI, and thus on consumption itself, before finalizing the numbers.

Projecting the Reconciliation Items between GNP and Disposable Personal Income

The items that must be projected in moving from GNP to DPI are shown in Table 16-1.

Capital consumption allowances   The simplest way to project capital consumption is on the basis of the average increase in recent quarters, since the movement is fairly regular. The average quarterly rate can be raised a little, if high fixed investment is projected, or shaded a little when fixed investment is expected to fall significantly.

A more precise method is first to estimate the major component, depreciation, as follows. Take the two most recent end-of-year estimates of fixed capital stock in current dollars. Take the change (net investment), and subtract this from gross expenditures for construction and producers' durable equipment in order to get implied depreciation. Compute the ratio of depreciation to the beginning-of-period stock, and apply the ratio to end-of-period stock in order to obtain an estimate for the coming period; subtract this from the gross investment projected to get the net investment to add to beginning-of-period stock to get end-of-period stock. Continue to "unwind" in this fashion for the entire forecast period.

The minor item of accidental damage to fixed capital is somewhat erratic, but an approximation can be obtained by computing the most recent ratio to fixed capital stock which can apply to the projected stock of capital figures obtained as described above.

Other items in the reconciliation with national income   For most purposes a three-way breakdown is sufficient to forecast indirect business taxes. Sales taxes and excises, which account for over half the total, can be estimated on the basis of their relationship to consumption expenditures. Customs duties, which are small but more volatile than the rest, can be estimated on the basis of their relationship to import volume. The remaining indirect taxes, of which the major type is property taxes, show little sensitivity to income and can be conveniently projected on the basis of past trend.

Business transfers are quite stable. Subsidies less current surplus of government enterprises is an erratic item, but small. The statistical discrepancy is the main swing item of this group—but obviously we cannot, nor would we wish to, predict a statistical discrepancy. The convention is to hold this component at its level in the takeoff period of the forecast.

Corporate profits and inventory valuation adjustment   Changes in corporate profits and inventory valuation adjustment (IVA) can be related to changes in national income, which has just been derived. During post-World War II expansions, 16 percent of the increases in national income has gone into corporate profits on average. During the expansion of 1958 to 1960, the ratio was 24 percent. During contractions, reductions in corporate profits and IVA have accounted for 75 percent of the drops in national income on average. Between 1960 and 1961, corporate profits and IVA fell more than national income. The precise relationship to be used in the forecast period will depend in part, of course, on the forecaster's judgment as to the net

TABLE 16-1

Relation of Gross National Product, National Income, Personal Income,
and Disposition of Personal Income, 1966–1968
(Billions of Dollars)

		1966	1967	1968
GROSS NATIONAL PRODUCT		749.9	793.5	865.7
Less:	Capital consumption allowances	63.9	68.6	73.3
EQUALS:	NET NATIONAL PRODUCT	685.9	725.0	792.4
Less:	Indirect business tax and nontax liability	65.7	70.1	77.9
	Business transfer payments	3.0	3.2	3.4
	Statistical discrepancy	−1.0	−1.0	−2.5
Plus:	Subsidies less current surplus of government enterprises	2.3	1.4	0.8
EQUALS:	NATIONAL INCOME	620.6	654.0	714.4
Less:	Corporate profits and inventory valuation adjustment	82.4	79.2	87.9
	Contributions for social insurance	38.0	42.4	47.0
	Wage accruals less disbursements	0	0	0
Plus:	Government transfer payments to persons	41.1	48.8	55.8
	Interest paid by government (net) and by consumers	22.2	23.6	26.1
	Business transfer payments	3.0	3.2	3.4
	Dividends	20.8	21.5	23.1
EQUALS:	PERSONAL INCOME	587.2	629.4	687.9
Less:	Personal tax and nontax payments	75.4	82.9	98.0
EQUALS:	DISPOSABLE PERSONAL INCOME	511.9	546.5	590.0
Less:	Interest paid by consumers	12.4	13.1	14.2
	Personal transfer payments to foreigners	0.6	0.8	0.8
EQUALS:	DISPOSABLE PERSONAL INCOME LESS PERSONAL TRANSFERS	498.9	532.6	575.0
Less:	Personal consumption expenditures	466.3	492.3	536.6
EQUALS:	PERSONAL SAVING	32.5	40.4	38.4

SOURCE: Adapted from *Survey of Current Business,* vol. 49, pp. 19, 26, July, 1969.

ECONOMIC ACCOUNTS AND THEIR USES

effect of probable policies, especially those of the central bank, management, and unions, as they affect cost-price relations.

Contributions for social insurance   These contributions are most clearly related to labor compensation, at present rates changing by about 10 percent as much. Compensation of employees, in turn, has shown a remarkably stable relationship to national income since 1948. During expansions, about 75 percent of changes in national income has gone to labor; during contractions, about 45 percent. Thus contributions for social insurance may be increased by about 7½ percent of the increases in national income, and by about 4½ percent of decreases. Allowance should be made for any known change in social insurance tax rates.

Wage accruals less disbursement can be entered as zero unless special circumstances of retroactive wage settlements dictate to the contrary.

Transfer payments   Government transfer payments to persons should be broken down between unemployment insurance benefits and the remainder. The unemployment insurance benefits depend on the number of insured unemployed and the average benefit. Total unemployed can be estimated from the preliminary GNP projection by dividing the deflated projection by projected production per employee, to obtain employment, and subtracting the result from a labor-force projection. The insured unemployed figure maintains a fairly consistent relation to total unemployment. The average benefit can be projected after a review of information from the Bureau of Labor Statistics concerning expected changes. Of the remaining transfers, veterans benefits are projected in federal budget documents, and others have shown a fairly steady upward trend, with some tendency to accelerate during recessions as older workers withdraw from the labor force in somewhat greater numbers and start collecting old-age and other retirement benefits.

Business transfers, consisting primarily of consumer bad debts and corporate gifts to nonprofit institutions, show little or no change from quarter to quarter, but a mild upward trend over a period of years.

Interest paid by government (net) and by consumers   Interest paid by government depends on the size of the net public debt and the average effective rate of interest on the debt. The federal budget documents contain a projection of interest payments. An alternative procedure is roughly to estimate total tax revenue by applying the overall national tax rate to the projected GNP, and subtract this from the projected government expenditure to get a projection of the change in debt. To this figure should be added the expected refundings, and an average interest charge applied based on the projected trend of rates and the composition of the new debt. These payments should be added to the payments on the bulk of the debt which is not maturing during the projection period. This is a slow-moving item because the bulk of payments are already determined, and on the remainder, substantial debt increases are often associated with rising rates.

Similarly, interest paid by consumers can be related to the net consumer debt and the average effective rate of interest on that debt.

Dividends   Dividend payments are far more stable than corporate profits and are an important stabilizer in the private economy. There is a fair relationship between dividends and a four-year moving average of profits after tax. The general picture is one of dividends moving up slowly as profits rise, and of their leveling off during declines in profits lasting less than one year.

Personal tax and nontax payments   Projections of the above items permit one to go from GNP to personal income. Disposable personal income is obtained by deducting projected changes in personal taxes from projected changes in personal income. During the period of expansion since the federal tax reductions in 1964-1965, approximately 26 percent of the increases in personal income has gone to governments. Declines in personal income have been infrequent and limited, and the relationship of tax revenues to income change has been rather irregular. It is clear, however, that the ratio of tax change to income change is somewhat larger on the downswing than in expansions. Two items, the relatively stable personal transfer payments to foreigners and the interest payments by consumers, must be deducted also to get the form of disposable personal income with which we worked out the behavioral relations.

Once the projections of disposable personal income less personal transfers are obtained, the past relationships of consumer spending to DPI can be applied, modified on the basis of surveys of consumer buying plans referred to earlier.

THE OBE ECONOMETRIC MODEL

There now exist a variety of econometric models of the United States economy. They differ in their complexity, purpose, and, no doubt, in the degree of accuracy of the prediction produced (see Selected References at the end of the chapter).

The model builder, working within the conceptual framework of the way he believes the economy to operate, must test hypotheses with actual economic magnitudes and decide upon a workable set of explicit relations. Thus, a forecasting model may be framed to determine the GNP. A set of equations representing the components of GNP would be developed, and the required interrelations of price, income, labor force, and other variables brought in.[16]

The OBE quarterly model of the United States economy is primarily a forecasting instrument.[17] It is a variant of one constructed by Lawrence R. Klein. The model consists of forty-nine equations, including identities. The equations may be divided into groups: (1) components of GNP, which will be discussed in greater depth, since our main interest lies in this group of equations; (2) prices and wage rates; (3) labor-force and employment-related magnitudes; (4) income components; (5) monetary variables; and (6) miscellaneous variables needed to round out the model.

---

[16] Short general explanations of econometric model building, depicting the economy in terms of GNP, are contained in Maurice Liebenberg et al., "A Quarterly Econometric Model of the United States: A Progress Report," *Survey of Current Business*, vol. 46, pp. 13-16, May, 1966; and in F. Gerard Adams and Peter E. de Janosi, "Statistics and Econometrics of Forecasting," in William F. Butler and Robert A. Kavesh, eds., *How Business Economists Forecast* (Englewood Cliffs, N.J.: Prentice-Hall, Inc., 1966), pp. 14-29.

[17] The discussion that follows is based on Liebenberg et al., *ibid.*, pp. 16-39.

The equations explaining the GNP components have been reproduced for reference. Personal consumption expenditure is explained by four equations, each of which is made a function of deflated disposable personal income, as would be expected from theory. Further, each equation contains other variables. The automobile equation contains relative prices, lagged average weekly hours, and a dummy variable that helps to bring in the effect of strikes in the auto industry. Expenditures on other durables are explained (in addition to disposable personal income) by the ratio of nonwage to wage income to allow for an income-distribution effect, and deflated liquid assets held by households. Lagged consumption enters the equations for nondurables and services, as does population in the latter case.

OBE Econometric Model: GNP Component Equations

Numbers in parentheses under coefficients are standard errors of the coefficients. Key to variables and other abbreviations follows equations.

Personal consumption expenditures, automobiles and parts

$$C_a = -134.0 - 11.0\frac{p_a}{p_c} + .104\frac{Y-T}{p_c} + 129.0(h_u)_{-1} + 1.85d_a;$$
$$\quad\ (.14)\quad (6.4)\qquad\quad (.006)\qquad\quad (19.4)\qquad\quad (.30)$$

$$TSLS,\ \overline{R}^2 = .91,\ \overline{S} = 1.0,\ D.W. = 1.25$$

Personal consumption expenditures, durables other than automobiles and parts

$$C_{od} = 28.0 + .060\frac{Y-T}{p_{od}} - 65.2\frac{P}{W} + .060\left(\frac{L_h}{p_{od}}\right)^{dev}_{-1};$$
$$\quad\ (.07)\quad (.002)\qquad\quad (15.2)\qquad (.008)$$

$$TSLS,\ \overline{R}^2 = .98\ \overline{S} = .5,\ D.W. = .88$$

Personal consumption expenditures, nondurables

$$C_n = 31.1 + .252\frac{Y-T}{p_n} + .210\frac{1}{8}\sum_{i=-1}^{-8}(C_n)_i;$$
$$\quad\ (.15)\ (.025)\qquad\quad (.083)$$

$$TSLS,\ \overline{R}^2 = .995,\ \overline{S} = 1.0,\ D.W. = 1.23$$

Personal consumption expenditures, services (except housing)

$$C_s = -44.2 + .069\frac{Y-T}{p_s} + .476\frac{1}{8}\sum_{i=-1}^{-8}(C_s)_i + .347N;$$
$$\quad\ (.06)\quad (.015)\qquad\quad (.161)\qquad\qquad (.118)$$

$$TSLS,\ \overline{R}^2 = .998,\ \overline{S} = .5,\ D.W. = 1.13$$

where $\quad C' = C_a + C_{od} + C_n + C_s$

One-family housing starts, private nonfarm

$$HS_s = -768 + .622\ (HS_s)_{-1} - .113\ (HS_3)_{-3}$$
$$\quad\quad\ (7.9)\ (.137)\qquad\qquad (.081)$$

$$- 43.9\ (r_m)_{-1} + 1530\left(\frac{R_h}{q_h}\right)_{-1} - .0216V_{-2}^{dev};$$
$$\quad\ (13.9)\qquad\quad (486)\qquad\quad (.0235)$$

$$OLS,\ \overline{R}^2 = .32,\ \overline{S} = 54.5,\ D.W. = 1.96$$

Residential structures, nonfarm

$$I_h = -.14 + .001022 \left[.41\left(\frac{c_h}{q_h}HS\right) + .49\left(\frac{c_h}{q_h}HS\right)_{-1} \right.$$
$$(1.06) \quad (.000060)$$

$$\left. + .10\left(\frac{c_h}{q_h}HS\right)_{-3} \right] - .19d_1 + .0d_2 + .38d_3 + I_{hr};$$
$$(.21) \quad (.23) \quad (.24)$$

$$OLS, \ \overline{R}^2 = .93, \ \overline{S} = .4, \ D.W. = 1.36$$

where $\quad HS = HS_s + HS_m$

Fixed investment, nonresidential

$$I_p = 11.0 + .804 I_p^e + .108(\Delta X)_{-1} + .524(I_p^a - I_p^e)_{-2} + .163t + .14C_a;$$
$$(1.5) \quad (.045) \quad (.026) \quad (.126) \quad (.012)$$

$$OLS, \ \overline{R}^2 = .96, \ \overline{S} = 1.0, \ D.W. = 1.25$$

Change in business inventories

$$I_i = 49.9 + .232(X - I_i - C_s) + .363(I_i)_{-1}$$
$$(0.2) \quad (.044) \quad (.084)$$

$$- .354 \sum_{j=-\infty}^{-1} (I_i)_j + .215(U_d)_{-1} + .72t + 4.34d_i;$$
$$(.053) \quad\quad\quad (.064) \quad\quad (.18) \quad (.86)$$

$$TSLS, \ \overline{R}^2 = .81, \ \overline{S} = 1.6, \ D.W. = 2.04$$

Imports other than crude materials and foodstuffs

$$F_{if} = 15.5 + .0573 \frac{Y - T}{p_i} - 49.4 \frac{P}{W};$$
$$(0.1) \quad (.0026) \quad\quad\quad (17.0)$$

$$TSLS, \ \overline{R}^2 = .97, \ \overline{S} = .6, \ D.W. = .60$$

Imports of crude materials and foodstuffs

$$F_{im} = 3.94 + .0027 \left(\frac{pX}{p_i}\right)_{-1};$$
$$(.03) \quad (.0005)$$

$$OLS, \ \overline{R}^2 = .35, \ \overline{S} = .2, \ D.W. = 1.18$$

where $\quad p_a C_a + p_{od} C_{od} + p_n C_n + p_s C_s + p_r C_r + q_h I_h$

$$+ I_{hf} + q_p I_p + p I_i + e_i - p_i(F_{if} + F_{im}) + F_e + G = GNP$$

Key to Abbreviations

(All variables except interest rates are seasonally adjusted. All components of the national income and product accounts are at annual rates; other flow variables are at quarterly rates unless otherwise noted. Variables preceded by * are exogenous.)

C' Personal consumption expenditures, except housing services, billions of 1958 dollars

C_a	Personal consumption expenditures, automobiles and parts, billions of 1958 dollars
$*c_h$	Average cost per new private nonfarm housing unit started, in thousands of dollars
C_n	Personal consumption expenditures, nondurables, billions of 1958 dollars
C_{od}	Personal consumption expenditures, durables other than automobiles and parts, billions of 1958 dollars
$*C_r$	Personal consumption expenditures, housing, billions of 1958 dollars
C_s	Personal consumption expenditures, services (except housing), billions of 1958 dollars
d_1, d_2, d_3	Seasonal dummy variables, housing expenditures equation; $d=1$ in quarter corresponding to subscript, 0 otherwise
$*d_a$	Dummy variable for auto equation (-1 during strike quarter; $+1$ following strike quarter; $+1$ in 1955 to reflect abrupt credit and taste changes; 0 otherwise)
$*d_i$	Dummy variable for inventory equation (-1 during strike quarter; $+1$ before and after strike; 0 otherwise)
dev	Deviation from least squares linear trend
e_i	Discrepancy in jumpoff quarter between change in business inventories in current dollars and pI_i
$*F_e$	Exports, billions of dollars
F_{if}	Imports other than crude materials and foodstuffs, billions of 1958 dollars
F_{im}	Imports of crude materials and foodstuffs, billions of 1958 dollars
$*G$	Government purchases of goods and services, billions of dollars
GNP	Gross national product, billions of dollars
h_u	Average weekly hours index, private employees (1957-59=1.000)
HS	Private nonfarm housing starts, in thousands at annual rate
$*HS_m$	Number of new 2 or more family units started, in thousands at annual rate
HS_s	Number of new single-family units started, in thousands at annual rate
I_h	Residential structures, nonfarm, billions of 1958 dollars
$*I_{hf}$	Residential structures, farm, billions of dollars
$*I_{hr}$	Residential construction expenditures on other than new units (additions and alterations, etc.), billions of 1958 dollars
I_i	Change in business inventories, billions of 1958 dollars
I_p	Fixed investment, nonresidential, billions of 1958 dollars
I_p^a	Actual plant and equipment outlays in billions of dollars deflated by q_p
$*I_p^e$	Anticipated plant and equipment outlays; first anticipations in billions of dollars deflated by q_{n-2}
L_h	End of quarter liquid assets held by households (currency+demand and bank savings deposits+savings and loan shares), in billions of dollars
$*N$	Total population in millions
p	Implicit price deflator, gross private output, except housing services (1958=1.000)
P	Nonwage personal income (sum of proprietors' income, rental income of persons, dividends, and personal interest income), billions of dollars
$*p_a$	Implicit price deflator, personal consumption expenditures, automobiles and parts (1958=1.000)
p_c	Implicit price deflator, personal consumption expenditures (1958=1.000)

$^*p_i$	Implicit price deflator, imports (1958$=$1.000)
p_n	Implicit price deflator, personal consumption expenditures, nondurables (1958$=$1.000)
p_{od}	Implicit price deflator, personal consumption expenditures, durables other than automobiles and parts (1958$=$1.000)
$^*p_r$	Implicit price deflator, personal consumption expenditures, housing (1958$=$1.000)
p_s	Implicit price deflator, personal consumption expenditures, services (except housing) (1958$=$1.000)
q_h	Implicit price deflator, residential structures, nonfarm (1958$=$1.000)
q_p	Implicit price deflator, fixed investment, nonresidential (1958$=$1.000)
R_h	BLS consumer rent index (1957-59$=$1.000)
r_m	Percent yield, secondary market, FHA-insured new homes
t	Time in quarters (1953$-I=$1.0)
U_d	Unfilled manufacturers' orders, durable goods at end of quarter, billions of dollars, deflated by p_{wd}
V	Number of vacant nonfarm housing units, end of quarter, in thousands
W	Wage and salary disbursements and other labor income, billions of dollars
X	Gross private output, except housing services, billions of 1958 dollars
Y-T	Disposable personal income, billions of dollars
OLS	Ordinary least-squares estimate
$TSLS$	Two-stage least-squares estimate
D-W	Durbin-Watson statistic: Test for serial correlation of residuals
$\overline{R}^2$	Adjusted coefficient of determination
$\overline{S}$	Adjusted standard error of estimate[18]

Gross private domestic investment is broken into three components. For residential construction, the first step is to estimate nonfarm, one-family housing starts. Use is made of an equation containing lagged housing starts, mortgage yields, a lagged representation of the relative cost of renting to building, and deviation from the trend in vacancies. Housing starts thus obtained are multiplied by a cost of unit started, and the result phased in to obtain quarterly expenditures. The other residential construction components are exogenous. Nonresidential fixed investment is made a function of anticipated expenditures and variables that may cause actual expenditures to deviate from those anticipated, namely, change in output, two-quarter lagged deviation of actual from anticipated investment expenditures, and personal consumption expenditures on automobiles. Inventory investment is explained by total sales of private GNP to final markets, prior period's inventory investment, durables manufacturers' unfilled orders, and total inventories on hand at the beginning of the period.

Imports are estimated in two parts: Crude materials and foodstuffs are explained by lagged, deflated private GNP, and all other imports by deflated disposable personal income and the ratio of wage to nonwage income. Exports, necessary to compute net exports as the item enters GNP, are determined exogenously. The remaining component, government purchases of goods and services, is also exogenous.

Very briefly, with regard to the other equations of the model, the major price indexes, mostly in the form of appropriate implicit GNP deflators, are determined endogenously. For example, the price deflator for private GNP is a function of the

---

[18] *Ibid.*, pp. 30-31, 35-37, Appendix A.

average unit wage cost of private output for the current quarter and the two previous ones, and the two-quarter change in private final sales, with the latter dependent upon capacity utilization to reflect increased sensitivity of prices as capacity is approached. The wage rate is related to the state of the labor market and two factors that have a major role in collective bargaining. The labor-force equation, expressed as a participation rate, is a function of the proportion of the working-age population employed and a time trend. Man-hours of labor employed reflect both secular and cyclical variations in production. Private employment is derived from the estimate of total man-hours and an index of average weekly hours that reflects both cyclical and secular movements. Of the income equations, the private wages and salaries component is obtained from private man-hours and the wage rate; government employee compensation is exogenous. Corporate profits are made to vary positively with sales and negatively with the ratio of money wage rate to the overall price deflator, man-hours per unit of output, and the ratio of capacity to actual output. Nonwage personal income and dividends are related to corporate profits and other variables. The monetary equations include equations for the short-term interest rate, the long-term interest rate, the mortgage yield, and liquid assets of households. The miscellaneous equations include equations for capital consumption allowances, output at capacity, taxes, unemployment insurance benefits, orders, and shipments.

The internal consistency of the relations, or the interdependent character of the system represented by these equations, is clarified by a condensed flow diagram which depicts a simplified version of the OBE model (see this chart reproduced below as Diagram 16-1). The lines indicate the direct dependencies among the variables, and the arrows indicate the cause-effect direction. That all the boxes except the predetermined variables (exogenous variables and lagged endogenous variables) have arrows entering as well as emanating from them reveals the simultaneous character of the system. The income-product loop is the major element of simultaneity. The high degree of simultaneity of relations achievable with econometric models is regarded as one of their chief advantages.

Work with the OBE model is regarded as experimental: OBE does not publish forecasts of the future based on the model, but they are produced for internal government use. Several tests to which the model was subjected give some indications of how close the model might come in predicting. With regard to predicting business-cycle turning points in the period 1953 to 1961, the criterion of exactly coincident timing was met only infrequently, but the criterion of predicting the neighborhood of the turning point—such as one quarter on each side—was met in fifteen out of eighteen trials. When a run was made for 1965, a year outside the period to which the equations were fitted, the model closely depicted the degree and pattern of economic expansion in terms of GNP, although the major components did not do quite as well.

COMPARISON OF FORECASTING TECHNIQUES

A project to assess the accuracy of short-term forecasting of aggregate economic activity is under way at the National Bureau of Economic Research. The first results of that project appear in *An Appraisal of Short-term Economic Forecasts* by Victor Zarnowitz. Eight sets of forecasts that represent a variety of sources and types, but excluding formal econometric models such as that just described, were analyzed.

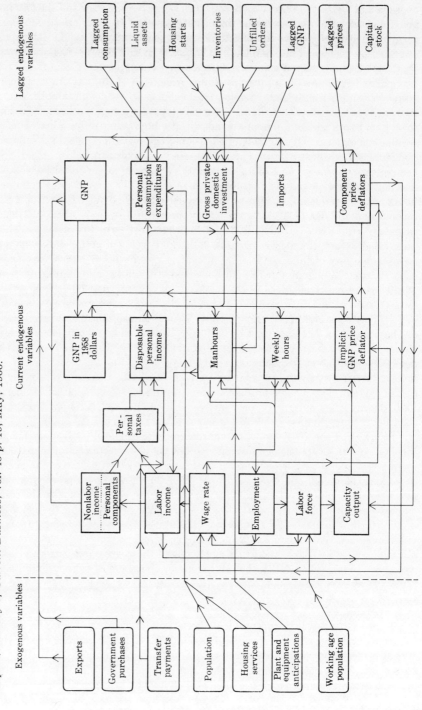

DIAGRAM 16-1

OBE econometric model: condensed flow diagram. Source: Maurice Liebenberg, Albert A. Hirsch, and Joel Popkin, "A Quarterly Econometric Model of the United States: A Progress Report," *Survey of Current Business*, vol. 46 p. 19, May, 1966.

Forecasts of GNP for a year ahead, covering the period 1953 to 1963, showed a mean absolute error of $10 billion, or no more than 2 percent of GNP. But when measured as a percentage of the change in GNP—a more significant figure—the error was approximately 40 percent. Typically the forecast for GNP as a whole was better than that for components, representing in part offsetting errors but also the fact that there are certain indicators used in forecasting that relate to aggregate economic activity but not to components. Most forecasts tend to be low, underestimating economic growth. It was found that there was no steady improvement in the quality of the forecasts over the period reviewed, although the forecasts continued to be more accurate than extrapolation of the preceding year's change or level.[19]

With this as the record of the judgmental forecasts, it has been asked: "Econometric Models: Is the New Age Dawning?"[20] Not necessarily quite yet. First, for the purpose of pure forecasting (and admittedly this is not the only purpose of econometric models), the very complex models, such as the approximately 150-equation Brookings model, have not proved themselves superior to the smaller models. When the discussion narrows to the smaller econometric models, the distinction between judgmental and econometric models begins to blur. Both kinds depend importantly on exogenous variables. For example, in the OBE model both government expenditures and exports are determined exogenously. Furthermore, actual forecasting practice by government officials in the United States and other countries suggests that to draw a sharp distinction between a rigorous, scientific but inflexible econometric approach and a subjective but flexible judgmental approach is misleading.[21] In practice, judgmental forecasts may encompass estimates of particular sectors derived by econometric techniques, or estimates arrived at using a judgmental approach may be checked with those produced by a formal model. Similarly, no realistically useful econometric forecast can be made without allowing for special factors. Therefore, there is a place for both approaches in short-term economic forecasting.

REVIEW QUESTIONS

1   What kinds of information must a forecaster have at hand in order to begin preparation of a forecast? What are some of the most useful secondary sources of information?
2   Discuss the role of symptomatic variables, including intentions surveys, in short-term forecasting.
3   Discuss the variables that a forecaster would wish to consider in preparing a forecast of any one of the more volatile components of GNP: residential construction, inventory investment, or net exports.
4   Discuss the approaches to forecasting personal consumption expenditure represented in the judgmental model described and the OBE econometric model.
5   Compare and contrast the judgmental and econometric approaches to short-term economic forecasting.

[19] Occasional Paper 104 (New York: National Bureau of Economic Research, 1967), pp. 4–8.
[20] Edwin Kuh, "Econometric Models: Is the New Age Dawning?" *American Economic Review*, vol. 55, pp. 362–369, May, 1965.
[21] *Techniques of Economic Forecasting*, with an Introduction by C. W. McMahon (Paris: Organization for Economic Cooperation and Development, 1965), especially pp. 26–27 and 150.

SELECTED REFERENCES

General

BUTLER, WILLIAM F., and ROBERT A. KAVESH, eds.: *How Business Economists Forecast* (Englewood Cliffs, N.J.: Prentice-Hall, Inc., 1966).

CONFERENCE ON RESEARCH IN INCOME AND WEALTH: *Models of Income Determination,* Studies in Income and Wealth, vol. XXVIII (Princeton, N.J.: Princeton University Press for the National Bureau of Economic Research, 1964).
Two papers present complete econometric models; others treat individual structural relations.

———: *Short-term Economic Forecasting,* Studies in Income and Wealth, vol. XVII (Princeton, N.J.: Princeton University Press for the National Bureau of Economic Research, 1955).

LEWIS, JOHN P., and ROBERT C. TURNER: *Business Conditions Analysis,* 2d ed. (New York: McGraw-Hill Book Company, 1967).
See part IV for a general discussion of forecasting techniques and sector demand analysis.

ORGANIZATION FOR ECONOMIC COOPERATION AND DEVELOPMENT: *Techniques of Economic Forecasting,* with an Introduction by C. W. McMahon (Paris: 1965).
Official forecasting techniques used in six countries are described. The eclectic method used by the U.S. Council of Economic Advisers is of special interest.

Econometric Models

DUESENBERRY, JAMES S., OTTO ECKSTEIN, and GARY FROMM: "A Simulation of the United States Economy in Recession," *Econometrica,* vol. 28, pp. 749–808, October, 1960.
This was reprinted in Robert A. Gordon and Lawrence R. Klein, eds., *Readings in Business Cycles* (Homewood, Ill.: Richard D. Irwin, Inc., 1965).

——— et al., eds.: *The Brookings Quarterly Econometric Model of the United States* (Chicago: Rand McNally & Company, 1965).

DE LEEUW, FRANK, and EDWARD GRAMLICH: "The Federal Reserve-MIT Econometric Model," *Federal Reserve Bulletin,* vol. 54, January, 1968.

KLEIN, LAWRENCE R.: "A Postwar Quarterly Model: Description and Applications," *Models of Income Determination,* Conference on Research in Income and Wealth, Studies in Income and Wealth, vol. XXVIII (Princeton, N.J.: Princeton University Press for the National Bureau of Economic Research, 1964).

LIEBENBERG, MAURICE, ALBERT A. HIRSCH and JOEL POPKIN: "A Quarterly Econometic Model of the United States: A Progress Report," *Survey of Current Business,* vol. 46, May, 1966.

THUROW, LESTER C.: "A Fiscal Policy Model of the United States," *Survey of Current Business,* vol. 49, June, 1969.

Economic Growth Analysis and Long-term Projections

17

Economic growth is usually defined as the secular rate of increase in real national product—preferably real NNP, since capital consumption is merely one of the costs of growth, although real GNP is often used as a proxy measure. Economic growth should be distinguished from economic progress, which refers to the rate of increase in real product per capita. Unless real product grows faster than population, or some variant measure of consumer units, it is clear that no progress has been made toward raising potential planes of living, which is virtually a universal goal in this age. Thus, the basic concepts of economic growth and progress are defined in terms of economic accounting aggregates. And the proximate analysis of these variables may be conducted largely in terms of various components of the accounts.

We say "proximate" explanations, since it is the basic values and motivations of a society, and the related socioeconomic institutions, designed to facilitate realization of individual and social material goals, that are fundamental. The economist must recognize that psychological, mental, or "spiritual" processes lie behind the material, which is not to say that attitudes and values may not in turn be conditioned by material circumstances. In this analysis, we are concerned with the proximate, material circumstances affecting economic growth, leaving aside the analysis of the infinitely more complex, and fundamental, psychological, social, and other factors that lie beyond the purview of economics, narrowly defined. We would not, however, discourage the student of economics from looking beyond and beneath the purely material phenomena. It makes life more interesting and fulfilling if we choose to be generalists as well as specialists.

TANGIBLE FACTOR INPUTS AND PRODUCTIVITY

As a first step in growth analysis, it is useful to divide the changes in real product into components, namely, real factor input and productivity. This may be done, in the first instance, through the statistical fitting of production functions. Most of us are familiar with the Cobb-Douglas form of the production function: $O = A L^a K^\beta$. O is real product; L is real labor input, usually measured by man-hours worked, sometimes weighted by base-period average hourly earnings by occupational and/or industry categories; K is capital input, often measured by the real stock of capital weighted by the base-period rate of return, possibly by industry components; and A is the scalar, representing the level of technology, organization, and other factors influencing the productivity of the basic factors. Actually, in this simple form of the production function, O is best interpreted as expressing the potential real product at optimum rates of utilization of the factors, and $L + K$ is real factor cost. An important part of short-term deviation of actual from potential output is due to fluctuations of output around the optimum potential, as has been shown by multiple correlations embodying a cyclical variable. In the absence of such a variable, cyclical forces must be included with the other factors reflected in shifts in A. The cyclical forces usually show up clearly in short-term (quarterly or annual) changes in A. When a time trend $(1 + r)^t$ is included with the logarithms of output and the input variables in multiple correlation analysis, the cyclical factor is not evident, although to the extent that departures from an optimum growth path affect investment and other relevant variables, the trend is indirectly affected by fluctuations. This form of the production function may be expressed as follows:[1]

$$\log O = a \log L + \beta \log K + (1 + r)^t$$

Under conditions of perfect competition, linear homogeneity, and the other assumptions of the Cobb-Douglas production function, the coefficients a and β represent the marginal productivities of the factors. When index numbers of the factor inputs are used, the coefficients indicate the factor shares of income, since under equilibrium conditions marginal product equals average product.

The "Total Factor Productivity" Approach

Rather than work with a productivity trend factor based on a statistical production function, we find it more convenient and flexible to derive a total factor productivity measure as the ratio of output to a weighted average of the factor inputs:

$$\log A = \frac{\log O}{a \log L + \beta \log K}$$

The author has developed such measures for the United States, except that he used

---

[1] See Solomon Fabricant, "Productivity," *International Encyclopedia of the Social Sciences*, vol. XII (New York: The Macmillan Company and The Free Press, 1968), pp. 523-536.

TABLE 17-1
Average Annual Percentage Rates of Change in Output, Inputs, and
Productivity Ratios in the Private Domestic Economy

	Periods			Subperiods			
	1889 to 1919	1919 to 1948	1948 to 1966	1948 to 1953	1953 to 1957	1957 to 1960	1960 to 1966
Real gross product	3.9	2.8	4.0	4.6	2.5	2.6	5.2
Inputs:							
Labor (weighted manhours)	2.2	0.9	1.0	1.1	0.0	−0.1	2.0
Man-hours	1.8	0.6	0.6	0.4	−0.2	0.1	1.5
Capital (net)	3.3	1.2	3.5	4.3	3.7	2.4	3.4
Total	2.6	1.0	1.5	1.8	0.6	0.4	2.3
Productivity ratios							
Real product per unit of:							
Labor input	1.6	1.9	3.0	3.5	2.6	2.7	3.1
Man-hours	2.0	2.2	3.4	4.1	2.7	2.6	3.6
Capital	0.5	1.6	0.4	0.2	-1.1	0.2	1.7
Total factor input	1.3	1.8	2.5	2.7	1.9	2.2	2.8

SOURCE: John W. Kendrick, *Productivity Trends in the United States* (Princeton, N.J.: Princeton University Press for the National Bureau of Economic Research, 1961), table AXXII; and "Postwar Productivity Trends" (unpublished manuscript).

weighted arithmetic means rather than a weighted geometric mean to obtain the output and input measures.[2] Since he changed weights every decade or so, the results are almost the same. Also, rather than use coefficients derived from a statistical production function as input weights, he employed the factor shares of national income. Actually, in many statistical investigations, the coefficients have closely approximated income shares.

The trend of total factor productivity closely approximates the trend rate of shift in the scalar *A* of the production function. The author's estimates of rates of change in productivity and the output and input components are shown in Table 17-1. The periods chosen are based on analysis of the trends in total factor productivity. Thus, in the period 1889 to 1919, productivity grew at the average rate of approximately 1.3 percent a year. During World War I and the decade of the 1920s, the trend rate accelerated to 2.3 percent a year. This was the period that saw the spread of scientific management, mass-production techniques, and the rise of industrial research and development as a regular, organized activity in the larger firms. As a result of the Great Depression of the early 1930s, the productivity trend line

[2] See John W. Kendrick, *Productivity Trends in the United States* (Princeton, N.J.: Princeton University Press for the National Bureau of Economic Research, 1961).

shifted downward, reflecting the low level of investment and a loss of capital and productive capacity that could never be recouped. But by 1936, the country was back on the productivity growth trend. Since 1948, the rate has averaged 2.5 percent a year, approximately the same as during the earlier period of rapid advance, 1916 to 1929 (see Chart 17-1).

CHART 17-1
Output, input, and productivity ratios, United States private domestic economy (index numbers, 1889-1965; 1958 = 100). Source: John W. Kendrick *Postwar Productivity Trends in the United States* (New York: unpublished manuscript for the National Bureau of Economic Research).

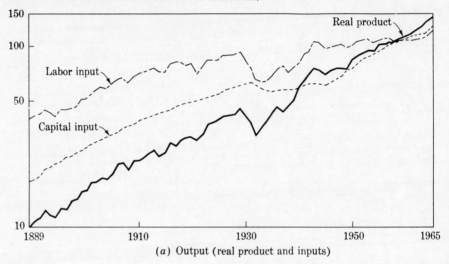

(*a*) Output (real product and inputs)

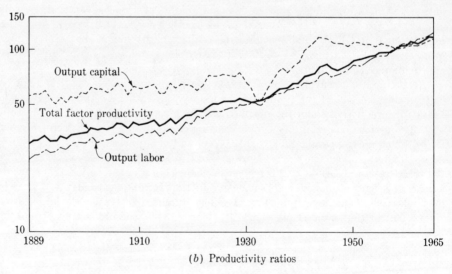

(*b*) Productivity ratios

ECONOMIC ACCOUNTS AND THEIR USES

The rates we have cited were obtained by the compound interest formula applied to index numbers for the first and last years of each period. They are almost the same as the rates obtained from a least-squares trend line through all the years of the period, since productivity is a much smoother series than output or input, and we chose boundary years representing relatively high levels of activity. The advantage of the compound interest approach is that rates of change in productivity, output, and input are all consistent, as indicated in the following comparisons. These are confined to the period since 1948, which is most pertinent to current growth trends.

Between 1948 and 1966, real GNP in the private domestic economy increased at an average annual rate of 4 percent. Total factor input grew at the rate of $1\frac{1}{2}$ percent, representing an average of the 1 percent rate of increase in labor input (weighted 0.80), and a $3\frac{1}{2}$ percent rate of increase in tangible capital (weighted 0.20). The resulting $2\frac{1}{2}$ percent a year growth in total factor productivity thus accounts for more than two-thirds of the economic growth of the period. Since total input grew about as fast as population, which rose $1\frac{1}{2}$ percent a year on average, we may say that all our economic progress, as measured by real product per capita, depended on the advance in productivity.

It has been stressed by a number of economists that merely labeling the difference between rates of change in output and tangible factor input as "productivity" does not really explain it. Abramovitz has called it a "measure of our ignorance"; Solow has termed it more simply the "residual." It has been a favorite sport of growth economists since the mid-1950s to try to explain away the residual. We shall first refer to one of the better known of these attempts, that of Edward Denison, which employs a national income framework. Then we shall give our own explanation, which employs the expanded concepts of investment and capital developed earlier (see Chapters 8 and 13).

Decomposing the Economic Growth Rate

In his study of the sources of economic growth in the United States, Edward Denison attempted to allocate the growth rate for past periods among the various inputs and the sources of increase in real national income per unit of input.[3] His results are summarized in Table 17-2. As a component of increase in total inputs, it will be noted, Denison includes factors affecting the quality of labor input. These factors—chiefly education and the effect of shorter hours on the quality of a man-hour of work—account for 1.10 percent of the 2.93 percent growth rate of 1929 to 1957. If these factors were excluded from input and included with the factors increasing output per unit of input (productivity), the average annual increase in total inputs would be 0.90 percent, or about one-third of the growth rate, and the productivity increase would be 2.03 percent a year, accounting for slightly more than two-thirds of the growth rate, which is consistent with the present author's results. In the last analysis, it does not really matter whether we count growth-producing forces as input or productivity, so long as we identify and measure the forces with reasonable accuracy.

Denison identifies seven factors that account for increasing productivity, as he

[3] Edward F. Denison, *The Sources of Economic Growth in the United States and the Alternatives before Us*, Supplementary Paper no. 13 (New York: Committee for Economic Development, 1962).

TABLE 17-2
Allocation of Growth Rate of Total Real National
Income among the Sources of Growth

	Percentage Points in Growth Rate			Percent of Growth Rate			
	1909–29[1] (Commerce)	1929–57	1960–80[2]	1909–29[1] (Commerce)	1909–29[1] (Kendrick-Kuznets)	1929–57	1960–80[2]
Real national income	2.82	2.93	3.33	100	100	100	100
Increase in total inputs	2.26	2.00	2.19	80	71	68	68
Labor, adjusted for quality change	1.53	1.57	1.70	54	48	54	51
Employment and hours	1.11	0.80	0.98	39	35	27	29
Employment	1.11	1.00	1.33	39	35	34	40
Effect of shorter hours on quality of a man-year's work	0.00	−0.20	−0.35	0	0	−7	−11
Annual hours	−0.23	−0.53	−0.42	−8	−7	−18	−13
Effect of shorter hours on quality of a man-hour's work	0.23	0.33	0.07	8	7	11	2
Education	0.35	0.67	0.64	12	11	23	19
Increased experience and better utilization of women workers	0.06	0.11	0.09	2	2	4	3
Changes in age-sex composition of labor force	0.01	−0.01	−0.01	0	0	0	0

Land	0.00	0.00	0.00	0	0	0	0
Capital	0.73	0.43	0.49	26	23	15	15
Nonfarm residential structures	0.13	0.05	NA	5	4	2	NA
Other structures and equipment	0.41	0.28	NA	15	13	10	NA
Inventories	0.16	0.08	NA	6	5	3	NA
U.S.-owned assets abroad	0.02	0.02	NA	1	1	1	NA
Foreign assets in U.S.	0.01	0.00	NA	0	0	0	NA
Increase in output per unit of input	0.56	0.93	1.14	20	29	32	34
Restrictions against optimum use of resources	NA	-0.07	0.00	NA	NA	-2	0
Reduced waste of labor in agriculture	NA	0.02	0.02	NA	NA	1	1
Industry shift from agriculture	NA	0.05	0.01	NA	NA	2	0
Advance of knowledge	NA	0.58	0.75	NA	NA	20	23
Change in lag in application of knowledge	NA	0.01	0.03	NA	NA	0	1
Economies of scale — independent growth of local markets	NA	0.07	0.05	NA	NA	2	2
Economies of scale — growth of national market	0.28	0.27	0.28	10	10	9	8

1 "Commerce" and "Kendrick-Kuznets" headings refer only to the growth rate of total product. Contributions in percentage points under the Kendrick-Kuznets heading would be identical with those shown under the Commerce heading except for "real national income," 3.17; "output per unit of input," .91, and "economies of scale — growth of national market." .32

2 ■Growth rate based on high-employment projection.

NA: Not available.

NOTE: Contributions in percentage points are adjusted so that the sum of appropriate details equals totals. Per cents of the growth rate have not been so adjusted.

SOURCE: Edward F. Denison, *The Sources of Economic Growth in the United States and the Alternatives before Us*, Supplementary Paper no. 13 (New York: Committee for Economic Development, 1962), table 32.

defines it. The chief factor is "advance of knowledge," which Denison estimates as a residual, accounting for 0.58 percent (one-fifth) of the 1929 to 1957 growth rate. The other significant factor is economies of scale due to the growth of local and national markets, which, together, account for 0.34 percent of growth, or 11 percent of the total.

It must be observed that many of Denison's estimates represent informed judgments. Also, it is not clear that he has adequately dealt with interactions among the forces. Yet, as Abramovitz pointed out in a review article, Denison provides us with "an agenda for future research."[4] He also succeeds in showing the large magnitude of investment required to raise the growth rate by even 0.1 percent. More recently, he has used his analytical framework for comparing components of growth rates for a number of countries.[5] Also, his framework can be used for projections as shown in the table.

INTANGIBLE INVESTMENT AND CAPITAL

In Chapter 8, we suggested that the term investment be defined broadly to include all outlays designed to expand future output- and income-producing capacity. By this interpretation, the capital account was expanded to include not only all purchases of durables and the accumulation of inventories by the nonbusiness as well as by the business sectors, but also the major types of productivity-enhancing intangible outlays: research and development, education and training, health, and mobility.

As shown in Table 17-3, intangible investments rose significantly in relation to GNP between 1948 and 1966, the period used in a study being conducted by the author for the National Bureau of Economic Research. This contrasts with the behavior of tangible investment, which has maintained a fairly stable proportion of GNP. The rising share of total investment indicates that as per capita real income has risen, the propensity to save has also risen.

In explaining productivity advance, however, we note that it is not the intangible investment itself that is of paramount interest; rather, it is the real stock of intangible capital resulting from the investment, relative to tangible factor inputs. That is, the stock of knowledge resulting from basic research is the fundamental pool of disembodied ideas that can be embodied in the productive agents: The stock of applied research and development represents the productive knowledge embodied in tangible instruments, processes, and organization of production; the stock of education and training represents the productive knowledge and know-how embodied in human beings; and the stock of health and mobility represents the cumulative outlays for these purposes embodied in the population. For purposes of productivity analysis, the real stocks of intangible capital embodied in human beings are reduced to that portion embodied in the employed labor force for that portion of potential hours which is utilized in production. That is, part of "human investment" has its payoff in enhancing the quality of nonproductive time.

[4] Moses Abramovitz, "Economic Growth in the United States: A Review Article," *American Economic Review*, vol. 52, pp. 762–782, September, 1962.

[5] Edward F. Denison, *Why Growth Rates Differ* (Washington, D.C.: The Brookings Institution, 1967).

TABLE 17-3

Real Tangible and Intangible Gross Domestic Investment and Stock
(Billions of 1958 Dollars and Percentages of GNP, Selected Years)

	1948		1957		1966		1975 (projected)	
	Billions of Dollars	Percentage of GNP	Billions of Dollars	Percentage of GNP	Billions of Dollars	Percentage of GNP	Billions of Dollars	Percentage of GNP
GROSS NATIONAL PRODUCT	323.7	100.0	452.5	100.0	657.1	100.0	950.0	100.0
Tangible investments (GPDI)	60.4	18.7	68.8	15.2	108.8	16.6	143.0	15.0
Nonresidential structures and equipment	38.0	11.7	47.4	10.5	73.8	10.9	101.3	10.7
Net change in business inventories	4.6	1.4	1.2	0.3	13.9	2.1	9.0	0.9
Residential construction	17.9	5.5	20.2	4.5	21.1	3.2	32.0	3.4
Intangible investments	65.5	20.2	95.8	21.2	155.3	23.6	248.8	26.2
Education	37.2	11.5	51.5	11.4	85.7	13.0	141.5	14.9
Training	7.3	2.3	11.8	2.6	21.4	3.3	38.0	4.0
Research and development	3.9	1.2	10.6	2.3	17.8	2.7	25.6	2.7
Health and mobility	17.1	5.3	21.9	4.9	30.4	4.6	43.7	4.6
Real stocks of capital								
Tangible—total	739.0	228.3	1,010.0	223.2	1,302.0	198.1	1,828.0	192.4
Intangible—total	1,165.7	360.1	1,658.4	366.5	2,423.6	368.8	3,773.0	397.2

TABLE 17-4

Private Domestic Economy:
Output, Input, and Productivity Ratios, 1948, 1957, 1966, and Projected 1975

	Index Numbers (1958 = 100)				Percentage Rates of Change		
	1948	1957	1966	1975*	1948-1957	1957-1966	1966-1975*
Real product	73.3	101.3	148.4	227.0	3.7	4.3	4.8
Factor inputs:							
Total (I)	92.2	103.6	120.5	146.3	1.3	1.7	2.2
Labor (L)	99.7	105.1	118.3	137.7	0.6	1.3	1.7
Man-hours (MH)	102.6	104.2	114.6	129.9	0.2	1.1	1.4
Capital (K)	68.7	98.0	128.7	180.7	4.0	3.1	3.8
Productivity ratios:							
Total (O/I)	79.5	97.8	123.2	155.2	2.3	2.6	2.6
Labor (O/L)	73.5	96.4	125.4	164.9	3.1	3.0	3.1
Man-hours (O/MH)	71.4	97.2	129.5	174.7	3.5	3.2	3.4
Capital (O/K)	106.7	103.4	115.3	129.8	-0.3	1.2	1.3
Other ratios:							
Labor input per man-hour (L/MH)	97.2	100.9	103.2	106.0	0.4	0.3	0.3
Capital input per man-hour (K/MH)	67.0	94.0	112.3	139.1	3.8	2.0	2.4
Total input per man-hour (I/MH)	89.9	99.4	105.1	112.6	1.1	0.6	0.8
Addendum:							
Real gross stock of intangible capital	67.7	96.3	140.7	219.1	4.0	4.3	5.0
Intangible (K/I)	73.4	93.0	116.8	148.7	2.7	2.6	2.7
Intangible (K/MH)	66.0	92.4	122.8	167.2	3.8	3.2	3.5

*Projected.

Insofar as the real stocks of intangible capital utilized in production expand faster than the tangible inputs, one would expect the productive efficiency, or productivity, of the tangible inputs to rise. The estimates necessary for this comparison are shown in Table 17-4. It should be noted that the real capital estimates are made in terms of costs, rather than in terms of the present value of an expected future income stream. For analysis of rates of return on invested capital, the cost approach is necessary to avoid circularity.

As shown in the table, the rates of increase in real intangible stocks per unit of tangible factor input and in total factor productivity are closely similar—2.6 compared with 2.5, on average, for the period 1948 to 1966.

STRUCTURAL CHANGES

As aggregate product changes levels, so usually does its composition in a dynamic economy with changing technology, resource availabilities, tastes, values, and institutions. Structural changes in the economy may be looked at from the viewpoint of the composition of final demand, the composition of national income and product by industry, the structure of inputs by industry and by type, the structure of financial flows and claims, and the distribution of income by factor, by size class, and so on.

Obviously, we cannot cover this immense area in any depth. Rather, we shall try to point out how the accounts may be applied in analyzing some of the chief forces affecting economic structure in several of its important dimensions.

Composition of Final Expenditures

Table 17-5 shows changes in the composition of GNP by broad expenditure classes for selected years from 1929 through 1968. In part, these changes must be explained in terms of institutional forces, largely exogenous to the economy. Thus, the relative growth of general government nonsecurity purchases reflects growth in population and its concentration in urban areas, increases in real income per capita, and changing views of the citizenry about the role of government in providing collective consumption and public investment. National security outlays reflect changing international relations, as interpreted by national leaders. The pattern of government purchases by functional and object classes must be interpreted in similar terms, with additional allowances for changing technology and relative prices as government agencies, to the extent that their decisions are based on analysis, attempt to provide the optimum combination of public services at the lowest feasible unit cost.

The share of gross private domestic (tangible) investment plus net foreign investment has remained relatively constant over the past century or so. If Simon Kuznets is right in saying that saving is the key element in constraining aggregate investment, then one must analyze the saving behavior of the several sectors in seeking to understand the relative magnitude of total saving and investment. Demand for each of the various types of investment—net foreign investment, net change in business inventories, producers' durable equipment, and new construction—must be analyzed separately. This is not the place to review specific techniques,

TABLE 17-5

The Composition of Gross National Product by Final Expenditure Groupings
(Percent Distributions, Selected Years)

	1929	1941	1955	1968
Government purchases	8.2	19.9	18.6	23.1
Federal	1.2	13.6	11.1	11.5
National security	–	11.0	9.7	9.0
State and local	7.0	6.3	7.5	11.6
Gross private domestic investment	15.7	14.4	16.9	14.6
New residential construction	3.8	3.2	5.9	3.5
Nonresidential construction	4.8	2.3	3.6	3.4
Producers' durable equipment	5.4	5.3	6.0	6.9
Change in business inventories	1.7	3.6	1.4	0.8
Net exports	1.1	1.0	0.5	0.3
(Exports)	6.8	4.7	5.0	5.8
(Imports)	5.7	3.7	4.5	5.5
Personal consumption outlays	74.9	64.7	63.9	62.0
Nondurable goods	36.6	34.4	31.0	9.6
Durable goods	8.9	7.7	10.0	26.6
Services	29.4	22.6	22.9	25.7

SOURCE: Calculated from estimates prepared by the Office of Business Economics, U.S. Department of Commerce.

but there are a number of good studies of the various types of investment demand;[6] the equations in the OBE model cited in Chapter 16 are representative.

In aggregate, personal consumption expenditure (PCE) in relation to GNP depends on the ratios of disposable personal income (DPI) to GNP, and of PCE to DPI. The chief factor that may alter the ratio of DPI to GNP is business and personal tax rates. Thus, the decline in PCE as a percentage of GNP shown in Table 17-5 mirrors the increasing share of government purchases and the increases in tax rates that were necessary to finance it.

Industry Composition of GNP and Factor Input

Table 17-6 shows the composition of GNP by major industry groupings for selected years. Note that the share of the farming industry has fallen, while the percentage of GNP originating in some of the service areas has risen. If the industry

[6] See, for example, John P. Lewis and Robert C. Turner, *Business Conditions Analysis*, 2d ed. (New York: McGraw-Hill Book Company, 1967), parts 4 and 5.

ECONOMIC ACCOUNTS AND THEIR USES

TABLE 17-6

The Composition of Gross National Product by Industry Groupings
(Percent Distribution, Selected Years)

	1948	1957	1968
TOTAL	100.0	100.0	100.0
Agriculture, forestry & fisheries	9.3	4.4	3.1
Mining	3.6	3.1	1.6
Contract construction	4.3	4.7	4.6
Manufacturing:	29.0	29.8	28.4
Nondurable goods	14.2	12.2	11.4
Durable goods	14.8	17.6	17.1
Transportation:	5.8	5.0	4.0
Railroads	3.2	2.1	1.1
Nonrail	2.6	2.9	2.9
Communications	1.4	1.9	2.2
Electric, gas & sanitary service	1.6	2.3	2.3
Trade:	18.7	16.7	16.4
Wholesale	6.7	6.5	6.5
Retail	12.0	10.2	9.9
Finance, insurance & real estate	9.8	12.4	13.5
Services:	8.6	9.2	11.0
Households and institutions	2.2	2.4	2.9
Other	6.4	6.8	8.1
Government:	7.8	9.9	12.5
General government	6.8	8.8	11.0
Government enterprises	1.0	1.1	1.5
Rest of the world	0.4	0.5	0.4

SOURCE: Calculated from estimates prepared by the Office of Business Economics, U.S. Department of Commerce.

breakdown of GNP were shown in detail, there would be more dramatic instances of growing and declining industries, relative to the aggregate. How are these relative industry trends to be explained?

In the first instance, changes in the composition of final demand, which we have just analyzed, cause changes in the industry composition of product—since industries are defined in terms of product groupings. But industries sell to each other as well as to final demand. So changes in the "technical coefficients," which indicate the proportions of intermediate products each industry purchases from all other industries in order to produce its end products, may also effect changes in industry shares of GNP (see Chapter 5 on input-output matrixes). The net effect of changes in all the technical coefficients linking industry inputs with outputs would show up in changes in the coefficients indicating the direct *and* indirect requirements from other industries of a given change in its sales. Changes in the technical coefficients reflect not only technological relationships, but possibly also changes in relative prices of substitute inputs, and changes in the output mix of a given industry, which no matter how narrowly defined will comprise more than one product.

In recent years, OBE has adjusted its latest input-output matrix for comparability with matrixes for earlier years.[7] This then makes possible analysis of changes in national product by industry along the lines just described.

Given the relative changes in real industry product, estimates of relative changes in productivity make it possible to calculate relative changes in factor inputs (or vice versa).[8] For example, real farm product has grown less rapidly than total real GNP; that is, farm product declined relatively, owing to low income and price elasticities of demand. Total factor productivity in farming has shown a relative increase in recent decades. Thus, the relative decline in real factor inputs has been even faster than the relative decline in real product. And reflecting a rapid rate of substitution of capital for labor, persons and man-hours engaged in farming have shown a more rapid relative decline than total inputs—which accounts for an important part of our farm problem and the associated urban growth problems!

Conversely, real product originating in services has risen relatively, reflecting high income elasticity and low price elasticity of demand for most services, while productivity has risen less than in the total economy (declined relatively). As a consequence, factor inputs generally and employment in particular have shown faster relative increase than real product. As a growing proportion of our resources are shifted to service industries, it becomes more and more important to find ways to accelerate productivity advance in this area if the rate of national productivity advance is not to slow down.

It should be observed that relative rates of change in productivity and in real product, by industry (excluding agriculture and services), interact. That is, relative industry changes in productivity are negatively correlated with relative changes in sales and output. Thus, relative industry changes in productivity are positively correlated with relative changes in output, or real product. The degree of correlation is so strong that, on balance, industries with above-average increases in productivity tend to increase their employment of capital and labor a bit faster than industries that lag technologically, as indicated by below-average productivity advance.[9]

---

[7] See B. Vaccara and N. Simon, "Factors Affecting the Postwar Industrial Composition of Real Product," *The Industrial Composition of Income and Product,* Conference on Research in Income and Wealth, Studies in Income and Wealth, vol. XXXII (New York: Columbia University Press for the National Bureau of Economic Research, 1968).

[8] See John W. Kendrick, *op. cit.,* chap. VII, pp. 212-213, table 62.

[9] *Ibid.,* pp. 203-216.

The Functional Distribution of Income

The estimates of real factor costs (inputs) and the associated factor-price indexes provide us with a means of analyzing changes in the functional distribution of national income. "Functional" distribution relates to the shares of labor and property in the national income, after imputing labor compensation to proprietors. In the private domestic economy, the labor share increased from 72 percent to 77.8 percent of factor income between 1919 and 1960.[10] This change may be statistically explained in terms of the relative changes in the input quantities and prices of the two broad factor classes. Implicit price deflators for labor and property compensation are a by-product of productivity studies, in which it is necessary to estimate the real factor costs, or inputs. From 1919 to 1960, labor input declined relative to total factor input at an average annual rate of 0.3 percent a year. But the relative price of labor rose by 0.5 percent a year. Thus, the "elasticity of substitution," which may be computed as the ratio of the two rates—assuming neutral technology and the conditions of a competitive model—was roughly 0.6. When the elasticity of substitution is unity, as assumed in the Cobb-Douglas linear homogeneous production function, factor shares remain constant. When it is less than unity, the share of the factor which is becoming relatively scarcer rises, since its relative price rise is larger than the relative decline in its quantity. The elasticity of substitution may be calculated more precisely as the difference between the growth rates of capital and labor inputs, divided by the difference between the growth rates of the real prices of labor and capital. Using estimates for the years 1919 and 1960, we obtain the following:

$$\frac{1.84 - 0.76}{2.56 - 0.71} = 0.58$$

This number compares with an estimate by Irving Kravis of an elasticity of substitution of 0.64, and one by Arrow, Chenery, Minhas, and Solow of 0.57.[11]

Over the period under review, the average annual increase in the labor share was 0.2 percent. This may be viewed as the sum of the annual percentage rate of change in the relative quantity of labor input, -0.3 percent, and the annual rate of change in its relative price, 0.5 percent. The corresponding numbers with respect to average annual rates of change in relative capital input and price are 0.8 percent and -1.4 percent, which explains the 0.6 percent a year decline in the capital share.

The increase in the labor share may also be analyzed as the difference between the average annual rates of change in real average hourly labor compensation, 2.6 percent, and in real product per man-hour, 2.4 percent. This excess is possible when real income per unit of capital input rises by less than the increase in capital productivity.[12]

The trends we have noted are not surprising in an economy in which the saving propensities and inducements to invest are strong enough to produce a significant increase in the real stock of capital relative to the labor force and a rate of return on investment which shows no secular tendency to increase or decrease significantly. The rising labor share helps to explain the tendency toward a more equal distribution

---

[10] See John W. Kendrick and Ryuzo Sato, "Factor Prices, Productivity, and Economic Growth," *American Economic Review*, vol. 53, p. 980, December, 1963.

[11] *Ibid.*, p. 986.

[12] *Cf. ibid.*, p. 979.

of income by size class. This is another important area for structural analysis, but one which lies beyond the scope of this volume. Occasional estimates of the distribution of personal income, and wealth, do provide the basis for such analyses which have become important as background for programs to reduce the incidence of poverty.

LONG-TERM PROJECTIONS

In economic parlance, "long term" usually refers to a period ten or fifteen years ahead. For a period of this length, there is some basis for projection. All the people who will be in the labor force fifteen years hence are now born, so labor-force projections do not have to involve assumptions about birthrates, which are notoriously difficult to forecast. Most of the inventions that will affect production during the next decade have already been made or are being worked on. In any case, much of the productivity advance and change in product mix for the next decade will come from the diffusion of innovations that have already been made. And there is a large degree of persistence and regularity of past trends and relationships over a period of one to two decades or even longer.

Of course, long-term projections usually rest on certain basic assumptions: no major war or revolution, continuation of basically the same socioeconomic institutions and value systems, and thus much the same degree of economic efficiency as in the past in allocation of resources, including the rate of shift of resources in response to dynamic economic changes.

Labor Force, Man-hours, and Real Product per Man-hour Approach

The simplest and most widely used method of projecting aggregate GNP is to project labor force, employment man-hours, and real product per man-hour in order to arrive at total real GNP. If the projection involves GNP in current dollars, a trend rate of change in the implicit price deflator is added. This method has been employed by the National Planning Association, among others, with a high degree of accuracy over the years.[13]

An aggregate projection for the year 1980 made in early 1968 by the author is shown in Table 17-7. The labor-force projection was based on projections made by the U.S. Department of Labor, in which extrapolations of labor-force participation ratios to 1980 are applied to population projections of persons sixteen years of age and over, by age-sex groups. The size of the armed forces is reduced from 3.5 million in 1967, which reflected the demands of the Vietnam conflict, to 2.5 million in 1980, to obtain the civilian labor force on the assumption of no major war. Unemployment is projected at the normal frictional rate of around 4 percent, on the usual assumption that the target year is one of relatively full employment. It would be foolish to try to predict the cyclical position of an economy more than a year or two into the future.

Employment is divided into public and private components, since real government product is estimated without allowance for productivity change, and we attempt to project official estimates, rather than some ideal aggregate. The reason we project

[13] See *Long-range Projections for Economic Growth: The American Economy in 1970,* Planning Pamphlet no. 107 (Washington, D.C.: National Planning Association, 1959).

ECONOMIC ACCOUNTS AND THEIR USES

TABLE 17-7
Economic Projections to 1980, with Comparisons for 1950 and 1967

	Actual		Projected	Average Annual % Rates of Change	
	1950	1967^p	1980	1950-67	1967-80
Total labor force (millions)	65.1	80.8	102.0	1.3	1.8
Civilian labor force	63.4	77.3	99.5	1.2	2.0
Unemployment	3.4	2.9	4.0	−0.9	2.5
Employment	60.1	74.4	95.5	1.3	1.9
Government	5.5	11.6	15.0	4.6	2.0
Private	54.6	62.8	80.5	0.8	1.9
Avg. hrs. worked per week	41.0	39.0	36.6	−0.3	−0.5
Total manhours (billions)	116.5	127.4	153.2	0.5	1.4
Real private GNP per manhour (1967 dollars)	3.03	5.49	8.27	3.6	3.2
Real private GNP (billions)	371.7	699.6	1,267.0	3.8	4.7
Real government GNP	44.7	85.3	102.0	3.9	1.4
Total real GNP	416.4	785.0	1,369.0	3.8	4.4
GNP price index (1967=100)	68.4	100.0	151.8	2.3	3.3
Private economy	71.0	100.0	146.9	2.0	3.0
Government	46.8	100.0	213.3	4.6	6.0
GNP, current dollars (billions)	284.8	785.0	2,078.8	6.1	7.8
Private economy	263.9	699.6	1,861.2	5.9	7.8
Government	20.9	85.3	217.6	8.6	7.5
Corporate profits, adjusted (billions)	37.7	79.0	186.1	4.4	6.8
Percent of private GNP	14.3	11.3	10.0		

p = preliminary; final 1967 GNP was $789.7 billion; preliminary 1968, $860.6 billion; and forecast 1969, $920 billion.

a smaller rate of increase in public than in private employment is that in 1967 federal civilian as well as military employment was somewhat swollen by the Vietnam conflict. In any case, the total employment estimate is more important than the allocation, although if our public proportion is low, it lends a slight upward bias to the projection because of the no-productivity-change convention for general government.

Average hours worked per week in the private economy declined from around sixty in 1900 to thirty-nine in 1967, and the secular rate of decline is assumed to continue, since a shorter workweek and more paid leave are in the demands of many labor unions, particularly those representing workers whose average hours exceed the economy average. The decline has been a bit less in recent years than the 0.5 percent per annum secular rate, but this has been due in part to the taut demand situation in the 1965 to 1970 period.

Having obtained projections of man-hours worked as the product of average hours worked per week (times 52) and employment, we next project real product per man-hour. The usual procedure is to project the past trend rate. Since World War II, the rate of increase, based on fitting a least-squares trend line, has been approximately 3.4 percent a year. This is higher than the 1919 to 1948 rate, owing chiefly to a higher rate of increase in capital per man-hour. The trend rate of advance in cost-reducing technology, as reflected in total factor productivity, has not varied much since World War I, except for a downward shift during the Great Depression.

The extrapolation of past rates of increase in real product per man-hour implies the assumption that there will continue to be about the same rate of increase of tangible capital per man-hour in the future as in the past two decades, and also the same rate of increase of intangible capital and the other elements affecting productive efficiency generally. In the next section, we explain a more sophisticated way of projecting productivity. But as a first approximation, the projection of past trends is not a bad approach, in view of the relative stability of trend rates during the modern period.

For 1980, real product in the private economy is, of course, the product of man-hours and real product per man-hour; government product is the product of employment (civilian plus military) and real product per employee without allowance for productivity change, to accord with present Commerce procedures.

For many purposes, real product projections suffice. For others, current-dollar figures are needed. This requires projecting the general price level as reflected in the implicit deflator for GNP. The margins of error in the price projection are likely to be greater than those in the real product projection. It involves estimating the degree of cost push and the extent to which it will be accommodated, or the degree of demand pull that will be generated by the monetary authorities. The chief element in cost push is an increase of average hourly labor compensation in excess of the increase in productivity (a weighted average of real product per man-hour, by industry). In the period 1950 to 1967, average hourly earnings rose at an annual rate of about $5\frac{1}{2}$ percent in the private economy, compared with the productivity increase of about $3\frac{1}{2}$ percent, on average. A price rise which averaged 2 percent a year was the means whereby the rise in average earnings in money terms was cut back to an increase in real terms in line with the productivity advance. The increase in money supply and velocity was sufficient to accommodate the cost push, and at times it initiated a demand pull, as in 1965–1966.

After 1965, the rate of increase in prices accelerated to more than 5 percent a year. But by 1969, a firm policy of slowing down price increases was initiated. It is the judgment of the author that some deceleration will take place in 1970–1971, but not enough to get back to the 2 percent rate that prevailed before 1965. A politically unacceptable rate of unemployment would be entailed in a return to 2 percent. The projected rate of $3\frac{1}{2}$ percent seems more realistic, taking account of political as well as economic factors.

The table also includes corporate profits, since this particular projection was made as a background for a stock market projection. Note that the ratio of profits to private GNP in current dollars is expected to decline, since even with a constant rate of return on investment, a declining capital coefficient (or increasing capital productivity), which we project, means a falling profit ratio. The reader who is interested in the further steps necessary to obtain a projection of stock market averages may refer to the original article.[14]

A more refined projection of productivity, this one in connection with a projection of real product from 1966 to 1975, is shown as part of Table 17-4. Here, we used the method just described, with a trend projection of productivity, to arrive at first approximations of real product for the years ahead. Then, we projected ratios of tangible and intangible investment to GNP to obtain constant-dollar investment magnitudes (see Table 17-3). The estimates were based chiefly on McGraw-Hill surveys of businessmen's plans to spend not only for plant and equipment, but also for research and development, for five years ahead. The outlays for the other intangible investments were obtained from past relationships.

The annual investment outlays made it possible to unwind capital stock estimates by the perpetual inventory method for the period ahead by adding gross investment, and subtracting retirements by applying retirement rates to beginning stocks in order to obtain ending stocks. The tangible and intangible real gross stocks per man-hour for the projection period were examined to see if they rose in line with past trends. If not, the projected productivity would have been modified accordingly. It so happened in this projection that the growth of tangible and intangible capital relative to labor input was very much in line with past trends, and thus substantiated the projection of productivity based on an extrapolation of the trend rate.

Of course, the average return on capital stocks, the trend of scale economies, or other factors might cause productivity in the future to deviate from its past relationships to stocks per man-hour. But certain eventualities are essentially unpredictable; any projection, even when hedged with conditions, is subject to probable margins of error. For this reason, it is often desirable to project a high-growth and a low-growth GNP, in addition to one's best judgment as to probable growth. This procedure serves to remind the user that there is a range of probabilities, although he will usually use the judgmental model, which presumably falls between the high and low aggregate projections.

Projecting Economic Structure

Projections of economic structure involve application of the structural analysis discussed above. That is, we must extrapolate government purchases based importantly on institutional factors, including governments' own longer-term budget projections. The saving-investment proportions would be based on past trends and relationships. The pattern of personal outlays would depend on projected real DPI per capita and relative prices in conjunction with income and price elasticities of demand, modified by expected shifts in tastes and possible changes in the elasticity coefficients.

Just as one may project a range for aggregate GNP, so also may the forecaster produce a number of structural models. This is the usual procedure of the National Planning Association (NPA), which has produced "high consumption," "high investment," and "high government" models, the alternatives depending importantly on assumptions about public policy as well as on alternative interpretations of underly-

[14] John W. Kendrick, "Why Stocks Remain Attractive for the Long-term," *Commercial and Financial Chronicle*, Sept. 16, 1965.

ing economic forces.[15] The NPA wisely presents a judgmental model, since most users wish a unique set of numbers, even when they realize the uncertainties that attach to any projection.

Considerable experience has been accumulated in the use of input-output tables for projection purposes. The latest and most comprehensive projection is that of industry structure to 1980 prepared by the U.S. Department of Labor, with guidance from a federal interagency growth committee.[16] This report, which should be studied by anyone concerned with long-run projections, describes the techniques used in projections of aggregates and final demand categories as well as the use of input-output tables in obtaining the industrial composition of output and employment in the target years.

Unfortunately, space limitations preclude consideration of projections of other aspects of economic structure. We conclude with the observation that the preparation of long-term projections of economic structure as well as of aggregates is an extremely complex undertaking. A really comprehensive projection should involve teams of sociologists, psychologists, political scientists, natural scientists, engineers, and historians, as well as economists. But regardless of the magnitude of the effort which can be mounted, it is obvious that the indispensable tool kit is a comprehensive, consistent, and reasonably detailed set of socioeconomic accounts. As we improve the accounts, we improve the potential ability of social scientists to analyze past developments, to predict and to project, and to evaluate alternative policies which are proposed to help achieve the goals of the community.

REVIEW QUESTIONS

1 Compare the production function and input-productivity approaches from the viewpoint of statistical analysis of economic growth.
2 What are the chief factors behind productivity advance?
3 How would you go about preparing a ten-year projection of real GNP?
4 What are the chief factors behind secular changes in the industry structure of GNP? How would you project industrial production trends?

SELECTED REFERENCES

DENISON, EDWARD F.: *The Sources of Economic Growth in the United States and the Alternatives before Us*, Supplementary Paper no. 13 (New York: Committee for Economic Development, 1962).

——: *Why Growth Rates Differ* (Washington, D.C.: The Brookings Institution, 1967).

KENDRICK, JOHN W.: *Productivity Trends in the United States* (Princeton, N.J.: Princeton University Press for the National Bureau of Economic Research, 1961).

LEWIS, JOHN P., and ROBERT C. TURNER: *Business Conditions Analysis*, 2d ed. (New York: McGraw-Hill Book Company, 1967).

NATIONAL PLANNING ASSOCIATION: *Long-range Projections for Economic Growth: The American Economy in 1970*, Planning Pamphlet no. 107 (Washington, D.C.: 1959).

U.S. DEPARTMENT OF LABOR: *Projections 1980: Potential Demand, Interindustry Relationships, and Employment* (1970).

[15] *Long-range Projections for Economic Growth: The American Economy in 1970, op. cit.*, table 5.
[16] See U.S. Department of Labor, *Projections 1980: Potential Demand, Interindustry Relationships, and Employment* (1970).

ECONOMIC ACCOUNTS AND THEIR USES

U.S. Summary National Income and Product Accounts, 1968

LIST OF NATIONAL INCOME AND PRODUCT TABLES[1]

[1] U.S. Department of Commerce, Office of Business Economics, *National Income and Product Accounts of the United States, 1929-1965: Statistical Tables,* A supplement to the *Survey of Current Business* (1966), pp. iv and v.

7. Supplementary Tables

8. Implicit Price Deflators

TABLE A-1

National Income and Product Account

Line			Line		
1	Compensation of employees	513.6	24	Personal consumption expenditures (2–3)	536.6
2	Wages and salaries	465.0	25	Durable goods	83.3
3	Disbursements (2–7)	465.0	26	Nondurable goods	230.6
4	Wage accruals less disbursements (5–4)	0.0	27	Services	222.8
5	Supplements to wages and salaries	48.6	28	Gross private domestic investment (5–1)	126.3
6	Employer' contributions for social insurance (3–14)	24.4	29	Fixed investment	119.0
7	Other labor income (2–8)	24.2	30	Nonresidential	88.8
8	Proprietors' income (2–9)	63.8	31	Structures	29.3
9	Rental income of persons (2–10)	21.2	32	Producers' durable equipment	59.5
10	Corporate profits and inventory valuation adjustment	87.9	33	Residential structures	30.2
11	Profits before tax	91.1	34	Change in business inventories	7.3
12	Profits tax liability (3–11)	41.3	35	Net exports of goods and services	2.5
13	Profits after tax	49.8	36	Exports (4–1)	50.6
14	Dividends (2–11)	23.1	37	Imports (4–2)	48.1
15	Undistributed profits (5–5)	26.7	38	Government purchases of goods and services (3–1)	200.3
16	Inventory valuation adjustment (5–6)	-3.2	39	Federal	99.5
17	Net interest (2-13)	28.0	40	National defense	78.0
18	**NATIONAL INCOME**	**714.4**	41	Other	21.5
19	Business transfer payments (2–17)	3.4	42	State and local	100.7
20	Indirect business tax and nontax liability (3–12)	77.9			
21	Less: Subsidies less current surplus of government enterprises (3–6)	0.8			

TABLE A-1 (Continued)

22	Capital consumption allowances (5–7)	73.3
23	Statistical discrepancy (5–9)	−2.5
	CHARGES AGAINST GROSS NATIONAL PRODUCT	**865.7**

GROSS NATIONAL PRODUCT	**865.7**

TABLE A-2
Personal Income and Outlay Account

Line		
1	Personal tax and nontax payments (3–10)	97.9
2	Personal outlays	551.6
3	Personal consumption expenditures (1–24)	536.6
4	Interest paid by consumers (2–15)	14.2
5	Personal transfer payments to foreigners (net) (4–4)	0.8
6	Personal saving (5–3)	38.4
	PERSONAL TAXES, OUTLAYS, AND SAVING	**687.9**

Line		
7	Wage and salary disbursements (1–3)	465.0
8	Other labor income (1–7)	24.2
9	Proprietors' income (1–8)	63.8
10	Rental income of persons (1–9)	21.2
11	Dividends (1–14)	23.1
12	Personal interest income	54.1
13	Net interest (1–17)	28.0
14	Net interest paid by government (3–5)	11.9
15	Interest paid by consumers (2–4)	14.2
16	Transfer payments to persons	59.2
17	From business (1–19)	3.4
18	From government (3–3)	55.8
19	Less: Personal contributions for social insurance (3–15)	22.6
	PERSONAL INCOME	**687.9**

TABLE A-3

Government Receipts and Expenditure Account

Line			Line		
1	Purchases of good and services (1–38)	200.3	10	Personal tax and nontax payments (2–1)	97.9
2	Transfer payments	57.9	11	Corporate profits tax liability (1–12)	41.3
3	To persons (2–18)	55.8	12	Indirect business tax and nontax liability (1-20)	77.9
4	To foreigners (net) (4–3)	2.1	13	Contributions for social insurance	47.0
5	Net interest paid (2–14)	11.9	14	Employer (1–6)	24.4
6	Subsidies less current surplus of government enterprises (1-21)	0.8	15	Personal (2-19)	22.6
7	Surplus or deficit (−), national income and product accounts (5−8)	−6.7			
8	Federal	−5.2			
9	State and local	−1.5			
	GOVERNMENT EXPENDITURES AND SURPLUS	264.2		**GOVERNMENT RECEIPTS**	264.2

TABLE A-4
Foreign Transactions Account

Line			Line		
1	Exports of goods and services (1–36) ⎯⎯⎯⎯⎯⎯⎯	50.6	2	Imports of goods and services (1–37) ⎯⎯⎯⎯	48.1
			3	Transfer payments from U.S.Government to foreigners (net) (3–4) ⎯⎯⎯⎯⎯⎯⎯⎯⎯⎯	2.1
			4	Personal transfer payments to foreigners (net) (2–5) ⎯	0.8
			5	Net foreign investment (5–2) ⎯⎯⎯⎯⎯⎯⎯⎯	–.3
	RECEIPTS FROM FOREIGNERS ⎯⎯⎯⎯⎯⎯	50.6		**PAYMENTS TO FOREIGNERS** ⎯⎯⎯⎯⎯⎯	50.6

TABLE A-5

Gross Saving and Investment Account

Line			Line			
1	Gross private domestic investment (1–28) --------	126.3	3	Personal saving (2–6) --------		38.4
2	Net foreign investment (4–5) --------	–0.3	4	Wage accruals less disbursements (1–4) --------		0.0
			5	Undistributed corporate profits (1–15) --------		26.7
			6	Corporate inventory valuation adjustment (1–16) --------		–3.2
			7	Capital consumption allowances (1–22) --------		73.3
			8	Government surplus or deficit (–), national income and product accounts (3–7) --------		–6.7
			9	Statistical discrepancy (1–23) --------		–2.5
	GROSS INVESTMENT --------	**126.0**		**GROSS SAVING AND STATISTICAL DISCREPANCY**		**126.0**

* SOURCE: Tables A-1 to A-5 from *Survey of Current Business*, vol. 49, pp. 14-15, July, 1969.

The Standard Accounts
of the United Nations
A System of National Accounts

Appendix B

LIST OF SUPPORTING AND SUPPLEMENTARY TABLES[1]

Supporting Tables in Current Prices to II. Production, Consumption Expenditure and Capital Formation Accounts

Tables in Constant Prices for II. Production, Consumption Expenditure and Capital Formation Accounts

[1] UN, *SNA*, 1968, p. 165.

Supporting and Supplementary Tables to III. Income and Outlay and Capital Finance Accounts

Supporting Table to All Accounts

I. CONSOLIDATED ACCOUNTS FOR THE NATION

TABLE B-I.1
Gross Domestic Product and Expenditure

1.3.1	Compensation of employees (3.3.1)	2.2.20	Government final consumption expenditure (3.2.20)
1.3.2	Operating surplus (3.3.2)		
1.3.3	Consumption of fixed capital (5.3.3)	2.2.30	Private final consumption expenditure (3.2.30)
1.3.4	Indirect taxes (3.3.4)	4.2.5	Increase in stocks (5.2.5)
1.3.5	*Less* Subsidies (3.3.5)	4.2.6	Gross fixed capital formation (5.2.6)
		1.2.10	Exports of goods and services (6.2.10)
		1.1.1C	*Less* Imports of goods and services (−61.10)
	Gross domestic product		**Expenditure on the gross domestic product**

TABLE B-I.3
National Disposable Income and Its Appropriation

3.2.20	Government final consumption expenditure (2.2.20)	3.3.1	Compensation of employees (1.3.1)
		3.4.2	Compensation of employees from the rest of the world, net (6.4.1 −6.3.1)
3.2.30	Private final consumption expenditure (2.2.30)		
3.7.1	Saving (5.7.1)	3.3.2	Operating surplus (1.3.2)
		3.4.10	Property and entrepreneurial income from the rest of the world net (6.4.9 − 6.4.8)
		3.3.4	Indirect taxes (1.3.4)
		3.3.5	*Less* Subsidies (1.3.5)
		3.6.23	Other current transfers from the rest of the world, net (6.6.22 − 6.6.21)
	Appropriation of disposable income		**Disposable income**

TABLE B-I.5
Capital Finance

5.2.5	Increase in stocks (4.2.5)	5.7.1	Savings (3.7.1)
5.2.6	Gross fixed capital formation (4.2.6)	5.3.3	Consumption of fixed capital (1.3.3)
5.7.5	Purchases of intangible assets n.e.c. from the rest of the world, net (6.7.5)	5.7.6	Capital transfers from the rest of the world, net (6.7.6)
5.7.8	Net lending to the rest of the world (5.7.9)		
	Gross accumulation		Finance of gross accumulation
5.8.0	Net acquisition of financial assets (6.8.0 + 5.9.0 − 6.9.0)	5.7.9	Net lending to the rest of the world (5.7.8)
		5.9.0	Net incurrence of liabilities (6.9.0 + 5.8.0 − 6.8.0)
	Net acquisition of financial assets		Net incurrence of liabilities plus net lending to the rest of the world

TABLE B-I.6
All Accounts — External Transactions

	Current Transactions		
6.2.10	Exports of goods and services (1.2.10)	6.1.10	Imports of goods and services (− 1.1.10)
6.4.1	Compensation of employees from the rest of the world (3.4.2 + 6.3.1)	6.3.1	Compensation of employees to the rest of the world (3.3.1*)
6.4.9	Property and entrepreneurial income from the rest of the world (3.4.10 + 6.4.8)	6.4.8	Property and entrepreneurial income to the rest of the world (6.4.9 − 3.4.10)
		6.6.21	Other current transfers to the rest of the world (6.6.22 − 3.6.23)
6.6.22	Other current transfers from the rest of the world (3.6.23 + 6.6.21)	6.7.3	Surplus of the nation on current transactions (6.7.2)
	Current receipts		Disposal of current receipts
	Capital Transactions		
6.7.2	Surplus of the nation on current transactions (6.7.3)	6.7.5	Purchases of intangible assets n.e.c. from the rest of the world, net (5.7.5)
6.7.6	Capital transfers from the rest of the world, net (5.7.6)	6.8.0	Net acquisition of foreign financial assets (5.8.0 − 5.9.0 + 6.9.0)
6.9.0	Net incurrence of foreign liabilities (5.9.0 − 5.8.0 + 6.8.0)		
	Receipts		Disbursements

II. PRODUCTION, CONSUMPTION EXPENDITURE AND CAPITAL FORMATION ACCOUNTS

A. Commodities — Accounts 1, 2 and 4

TABLE B-II.A

Illustrative Account b. Characteristic Products of Mining and Quarrying, Manufacturing, and Electricity, Gas and Water

1.1.1.1	Industrial commodities from domestic industrial activity (Cb 1.1.1.1)	1.2.1	Intermediate consumption, industries (CΣn 1.2.1*)	
1.1.1.2	Industrial commodities from other domestic industries	1.2.2	Intermediate consumption, producers of government services (D 1.2.2*)	
1.1.2	Industrial commodities from producers of government services (D 1.1.2*)	1.2.3	Intermediate consumption, producers of private nonprofit services to households (E 1.2.3*)	
1.1.3	Industrial commodities from producers of private nonprofit services to households (E 1.1.3*)	2.2.4	Final consumption expenditure in the domestic market, households (Bd 2.2.4*)	
1.1.11	Imports of industrial commodities c.i.f.	4.2.5	Increase in stocks	
1.3.4.1	Import duties, industrial commodities	4.2.6	Gross fixed capital formation	
		1.2.11	Exports	

Supply	Use

B. Other Goods and Services — Accounts 1, 2 and 4

TABLE B-II.B.a

Sales of Other Goods and Services and Direct Imports of Government Services

1.1.4	Noncommodity sales, producers of government services (D 1.1.4)	1.2.2	Intermediate consumption, producers of government services (D 1.2.2*)
1.1.6	Noncommodity sales, producers of private nonprofit services to households (E 1.1.6)	2.2.4	Final consumption expenditure in the domestic market, households (Bd 2.2.4*)
1.1.8	Domestic services of households (F 1.1.8)		
1.1.12.2	Direct purchases abroad on current account, producers of government services		

Supply	Use

TABLE B-II.B.b

Final Consumption Expenditure of Government Services

1.1.5	Services produced for own use (D 1.1.5)	2.2.20	Final consumption expenditure

Supply	Use

TABLE B-II.B.c
Final Consumption Expenditure of Private Nonprofit Services to Households

1.1.7	Services produced for own use (E 1.1.7)	2.2.31	Final consumption expenditure
	Supply		Use

TABLE B-II.B.d
Final Consumption Expenditure of Households

2.2.4	Final consumption expenditure in the domestic market, households (AΣn 2.2.4 + Ba 2.2.4)	2.2.32	Final consumption expenditure, resident households
2.1.12.1	Direct purchases abroad, resident households	2.2.12.1	Direct purchases in the domestic market, non-resident households
	Supply		Use

C.   Industries — Account 1, Production Account

TABLE B-II.C
Illustrative Account b. Mining and Quarrying, Manufacturing, and Electricity, Gas and Water

1.2.1	Intermediate consumption (AΣn 1.2.1)	1.1.1.1	Characteristic products of industrial activity (Ab 1.1.1.1)
1.3.1	Compensation of employees	1.1.1.3	Other products
1.3.2	Operating surplus		
1.3.3	Consumption of fixed capital		
1.3.4	Indirect taxes		
1.3.5	*Less* Subsidies		
	Gross input		Gross output

TABLE B-II.D
Producers of Government Services — Account 1, Production Account

1.2.2	Intermediate consumption (AΣn 1.2.2 + Ba 1.2.2)	1.1.5	Services produced for own use (Bb 1.1.5)
1.3.1	Compensation of employees	1.1.4	Noncommodity sales (Ba 1.1.4)
1.3.3	Consumption of fixed capital	1.1.2	Commodities produced (AΣn 1.1.2)
1.3.4	Indirect taxes		
	Gross input		Gross output

TABLE B-II.E

Producers of Private Nonprofit Services to Households—Account 1,
Production Account

1.2.3	Intermediate consumption (AΣn 1.2.3)		1.1.7	Services produced for own use (Bc 1.1.7)
1.3.1	Compensation of employees		1.1.6	Noncommodity sales (Ba 1.1.6)
1.3.3	Consumption of fixed capital		1.1.3	Commodities produced (AΣn 1.1.3)
1.3.4	Indirect taxes			
	Gross input			Gross output

TABLE B-II.F

Domestic Services of Households

1.3.1	Compensation of employees		1.1.8	Domestic services (Ba 1.1.8)
	Gross input			Gross output

III. INCOME AND OUTLAY AND CAPITAL FINANCE ACCOUNTS

A. Nonfinancial Enterprises, Corporate and Quasi-corporate

TABLE B-III.A.3

Income and Outlay Account

3.4.4	Withdrawals from entrepreneurial income of quasi-corporate enterprises		3.3.2	Operating surplus
3.4.6	Property income		3.4.5	Withdrawals from entrepreneurial income of quasi-corporate enterprises
	1. Interest		3.4.7	Property income
	2. Dividends			1. Interest
	3. Rent			2. Dividends
3.5.1	Net casualty insurance premiums			3. Rent
3.6.1	Direct taxes		3.5.2	Casualty insurance claims
	1. On income		3.6.7	Unfunded employee welfare contributions imputed
	2. Not elsewhere classified			
3.6.2	Fines and penalties			
3.6.8	Unfunded employee welfare benefits			
3.6.13	Current transfers n.e.c., net			
3.7.1	Saving (A 5.7.1)			
	Disbursements			Receipts

TABLE B-III.A.5

Capital Finance Account

5.2.5	Increase in stocks	5.7.1	Saving (A 3.7.1)
5.2.6	Gross fixed capital formation	5.3.3	Consumption of fixed capital
5.7.4	Purchases of land, net	5.7.6	Capital transfers, net
5.7.5	Purchases of intangible assets n.e.c., net		
5.7.8	Net lending (A 5.7.9)		

Gross accumulation		Finance of gross accumulation	
5.8.1	Gold	5.7.9	Net lending (A 5.7.8)
5.8.2	Current and transferable deposits	5.9.4	Bills and bonds, short-term
5.8.3	Other deposits	5.9.5	Bonds, long-term
5.8.4	Bills and bonds, short-term	5.9.6	Corporate equity securities, including capital participations
5.8.5	Bonds, long-term		
5.8.6	Corporate equity securities, including capital participations	5.9.7	Short-term loans n.e.c.
		5.9.8	Long-term loans n.e.c.
5.8.7. and 8	Loans n.e.c.	5.9.10	Proprietors' net additions to the accumulation of quasi-corporate enterprises
5.8.10	Proprietors' net additions to the accumulation of quasi-corporate enterprises	5.9.11	Trade credit and advances
		5.9.12 and 13	Other liabilities
5.8.11	Trade credit and advances		
5.8.12 and 13	Other financial assets		

Net acquisition of financial assets	Net incurrence of liabilities plus net lending

B. Financial Institutions

TABLE B-III.B.3

Income and Outlay Account

3.4.4	Withdrawals from entrepreneurial income of quasi-corporate enterprises	3.3.2	Operating surplus
3.4.6	Property income	3.4.5	Withdrawals from entrepreneurial income of quasi-corporate enterprises
	1. Interest		
	2. Dividends	3.4.7	Property income
	3. Rent		1. Interest
3.5.1	Net casualty insurance premiums		2. Dividends
3.5.4	Casualty insurance claims		3. Rent
3.6.1	Direct taxes	3.5.2	Casualty insurance claims
	1. On income	3.5.3	Net casualty insurance premiums
	2. Not elsewhere classified	3.6.7	Unfunded employee welfare contributions imputed
3.6.2	Fines and penalties		
3.6.8	Unfunded employee welfare benefits		
3.6.13	Current transfers n.e.c., net		
3.7.1	Saving (B 5.7.1)		

Disbursements	Receipts

TABLE B-III.B.5

Capital Finance Account

5.2.5	Increase in stocks		5.7.1	Saving (B 3.7.1)
5.2.6	Gross fixed capital formation		5.3.3	Consumption of fixed capital
5.7.4	Purchases of land, net		5.7.6	Capital transfers, net
5.7.5	Purchases of intangible assets n.e.c., net			
5.7.8	Net lending (B 5.7.9)			
	Gross accumulation			*Finance of gross accumulation*
5.8.1	Gold		5.7.9	Net lending (B 5.7.8)
5.8.2	Currency and transferable deposits Of which by monetary institutions, liability of:		5.9.2	Currency issued by the central bank and transferable deposits
	i. Resident institutions		5.9.3	Other deposits
	ii. Rest of the world		5.9.4	Bills and bonds, short-term
5.8.3	Other deposits		5.9.5	Bonds, long-term
5.8.4	Bills and bonds, short-term		5.9.6	Corporate equity securities, including capital participations
5.8.5	Bonds, long-term			
5.8.6	Corporate equity securities, including capital participations		5.9.7	Short-term loans n.e.c. Of which by monetary institutions to:
5.8.7	Short-term loans n.e.c.			i. Resident institutions
	i. Of which by the central bank, liability of the rest of the world			ii. Rest of the world
			5.9.8	Long-term loans n.e.c.
5.8.8	Long-term loans n.e.c.		5.9.9	Net equity of households on life insurance reserves and on pension funds
5.8.10	Proprietors' net additions to the accumulation of quasi-corporate enterprises			
			5.9.10	Proprietors' net additions to the accumulation of quasi-corporate enterprises
5.8.11, 12 and 13	Other financial assets		5.9.11, 12 and 13	Other liabilities
	Net acquisition of financial assets			*Net incurrence of liabilities plus net lending*

C. General Government

TABLE B-III.C.3

Income and Outlay Account

	Disbursements			Receipts	
3.2.20	Final consumption expenditure		3.3.2	Operating surplus	
3.4.6	Property income		3.4.5	Withdrawals from entrepreneurial income of quasi-corporate government enterprises	
	1. Interest on public debt				
	3. Rent		3.4.7	Property income	
3.5.1	Net casualty insurance premiums			1. Interest	
3.3.5	Subsidies			2. Dividends	
3.6.4	Social security benefits			3. Rent	
3.6.5	Social assistance grants		3.5.2	Casualty insurance claims	
3.6.6	Current transfers to private non-profit institutions serving households		3.3.4	Indirect taxes	
				1. Import duties	
3.6.8	Unfunded employee welfare benefits			2. Other indirect taxes	
3.6.9	Current transfers n.e.c. to:		3.6.1	Direct taxes	
	1. Residents			1. On income	
	2. The rest of the world			2. Not elsewhere classified	
3.7.1	Saving (C 5.7.1)		3.6.2	Compulsory fees, fines and penalties	
			3.6.3	Social security contributions	
			3.6.7	Unfunded employee welfare contributions imputed	
			3.6.10	Current transfers n.e.c. from:	
				1. Residents	
				2. The rest of the world	

TABLE B-III.C.5
Capital Finance Account

5.2.5	Increase in stocks	5.7.1	Saving (C 3.7.1)
5.2.6	Gross fixed capital formation	5.3.3	Consumption of fixed capital
5.7.4	Purchases of land, net	5.7.6	Capital transfers, net, from:
5.7.5	Purchases of intangible assets n.e.c., net		i. Residents
			ii. The rest of the world
5.7.8	Net lending (C 5.7.9)		

Gross accumulation	Finance of gross accumulation

5.8.1	Gold	5.7.9	Net lending (C 5.7.8)
5.8.2	Currency and transferable deposits Of which by central government, liability of:	5.9.2	Currency issued by the treasury and transferable deposits
	i. Resident institutions	5.9.3	Other deposits
	ii. Rest of the world	5.9.4	Bills and bonds, short-term
5.8.3	Other deposits	5.9.5	Bonds, long-term
5.8.4	Bills and bonds, short-term	5.9.7	Short-term loans n.e.c.
5.8.5	Bonds, long-term	5.9.8	Long-term loans n.e.c
5.8.6	Corporate equity securities, including capital participations	5.9.11, 12 and 13	Other liabilities
5.8.7	Short-term loans, n.e.c		
5.8.8	Long-term loans, n.e.c.		
5.8.10	Proprietors' net additions to the accumulation of quasi-corporate government enterprises		
5.8.11, 12 and 13	Other financial assets		

Net acquisition of financial assets	Net incurrence of liabilities plus net lending

D. Private Nonprofit Institutions Serving Households

TABLE B-III.D.3
Income and Outlay Account

3.2.31	Final consumption expenditure	3.3.2	Operating surplus	
3.4.6	Property income	3.4.7	Property income	
	1. Interest		1. Interest	
	3. Rent		2. Dividends	
3.5.1	Net casualty insurance premiums		3. Rent	
3.6.1	Direct taxes	3.5.2	Casualty insurance claims	
	1. On income	3.6.6	Current transfers to private non-	
	2. Not elsewhere classified		profit institutions	
3.6.2	Fines and penalties	3.6.7	Unfunded employee welfare contri-	
3.6.5	Social assistance grants		butions imputed	
3.6.8	Unfunded employee welfare bene-			
	fits			
3.7.1	Saving (D 5.7.1)			
	Disbursements		**Receipts**	

TABLE B-III.D.5
Capital Finance Account

5.2.6	Gross fixed capital formation	5.7.1	Saving (D 3.7.1)	
5.7.4	Purchases of land, net	5.3.3	Consumption of fixed capital	
5.7.5	Purchases of intangible assets n.e.c., net	5.7.6	Capital transfers, net	
5.7.8	Net lending (D 5.7.9)			
	Gross accumulation		**Finance of gross accumulation**	
5.8.1	Gold	5.7.9	Net lending (D 5.7.8)	
5.8.2	Currency and transferable deposits	5.9.7 and 8	Loans n.e.c.	
5.8.3	Other deposits			
5.8.4	Bills and bonds, short-term	5.9.11, 12 and 13	Other liabilities	
5.8.5	Bonds, long-term			
5.8.6	Corporate equity securities, including capital participations			
5.8.7, 8, 11, 12 and 13	Other financial assets			
	Net acquisition of financial assets		**Net incurrence of liabilities plus net lending**	

E. Households Including Private Unincorporated Nonfinancial Enterprises

TABLE B-III.E.3

Income and Outlay Account

3.2.32	Final consumption expenditure		3.4.1	Compensation of employees	
3.4.6	Property income		3.3.2	Operating surplus	
	1 i. Consumer debt interest		3.4.5	Withdrawals from entrepreneurial income of quasi-corporate enterprises	
	1 ii. Other interest				
	3. Rent				
3.5.1	Net casualty insurance premiums		3.4.7	Property income	
3.6.1	Direct taxes			1. Interest	
	1. On income			2. Dividends	
	2. Not elsewhere classified			3. Rent	
3.6.2	Compulsory fees, fines and penalties		3.5.2	Casualty insurance claims	
3.6.3	Social security contributions		3.6.4	Social security benefits	
3.6.6	Current transfers to private non-profit institutions		3.6.5	Social assistance grants	
3.6.7	Unfunded employee welfare contributions imputed		3.6.8	Unfunded employee welfare benefits	
3.6.11	Current transfers n.e.c. to:		3.6.12	Current transfers n.e.c. from	
	1. Residents			1. Residents	
	2. The rest of the world			2. The rest of the world	
3.7.1	Saving (E 5.7.1)				

Disbursements	Receipts

TABLE B-III.E.5

Capital Finance Account

5.2.5	Increase in stocks	5.7.1	Saving (E 3.7.1)
5.2.6	Gross fixed capital formation	5.3.3	Consumption of fixed capital
5.7.4	Purchases of land, net	5.7.6	Capital transfers, net
5.7.5	Purchases of intangible assets n.e.c., net		
5.7.8	Net lending (E 5.7.9)		

Gross accumulation		Finance of gross accumulation	
5.8.1	Gold	5.7.9	Net lending (E 5.7.8)
5.8.2	Currency and transferable deposits	5.9.7	Short-term loans n.e.c.
5.8.3	Other deposits	5.9.8	Long-term loans n.e.c.
5.8.4	Bills and bonds, short-term	5.9.11	Trade credit and advances
5.8.5	Bonds, long-term	5.9.12	Other liabilities
5.8.6	Corporate equity securities, including capital participations	and 13	
5.8.7 and 8	Loans n.e.c.		
5.8.9	Net equity of households on life insurance reserves and on pension funds		
5.8.10	Proprietors' net additions to the accumulation of quasi-corporate private enterprises		
5.8.11	Trade credit and advances		
5.8.12 and 13	Other financial assets		

Net acquisition of financial assets	Net incurrence of liabilities plus net lending

* SOURCE: Tables B-I.1 to B-III.E.5 from Department of Economic and Social Affairs, Statistical Office, United Nations, *A System of National Accounts*, Studies in Methods, ser. F, no. 2, rev. 3, annex 8.2, pp. 152-163.

Name Index

Abramovitz, Moses, 289, 292
Adams, F. Gerard, 276n.
Arrow, Kenneth J., 299
Atkinson, Sue N., 244n., 256–257

Bailey, William R., 254n.
Ball, Claiborne M., 244n.
Barna, Tibor, 255n.
Bauer, Raymond A., 233n.
Becker, Gary, 122
Beckerman, Wilfred, 190, 191n.
Bhatt, V. V., 245n., 260n.
Blaug, Mark, 56n.
Bombach, Gottfried, 188n., 189n.
Brown, Murray, 265n.
Bruno, Michael, 244n., 256n.
Butler, William F., 243n., 276n.

Carson, Carol S., 17n.

Carter, Anne P., 244n.
Cassel, Gustav, 57
Chenery, Hollis B., 76n., 87n., 254, 299
Christ, Carl F., 87n.
Clark, Paul G., 76n., 87n., 254
Cohn, Samuel M., 264n.
Cole, Rosanne, 214
Copeland, Morris A., 19, 144, 244n.
Cornfield, Jerome, 254n.
Creamer, Daniel, 245n.
Croft-Murray, Giovanni, 3n.

de Janosi, Peter E., 276n.
Denison, Edward F., 18n., 243n., 289–292
Dimitrijevic, Dimitrije, 161n.
Dorrance, Graeme S., 161n., 163n.

Eisner, Robert, 266
Emerson, F. W., 162n.

Ensley, Grover W., 243n.
Evans, W. Duane, 254n.

Fabricant, Solomon, 40
Ferber, Robert, 269n.
Firestone, John M., 264
Fisher, Irving, 24
Freund, William C., 245n.

Geary, R. C., 40
Gilbert, Milton, 186, 187n., 190, 246n.
Goldberg, Kalman, 196n.
Goldman, Morris R., 61n., 244n.
Goldsmith, Raymond W., 19, 168, 170-179, 245n.
Gorman, John, 212
Griliches, Zvi, 99n., 101n.
Grose, Lawrence, 179n.
Gurley, John G., 245n.

Handfield-Jones, S. J., 162n.
Harberger, Arnold C., 269n.
Harkins, Claudia, 92n.
Hermann, B. F. G., 13
Hicks, J. R., 35
Hochwald, Werner, 197, 201n.
Hoffenberg, Marvin, 254n.
Hood, W. C., 162n.
Hoover, Ethel D., 98n.
Hyams, David J., 202n.

Jaszi, George, 26, 97n., 99n., 205, 207n., 214n.
Jaycox, C. Milton, 200, 201n.
Jones, Carl E., 40n.
Jorgensen, D. W., 101n.

Kalecki, Michael, 14
Kavesh, Robert A., 243n., 276n.
Kendrick, John W., 14, 26, 28, 32, 37n., 40, 91n., 97n., 122n., 126n., 129n., 175-178, 200-202, 245n., 286-287, 292-295, 298-300, 303n.
Keynes, John Maynard, 14, 16, 17, 117, 169, 226, 256, 269
King, Gregory, 11, 12

Kircher, Paul, 244n., 252
Klein, Lawrence R., 168n., 276
Kravis, Irving B., 30, 186, 190, 299
Kuh, Edwin, 283n.
Kuznets, Simon, 17, 24-26, 206, 243n., 245n., 295

Landau, Ludwik, 14
Lauderdale, Lord, 13
Leontief, Wassily, 19, 56n., 57, 61, 88, 244n., 255
Levy, Emanuel, 217n.
Lewis, John P., 246n., 296n.
Lewis, Wilfred, Jr., 264
Liebenberg, Maurice, 276n.
Lipsey, Robert E., 171n., 173n., 174n., 176n.

McCulloch, John R., 13
Machlup, Fritz, 123n.
Maisel, Sherman J., 265-266
Marimont, Martin L., 52n., 61n., 243n., 244n., 246n.
Marshall, Alfred, 13
Marx, Karl, 13
Matolcsy, M., 14, 24
Mayer, Lawrence A., 245n.
Meade, James, 17-18
Mendelson, Morris, 173n.
Meyer, John R., 196n.
Miernyk, William H., 76n., 201n., 202n.
Mill, John Stuart, 13, 168
Mills, Frederick, 26
Mincer, Jacob, 122
Minhas, B. S., 299
Mintz, Ilse, 268
Mitchell, Wesley C., 144, 267
Muskin, Selma J., 123n.

Nathan, Robert R., 17

O'Leary, James J., 244n.
Oshima, Harry T., 217n.

Paige, Deborah, 188n., 189n.
Pareto, Vilfredo, 57

Petty, Sir William, 1, 10-12, 16
Pigou, A. C., 14, 30
Popkin, Joel, 202*n.*
Powelson, John P., 3

Quesnay, François, 12, 56

Read, L. M., 162*n.*
Revell, Jack, 174*n.*, 175
Ricardo, David, 13
Rottenberg, Irving, 179*n.*
Rowley, Jennifer A., 126, 129*n.*
Ruggles, Nancy D., 7, 8*n.*, 201*n.*, 202*n.*,
    220, 222, 225, 226*n.*, 232*n.*, 233*n.*
Ruggles, Richard, 7, 8*n.*, 27, 201*n.*, 202*n.*,
    220, 222, 225, 226*n.*, 232*n.*, 233*n.*

Salant, Walter S., 245*n.*, 258-259
Sato, Ryuzo, 37*n.*, 299*n.*
Saunders, Christopher, 245*n.*
Say, J. B., 13
Schultz, Theodore W., 122
Senior, Nassau W., 13
Shaw, E. S., 245*n.*
Sigel, Stanley J., 110
Simon, Nancy, 298*n.*
Smith, Adam, 12-13, 168
Solow, Robert M., 243*n.*, 289, 299
Stanback, Thomas M., Jr., 267

Stockwell, Eleanor J., 150*n.*
Stone, Giovanna, 4*n.*
Stone, Richard, 3, 4*n.*, 17-19
Storch, Heinrich, 13
Studenski, Paul, 11, 14, 15*n.*, 25, 39
Suits, Daniel B., 269*n.*

Taubman, Paul, 265*n.*
Taylor, Stephan, 244*n.*, 257
Terleckyj, Nestor, 268
Tucker, George, 246
Turner, Robert C., 246*n.*, 296*n.*

Vaccara, Beatrice N., 61*n.*, 244*n.*, 298*n.*
Van Cleeff, Ed., 18
van der Weide, T., 245*n.*
Varga, S., 14, 24

Walras, Leon, 13, 56
Wasson, Robert C., 179*n.*
Watson, Donald S., 56*n.*

Young, Allan H., 92*n.*

Zarnowitz, Victor, 281-282
Zinbarg, Edward D., 245*n.*

Subject Index

Business accounting:
  as a basis for value-added estimates, 41-48
Business sector account:
  suggested expansion, 130-131
  in United Nations system, 105, 113-114
  in United States system, 107, 220
Business transfer payments (see Transfer payments, business)

Canadian National Transactions Accounts, 143, 161-162, 164-165
Capital:
  human, 122, 124-125, 127, 177, 292-295
  nonhuman: for development planning, stocks of, 253, 254
    estimating returns to, 37, 299-300
    in nonbusiness sectors, 50-51, 119-120, 128-129
    stocks of, 29, 101-102, 122, 169, 292-295
    (See also National wealth; Wealth statements)
  total, 122, 168
Capital consumption allowances, 28-29, 52, 118, 131
  on human capital, 127
  projection of, 273
  sources and methods for, 211
Capital flow matrix, 88-89
Capital formation account:
  in an integrated system, 7-9
  in United States income and product accounts, 118-120, 225-226
  (See also System of National Accounts, capital finance accounts in)
Capital gains and losses, 33, 37, 210
Capital-output ratios, 260-261
Census, United States Bureau of, 40, 41, 51, 93, 95, 111, 205, 208, 209, 211, 214, 265, 269
Commerce, United States Department of, 16-19
  deflated estimates of GNP, 92-93
  gross saving and investment account, 118-120, 225-226
  imputations included in income and product accounts, 31, 119, 210
  input-output studies, 56, 57
    for 1963, 60-77, 87

Commerce, United States Department of:
  institutional sectoring, 105
  market criterion of economic production, 30-31
  nation, definition of, 33-34
  national income, definition of, 34
  national product, definition of, 22, 26-27
  production, appropriation, and saving-investment accounts, rearrangement of, 106-109
Commodity flow procedure, 201, 206-208
Commodity X commodity input-output table, 77, 86
Comprehensive product concept of national income, 10, 11, 13, 31
Conference on Research in Income and Wealth, 18
Constant price data, 90
  (See also Deflation)
Corporate profits, 36-37, 52, 281
  projection of, 273, 302
  sources and methods for, 210
Council of Economic Advisers, 233, 248, 259, 264
Cyclical biases, 99
Cyclical indicators, 263, 264

Deflation, 222, 254
  basic approaches, 91-92
  problems of: in input measurement, 100-102
    in output measurement, 97-99
  techniques of: for capital stock, 177-180
    for final expenditures, 92-93
    by industry, 93
  in United Nations system, 102
Depreciation valuation adjustment, 33, 131, 222
Developing nations:
  efforts to improve economic accounting in, 215-217
  estimating methods in, 217-218
  uses of income and product accounts in, 252-254
Diffusion indexes, 263
Direct requirements table, 76
Disposable personal income, 110, 204, 269, 272-276, 296
  deflation of, 93
Dividends, 110, 276

Dodge, F. W., Division, of McGraw-Hill, 208, 266, 267
Double deflation method, 53, 93, 223-224

Econometric model, 276-281, 283
Economic accounts:
  definition of, 2-3
  development in United States, 16
  structure of, illustrated, 6-7
Economic Commission for Latin America, 190, 252-254, 260
Education and training expenditures, 24-25, 118, 122-126, 292-293
Elasticity of substitution, 91, 299
Employees:
  compensation of, 36, 52
  projection of, 275
  sources and methods for, 209
Employment Act of 1946, 248
Exchange rates, 186
Exports of goods and services, net: background for forecasting, 268-269
  sources and methods for, 209

Factor of production (factor inputs):
  by industry, 100-101, 298
  in input-output tables, 59
  real services of, estimating, 100-102, 286
  returns to, estimating, 34, 37, 299-300
Factor-cost valuation, 34-35, 94-95
Factor shares, 287
Federal Reserve System, Board of Governors of, 93, 95-96, 107, 169-171, 181, 211, 226, 257-258
  (See also Flow-of-funds accounts)
Federal Statistics Users' Conference, 249
Final product:
  official United States definition, 22-23
  shown in accounts, 106
  welfare-oriented definitions, 24-27
Financial interrelations ratio, 174-175, 261
Financial investment, net, 145, 226
Financing accounts:
  in Canadian National Transactions Accounts, 161-162, 164-165
  in United Nations system, 163-166
  (See also Flow-of-funds accounts)
Float, 152

Flow-of-funds accounts:
  development of, 16, 19, 144
  in an integrated system, 9
  sector-by-transaction matrix, 145-148
  structure of, 144-148
  supporting tables, 152-161
  uses, 256-258
    in developing nations, 254
    for regional analysis, 202
Foreign (rest-of-the-world) account, 7
  flow-of-funds sector statement, 154-161
  in 1963 input-output tables, 75
  suggested expansion, 131-132
  in United States current accounts, 112-113
Full-employment surplus, 248-249, 252
Functional distribution of income, 35-37, 91, 299-300

Gap analysis, 248-249
Government account:
  suggested expansion, 130
  United Nations general government income and outlay accout, 114-115
  United States current account, 111-112
Government purchases of goods and services, 295
  background for forecasting, 264-265
  in 1963 input-output tables, 75
  sources and methods for, 209
Government services:
  problems of measurement, 25
  United States method of measurement, 49-50
Gross domestic product, 34, 52-53, 221, 254
Gross income versus net income or product, 13, 17, 28-29, 221
Gross national product:
  concept of, 28-29
  deflated estimates of, 92-93
  by expenditure category, 246, 254
    in input-output tables, 59
  gap between actual and potential, 248-249
  by industry, 51-52, 246, 296-298
Gross private domestic investment, 280, 295-296
  background for forecasting, 265-268
  sources and methods for, 208-209

Gross product originating, 39
  equals gross income originating if no nonfactor charges, 48-49
Gross state product, 200-201
Gross world product, 192-193
Growth, economic, 90, 118, 132, 252, 253, 255, 260, 285, 289-292

Harrod-Domar model, 260
Household (personal) account:
  flow-of-funds sector statement, 153-154
  in 1963 input-output tables, 75-76
  suggested expansion, 128-130
  United Nations income and outlay account, 115
  United States current account, 110-111
Human capital, 22, 124-125, 127, 177, 292-295

Implicit deflators, 92, 246, 265, 280, 300, 302
Imputations, 14, 30, 119-120
  in official United States estimates, 31, 119, 210
    in financial intermediaries, 31, 36, 46-48
    for owner-occupied dwellings, 31, 36, 119, 210
  suggested additional, 31-32, 127-128, 221
Income and outlay accounts (*see* Appropriation accounts)
Index number problem, 95-97, 187-188
Indicators:
  cyclical, 263, 264
  in social statistics, 234
Indirect business taxes, 52, 273
  included in United Nations national income aggregate, 37
  and valuation of income and product aggregates, 33-35, 94
Industry:
  dummy industries, 75
  special industries, 75-76
  (*See also* Gross national product, by industry; National income, distribution of, by industry; Sectoring)
Industry X industry input-output table, 55, 77, 86

Input-output matrix (transactions table):
  applications of, 87, 201-202, 254-256
  assumptions of use, 87
  development of, 19
  in an integrated system, 7
    projections of, 87-88, 304
    quadrants of, 59-60
  from rearrangement of production statements, 59, 221, 224
Integrated system of economic accounts:
  restructuring United States accounts for, 231-232
  schematic representation of, 8
  summary, 220-231
Interest:
  net, 36, 52
    sources and methods for, 210-211
  rate of, for imputations, 50, 120
Interest paid by government (net) and by consumers, 110, 275
Intermediate product:
  definitions: official United States, 22-23, 26
    welfare-oriented, 24-25
  flows of, highlighted in input-output table, 59
  included in value of total production, 28, 29
  in production approach to value added, 40, 53
Internal Revenue Service, United States, 36, 41, 51, 181, 205, 207, 209-211, 214
International Association for Research in Income and Wealth, 18
International comparisons:
  methods of preparing, 186-191
  problems of, 185-186
  uses, 184-185
  (*See also* Gross world product)
Invariance to institutional change, rule of, 32
Inventories, change in business, 213, 214
Inventory valuation adjustment, 33, 37, 52, 118, 131, 273
  sources and methods for, 210
Investment:
  definitions of, 117, 118, 225
  expanded concept, 122-126, 225, 292-295
  in flow-of-funds accounts, 148
  (*See also* Capital)

ECONOMIC ACCOUNTS AND THEIR USES

Joint Economic Committee, 247, 248, 264
Judgmental model, 269-276, 283

Keynesian theory, 6, 246, 263, 270

Labor, estimating returns to, 37, 299-300
Labor Statistics, United States Bureau of,
57, 61, 92, 99, 205, 236, 254, 275
capital flow matrix, 88-89
input-output table for 1939, 57
projection of input-output tables, 87-88
League of Nations, 17-18, 185

Manhours, 100-101, 286
projection of, 300-301
Market-price valuation, 33-35, 94-95, 178-
180, 228
Market transactions, 13, 27, 30-31, 221
(*See also* Developing nations, estimating
methods in)
Material product concept of national income, 10
use in Communist nations, 13, 31, 192
Matrix, as a form of presentation, 5-6
(*See also* Flow-of-funds accounts, sector-
by-transaction matrix; Input-output
matrix; Population matrix; System
of National Accounts, structure of,
summary matrix)
Medical and health expenditures, 123-126,
292-293
Mobility costs, 123-126, 292-293
Modified nonmonetary indicator method,
190-191
Multiplier, 271-272

Nation, limits of, in defining income concepts, 33-34
National Accounts Review Committee, 61,
152, 211, 212, 244n.
National Bureau of Economic Research, 16,
32, 96, 126, 197, 214, 256, 263, 281, 292
National income:
approaches to estimating, 10, 39, 212,
218, 237
definitions of, 11-13, 34

National income:
distributions of: functional, 35-37, 299-
300
by industry, 52
relation to other major aggregates, 273-
276
(*See also* Net national income)
National income and product account:
as cornerstone of economic accounts, 7
development in Great Britain, 17
sources and methods for, 207-211
(*See also* Production account)
National Industrial Conference Board, 266,
269
National Planning Association, 244n., 300,
303-304
National wealth, definitional identity and
estimates of, 176-177, 231
(*See also* Wealth statements)
Nation's Economic Budget, 18, 247-248,
250-251
Net national income, 127-128
Net product (*see* Gross income versus net
income or product)
Net worth, 161, 176-177, 222, 228
Nonfactor charges, 21, 39, 40, 48, 52, 59,
110
Nonprofit institutions, private, 20, 32, 50,
105-106, 225
Nonstandard products, 97-98

Operating surplus, 37, 113-114
Organization for Economic Cooperation and
Development, 247, 268
efforts to improve economic accounting
by, 216-217
Organization for European Economic Cooperation, and development: of alternatives to exchange rate conversion,
186-189
of national income, 19

Perpetual inventory method, 179-180, 224,
303
Personal consumption expenditure, 76, 110,
214, 277, 296
background for forecasting, 269
estimates of, in developing nations, 218

Personal consumption expenditure:
  with expanded investment concept, 129
  projection of, 272
  sources and methods for, 207-208
Personal income, 110, 276
  local-area personal income, 200
  relation to other major aggregates, 273-276
  state personal income, 197, 200
  (*See also* Disposable personal income)
Personal tax and nontax payments, 276
Plant and equipment expenditures, surveys of, 208, 266
Population matrix, 233-234
Presentation of economic data, modes of, 5-6
Primary income, 39, 104-106
Producers' prices, 61, 86
Production:
  gross flows of, 28
  national product aggregate as indicator of, 28
  of utility, given priority, 21
Production account, 7, 39
  definition of national product in, 22
  in an integrated system, 7, 221-224
  relation to sector current accounts, 106-107
  suggested expansion of, 126-128
Production approach to estimation of national product (*see* Value-added approach to estimation of national product)
Production function, 16, 91, 286, 299
Productivity, 91, 260-261, 286, 302-303
  factor-cost valuation in analysis of, 33, 35, 94
  (*See also* Total factor productivity)
Profit-type income, 52
  (*See also* Corporate profits; Proprietors, income of)
Progress, 285, 289
Projections, 236, 247
  of balance-of-payments, 259
  of employment distribution, 255
  with flow-of-funds accounts, 257-258
  of input-output tables, 87-88
  long-term, 300-304
Proprietors, income of, 36, 107, 115, 221
  components of, separation of, 37
  sources and methods for, 210

Quality changes, 98-99

Real flow (and stock) estimates, 90
  (*See also* Deflation)
Region, definition of, 196
Regional economic accounts:
  gross state product, 200-201
  local-area personal income, 200
  other economic accounts, 201-202
  problems of, 195-197
  state personal income, 197-200
  uses, 195, 253
Reliability, 211-213
  in developing nations, 215
  in international comparisons, 192, 194
Rental income of persons, 36
  sources and methods for, 210
Research and development expenditures, 24, 118, 122-126, 292-293
Rest-of-the-world account [*see* Foreign (rest-of-the-world) account]
Revaluation of assets, 224, 228
Review Committee for Balance of Payments Statistics, 245*n.*
Revisions, 213-214

Saving, 107, 118, 167-168
  business retained earnings, 107
    with expanded investment concept, 131
  in flow-of-funds accounts, 148
  government surplus or deficit, 111
    with expanded investment concept, 130
  personal saving, 110
    with expanded investment concept, 129
  in United Nations sector accounts, 113, 121
Saving and investment account, 118-120, 225-226
  relation to flow-of-funds accounts, 144-145
Secondary income, 104-106
Secondary products, 75, 86, 224
Sector:
  definition of, 4, 51, 57*n.*
  sector accounts: alternatives to, 5
    development of, 7, 11, 16, 18
    income and outlay accounts, 106-107
    suggested expansion, 128-132

Sector:

    [*See also* Business sector account; Foreign (rest-of-the-world) account; Government account; Household (personal) account]

Sectoring:

    in flow-of-funds accounts, 150–151, 166

    industrial sectoring: for input-output tables, 75, 86

        in United States income and product estimates, 51–52

    institutional sectoring, 105–106, 150, 224–225

    types of, 4, 51–52

Social (economic) accounting, definitions of, 3–4

Social accounts and indicators, 233–234

State, U. S. Department of, 192–193

Subsidies less current surplus of government enterprises, 273

    sources and methods for, 211

Symptomatic series, 266–267

System of National Accounts (SNA), 2, 5–6

    balance sheets in, 228–231

    capital finance accounts in, 120–121, 163, 166

    deflated estimates in, 102

    developing nations, recommended economic accounts for, 215–216

    factor income in, 37

    gross domestic product in, 34

    input-output data in, 77, 83–86

    social data in, 233–234

    structure of, 227

        summary matrix, 228, 230

    value-added estimates in, 52–53

Tangible human investment, 123–126

Theory and relation to economic accounting, 1, 4, 11, 14, 236

Total factor productivity, 100, 222, 224, 260–261, 286–289

Total requirements (inverse coefficient) table, 76

Transactions, 27, 28

    in Canadian National Transactions Accounts, 162

    in flow-of-funds accounts, 150

    groupings of, 4

    in United Nations financing accounts, 163, 166

Transfer payments, 104–105, 110, 112

    business, 110, 211, 273, 275

    government, 110, 112, 275

Unified budget, 111, 265

United Nations, 190

    in development of national income, 19

    efforts to improve economic accounting, 215–216

    exchange rate conversion, use of, 186

    (*See also* System of National Accounts)

United States, government agencies of (*see* specific agencies)

Valuation:

    factor-cost, 34–35, 94–95

    market-price, 33–35, 94–95, 178–180, 228

    problems of, in international comparisons, 186–190

Value-added approach to estimation of national product, 40, 221–224

    developing nations, use of, 217–218

    implementation of, in United States: for financial intermediaries, 46–48

    for general government, 49–50

    for government enterprises, 48

    for households, 50–51

    for nonfinancial corporate business, 41–43

    for private nonprofit institutions, 50

    for the rest of the world, 51

    for unincorporated enterprises, 43–45

    in United Nations system, 52–53, 222

Wealth Inventory Planning Study, 50, 150, 169–171, 174, 179–182, 202, 245*n*.

Wealth statements, 16, 168–169, 229, 231, 260–261

    development of, 19, 29

    in an integrated system, 9

    (*See also* Balance sheets; Capital; National wealth)

Weighting, problems of, 93–97

Welfare:

    product aggregate no indicator of, 28

    welfare comparison, use of market-price valuation for, 33, 35, 94

    welfare-oriented measures of income and product, 24–25